Highland Papers

Angus Matheson

PUBLICATIONS

OF THE

SCOTTISH HISTORY SOCIETY

SECOND SERIES

VOLUME

XX

HIGHLAND PAPERS

VOLUME

III

MARCH 1920

Archibald, 7th Earl of Argyll

HIGHLAND PAPERS

VOLUME III

Edited by

J. R. N. MACPHAIL, K.C.

EDINBURGH
Printed at the University Press by T. and A. Constable
for the Scottish History Society
1920

HIGHLAND PAPERS

VOLUME III

Edited by

J. R. N. MACPHAIL, K.C.

EDINBURGH

Printed at the University Press by T. and A. Constable

for the Scottish History Society

1920

PREFACE

THE contents of this volume relate to a much shorter period of time than was covered by the materials printed in either of its predecessors. But it is hoped that it may not, on that account, be found less interesting by members of the Society or less useful to students of Highland history.

As before, a short introductory note has been prefixed to each item, and a few footnotes have been added.

The Society is indebted to Mr. Mill for another excellent index, and to Mr. Joseph Davidson for his careful transcription of the documents from the Denmylne Collection.

CONTENTS

PAPERS RELATING TO WITCHCRAFT
1662-1677

INTRODUCTORY NOTE

PRESERVED in the Charter Room at Inveraray is a thin unbound quarto volume which has been used by some one for the purpose of informally recording matters connected with certain charges of witchcraft in Rothesay in 1662. It bears no title and there is nothing by which the writer can be identified. Many words have become illegible, but otherwise the MS. has been transcribed verbatim, and the transcript has most kindly been placed at the disposal of the Society by His Grace the Duke of Argyll.

For the next item, which shows how far-reaching was the belief in the effects of witchcraft, the Society is indebted to the Trustees of the late Sir William Fraser, K.C.B.

For the third document, which would seem to concern fairies rather than witches, the Society has again to thank the Duke of Argyll.

I

WITCHCRAFT IN BUTE, 1662 [1]

DECLARATION Robert Stewart the 16 January 1662.

of Jonet Morisone.

Declares that about twa yeirs sine ther fell a contest betwixt . . . and Jonat Morisoun who came to his spouse to seek some quhat geir she aleged she promised her. Quhen his wife said to her that she would get a peek or two, if she serve not some as she desyred, the said Jonet said I garne to have it and I will garr yow rue it or it be longer; and within a quarter of ane yeir ther after the said Glens wife as she was going in the byre felt something strik her there; the whole house darkened which continued a long space with her, she still compleins that it was Jonet Morison that did'it.

of Jonet Morisone.

Nans. Mitchell declares that about two years syne she took a dreaming of Jonet Morisone in her bed in the night, and was afrighted therewith and, within half ane hour after wakning, her young child took a trembling a very unnaturall lyke disease quhair of he died and Jonet Morisone being desyred to heal the said child said it was twice shot and could not be healed.

About NᶜWilliam.

Major Ramsey declares that upon a tyme quhen he duelt in the Rosland that his ky gert no milk and suspecting that it was McWilliam, who was bruted for a witch and being

---

[1] Copied from the original in the Argyll Charter Chest. Many words have become faded away, otherwise verbatim —ARGYLL

his nichbour, he cam to her and upbradded her and said to her give my ky ther mulk agane or Ill burn thee myselfe and she said to him goe your wayis home and if ye wait Ill be giffend yow, and upon his retuinc the ky gave their milk.

About Jonet Nicoll.

Janet Huggin declaires that Preston told her that she sed at the fyresyd these that wronged her children was Jonet Nicoll.

About Jonet N^cNeill.

Jonat Man declares that Jonat McNeill used a charme to hir bairne, being extremely sick of the diseased called the Glack, that the said charme was in Irish [1] quhich she understood not and that after the charme [she] did put a threid about the bairnes neck, crossing the same upon his breist, and bringing the samin under his auxters knit it behind his bake quhich the said Jonat McNeill desired hir to let be about the bairne 48 hours and therafter to cut it and burne it in the fiie quhich she did. Item being demanded if she bund it about the catt that the catt died, denyed the samin but that Jon Campbell said to hir that a catt of his died that day. (Memo to inquire farder in this particular.)

Of Katherin Moore.

Memorandum. M^clevin sayes that Finley Gelic and Donald Gelic in   saw Katherine Moore and her sone feiding twa halked ky at Glenbeg and that immediately they vanished out of sight.

Declaration Margaret N^clevin the 26 January 1662, immediately after she was aprchended, before Mr. Johne Stewart minister, John Glasse provest, Ninian Banatyne of Kames, Mr. James Stewart.

Quhilk day she confessed that she had the charme for ane evill eye and that she did severall tymes charme both

[1] It is to be noted that the charms seem to have been in Gaelic. Cf *post,* pp. 5, 6, 9, 19.

men and Beasts therewith and that it proved effectuall and did good to any she applyed it. Item that she charmt therewith about midsummer last a calfe of Allan McConaghyes in Ballenlay which charme shee repeited in Yrish and that she put it in watter or in a curchif or some such lyke.

Johne McFersoune declares that about three yeires since [he] went in a good day In Robert Clerks boat In Company with James Cuninghame, Johne McKinlay and William Gillespie out of the toune of Boot to Rowniheirine at the back of Arran and there haveing cast out thair anker waiting their opportunitie to mak for coast of Ireland there arose sudenly a mightie great storme quhich drove them to hazard of the losse of Lyfe and boat quhich continued the mater of three or four hours ther after it calmed and they went for Ireland. At the said John McFersons returne from Ireland within seven or eight weeks therafter being sitting at John McIntalars fire side besid Margrat McLevin the said Margrat did say unto him, give me some thing Johne for ye are in my common, who said how or quhat way am I in your common? She said remember in the night ye reedde at the back of Arran ye may acknowledge your self in my common. I remember of that said John and will alse long as I live bot how am I in your common for that? She answered I helped you that night quhich if I had not done ye had gone to parteins and become lost.[1]

. Declaration Margaret NcLevin 27 January 1662 before James Stewart of Auchinlick and Mr. John Stewart minister.

Quhilk day she confessed that she had ane charme for wristing or brising quhilk she repeitted in the yrish language begineing Obi er bhrachaadh etc. Quhilk proved effectuall to all such as she applyed it to and that she

---

[1] I.e. have become food for crabs.

layd the charme in tallow or herbs and applyed it. Item
that she charmed John M^ctyre the taylor therewith that
hade ane sore shoulder. Item confesses that she applyed
the said charme of ane evill ey to some fishermen and
particularly to one . . . M^cintaggirt that came home
sick to Ballicurrye. Item confesses that she hes another
charme which is good for preserveing from mischance
quhilk she repeited in the yrish language.

January 28, 1602.

Confessed Margret N^cLevine befor thir witnesses John
Glasse provest, Niniane Ballantyne of Kames, Major
David Ramsay, Walter Stewart bailie.

That being in a litle chamber in Balichtarach the devill
came to her in the lyknes of a man and deseired hir to
goe with him and that she refusing he said I will not . . .
and she gave him . . . she never saw afterward and that
she knew it was the devill and after he went that he came
bak and asked hir to give him hir hand quhich she refusing
to doe he took hir by the midle finger of the rycht hand
quhich he had almost cutt off hir and therwith left
hir. Her finger was so sorely pained for the space
of a moneth ther after that ther was no paine comparable
to it, as also took her by the right leg quhich was sorly
pained likewayes as also be the devill. Item he came to
her againe as she was shaking straw in the barne of
Ardroscidell in a very ugly shape and that there he desired
hir to goe with him and she refusing he said to her I will
either have thy self or then thy heart. Item that he
healed her sore foot and finger quhich finger is yet be
nummed. Item that before he haled her that she made
a covenant with him and promised to doe him any service
that he wold imploy hir in. Item that he asked quhat was
her name. She answered him Margret the name that
God gave me, and he said to her I baptise the Jonat.
Item that she met with him a third tyme. Item that he
imployed hir in a peice of service about three yeirs since
quhen Robert Clarks boat was going to Irland quhair

in was John McFerson and William Gillespie and other
two quhom she remembred not of and the devill haveing
a desing to destroy them and the boat did cary hir under
his auxter unto the bake of Inchmernoch [1] quhair the said
boat was sailing to Arran to the end that she might droun
the said boat by putting in hir hand betwine two boards
of the boat and by pulling the mast out of the root
and flinging it over, but the same was preveined by God
who turned the boat upon another course, yet albeit the
same did no harme there was a stoime raised quhich
followed the said boat a space. Item confesses that its
foure yeirs since she entered in his service. Item that
at the divals comand she had a purpose to droun the boat
that John Moore went in to Lochfine with and quhen the
boat loused from Illa McNeill she went to the shore side
and raised a storme by casting a stane in the sea. Item
that quhen the devill broucht hir bake from InchMernoch
she being disapointed of drouning the boat that John
McFerson was in he did let her fall out of his auxter (as
she thought) in the midest of the sea yet it was not so
but upon a rocke beside the seashore under Balicharach
and that she was so creesd that she was not able to stir
till another woman whose name she cannot remember
drew her off the rocke it being about 12 hours of the day.
Item confesses that at that tyme quhich Jonet Morisone
mentioned she met the divell and a great company with
him about three nights before hallow day,[2] that she saw
the samine also as she was comeing from Ardbeg to the
toun and that they stood in a knot at the foot of the fauld
and they went away very swiftly. Item declairs that
ther irrand was to doe harme to Mr. John Stewart minister
and to John Glasse proveist and that they have a great
pick at them, also declairs that the very last meiting that
ever she was at that Margret McCuillem and her daughter
Ket said that they wold be about with the saids persons.
Item confesses that McCuillem and her daughter did vitch

[1] A small island off Bute
[2] All Saints' Day.

Donald MᶜGilchrist that nothing did thrive with him and that they put a pock with witchcraft under his bed and a catt to effectuat the samine and that their quarrell against him was that the said Kathrine stole a bairns coat from Donald MᶜGilchrist which was fund with hir. Item that the saids persons wronged Neil MᶜNeill by witchcraft that nothing threves with him. Item that John Gely in Barmore and Jonat MᶜConachie his wife, Cirstine Ballantyne, Margret MᶜNickell, Jonat MᶜNickell, Jonat MᶜNeill and all hir goodams bairnes were witches and that she saw them at meitings.

Item that Margret NᶜCuillem and hir daughter Kathrine did witch Alexander MᶜNeiven and bind him to a post till he died.

Item that Margret NᶜCuillem and hir daughter Kathrine did put witchcraft about hallowday last under Mr. John Stewart minister his bed.

Item that about a yeir or two since whe was at a meeting at Corsmore quhair there was a great number and that they were carying a corps on a beirtree and that a young man fell under the beirtree and that Kathrine Largizean lifted him and there was nothing but the stock of a tree. Item that the said Kathrine was a great witch and was at all meitings.

Item that Annie Heyman at the bay head on hir ordinarly to be their maiden and that she danced ordinarly in the midst of them.

Item NᶜillMartine Patrick Na Muicks wife and Kathrine frissell were witches and at meitings.

Item a daughter of Alexander MᶜillMartins in Kelspoge being a young lasse blake haired broad faced mirry disposed was maiden at a meitings.

Item that at a voyage they went to Scoulage side and took the life of a child of [*blank*] MᶜCurdie and that their maiden there was [*blank*] Ballantyne with the one hand and that at that meiting she saw Donald MᶜCartour in the reir of the company carying flesh upon his bak. Item that Kathrine Moore and [*blank*] did put witchcraft in Mr. John Stewart's house quhen he dwelt in Kingarth quhich

occasioned the sickness and death of his wife and was set
for himself also but God gave them not liberty.

Item declares that N^callen is a witch and elspeth . . .
[*illegible*].

> Declaration N^cLevine the 28 day of January 1662 be-
> for Mr. John Stewart and Alexander M^cintyre.

That she used the charme quhich keeps from mischance
quhich sche repeited in Irish to severals and that they were
not the worse of it quhich charme begineth thus er brid
na bachil duin etc.   Item that she hath a receipt for the
disease in childrine called the Glaick quhich she heiles by
a herbe called achluiuisge after this maner she takes the
child with hir in hir armes to the part quhair the herbe
groweth eschewing meiting or speiking with anybody by
the way and eshewing also all high wayes and quhen she
comes to the place quhair the herbe is she takes a broch
and layes upon the herbe and plucks up the samin throw
the broch in the childs name and then brings it home
eshewing speiking or meiting with any by the way and
seiths it upon the fire without suffering either a dog or
catt or anything to passe betwixt hir and the fire till
it be boiled quhair of she administers drink to the child
three severall tymes and heales it.

> Confession Margret N^cLevin the 29 January 1662
> before Mr. John Stewart minister and John glas
> Proveist.

Item that she was at a meiting with severall other
witches betwixt Kilmachalmok and Edinmore and in
the said meiting Patrick McKaw in Tonaghuil was there and
that he and all of them went up through the moores to
Elanshemaroke and there the said Patrick McKaw shot
a bearne of Donald roie McKerdie who dwelt there.   Item
she declared that she was at another meiting at Crosmore
about this time twel month at quhich meiting Kathrine
Stewart good wife of Largizean was Annie heyman, Kathrine

Cristell, NᶜIllemartine, Patrick McKawes wife, Isobell More NᶜKaw; James Frissells wife, Katharine Moore and her eldest sonne and Margret NᶜWilliam and that they went to Birgadele broch and in a window Margret NᶜWilliam shot James Androws son and that Marie More Nᶜcuill was appointed by them to take away the body and leave the stoke of a tree in his place quhich she gat nocht done, she not being so skilfull as she sould have been. Item she declared that she was with another meiting with Margrat NᶜWilliam, Kathrine Moore and Donald Mᶜcartour with several others and that Donald Mᶜcartour had a peice of the severall bits of flesh upon his shulder quhich they were to put in the place of Elspa Kelso sister to Donald Kelso who was then servant to· Kathrine NᶜIllmoon and declared that she not being so able to hold fit with them, they went away and she knew not how they lost their prey. Item she declared that she was at another meiting at Hallowday last betwixt Mikell Kilmorie and Killeferne and at that meiting Margret NᶜWilliam Kethrine Moore, John Gely in Barmore and his wife and severall others were at a dance there and was purposed to shoot one of Robert More MᶜKennies bearnis (haveing taken two of them before) but was disappointed that night and then came down to the tounward be Ardbeg and that Margret NᶜWilliam and Kathrine Moore had a purpose to put a pock of witchcraft under Mr. John Stewart minister his bed and another pock with witchcraftis in John Glasses stable quhich she knew was done. Item she declared that in hervest last she was at a meiting in Lochfine with Donald Mᶜcartur Kathrine Moore and a wife out of Kildavanane and Soirle Mᶜallesters midmost sone and severall other heiland people there (quhich she knew not) and one McKeraish out of Glendaroil (as she thought) quho was on a fisher boat and that the said MᶜKeraish shot Robert MᶜKomash after dinner being sitting on the craft.

Item she declars that Marie Stewart mother to Neil MᶜLachlane in Kilbride [blank] Stewart daughter to black Heug are great witches and was at severall meitings and that John Gely in Barmore and Patrick McKaw in Tonagheill and their wifes are for the most part at every meitings.

Item she declard all her former declarations to be of truth.

Item she declard farder that Kirstine Ballantyne and Jonat NcNeill her good daughter and all the saidis Jonats gooddam beains were all witches and particularly Soirle Mcallexanders wife.

Confession Margrat Nclevin february 2 [1662] before John Glas proveist Mr. John Stewart minister and Ninian Allane.

Quhilk day declared that Margrat NcWilliam [blank] Stewart in Arran [blank] McKaw More his wife the witch and [blank] her dochter with diverse others went on a woyag from Corsmore overseas to Kerramorrie in Kingarth and ther killed a bairne of Donald Moir McKawes and laid by witchcraft a disease upon Donald Moies wife and that for effectuating heirof they took a boy out of Patrick Glas house being a coosine of his and that it was the said boy that shot the child And after they came home to Corsmore to William Moores house that they got to their supper eggs. Item that it was NcWilliam and John Mcfie falling at variance for breaking the slap of a dyk at Corsemorre and flighting together the said McWilliam did by witchcraft lay a heivy disease on the said John about the midle of hervest and that John McPhee's wife came to the said Margrat Nclevin who then dualt at Knokankamis and desyred her to com sie her husband and help him if she could doe him any good and that as she was goeing in at the dore she mett NcCullem beg the witch, comeing out after the aplyeing of some herbs to him and that she herself came home again but that it was NcCullem beg the witch that hailed him. Declares that the said NcWilliam went three 9 tymes about the house and barne that Neill McNeill dwells in quhen McNilas duelt ther and laid witchcraft in the said house then and

that some of the vinume therof sticks to that house,
yet.

John roy Hyndman declares that being at Kilkatten
in Johne Hyndmans house before he went to the herring
fishing that the said John confessed to him that he hade
received a charme and something in a clout to weare about
him quhairby she said that he wold further the better with
as they were both goeing up to Kilkatten quhich the said
John took out of his pouch and cuist from him. Item
that she offered the said Johne roy a charme quhilk he
refused.   Memo. speik to John roy about this.

Confession Issobell NcNicoll upon the 21 of februar
[1662] befoie Mr. John Stewart minister, Duncan
Mconlea late bayly of Rothesay. She was apprehended upon Tysday at even and this was upon the
friday.

Quhilk day Issobell NcNicoll with a great deale of seeming remorse and praying God to deliver her soule from the
power of Satan confessed that as she was in her owne
house her alone drawing acquavittie the devill came to
her in the lyknes of a young man and desyred her to goe
with him and confesses that she made a covenant with him
quhairin he promised that she should not want meanes
enough and she promised to be his servand.

Item that he baptised her and gave her a new name
and called her Caterine.

Item that about a moneth therafter in the night as she
went out at her own back dore she met with the devill
and spok with him.

Item that about a moneth therafter the devill came
to her againe as she was ther alone brewing with quhom
she hade speiches and conference. Item confesses that
she was at a meeting with the devill and severall other
associats about Hallowday last at Cregandow or Butt
key.[1]

---

[1] Bute Quay.

Confession Jonet McNicoll february 22, 1662, present John Glas proweist, Mr. John Stewart, Robert Stewart leiche, John Campbell being the morne after her taking.

Confesses with remorse praying to God to forgive her sins that about hallowday as she was in Mary Moores house that there appeared to her two men the on a gross copperfaced man and the other a wele favored young man and that the copperfaced man quhom she knew to be ane evil spirit bade her goe with him. Item confesses that she made a covenant with him and that he promised she wold not want meines eneugh and she promised to serve him and that he gave her a new name saying I baptise the Mary. Item she confesses that she was at that meitting with the devill at Butt Key about hallowday last (which the other witches maks mention off) quhair ther was a company with hir and as she was comeing over the burne that the yong man quhilk spok to her before reached her a cog with watter to drink which as she was taking out of his hand her foot slipped and she fell in the burne and that the said young man lifted her and as she rose the company left her and only the yong man abode with her and convoyed her till the foot of the broad waast.

Confession Jonat N^cNicoll february 23, 1662. Present Mr. John Stewart minister, Ninian Banatyne of Kames, Robert Wallace and Thomas McKinlay.

Quhilk day she confessed her former declaration in the whole substance and tenor therof viz. her speiches with these 2 men that apeired to her, her covenant with him and her recieving a new name from him and her being at the meitting about Hallowday and further added that she saw at the said meiting Jonet Morisone and Elspeth Spence spouse to Patrick glass. Item that the devill conveyed her be the left arm.

Jonet Hugin Robert Walleis wife declares that Prestoun the slater told her that she sedd at her fyresyd (meaning Jonet N^cNicoll) . . . those that wronged her gedem.

23 Feb. 1662.   Present Mr. John Stewart, Donald McGilchrist, Duncan McNicoll.

Quhilk day she confessed her former declarations and added further that she saw at that meiting about Hallowday Maigrat N^cWilliam, Christin Banatyne and John Galie in Barmoire.

Proces Margrat N^cWilliam.

1. Since memory of any alive that knew the said Margret she went under the name of a witch.

2. Anno 1631.   She was delated be confessing witches who dyed in prison in the Castell of Rothesay.

3. Anno 1645, July 13.   Ther was a clame given in against her to the Session of Rothesay accusing her of witchcraft quhairanent the Session concluded nothing but took the same to ther advisment.

4. Anno 1645, January 16.   The Session of Rothesay ordained that ane accusation should have beine drawne up against her upon these grundis 1° The evills quhilk she threatened to doe and came to pas.   2° the crymes that were delated and made out against her in the sessions book quhen Mr. John boyle and Mr. John Auld wer clerks to the Session.   3° the ill report and brute she has amongst her nichbouris.

5. Anno 1649.   The said Margrat was apprehended for a witch and imprisoned and being tryed the devills merk was found upon her in severall pairts of her body. But throw the confusion of the tymes then she was lett out upon bands.

Presumptions against her.

John M^cfie declares that quhen his father flitted out of Kerecresoch to Lochly that his father and Hector his brother and the said John was comeing with three horse load of flittings throw a fald of the said Margarets and, comeing to the slap which they hade casten downe before, they found the said slap bigged up and N^cWilliam lyeing thairupon and his father preasseing to cast downe the slap she resisted him and bigged up as he cast downe and that he and she strugled till they fell and after ryseing the said N^cWilliam flett with him and came to Hector and pulled the helter out of his hand and turned the horse back from the slap. Item quhen his father brocht his horse over the slap the horse fell doune and lay for halfe ane hour and could not stir. Item after that within a short space the said John M^cfie took a sudden sicknes quhich keeped him neire a quarter of a yeire which was very unnaturall, lyk a weeman travelling with sicknes, he suspected the said N^cWilliam to have laid on him. Memo to speek Hector about this. Item a child of his dyed suddenly in 3 or 4 hours space.

Agnes N^cgilchrist declares that her husband Alester McNevan threatening to poynd Kate Moore N^cWilliam's dochter fer some malt silver she owed him the said N^cWilliam said that she would gar him repent it if he wold not tak so much as she hade to give him and mediately as he went home to his owne house that he took a very unnaturall disease lyk a weeman travelling in which agonie he continued three dayes and that her said husband suspecting it was the said N^cWilliam that laid it on him desyred her to goe to N^cWilliam and desyre her to come sie him which she did and told N^cWilliam how her husband was and that he was sorely tormented ever since he threatened to poynd her dochter. The said N^cWilliam answered ye neid not feare nothing will aile him he will be wele enough and she goeing imediately home she found her husband seased of his sicknes quhom she left in great agonie. Item as she went home from N^cWilliams house she imagined she fell in a dub and was all wett notwithstanding ther was no watter where she was. Item that about 2 yeires therafter her husband went into her house to poynd for the comon maills as he was taking away a seck the said N^cWilliam and Katt her dochter did tye him fast to a post with the said seck untill John Moore her sone loused him. Item N^cWilliam said to him she

would gar him repent quhat he hade done and he saying
to her quhat can ye doe to me she said Ile slay your wife.
Item shortly after his homecoming he took sicknes quhairby
he was pitifully tormented most unnaturally till he dyed,
and the said Agnes took a very unnaturall sicknes lykwise
for a quarter of a yeire and suspected her. Item quhen
her husband was lying sick still crying that it was NᶜWilliam
that hade witched him the said Agnes his wife came to
NᶜWilliam and desyred her to come see him and that now
being at poynt of death he might forgive her and she
. . . is he hade wronged her. The said NᶜWilliam said
the devill one bit she would goe see him.

Jonet Stewart declares that quhen Alester MᶜNivan was
lying sick that Jonet Morisone and NᶜWilliam being in
her house the said Jonet desyred NᶜWilliam to goe see the
said Allester the said NᶜWilliam lifting up her curcheffe
said ' devill let him never be scene till I see him and devill
let him never ryse.'

Major David Ramsey declares that a stirk of NᶜWilliams
eating his corne severall tymes, he bound the said stirk
and the said NᶜWilliam loused it agane and that therafter
his kowes lost ther milk and gave nothing but blood and
the said Ramsey haveing fletten with her and saying if she
wold not give his kowes thair milk he wold cause burne
her. She bade him goe home and if he wanted his milk
could send him it. Item imediatly his kowes gott ther
milk.

Item that quhen his kowes came out of thair land and
Elspeth NᶜLene keping them she came to the said ky and
went severall tymes about the said ky suspitious lyk
and at every tyme wold sit downe with the las and then
ryse agane and goe about them. This she did [blank]
tymes. Interrogate MᶜLen and Major's wife.

Donald Mᶜgilchrist causing ryve MᶜCarturs house for a
childs coat that was stolne and the said coat being gotten
in that house the said MᶜCarturs was unlawed and imediatly thereafter William Moore and NᶜWilliam came
to the said Donald Mᶜgilchrist and said to him why reckis
ye ane unlaw upon MᶜCarthur and shamed us they will

not be the worse of it and ye will not be the better and within a fortnight his chamber was brunt and sen thence nothing threave with him quhairof he suspected N^cWilliam and her dochter Kat.

Item ther being a controversie in the toune court betwix her and her dochter and the said N^cWilliam challenging Donald M^cgilchrist that he hade wryten her dochters clame before hers said if he knew quhat all that good bird did yow wold not pitie her.

Jonet Stewart Ambrisbegs wife declares that N^cWilliam her two dochters and another man haveing shorne some rushes in the bog of Ambrisbeg that she and her husband came to them and hindered them to tak the said rushes being shorne away. The said N^cWilliam said it were alse good to yow to let the rushes gang as to hinder them and her dochter said that she wold repent the hindring them and shortly therafter the said Jonet turned distracted a while and being with child took her panes and was sorely handled being 20 dayes in labour. Item that sensyne she nether bade her haily wele and that nothing thrave with them but all ther kowes dyed suddenly.

Margaret N^cWilliam was tryed for the merk february 7 there was 3 merks fund, one up her left leg, next hard be the shine bone, another betwixt her shoulders a 3° ane uthyr up her hensh, blew. Present young Kames John Glas Robert McWilliam Niniane Allane Quhilk day Kat Moore was tried,[1] and it was found undernethe her richt shoulder a little whyt unsensible spott. Item being pressed whether she went afeld the day that Adam Ker dyed answered that she was at her owne house and went not from home. Item being pressed if she said to Donald M^cgilchrist if he knew quhat her dochter hade done to him he wold not pitie her so much as he did, she denyed that ever she spok such words. Item being posed if she lifted up her curcheffe quhen Jonet Morisone desyred her to goe see Alester McNivan, saying ' god let him never ryse till I goe see him.' The said N^cWilliam denyed the

---

[1] For the mark

samen that she nether lifted up her curcheffe nor spok the words. Jonet Stewart Donald Bannatynes wife testifies this part hereof.

Memorandum there it is remarked that she never flett or cast out with other but some harme came to the partie sik as contended with her.

Of Elspeth Moore.

Memorandum that Mᶜconochie, Neill McNeill and John Allane refuseing to plew a litle peice land of NᶜWilliams they saw Elspeth Moore her dochter sitting upon the grund and goeing severall tymes about.

Confession Margrat NᶜWilliam february 14, 1662, before John Glas Proveist and Mr. John Stewart minister.

Item that the yeire before the great Snaw about 28 yeires syne quhen she was duelling in Corsmoire about Candlemes about 12 hours of the day she went owt to a fald beneath her hous called Faldtombuie and out of a furz in the mids of the fald ther apeared a spreit in the lyknes of a litle browne dog and desyred her to goe with it which she refused at first, it followed her downe to the fitt of the fald and apeared in the lyknes of a wele favored yong man and desyred her agane to goe with it and she should want nothing and that tyme griped her about the left hench quhlch pained her sorely and went away as if it were a grene smoak.

(2) That betwixt and the May therafter she being in a fald above the said house the devill apeired to her first in the lyknes of a catt and speired at her How doe ye? will ye not now goe with me and serve me? at which tyme she said she made a covenant with him quhairin she promised to be his servand and he said that she should want for nothing and put his mouth upon the sore and hailled it. Item that she renounced her baptisme and he baptised her and she gave him as a gift a hen or cock.

(3) That about 18 yeires syne being duelling in Chapel-

toune the devill apeired to her at the back of the
Caleyaird and she haveing sustained losse by the death of
horse and kye was turneing to great poverty he said unto her
be not affrayed for yow shall get ringes eneugh and requiring . . . he sought her sone William a child of 7 yeires
old which she promised to him and he gave her ane elf
errow stone to shott him which she did ten dayes therafter that the child dyed imediately therafter which
grieved her most of anything that ever she did.

(4) That about Hallowday last she was at a Meiting and
danseing upon the hill of Kilmory with severall other
witches and came doune under Broadsyde amongst quhom
was John Galy in Barmoire and his wife Elspeth Gray
Agnes [blank] in Gortenis and N^cNeill her dochter in law
Margrat N^clevin Jonet . . . Issobell Margrat and Jonet
N^cNiells Elspeth Spense and her owne dochter . . .
McIlmertine Patrick Mucks wife and Issobell and Marie
McKaw. She confesses haveing the charme for ane ill ey
quhilk she repeited over in the yrish language but that
she made no use thair of but to her selfe only.

February 28, 1662, before Mr. John Stewart,
John Glas, John Campbell.

Confesses Margaret N^cWilliam her former declaratione
over againe and added farther that at the meitting about
hallowday last she saw ther N^cIlduy Donald McKeresches
wife [blank] N^clevine M^cvicars wife. Item that Elspeth
Stewart fell at the neirrest stony slap above Restyouel
and that   Nicoll fell at the flash
          and that Jean grey being . . . reached the blude
to her and lifted her haveing the blude lyk the . . . of a
most upon a atstack [?].

Jonet Boyd declares that about six quarters of a yeire
syne haveing a child upon her breist and abundance of
milk did upon a night dreame that Kat. Moore came
violently upon her and took a great nipp out of her pape and
said help me quhat should yow doe with milk and mediately
as she wakened that her milk was gone out of her brest

and hade not a drop, and that the place quhair she dreamed
that the said Kat. nipped her was blue. Item the said
Katheine being bruted for a witch she came to her to
her owne house and told her how she had dreamed of her
and lost her milk and that she suspected it was she that did
it desyring her for God sak to give her her owne milk
and that within 2 or 3 dayes therafter she hade her milk
as formerlie. Item Jonet Boyd declares that after this
McCarthur came to her house and challenged her for seeking her milk of his wife and said to her that he should
mak her repent it before that day month and within a
quarter of yeire her husband dyed suddenlie.

The Declaratione of Jonet [Morison] haveing sent for
Mr. John Stewart to speik with her at her own house
the 19 Januar 1662 before John Glas proveist of Rothesay,
Mr. John Stewart minister there and Johne Gray burgess
in the said Burgh.

First that, about a fourtnight afore halountayd last, as
shee was going from the toune of Boot till her owne house
in the tweilight she forgathered on the way at the loning
foot with a black rough fierce man who cam to her and
desired her till goe with him fer that thou art but a poor
womune and are begging amongst hailots and unchari-
table people and notheing the better of them and I will
make the a Lady for thow mayst gett Adam Ker brought
home for his father and mother sister and wife are witch
people and will give the a Kayre and make the a Lady.
Item he drew near her and wald have taken her be the hand
bot she refused bot traysted to meet him that same night
eight nights at Knockanrioch and being enqueired be us
if shee knew quhat that man was shee said she knew him
to be the divill and at the first she grew eyry.

2. Item . . . she declared that according to her promise
shee keeped the trayst with him and meet in the place
appointed and that he appeared clad with a wheit midell
and that he said to her thow. art a poor woman and beggar

among a cumpanie of harlots, goe with me and I 'll make the a Lady and put the in a brave castall quhair thou shalt want nothing and I will free the of all the poverties and troubles thou art in and learn the a way how to bring home Adam Ker.

3. Shee declared that on a tyme heirefter being cuming from Kilmorie in the evening there appeared as it were a great number of people and there cam ane from them to her in wheit or as a mane naked with a great black head, and bid her goe with him. Shee asked quhair? it said in to the Knockane.

4. Shee declared that therafter she and her husband being laying in bed there cam one to the window and said Robert rise and goe to the toune and ile give you a penny (werth) of ale for its long since yow wer in the toune and far longer (since) I was in it. Shee hearing the voice did put upon her husband to waken bot could not gett it done bot spake herself and asked who was there. The voice answered and said I am Adam Kerr; rayse and let me in, her answer was and thois were a good Spirit Ile let the in bot and thou be ane evill spirit God be between me and the. With that it ged mourning and greeting from the window.

5. Shee declared (after being challenged at the Session) one frayday thereafter being the liventh [11th] of January 1662. She was cuming home from the Waster Kams and at the Lochtie shee grew faint and satt doune and a voice spake to her and forbad her to goe hom bot goe in a hole and droune herselfe. Shee raise and cam forward the voice spake to her againe and said goe not home. I am not scorning the for thow will be bot troubled and vexed Shee came forward neare the deck of the gortans. Shee grew faint and satt doune and, as shee thought, the stalk of heather that was at her foot said to her belive not, you goe hom for they will be bot troubled seeking the. Shee raise and as she was cuming to the deck the voice spake to her and said belive in me and goe with me and Is' warrand the.

The Declaratione of Jonet Morisoune in the Tolboothe
of Rothesay imediately after she was apprehended,
the 18 of January 1662 in presence of Johne Glas
proveist, Mr. Johne Stewart minister, Nimane
Ballantyne of Kaims, Nimane Ker baylie, Johne
and Johne Kelburnes elder and younger burgesses
of Rothesay, Mr. James Stewart, Robert Beith,
Aichibald Glas burgesses of Rothesay.

1. Shee declaied over againe her declaratione made
at her owne house the 15 of Januar 1662 word be word
and farder declared that that night shee traysted with
the divill at the Knockanrioch, being the secound tyme
of her meeting with him, that shee made covenant with
the devill quhairin the divill promised to give her any
thing shee desyred and to teach her how to bring home
Adam Ker and woon her hayre quairin she promised
to be his servant etc. that shee asked quhat was his name his
answer was my name is Klareanough ˣand he asked quhat
was her name and she answered Jonet Morisoun, the name
that God gave me, and he said belive not in Christ bot
belive in me. I baptize the Margarat and also declared that
the first service he imployed her in was to bring home
Adam Ker and to put Nimane Ker baylie in his stead by
shooting of the said Nimane.

2. Shee declared that in Summer last being gathering
hearbs to heall Patrick Glas daughter who was laying
seick of a very unnaturall disease that she got a sore strok
upon the hafet the paine quhairof continued for the space
of a moneth thereafter.

> Declaiatione Jonet Morisone the said day being the
> 18 day of January 1662 in the afternoone before
> John Glas proveist, Mr. John Stewart minister,
> Ninian Bannatyne of Kames, Walter Stewait, Neill
> McNeill, Duncan McAlester.

Quhilk day the said Jonet Morisoune did declare and
stand by her former declarationes and repeitted the
most part of the particulars formerly confessed and said

ˣ Clàn eineach ??

she would not deny anything that she had spoken. As also added further that the devill desyred her to tak the lyfe of John Glas proveists dun horse by shooting him and to put him for William Stephen who was lying sick sore payned which she refused to doe. Item that the devill desyred her to tak Walter Stewart, bayly, his lyfe by shooteing him to put him for ane nighbour of his that dwelt in the highlands which she refused to doe. Item declares the devill told her that it was the fayries that took John Glas child's lyfe, and that the Spirit which spok to her told her the same that they were minded to tak his lyfe as they did. Item declares that at the time she met with the devil quhen he was goeing by with a great number of men that she asked at him quhat were these that went by who answered they are my company and quhen she speired where they were going he answered that they were going to seek a prey.

Declaration Jonet Morisone the 21 January 1662 before John Glas proveist, Mr. John Stewart Minister, Major William Campbell, Mr. Archibald Beith, Walter Stewart bayley, Peter Gray, Alester M^{c}tyre, James McNivane, James Stewart, William Gillespie, Archibald Steuart Provost.

Quhilk day she repeitted severall particulars of her former declarationes viz. her meiting with the devill severall tymes and her trysting with him, her covenant with him and that the devill bade her tak Walter Stewart bayly and put him for a nighbour of his in the highlands quhilk she knew not and that he told her that he was intended to tak John Glas his barne and to tak John Glas dun horse and put for William Stephen. And being questioned anent her heiling of M^{c}feisone in Keretoule his dochter who lay sick of a very unnaturall disease without power of hand or foot both speichles and kenured [?]. She answered The disease quhilk ailed her was blasting with the faryes and that she healed her with herbes. Item being questioned about her heileing of

Alester Bannatyne who was sick of the lyk disease answred
that he was blasted with the fairyes also and that she
heiled him thereof with herbs and being questioned anent
her heileing of Patrick Glas dochter Barbra Glas answered
that she was blasted with the faryes also.

Upon the 22 of January 1662 Jonet Morisone sent for
Mr. John Stewart minister and before James Stewart,
Adams sone and Coline Stewart burges of Rothesay declared to him as followes That about three nights before
Hallowday last as she was goeing out of the towne home
at But Kyie She saw the devill and a company with him
comeing downe the hill syde underneath Brod cheppell,
and that himself was foremost and after him was John
Galie in Barmore and his wife Jenat NᶜConachie, Elspat
Galie in Ambrisbeg Margaret NᶜWilliam Katrine Moore
[blank] NᶜLevin Cristen Banantyne Jonet NᶜNeil her
good daughter who came all orderly doune the brae and
quhen they came to the craft went in a ring and himself
in the midst of them and that she hearkened and heard
them speiking to him and that the devill came out from
among them to her and convoyed her to the Loaning fitt
quhair he and she sett a tryst to meit against that day
8 dayes. Item that all these were witches and that
MᶜLevin Margaret NᶜWilliam and Kathain Moore her
dochter did by witchcraft shoot to deid William Stephen
and that the cause therof was because a long space before
John Stephen was blasted with ane evill ey quhen he
dwelt in Balskye. NᶜLevine offered to heale him of that
blasting bot he would not, saying till her that he would
have none of the devils cures which was her quarrell with
him and that he was shott underneath the short ribbs
and that quhen she found him there was a hole in it that
ye might put your neive in.

Item it was Margaret NᶜWilliam ·and her dochters
Katharine and Elspeth that took Adame Kerr's lyfe and that
they had contrived it the night before and that they laid
the cantrapes or witchrie in the burne quhilk the milstane
was to come throw and the maire for taken that the said
Margrat NᶜWilliam fled and went away to Kingarth or

some other quhair from home upon the morne in the morneing that the milstane was drawne that she might not be suspected And that before that tyme they hade taken the power of his syde from him making two onsets on him for he was a man litle worth and as he hade litle ill in him so he had also litle good that therfor they got overtane of him. Item that Margaret N^cWilliam and her dochter Katharine took by witchcraft the lyfe of a cow of Neill McNeills quhen they wes bigging the stind falds.

Item that the said Margaret and Kate took or was intended to tak the milk of a cow of Mr. John Stewarts.

Item that the said N^cWilliam and her dochters took be witchcraft the lyfe of Alester McNiven and that they keeped him long in truble but at last got his lyfe ; the quairell was that becaus he craved sorely some malt silver that Katrine Moore was owing him.

Item that N^clevin did put a pock of Witchcraft in the east roof of Finley M^cconochie in Ballicailes stable above the horse on the north side of the house and that she said to the devill at that meiting that quhilk finley M^cconochie got he is litle the worse of it, it wold be the better to be doubled.

Item that N^cConochie in Barmoire and Elspath Galie was at a meitting in the lowlands with one Jonet Isack in Kilwineing and Margaret Smith ther, dochter to [blank] Smeth at the Crosse, and they wronged by witchcraft Hew Boyd in Kilwinning quho had four wives and they lived no longer nor they bore a child and that the child never lived and lyes sick himself.

Item that the said N^cConoche took by witchcraft the lyfe of a horse of Neill McNeills.

Item that the said N^cConoche and Elspath Galie hade almost taken the lyfe of Jonet Stewart wife to Donald M^cconochie in Ambrisbeg quhen she was lighter of her first bairne and that they laid some pocks of witchcraft under the threshold of his dore but whether it be ther yet or not she knew not but she suspects it be and though the pock or the clout it was in may be rotten yet the thing itselfe and vertue might remaine. Item that the thing

✗ they put in the pocks is the mooles of ane unchristened
bairnes threid nailes and was resolved to shoot a cow of
his at that same time.

Item that N^cWilliame and hir daughter Katherine
wrongd by witchcraft Donald McGilchrist and that nothing
threave with him since they did medle with him and that
they did lay a Pocke with witchcraft in the eising of the
east side of the house without, betuix the window and the
Doore. Quhether it be ther yet or not she knowes not bot
that Mary Moore hir daughter who duelt ther afterhinde
quhen hir child died left that house upon that occasion.
Also declares that Isobell N^cNicoll and Elspa Spence
and Margrat N^cWilliam said [1] a pocke of witchcraft in
Patrick Glas his back chamber In the eising therof in
the east side fore against the doore.

Being asked if she saw Elspa Spence at the meeting
answered No but that she heard one of the witches say to
the divell We want one of our Cummers yet viz. Elspa
Spence Patrick Glas his wife. He answered that is a great
fault.

Item declares that she saw with Isobell N^cNicoll, at a time
that she was in her house opened her Kist a clout she took
in hir hand and found in it a thing like ridd clay, quhich
she said she had gotten from an other woman quhich
she supposed to be witchcraft.

Item that the devill asked at Kathrine Moore quhair
hir Husband was that he came not she answered there was
a young bairne at home and that they could not both
come. Also declared that the errand quhich that Companie
was about was to take Johne Glas the Provist his lyfe.

Item that Christen Ballantyne did wrong by witchcraft
Peter Gray.

Also declares that at that tyme quhairin she spoke with
the devil in the Ferne quhen the great army went by she
knew none of the companie bot only Jonet N^cNicoll In
the great armie that was goeing away more swiftly nor
herself. Item that at that meeting with the devil at

---

[1] *Quære* set.

But Kyie she hard one speake to him like Donald McConochies wife in Ardroskadill, Margrat N^cilduy, She saw hir bot she wold not know her wele bot she knew that it was hir ·voice. Againe being inquired quhat difference was betwix shooting and blasting sayes that quhen they are shott ther is no recoverie for it and if the shott be in the heart they died presently bot if it be not at the heart they will die in a while with it yet will at last die with it and that blasting is a whirlwinde that the fayries raises about that persone quhich they intend to wrong and that tho ther were tuentie present yet it will harme none bot him quhom they were set for, quhich may be healed two wayes ether by herbs or by charming and that all that whirlwind gathers in the body till one place if it be taken in time it is the easier healed and if they gett not meanes they will shirpe away.

Declares that day quhich she was challenged at the Sessione, that Jenet N^cNicoll came to hir in Patrick Rowans house and said Jenat, Look that the fyle none bot yourself.

Item she declared that N^cWilliame had Alexander Woods milk all the summer over.

Item Cristen Banantyne bewitched the Ladie Kames quhich was the cause of her sicknes.

Declaration Jonet Morisone January 22, 1662, afternoone before John Glas proveist, James Stewart adamsone and Coline Stewart.

Quhilk day she repeited her foresaid declaration made the forenoone in all the particulars thereof and declared the same to be of truth adding further that Margaret N^cWilliam and her dochter Katherine notwithstanding of quhat witchrie they hade put formerly in Donald McGilchrist's house did after his comeing out of Cumray put a pock under the bed that stands in the insett of the house. Item that Jonet N^cNeill did heale a bairne of Jonet Mans by putting a string with Knots and beids about the bairne which the said N^cNeill desyred the said

Jonet Man to let it byde about the bairne 48 hours and therafter to tak it off and bind it about the catt quhich the said Jonet Man did and imediately the Catt dyed.

> Declaration Jonet Morisone the 23 of January 1662 before Mr. John Stewart Minister, John Glas proveist and Ninian Bannatyne of Kames.

Quhilk day she declared the foresaid declaratione made the 22 in the whole particulars therof about the samen to be of truth.

Item upon the said day afternoone she declared the samen to William Glas and added that John Glas his bairne quhilk he hade in fosteiing was shot at the window.

> Declaration Jonet Morisone the 29 Januaiy 1662 to Mr. John Stewait Ministei.

That it was Donald Mccaitour his wife and goodmother who did drinke out his aile and camped about it.

Saia Stewart declaies that she haveing a Kow sick and Jonet Morisone comeing into her house she told her therof and desyred her to goe see the kow if she could doe her any good the said Jonet went into the byre and took off her curcheffe and Strek thrie straiks of her curcheffe upon the kow and that theiafter the kow grew wele. Item that the said kow therafter had neither milk nor calfe.

March 26, 1662. Issobell More NcKaw haveing confessed about 20 yeires sine did delate Amy Hindman, Alester McNiven and Mary Frissell his wife, Jonet Nctyre McNivans wife in Keighs. Item Jonet Ncilmertine haveing confessed covenant and baptisme delated Amy Hyndman elder and younger, Katrine Fiissell, Marione Frissell and Mary NcNivan her dochter, Jonet Ncintyre McNivans wife.

Dittay Issobell NcNicoll.

Upon the 21 of Februar 1662 deponed Jonet Glas that Issobell NcNicoll comeing into her house said to her that she was in Walter Stewarts house seeing his bairne and that Walters wife seemed to be displeased with her but sayes she Walter put a paper on my face and therefter he or his will rew it within 5 yeiris and les and that it might best it were long, that he wold have also few children as she hade.

Margrat Glas deponed that she heard Issobell NᶜNicoll say I had a whyt face and its gods will that she (meaneing Walters child) should have a black face and its not come in yet quhat was done to me.

Margrat Galy deponed that She heard Isobel say Walter Stewart put a paper on hir face, God let him nor his never prosper and god tak a revenge of quhat he did to me. Item Walteis child David took a sudden disease with crye-. ing and dyed within 8 days the day that he was buryed his dochter took ane veiy unaturall disease her face dying and growing black quhair of she dyed in short space.

NᶜWilliam.

Memo. The first yeire that Jonet Stewart Ambrisbegs wife was mayed big with child that NᶜWilliam and Kat her dochter came to the bog of Ambrisbeg to sheir bent and the said Jonet comeing to her reproved her for sheiring therof and hindeied her from taking it with her. She said NᶜWilliam said to her that she wold as good let it goe and shortly therafter the said Jonet distracted and took her paines and was soiely handled.

Memo about Donald Mᶜgilchrist.

Memo about Margarat Nᶜilchiist McNivan's wife.

Memo that Jonet Morisone and Margarat NᶜLevin confronted Margarat NᶜWilliam upone the 5 day february 1662 before Mr. John Stewart minister, Ninian Banatyne of Kames, Major David Ramsay and Kilchunlik. Quhilk day alsoe the said NᶜLevin confronted Ceatherin Moore.

Memo Major Ramsay and his wife be spoken to.

Memo that NᶜConaghy Barmoire uses phisik and charmes.

Item that NᶜKinley the miller of Scapsys wife said to James Crafurd that upon a tyme quhen the said Jonet was travelling she had a string and 9 poks bound about her at quhich tyme Robeit Warkes doughter was in the house.

Memo that bothe her daughters are charmers and that Neall McKenans wife recovered by charming a meere of yong Kirilamonts and that John Bannatyne and the said Kinlamonts knowes. Item Alexander McCurdyes wyfe in Baron charmed a Bairne·of William Glasses. Item to trye if NcWilliam was at home the day that Adam Ker dyed Alester Mcconochie they say will prove this.

Memorandum that NcMaister in Barone is a charmer Sara Stewait can prove this.

Memorandum that John Allane having a cow that was crooked he told his father thereof who sent up to him Jeane Stewart, Thomas dechter to charme the said kow but Kat Ncphune wold not suffer the samen to be done.

Item that imediately therafter a kow of heis dyed suddenly in the byre.

II

THE CASE OF ROBERT DOUGLAS [1]

Endorsed.—For the R[t] hon[ble] the Earle of Lauderdall,
Lord Secretary of Scotland. At Whitehåll.

Edin., 24 *July* 1665.

RICHTT HON[BL],—These ar earnestly to Recomend unto
yor Lo[ps] caire a petition heirwith—profer'd to his Matie
in favo[r] of—Robert Douglas who the last yeere fell in ane
accidentall slaughter neare the place where his dwelling
is above Dumberton. Wee ar certainly informd that the
tyme of the act and divers weeks before he was in a distraction bewitchd as is alledgd by some highlanders there
for his strict exacting of the customes deu to the Castle
of Dumbarton.[2]

---

[1] Robert Douglas was proprietor of Auchintulloch on the west shore of Loch
Lomond, some two miles south of Rossdhu. Some light is shown on his
identity by the following writs.—

1 Charter of Daniel Clerk of Auchintulliche with consent of his wife in
favour of Robert Douglas son of John Douglas in Auchindinnane and Mary
Schaw his spouse and the longest liver in conjunct fee of the lands of Auchintulliche in Moane, etc , dated at Glasgow 24 January 1652 (*Cartulary of
Colquhoun*, p. 92)

2. Disposition by William Douglas advocate with consent of Robert
Douglas of Auchintullich and John Shaw of Bargarran in favour of Sir John
Colquhoun of the teinds of Mawmore, etc , originally disponed by Archibald
Earl of Angus to the said Robert Douglas and by him assigned to the granter,
dated at Edinburgh 15 July 1670 (*ibid.*, p. 425).

[2] On 26 November 1661 the Duke of Lennox presented a petition to the
Privy Council setting forth that he and his predecessors 'as having rights to the
rents, customes and deuties belonging to the Castle of Dumbartonne have
bein in use constantlie to receive four shilling Scots for the custome of ilk ox,
bull, cow, or stott which were brought furth of the said Sheriffdom of Argyle
or from any other part be the said Castle. or otherwayes did receave ane cow of
ilk threttie, giving back to the owner eight pounds Scots of the said cow and

31

However the matter be wee find the desire reasonable for a mercifull prince to grant. And wee can crave no farder but yor Lo^{ps} assistance for charitie and this mediation of Right hon^{bl}, yor Lo^{ps} most affectionat humble servants,

HAMILTON,
ANNANDALE,
KELLIE,
DRUMLANGRIGS.

To the King's Most Excellent Majestie The humble petition of Robert Douglas gentleman.

Humbly sheweing

That 27 May anno 1664 yor Maties Pet^r being unwell and in a fitt of distraction att that tyme unhappily fell unto manslaughter, never intended or forethought by yor Maties Pet^r which yor Maties Pet^r cann Justify by severall and of the best in Scotland and that it was never his intention to wrong that person hee unhappily then ramcountered with beinge almost the ruine of yor Maties Pet^r since.

The premisses Considdered and the Condition of yor Maties Pet^r here laid out before yor Matie yor Maties Pet^r most humbly implores that out of yor Maties goodness yor Matie (for God's sake) wold graciously bee pleased to commiserat this sadd condition he is in for the present and hath been these two yeares bygone and to grant him

---

now the drovers and bringers of the forsaid Ky from the said bounds most wilfullie refuses to pay the forsaid custome and in defraud thereof take their Ky be ane other new way then be the said Castle wherby his majestys garrisons in the said Castle is mightilie prejudged.' On these representations he obtained an order from the Council ordaining 'all and sundrie drovers of Kyne and other bestial as aforsaid from the forsaid bounds to bring the same be the said Castle of Dumbarton as of old and to pay the afor written custome therfor, wherin if they faill, taking any new uther way without paying the ordnary custom above specifit, the said Lords doe give warrant to seaze upon the forsaid Kyne and upon the personnes drovers of the same when they can be apprehended until the custome be payed ' Representations being made against the order the matter was remitted to the Court of Session (*Privy Council Register*, vol 1 pp. 100, 553, 654) It is easy to understand how Robert Douglas by his exertions in exacting the payment of the custom may have become extremely unpopular in Argyll and the Lennox '

a remission or respit for so long tyme as it shall please yor Matie whereby hee may have the freedoms to act for himselfe his wife and eleaven children According to the Lawes of the Land for that purpose made therefore. And yor Maties pet^r shall ever pray etc.

ROBERT DOUGLAS.

At the Court at Whitehall, March 7th, 166⅘.

His Majesty is graciously pleased to referr this Petition to the Right Honble the Earl of Lauderdale, to examine the Particulars within alledged, and to Report the Truth thereof to his Majesty who thereupon will farther declare His Royal Pleasure.   JO: BERKENHEAD.

Whitehall, 4 May 1667.

His Maj^{tie} is graciously pleased to referr the examination of this busines to his Th^r Principal Th^r Depute and Comissioners of Exchequer who are to make report of what they finde to the end his Maj^{tie} may declare his further pleasure.   LAUDERDAILL.

Endorsed.—Testificat of the furiositie of Robert Dowglas in the committing the accidentall slaughter of Wm. Lindsay, Ferrier, at Bonill,[1] upon the 27 May 1664.

We undersubscryvers do hereby declair that to our certane knowledge Robert Dowglas somtyme in Auchintulloch was not in his naturall witts the tyme of the unhappie slaughter committed by him upon William Lindsay at the boat of Bonill.[2] As also to our certane knowledge and best information thair was no former grudge nor

---

[1] From an early date the lands of Bonhill included the eight-pound lands of Bonhill-Lindsay, the fifty-shilling lands of Bonhill-Noble, and the ten-merk lands of Bonhill-Napier—so called after the families to whom they belonged The victim may have been a member of the Lindsay family who at the time still owned Bonhill-Lindsay.

[2] There was a ferry there over the Leven. Cf. Boat of Garten on the Spey.

privat quarrell betwix the said Robert Dowglas and
William Lindsay bot onlie ane accidentall encounter the
tyme of the said Robeit his distraction which continued
for considerable tyme both befoir and eftir the said
slauchter. As witnes our subscriptions,

GLENCARNE,   —— FRAW,
                               ADAM COLQUHOUN,
                               GEORGE RICHART,
                               HEUGH CRONYGHAME.

I master William Dowglas advocat do hereby declare
upon my credit and certane knowledge that I being at
Rosdo the laird of Luss house in the beginning of May 1662
Robert dowglas came and spok with me there some twentie
dayes before this accidentall slaughter and as he came to
me in a very strange poster with sword durk and pestole
bended so I perceived him to be in deape fit of melan-
cholie and destraction as was knowen to all the countrie
round about.   Witness my hand etc. the 6th of July 1665,

                               W. DOWGLAS,
                               JAS FRIELAND.

I Walter Watsone towne clerk of Dumbartane doe upon
my credit and most certaine knowledge testifie and declair
that ye forsaid Robert Dowglas was in ane reall distractione ane moneth and ane half before his comiting of the
foirsaid slauchter and that thair was no former grudge nor
quarrell betwixt him and ye detunct.   And this the whole
magistrats of Dumbartan will declair also, as witness my
hand the 21 July 1665.   WALTER WATSONE.

Unto the right reverand father in god Alexander Lord
Archbischope of Glesgow his graice and remanent members
of his graices reverand Synod within his Lordschipis diocie
the humble petitioune of Marie Schawe spous to Robert
Dowgles of Auchintuluche.
Humblie scheuethe,
That wherupon the 27 day of may 1 m vic three score four
yeares the said Robert Dowgles being then and divers

weekes befoire beuitched in ane distractioune as is weill
knouine to all the countrie about the place wher he leivid,
did committ ane accedentall slaughter haveing no for-
thought ffellonie in his heart to the pairtie nor any malice
whatsomever as all the countrie wher he leivid can informe,
and now the said Robert ffor fear of his lyfe and giving
offence to the pairtie did fliee and lye out ever since in
great miserie being sadlie affected before God in his con-
schience ffor the horrid sin of bloodshed and being ex-
treamlie punishid in his persoune through extreame want
beeing bot ane verie poore man, and wandering from place
to place doeth notwithstanding seik out all possible meanes
to satisfie the pairtie and to be reconcilid to God and his
Majesties Lawis, bot they ar all togider obstinait from
any agreement so that the said Robert darres not appeere
to act for himselfe.

May it theirfor plees your Grace and remanent members
of your Grace's honourable Synod ffor thee mercie of
Cryst Jesus to grant to the said Robert Dowglas respyt as
anent your Lo^p church censoure to dale with the pairtie
and the petiouneres schall not onlie be readie to give all
dew obedience to any censoure your grace will Impose
upon him But schall ever pray for your Graces happie
prosperitie and success etc.

At Glasgow the nintene of aprill 1 m vic sextie sex yeeres.

The Archbishop and Synode upon Consideratione of the
premisses and out of compassione to the poor woman and
her eleven children finding a certificat under the hands of
creditable and considerable persones that the foremen-
tioned Robert Dowglasse was under a fitt of distractione
q^n that lamentable slaughter was committed, did recommend to the Brethren of Dumbartane to forbear any
ecclesiastick procedor against him till my Lord Archbishop
be acquainted theirw^t.   ALEX. GLASCUEN.

EXTRACT FROM THE PROCEEDINGS OF A JUSTICE COURT HELD AT INVERARAY TOLBOOTH, 27 October 1677, by Mr John Campbell of Moy, Justice Deput of Argyll, by command of Archibald 9th Earl of Argyll

John McIlverie in Dalavich persews Donald McIlmichall vagabond without residence and Donald dow McGregour in Dalavich for a cow they stole from him upon 4 or 5 October last. Donald McIlmichall examined confesses that he and John dow M^cdonald v^cranald in Glentendill [1] and Allister oge m^cdonel v^cgorie in Ardnaclach in Appyne coming from Kilmichall in Glastrie met with the said Donald dow McGregor at Dalavich and after cloud of night bought the said kow from him for 11½ marks. The culprits had previously trysted at the Michaelmas Fair at Kilmichael and agreed to steal something 'worth ther paynes.' Donald the vagabond also admitted other thefts of cattle & horses from the Laird of Lochnell, in the Lands of Lorne etc. which he had ' taskalled,' [2] others from Lismore and Appin. The names of other common thieves were given up.

The above Justice Court was continued on the 15 November 1677, when Donald dow McIlmichall and the above Donald dow McGregour again appeared. Donald (the Vagabond) was particularly pursued ' for that horrid cryme of corresponding with the devill and consulting him anent stollen goods and getting informatione for

---

[1] Glentendil, a small glen in the Benderloch near Barcaldine House.

[2] ' Tascal money. The money formerly given in the Highlands to those who should discover cattle that had been driven off, and make known the spoilers.' —Jamieson.

discoverie thereof being expressly contrare to the **73 Act, Queen Mary Parl. 9.**

'And the said Donald being thereupon interrogat con-
' fesses judiciallie that on a night in the moneth of Novem-
' ber 1676 he travelling betwixt Ardturr and Glackiriska [1]
' at ane hill he saw a light not knowing quhair he was.
' And ther a great number of men and women within
' the hill quhair he entered haveing many candles lighted,
' and saw ane old man as seemed to have preference above
' the rest and that sum of them desired to shutt him out
' and others to have him drawine in And saw them all
' danceing about the lights and that they wold have him
' promise and engadge to come ther againe that night
' eight nights and for a considerable space thereftir.
' Being interrogat what night it wes he mett first and
' quhair he went efter he parted with them Answers that
' it wes on the Sabath night and eftir he left them that
' night he went to Robert Buchanan his house in Glac-
' kiriskay and that he wes forceit to com againe the second
' tyme on the Sabath thereftir.
  ' 2°. Interrogat what tyme he continowed his meitting
' answers that he entered 20 dayes eftir Hallowday and
' continowed till 20 days before Candlemes.
  ' 3°. Interrogat with quhom he engadgeit and what he
' judget them to be and if his name wes enquyred or got
' a new name Answers that it wes a woman among them
' that took the promise of him, and that he cannot weill
' tell quhat persons they wer bot he judges them not to
' have bein *wordlie* men or men ordayned of god, and
' that they enquyred if he wes baptized and that he said
' he wes, bot that they gave him no name nor that he told
' them his own name bot still called him by the name of
' that man.
  ' 4°. Interrogat if he mett with them in other places
' Answers that he mett them in Leismore and at the Shian

---

[1] Both in Appin   Ardturr is on Loch Linnhe opposite Lismore, and Glackiriska on Loch Creran opposite Eriska.

' of Barcalden [1] and still saw the old man that seemed to
' be cheif being ane large tall corporal Gardman and ruddie
' and that he wes engadgeit to conceall them and no to tell
' other. Bot that he told it to the forsaid Robert Buchanan
' once fer which he was reproved and stricken be them in
' the cheik and other pairts, and that he mett them still
' on ilk Sabaths nights and that he playd on trumps [2] to
' them quhen they danced.

' 5°. Being interrogat as he consulted the devill and these
' evill spirits anent stollen goods answers that he went
' and enquyred anent stollen goods and that it wes told
' him especiallie of the stealling these twa horses from
' —— McAllister VcLauchlane in Ballegowine in Leismore.
' And that at other tymes loist goods wes told him without
' asking quhilk he wes discovering to the owners. Upon
' all quhilks haill foresaid confessione the Procurator
' Fiscall taks instruments.' (Signd) NICOLL ZUILL.

As a result of this confession the Jury unanimously
found him guilty of theft and of consulting with evill
spirits sundry times (Mr. Archibald McCorquidill in Auchna-
maddie being Chancellor).

On 17 November 1677. Sentence was pronounced by
the Justice Depute ' the said Donald McIlmichall to be
taken on Moonday 19 Nov. instant be 2 acloak in the
efternoon and on the Ordinare gibbet at the gallow farlane
ther to be hangit to the death, and to forefault his haill
moveable goods and gear, Requyreing the Magistrats of
Inveraray to sie this sentence put to executione.'

The other culprit was tried subsequently, and also
apparently hung at a later date.

---

[1] A typical fairy mound, on the south side of Loch Creran, near the ferry
to Appin. Much fairy lore will be found in *Superstitions of the Highlands and
Islands of Scotland*, by the Rev John Gregorson Campbell, minister of Tiree
[2] Generally means a Jew's-harp

MEMORIAL FOR FFASFERN

INTRODUCTORY NOTE

JOHN CAMERON of Lochiel, the son and successor of the famous Sir Ewen, by his wife, Isabell Campbell of Lochnell, had at least four sons :

1. Donald, his successor. This is the gentle Lochiel of the '45, and from him the present Lochiel is descended.

2. John of Fassifern.

3. Alexander, a priest, who died from the treatment which he received after the '45.

4. Dr. Archibald, whose execution, at Tyburn in 1753, aroused widespread indignation.

At an early age the second son, John, seems to have resolved on pushing his fortune in the south. He is said to have lived for some time in the West Indies, where, curiously enough, his grandfather, Sir Ewen, had owned a plantation.[1] In 1734 he married Jean, daughter of John Campbell of Achallader, and in 1735 he became a merchant burgess of Glasgow. He was not out in the '45, though he is believed to have given financial assistance to his brother and chief.

After his brother's escape to France he became, for practical purposes, the head of the House, and was regarded with much animosity by the Hanoverian Government. In one way or another it was determined to get rid of him, and the methods employed were as clumsy as they were

---

[1] *Memoir of Colonel John Cameron, Fassiefern, K.7.S , Lieutenant-Colonel of the Gordon Highlanders or 92nd Regiment of Foot,* by the Rev Archibald Clerk, minister of Kilmallie, p 102. Dr Clerk gives also another son named Ewen, and says that in 1734 he took a number of people out to the West Indies

dishonest. The late Dr. Andrew Lang has brought together a great deal of the material bearing on the ' Uprooting of Fassifern,' as the process was termed by Colonel Crawford, one of the instruments employed. But what is now printed was not known to him. It is a memorial, in Fassifern's own writing, apparently for the instruction of his agent, Mr. John Macfarlan, W.S., well known as the doer of Lovat and other Jacobites, and perhaps still better known as the husband of the beautiful Mrs. Macfarlan, who shot the ruffianly exciseman Cayley. For its presence here the Society is indebted to the Trustees of the late Sir William Fraser, K.C.B.

Fassifern had been arrested and placed in Edinburgh Castle in May 1753, and in this Memorial, which bears to have been written in August, he tells the story of his persecution down to that date. He, of course, puts in the forefront everything tending to show that he must be regarded as well-affected to the Hanoverian Government. And apparently it was found impossible to counter this successfully. Different charges accordingly were vamped up against him. It was alleged that he had forged some deeds in order to bolster up false claims on the forfeited estate of Lochiel, and after being kept prisoner in Edinburgh Castle till January 1755, he was sentenced, not by any Criminal Court, but by the Court of Session to ten years' banishment from Scotland. He finally returned to Fassifern, where he died in 1785, and is buried at Kilmallie. His son Ewen was the father of the famous Colonel John Cameron.[1]

---

[1] *Memoir of Colonel John Cameron*, etc , p 15.

MEMORIAL FOR FFASFERN

Aug[1] 1753 [1]

AFTER I was some days prissoner at Fort William when I represented my Innocence to Governour Campbell and Captain Scott,[2] they being sensible of it gave me a Protection dated 23rd May 1746. When his Royall Highness the Duke came to Fort William where I was at that time Prissoner I was introduced to Collonell York by Major Coffild to whom I gave a Petition and Memoriall to be presented by him to his Royall Highness which Colonell York very civily accepted and desired me to send him ane express next day to Fort Augustus which accordingly I did with a letter to him the Copy of which [is] to be seen dated 1st June 1746 allso the Copy of my Petition and Memoriall to his Royall Highness. I received by the return of my Express a leter from Colonell York dated June 2nd allso a letter of the same date to Governour Campbell from Sir Everad Fawkener ordering my liberation, of which I have ane attested Copy. Accordingly I was sett at liberty and next day Captain Scott came to my house in his way to the Isles with a party where he received some Arms and lodged them in my house as by his certificate dated the 8th June allso a leter of the same date to me ane other leter from him dated the 6th June desireing the favour of me to keep some Rebell horses Certificate from Governour Campbell dated the 11th June acknowledging that the Arms and horses were returned, Copy of a leter from me

---

[1] So endorsed on the back.

[2] Captain Caroline Scott, one of the most infamous of Cumberland's officers Vide *The Lyon in Mourning*, passim

to Colonell York upon my being liberate. Some few days after I was liberate a Party from Lord George Seckviles [1] Camp at the head of Locharkak took up out of a ffarm of mine above a hundred head of cows of which I sent ane Express to acquaint Captain Scott, he sent me a return dated 8th June I immediately waited of Lord George but he would not return my Catle so went from that to ffort Augustus to complain to Collonell York, in the mean time while I was soliciting about these Catle my wife came to ffort Augustus and told me that Collonell Corwallace came to our house with a Regiment of men whom she entertained the best she could and they caryed of sixty of my hill horses and all our sheep and goats. When I acquainted Collonell [York] of this he assured me that my Catle would be returned and desired me immediately to write a petition representing my Case to his Royall Highness which he would deliver, which I saw him deliver, and next day when I waited of him he told me that he would soon procure ane order to get my Catle returned but the next time I waited of him he told me that he was sory to tell me that my wife had ruined me for that one of the officers that was at my house with Collonell Corwallace did tell his Royall Highness that he heard my wife say that it was owing to her that I was not engaged in the Rebellion for that she had made me grant a bond of 1000£ to Governour Campbell obligeing myself not to engage in it and that she was sory for what she had caused me do as I was as ill treated as the Rebells, and that it was owing to this information that my catle were not returned. I assured Collonell York that my wife never said any such thing nor had it not to say as it was both ridiculous and false and beged as she was in the place that that Gentleman and she should be brought face to face or that the other Gentlemen that were present should be asked if they

---

[1] Also known as Lord George Germain, son of the first Duke of Dorset. He had a somewhat chequered career. After Culloden he proved himself an expert cattle thief. For his conduct at the battle of Minden in 1759 he was tried by court martial and dismissed the service. He afterwards entered politics and became a Secretary of State.

heard her express herself in that manner. The Collonell advised me not to give myself any further trouble about the Catle that were taken away but that I should go home and take care of what was remaining and accordingly procured me a pass dated the 12th June. Some time therafter I sent a Compliment of such things as I thought would be acceptable to Collonell York in return of which he sent me a leter dated the 9th July, there is allso a Certificate from Achchalider,[1] dated 6th ffeb^ry 1746, also a leter from Governour Campbell dated the 9th Oct^bre 1746. I believe these two are for litle use. The next Party that came to my house was commanded by one Mr. Dalrymple a relation of the president Dalrymples who told me he was ordered to take up all the Catle in my neighbourhood and in Ardgour but that he was ordered not to cary of [any of my own] or of my tenants Catle and desired I should send a [servant] with him who would let him know my Catle and my [tenants] which accordingly I did. Next day Mr. Dalrymple returned [with] a great number of Catle but not medle with any of mine. After that time there was none of my Catle taken away, all the officers that came upon parties to that Country haveing the same orders, which I'm persuaded was owing to his Royall Highness being made sensible that I was unjustly accused. By all which it's evident that my conduct in the 1745 and 1746 was without exception otherwise Collonell York and Captain Carrolin Scott would not have befriended me so much as they did.

In the winter 1746 I came to E^dn about my own private affairs and was told after I was some days there by a friend of mine that there was a warrand comeing out against me upon which my Agent waited of My Lord Justice Clerk [2] and asked him if it was so and upon what acctt. His Lordship owned that there was ane information against me by Governour Campbell, upon which my Agent made his Lordship sensible that it was all owing to malice and

---

[1] Fassifern's wife was a daughter of John Campbell of Achallader.
[2] Andrew Fletcher of Milton, Lord Justice Clerk, 1736-1748.

design in the Governours son in law McLauchlin[1] who made
of the Governour what he pleased upon which I was no
further troubled at that time. This McLauchlin continued
always to do me clandestinly all the bade offices in his
power whose Character is known by all that heard of him.
In winter 1748 I came the North road to Town to advise
about Lady Lochiel and her Childrens' Claims and other
Claims upon some of the forfeited Estates, and in the end
of Harvest 1749 I came from my own house in company
with Donald Cameron the North road to Town which was
the last time I travelled that road. When Mr. David Bruce[2]
came to survey the Estate of Lochiel he held his Courts
at my house and I appeall to himself if I did not do him
all the service in my power in assisting him in the execution
of his office, and I allso appeal to Mr. Patrick Campbell
ffactor apon the Estate of Lochiel if I did not assist him
all in my power to levy the Rents and sett the Lands and
as he knows perfectly weel by my concurring with him
I dissobliged the whole country. In the end of Harvest
and beginning of Winter 1751 Collonell Crawford who
commanded then at Fort William sent Captain Johns and
Mr. Gardiner to my house with orders to bring all my
papers to Fort William and me Prisoner there which
accordingly they did and brought every paper I had in
my house, not only mine but every paper they found in my
wife's drawers and in my Cousine Peggy Cameron's drawers.
Next day all my papers were read and examined by Mr.
Douglass the Sherife, Mr. Gardiner, the Agitant and Captain Johns, and after the narowest examination they could
make, haveing found nothing in them that they could in
the least challenge were all returned to me and I was sett

---

[1] John Maclachlan of Greenhall   He had been tenant of the farm of
Achintore at a very low rent   This rent was raised by the Barons of Exchequer
and he would not pay the increase   So the tenancy was exposed at public
roup and Fassifern outbid Maclachlan

[2] David Bruce, a Hanoverian official   Having been attached as Judge
Advocate to Cumberland's army in the '45 he was subsequently employed to
survey the forfeited estates, and still later as a spy in conjunction with Pickle
(vide *The Highlands of Scotland in* 1750, with introduction by Andrew Lang)

at liberty upon giveing a Bond for my compearance in six months if desired.

When I was Prissoner at Fort William in 1746 I heard Captain Scott frequently say that he wanted to aprehend Glenavash [1] as he was informed that he was in Company with the Enginer that came to take over of the ffort when they began the sige and in the time of the sige was offering rewards to those that would kill any within the ffort and continued still with the Rebells and had a Company of men commanded by his brother [2] the whole time of the Rebellion mostly his own tennants and that he received after Collodin 120 Luidors from Doctor Cameron as the Arrears due his Company and 160 Luidors from Charles Stewart.

Some time after Glenvash came home from his Imprisonment in Ed[n] Castle either in the 1747 or 48 the first time he came to my house he told me that as he was going in to his boat at Marybrough Governour Campbell and Mclauchlin his son in law in a manner forced him to go and dine with them and after dinner that they called him to a Closett where they pretended a great deal of friendship for him and that his answer to them was how could he belive them as Generall Campbell showed him a leter from the Governour wherein after laying a great deal to his Charge he said that besids that his son in law had much more to lay to his Charge, and that the Governour's answer was that it was that villant Douglass wrote that leter and that he signed it without knowing the Contents of it, and that then Mclauchlin said he thanked God he was in

---

[1] Alexander Cameron of Glenevis He married Mary, daughter of Archibald Cameron of Dungallon, whose daughter, Jean, was the wife of Dr. Archibald Cameron Though he took no part in the '45 he was imprisoned for nearly a year on suspicion He was released from Edinburgh Castle, 7th July 1747 (*The Lyon in Mourning,* 1 124) His wife and family also suffered the usual brutalities at the hands of the Hanoverian troops

The relation between the Camerons of Lochiel and the Camerons or MacSorlies of Glenevis were never cordial In fact there was a tradition that the latter were not Camerons at all, but a sept of Clan Donald

[2] Glenevis had three brothers—Alan, killed at Culloden; Angus, mentioned in the Memorial, and Samuel, the spy, who betrayed Dr. Archibald Cameron (*The Lyon in Mourning,* III. 137, *note*)

good friendship with the whole Country except ffassfern
and that he was very indifferent about him and Glenavash
said that his answer to him was how could he expect to be
in friendship with the Country and be at variance with
Fassfern. Its very well known that while Glenavash was
prissoner at Inveraray at Glasgow and E^dn that he made it
his business in all companies to run down the Governour
and McLauchlin. Some time after Glenavash had this
conversation with me at my own house, I was informed
that he and Mclauchlin had Joined in Copartnership of
trade, and hapning to meet him in August 1749 at Cul-
chenas buriall after the Interment he and I and a great
many others returned to Culchena's[1] house where we took
a hearty Glass ; at which time I told him I was surprised
after what he told me at Fassfern that he should join in
Company with Mclauchlin he began to vindicate Mclauchlin
and denyed that he had told me a word of the conversation
at ffasfern which provoked me so much that I threw a glass
of punch in his face and tossed him over on the bed wheron
we were sitting. Immediatly Blairmacfildich[2] and younge
Kenloch appeared for Glenavash and blustered a good
deal however he and his two friends were turned out of
the Room and did not appear till next morning and then
ther was no more mention of it. Its to be observed that
at my own house at the head of Locharkak and in all
places where I had occation to see Glenavash his conversation was mostly running down Mr. Douglass and
calling him a thousand Villants and that the Country would
never be hapy while he was in it. The greatest dispute
betwixt us allways was he running down Mr. Douglass and
I takeing his part.

Mrs. Cameron came to my house in Winter 1751 and told
me at Glenavash's desire she was come to receive py^t of
money due by him and his brother. I told I would not
interfire betwixt them, she went to Glen's and when she

---

[1] The Camerons of Cuilchenna, near Onich at the mouth of Loch Leven, are
said to have been cadets of Callart

[2] A farm near Fort William on Wade's road.

returned to my house she told me Glen would not give her one halfe peny. She sent severall messages to him and to his brother upon that subject but all to no purpose. About the time she was leaving the Country she then threatned she would put the debt in other peple's hands. Some little time befor this hap'ned the barbarous murther of Glenuire.[1] There was a precognition taken upon Oath of Glenavash Blarmcfildich and Kenloch when the rest of the Country was sworn [2] and they deposed then that they knew of none that had any manner of hand in that murther by advice threatning or otherwise. In about eight days after this first Oath, Glen, Blair, and Angus, Glen's brother, sent a message to me by William Steuart if I would not keep Mrs. Cameron from puting her threats in execution that they would ruin me, which accordingly they attempted by the second Oath they gave quite contrary to the first. Upon my hearing of this I went directly and waited of Collonell Crauford and Barcaldine and showed them Blair's leter to me and represented to them the malice of these people against me. They both seemed to be satisfyed of

---

[1] Colin Campbell of Glenure, son of Patrick Campbell of Barcaldine by his second wife, Lucy, daughter of Sir Ewen Cameron of Lochiel, and therefore cousin-german of Fassifern He was factor on the forfeited estates of Callart, Mamore, and Ardsheal, and was shot in the wood of Lettermore, in Appin, on 14th May 1752 As is well known, the story is the basis of *Kidnapped*, by R L Stevenson

[2] The story of how the whole country was raked for evidence is told in an article, based on original documents, which appeared in *Chambers's Journal* for 1903, p 716, entitled 'Side Lights on the Appin Murder Trial '

A number of persons mentioned in the Memorial appear in the ' Report of the Trial of James Stewart of Aucharn in Duror of Appin Edinburgh, 1753 ' In the list of witnesses for the Crown are the names of Charles Stewart, Writer in Banavie, and Notary Public, Alexander Cameron, sometime Forester of Mamlorn, now in Inneruskievoulin; Archibald Cameron, son of Allan-dow-Cameron, sometime Change Keeper in Maryburgh, Duncan MacVicar, Collector of the Customs at Fort William, John Cameron, younger of Kinlochleven; Alexander Cameron of Glenevis; John Cameron of Fasfern ; George Douglas, Sheriff Substitute of the Sheriffdom of Inverness, John Crawford, Esq , Lieutenant-Colonel of General Pultney's regiment of foot

Several of these also appear in the list of witnesses for the panel (*ibid.*, App., p 147), along with Alexander Cameron of Dungallon, and Allan Cameron, Tacksman of Lundavra In the list Archibald Cameron, *supra*, is designed son of Allan Cameron, sometime Innkeeper at Maryburgh, Drumnasaille

the falsehood of what Glen and his Knights of the Post declared. The precognitions in Mr. Mcfarlans hands will show the threatnings and suborning of witnesses against me. Charles Stevart told me that in Spring 1752 at Drimnifallies buriall Duncan Cameron Toullie insinuate to him that he would have what money he desired provided he would make discoveries against me.

About the end of Harvest 1752 there was a party went from Lagan Achdrom to search Glen's house for Arms where they found five or six Guns. They brought himself and his Arms into Fort William. It is to be observed that Glen's rentale does not intitle him to cary Arms though he qualifyed, and instead of being prosecute for the Arms found with him, in a few days therafter he got warrands for six stand of Arms. The next attempt he made upon me, being disapointed in the first, was in Winter 1752. He came to the Shirif Mr. Douglas and swore to him that, haveing left Marybrough at twelve of the clock at night in his way to his own house, within pistole shote of the Garison, there was a priming burnt at him and when he went forward a short mile further two men mett him and asked him if he was Glenavash to whom he answered, what if he was, upon which they fired two shott at him. Its to be observed that he was then two miles from his own house and but a mile from ffort William and a house aside him and several houses betwixt him and his own house that he did not call at any of these houses nor return to Fort William but went straight to his own house and neither his cloaths nor his horse touched. Upon this there was ane order to take precognitions of every one he suspected and the first question asked at each of them was if ever they heard me threaten him or proposed to do him ane Injury. Notwithstanding of the strictest inquiry that he could make it came to nothing and though there was people, close to the place he pretended he was fired at watching a Corps, there was none of them heard a shott, so that all he gained by this adventure was that every person belived that he perjured himself, beside it can be proven that a few nights after the shoting match he traveled home all alone under night. And when this second attempt upon me failed he has now made a third in which, though he has put me to a great deal of expences and trouble, yet I hope he will be dissapointed as I understand after the strickest enquiry he could point out of Evidence against me that they could lay nothing to my charge. Its to be observed that Duncan M'Vicar Collector of the Customs at Marybrough was the only person allowed to be present at the first examinations and directed the Judge what questions he was to ask those that were examined, and at the second examination Glenavash pointed out the witness and, I'm told, directed the Judge as to the Questions. Its to be observed that this M'Vicar has been most intimate with Glenavash these severall years and they go hand in hand in everything and when Blair and younge Kenloch gave the last oath in regard to Glenuire M'Vicar made it his business to represent to every person that Blair and Kenloch were men of good Characters and never known to tell any thing that was false, particularly to Corronan, to whom he made some insinuations about me and to old Kenlochlivin desiring him to stand Glens friend against me. And in the time that Mr. Douglass and he had a law plea he threatned he would do me all the hurt in his power which William Stewart Mer^ct in Marybrough can testify and severall others and Doctor M'leran residenter there. The s^d M'Vicar has got possession last Whitsunday of the Lands I was dispossessed of and wants to ruin me in order he may get all my possessions in that Country.

Its to be observed that Blairmacfildich is cousine german to Glenavash and maryed to his Cousine German and received some of the pretender's gold from him, and younge Kenloch is in love with Glen's Daughter and received of the Pretender's gold from Glen by which he has forced him to say or do whatever he directs them. To be remembered to ask Sanders Cameron Possessor of Inveriskilivuln what he has frequently heard C: Cr.[1] direct him in regard to me and Glen.

---

[1] Colonel Crawford

To be enquired of Doctor Mcleron what he heard the Doctor of that Regiment say in regard to ane expression of Co. Cr. in a publick Company of his Officers. To be enquired of Charles Steuart what was proposed to him by C. C. Captain Steuart, and Collector M'Vicar if he was offered any money or if he received any.

The Captain that was stationed at Erict and Sherife Douglass can testify it was I put them on the schem of employing Sanders Cameron to aprehend the thievs which has had very good effect in civilizing the Country. All the Gentlemen in the Neighbourhood of the Country where I live can testify that I always contributed all in my power to curb all disorders in the Country and to discourage theft and depredations and my behaviour in the 1745 and 1746 is without exception as is attested by his Royall Highness the Duke, my Lord Breadalbine, Collonell York, and Captain Carroline Scott and the deceast Governour Campbell and I belive all the officers that have been at Fort William since will attest my Character, particularly Major Pim Captain Scott, Captain Duprisinie, and the rest of the officers stationed there at present.

To be observed that when we were at Lithgow in our way here in presence of Captain Duprisinie and the other officers and Charles Steuart talking of a woman in Glasgow Glen said that the servant he had with him at present offered to him to take off that woman's head for five guinaes and comeing up to the Castle in Coach where Ensign Gordon, Glen, Charles and I was Glen observing his servant walking by the side of the Coach pointed him to us and said there is the man offered to take off the woman's head. His name is McMillan he is a cliver fellow, which shows what kind of man Glen is and what rascally servants he keeps.

PARTICULAR CONDESCENDANCE
OF SOME GRIEVANCES

INTRODUCTORY NOTE

IN vol. iii. of the *Miscellany of the Maitland Club* (pp. 387 *et seq.*) are printed various lists of Popish Parents and their children in Scotland during the period 1701-1705. These lists appear to have been made up locally by order of successive General Assemblies for transmission to the Privy Council, 'with an earnest application for the vigorous execution of the laws against the enemies of the Reformation.' Prefixed to these lists is a Proclamation against Priests and Papists dated March 17, 1704, in which Queen Anne refers to 'ane address made to us with a particular condescendence given in to our Privie Councell by the late Generall Assemblie.' And this is followed by a Memorial to the Privy Council by the Commission of the General Assembly, dated December 1, 1703, which narrates how the Assembly had laid before the Privy Council 'sundrie grievances of this Church occasioned through the increse of poperie, the multitude and restless endeavours of trafficqueing Priests and Jesuites, the abounding of profanity, and the disorders of some of the episcopall clergie.'

The document that follows seems to be another such Particular Condescendance submitted in 1714. It throws a good deal of light on the religious condition of those parts of the Highlands with which it deals, and contains names and details that seem worthy of preservation. Incidentally it illustrates the views held, not by the extreme Cameronians, but by the General Assembly of

the Church now by law established, with regard to that
'civil and religious liberty' which is frequently assumed
to have been both the object and the result of the Revolution of 1688.

The original document has not been seen.   What has
been printed is a contemporary copy *penes* the Trustees
of Sir William Fraser, K.C.B., who have kindly placed it
at the disposal of the Society.

PARTICULAR CONDESCENDANCE OF SOME GRIEVANCES FROM THE ENCREASE OF POPERY AND THE INSOLENCE OF POPISH PREISTS AND JESUITS [1]

In the bounds of the presbytery of Strathbogie popish preists are very Insolent. Some of them have their dwelling houses and farmes and live as openly and avowedly as any minister within the presbytery particularly Mr. Alex. Alexander at Burnend and the papists in that countrey do repair to their Idolatrous Mass as publickly as protestants do to the Church. Preist ffraser and severall papists in the neighbourhood of that countrey, avowed resettors and harbourers of preists, were banished by the Lords of Justiciary and yet they live openly and avowedly in their former dwellings, and this preist ffraser is entertained in the Marquess of Huntly's family. As also there is one Mr. Peter Reid preist who preaches and says Mass in the said bounds particularly at Kinnore, Abathie and Rabston and Mr. Charles Stewart sayes Mass and preaches at Dumbennan.

Mr. Alexander surnamed Mein has lived at Burnend in Dumbennan these eight or nine years, He sayes Mass and preaches ordinarly in the house of James Dalgarno in Raws of Huntly, Mr. John Gordon preist lives at Cormclat in the parish of Rathven and Bolarie and is a busie traffrequer. By means of these there is above an hundred in the paroch of Rathven perverted to popery

---

[1] A good deal of information regarding the priests and districts mentioned is contained in *The Catholic Highlands of Scotland*, by Dom Odo Blundell, O S B, and *Memoirs of Scottish Catholics*, by W Forbes Leith, S J. So far as Jesuits are concerned short biographical notices will be found in *Records of the English Province of the Society of Jesus*, by Henry Foley, S J, vol vii.

within these two years or thereby. Mr. Alexander Bruce
alias Bishop Bruce and James Donaldson preist have
their dwelling at Presham,[1] and they with Charles Stewart
preist have frequent Meetings and Masses at Letterfurie
Gollochie and Cosurrach. Mr. John Irvine preist keeps
Mass at Castle Gordon and Mr. Patrick Fraser preist at
Fochabers in a fixed place in the house of Robert Edward
there. There are above six hundred papists in the parish
of Bellie, and in Kinnore and Dumbennan the papists
are equall in number to the protestants.

In the Countreys of Glenlivet and Strathaven in the
presbytery of Aberlour preists are very Insolent and busie
and have seduced some to apostatize and others who had
renounced popery are now fallen back to their former
delusions. William Gordon in Upper Drummen an
Apostat resets Mr. John Gordon a preist and has built
a Mass house, to which the people do as openly resort to
hear Mass as protestants do to their paroch Churches.
The said preist Gordon travels up and down that countrey,
and sayes Mass and Baptises children. They proclame
banns in that Mass house in order to marriage and do
marry avowedly. One of the teachers of the Grammar
School at Fochabers is popish and children of popish
parents from diverse remote places are sent thither to be
taught and preist Stewart brother to Stewart of Boigs in
the Enzie not long agoe Gathered about thirty boyes of
good expectation having the Irish tongue and carried
them abroad in order to qualify them at their returne to
make proselyts to Rome. The papists in the said bounds
have of late sett up privat schoolls which are taught by
popish women. The preists also instruct women and send
them through the Countrey to propogat their Delusions
who when they find any easie to be practised upon, they

---

[1] Preshome in the Enzie, where Bishop Thomas Nicolson lived. A younger
brother of Sir George Nicolson of Kemnay, who was a Lord of Session, he was
Bishop of Peristachium *in partibus*, and the first Vicar-Apostolic in Scotland
after the Reformation. It would seem from a letter from Father Levistone
(Forbes Leith, vol. ii. p. 258), as well as from passages in the present document, that Bishop Nicolson sometimes passed under the name of Bruce.

acquaint their preists and the preists perfect what they
have begun.   In that countrey some protestant ministers
have no house to preach in, or any Shelter against the cold
in winter or heat in summer, and yet not only is the preist
provided in a convenient house there but in the neigh-
bouring paroch of Kirkmichaell his hearers have bought
for him a large and convenient house, to which he and they
do ordinarily resort for worship.   There are in the paroch
of Inveraven two hundred and seventy papists of whom
fifteen have apostatized within these two years.

In the paroch of Lochaber the preists swarme like
Locusts, running from house to house Gaining Multitudes
to their Ante Christian Idolatry, Baptizing and Marrying.
In the presbytery of Abernethy the preists keep publick
meetings, visite, preach, declare people married, and say
Mass without fear of the Laws.

There are four large tracts of ground in the presbytery
of Lorne upon the Continent vizt Moydart Arrisaig
Morhirr and Knoidart contiguous to one another, which
are altogether popish except one Gentleman.   They have
one Mr. Gordon a preist residing allwayes among them,
saying Mass publickly each Sabbath, and who of late is
become so bold that he encroaches on the paroches adjacent
which are planted with ministers of the Established Church,
he perverts the people and marries and Baptises particularly he baptizes children begotten in ffornication, and
takes the parents obliged to be of the Communion of the
Church of Rome and such delinquents resort to him to
evade discipline, which weakens the hands of the protestant ministers, He frequents Glenavayle Kenloch and
Moydart their houses, where he keeps Mass openly.   The
Isles of Rum Egg and Canna are all popish.   They keep
their preist and pay him their teiths.   The Isle of South
Uist is all popish.   They have a preist who resides with the
Captain of Clanronald and Benbecula and sayes Mass
publickly.   These Countreys and Islands were never
reformed from popery, and generally all the relations,
followers and tennents of the Captain of Clanronald through
all his lands both in the Continent and Isles are all papists.

The Isle of Barra [1] and other adjacent Lesser Isles have a preist who resides in the house of M'Neill of Barra. In these Countreys there are to the number of two thousand papists. There are six preists and a Mendicant ffrier still residing and officiating among them. They have their respective paroches where they ordinarly reside and officiat as if formally fixed and countenanced by authority, and it's said they are duly maintained from abroad. They keep their meetings under the inspection of their Popish Bishop, who comes to their bounds to administrat their pretended sacrament of Confirmation. The proprietors of these countreys are but fourteen of whom eight are popish viz[t] The Earl of Seaforth, the Laird of Killdin, the Captain of Clanronald, the Lairds of Moror, Benbecula, Bara Glengerry and Knockeiltaig, who all countenance the preists in perverting the people.

There are two preists that frequent the braes of Lochaber and Glengarden and sometimes go to Knoydart and Morhir, who have perverted the most part of the people of the braes of Lochaber especially Glen Rey, they have infected a great part of the paroch of Kilmanivoig. They haunt also the Braes of Locherkaig in the paroch of Kilmalie and are like to over run all that Countrey if not speedily and effectually prevented.

In the bounds of the presbytery of Auchterarder in the shire of Peaith, there are many papists, and Mr. Alexander Drummond a preist resides constantly there, and he and other preists who haunt the family of Drummond have latly perverted diverse persons. The Lord Drummond had latly a son baptized publickly by a popish preist and a popish Bishop was sent for, to be Godfather, and many Gentlemen in the Countrey about were invited to be there,

---

[1] The following curious passage occurs in a Visitation Report to Propaganda, by Bishop Nicolson, in 1700: 'In this island (Barra) many people are under the power of a kind of vision, called by the natives second sight, in virtue of which they foresee and predict unexpected and wonderful events This power is quite beyond their own control, and the effects actually correspond to the predictions The bishop proposes certain spiritual remedies with a view to delivering these poor people, but desires to refer the matter to the impartial judgment of your eminences' (Bellesheim, *Hist. of Catholic Church*, vol. iv. p 372).

and came accordingly. Most of whom were said to be present at the Baptisme.

There are in the united paroches of Tullich Glenmuick and Glengarden in Aberdeenshire two hundred and sixty five papists, ffour hundred in the united paroches of Crathie and Kindrochet, twenty one in Aboyne and Glentanner, and preists Jesuits and others in popish orders have their ordinary residence in those paroches particularly Mr. Hugh Strauchan a Jesuit resides in Ardoch which belongs to Callum Grierson alias M'Grigor of Dalfad who has built an house for him and a garden and furnishes him with other necessaries. They keep publick Mass and all other parts of their Idolatrous Worship in and about the said place almost every Lord's Day, and there are other preists residing for ordinary there, such as Mr. John Innes, Mr. Robert Seton brother to Seton of Garltoun both Jesuits. They have their ordinary residence with John Stewart of Balletrach and James Mackie in the Muir of Tullich which last named has built a Mass house for them, where they have their Popish Meetings At Least once a moneth. Mr. Walter Innes, prior of a convent in Burgundie and Mr. George Innes son to Innes of Drumgask one Mr. [Stephen] Maxwell provinciall of the Jesuits frequents those parts and Mr. —— Bruce who goes under the name of Lord Bishop of Aberdeen [1] comes once a year and sometimes oftener and with great solemnity administrats their pretended Sacrament of Confirmation in these paroches. Papists do meet on the Lords Day and their popish holy dayes and solemnize Marriage and Baptize children openly in the view of the world without regard to authority. Within these few years there are two hundred in the paroches of Crathie and Kindroucht who have apostatized to popery, and twenty eight in the paroch of Tullich, Glenmuick and Glengarden. Beside these preists there are trafficquing papists that do much harme in the places such as Callum Gregory, Alexander Cattanach and the said Callum Grierson of Dalfad and James Michie and

---

This seems to refer to Bishop Nicolson, *vide ante*, p 59, note.

others. Yea so barefaced are those papists, that such as
were banished by the Lords of Justiciary are returned
home particularly Patrick Grant in Tomnaraw.

In the bounds of the presbytery of Aberdeen there are
above thirty popish families and several preists vizt Mr.
Nicolson Mr. Buchan Mr Donaldson Mr. Abernethie
Mr. Strauchan and Mr. ffordyce who keep meetings
and say Mass in the houses of Lady Pitfoddells Lady
Cairnfeilds George Duncan and ffrancis Innes.

In the bounds of the presbytery of Garioch there are five
popish preists vizt Mr. John Innes alias Litle Innes, Mr.
[Alexander] Seton alias Ross, natural son to the late Earl
of Dumfermline and Mr. —— Halket. These all haunt the
house of Lesly of Balqhain at ffetternier. This is the comon
receptacle of the Superior of the Jesuits in Scotland, In
this house there is a consecrated Chaple put to no other
use but their Idolatrous worship, There they have an
altar, rich Vestments and all other coastly appurtenances
for their service, from that place popish youths are recommended when they go abroad and thither they first return
when they come home Missionaries, and from thence are
dispersed through Scotland, ffor the family of Balquhain
as is informed has the disposall of most if not all the
Bursaries in the Scots Colledges at Dowie and Rome.

In the bounds of the presbytery of ffordyce particularly in the paroch of Rathven there are a great many
preists trafficquing among the people and do pervert many,
such as Mr. Nicolson alias Bishop Bruce, preist Donaldson,
preist Gordon alias Bishop Gordon brother to the Laird
of Glastirum and diverse others who keep their staited
meetings every Lords day in a most publick manner
without the least disturbance.

In the paroch of Kirmorack[1] there are above an hundred
families within these two or three years perverted to
popery who with the many preists that were there formerly
make up the farr greater part of that paroch Mr. Alexander M'Craw a Jesuit and Mr. Æneas M'Laughlan a preist

---

[1] The reference seems to be to Strathglass in the parish of Kilmorack.

latly come from ffrance Reside in that paroch and keep Mass openly.

One, father Peter M'Donald resides near Abertarfe and sometimes in Glengarden and keeps Mass openly in the house of M'Donald of Kiltrie and now the farr greater part of the paroch of Abertarf are popish.

Mr. ffrancis Murray preist and other preists and Jesuits do frequent the bounds of the shires of Dumfrees Galloway and Tweeddale and say Mass there particularly at Kirkconnell and of late have perverted diverse persons to popery about sixteen in one paroch.

Some of these popish Bishops preists and Jesuits above named are several times named Because they trafficque in diverse places.

And besides these popish Bishops preists and Jesuits above mentioned there are a great many others latly come from abroad whose names by their Artifices to conceal them cannot certainly be known.

By the Laws of Scotland no papist can succeed to heretages and the children of popish parents are appointed to be taken from them and put in the custody of their nearest protestant relations and all papists are discharged under severe penalties to keep schoolls or teach any science, art or exercise or to be Imployed in the Education of youths or the Mannagement of their affairs, or to be Governours, Chaplains Pædagogues Schoollmasters tutors curators Chamberlains or ffactors. Yet these good Laws are not put in execution.[1]

---

[1] These Penal Laws were not repealed till 1793 But in spite of many 'an earnest application for the vigorous execution of the laws against the enemies of the Reformation,' the authorities as a rule refused to interfere; e g. in 1756 Bishop Hugh Macdonald, a brother of Allan Macdonald of Morar, and Vicar-Apostolic for the Highlands, being delated by a dishonest debtor of his brother, was tried before the Court of Justiciary on the charge of being a Jesuit, priest, or trafficking papist, refusing to purge himself of popery by taking the statutory formula. He was found guilty by the jury and sentenced to be banished furth of the realm, with certification that if he ever returned, being still papist, he should be punished with death (*Scots Magazine*, vol xviii p. 100) However, he merely changed his name and went on with his work as before, and the government took no notice.

PARTICULAR CONDESCENDANCE OF SOME GRIEVANCES from the Insults and Intrusions of those of the Episcopall Perswasion

DOCTOR John Sharp who designs himselfe Chaplain to her Majesties forces in America, and who is of the Episcopall perswasion, Having got a presentation from two of the Masters of the King's Colledge of Aberdeen has intruded into the paroch Church there, and performes worship after the manner of the Church of England, notwithstanding that there was a prior presentation given by all the qualified Masters of the said Colledge, to Mr. Alexander Mitchell [1] a Minister of the Established Church, and who is now appointed to go and be admitted Minister there, and a rable of people who did attend the said Doctor did break open the doors of the Church and Insulted and abused the preacher sent by the presbytery to supply that vacant Church.

Mr. William Law [2] once a Minister of the Communion of this Church but who several years ago, has gone over to those of the Episcopal way, has latly intruded and sett up the English service in the paroch Church of Slains.

Mr. George Scott an Episcopall Clergieman latly ordained, Did in the moneth of May current Raise and excite a rable of people and with their assistance broke open the doors of

---

[1] Alexander Mitchell, minister of Belhelvie, was presented to Old Machar in May 1713 and admitted 31st August 1714 (*Fasti*, vol iii p 485)

[2] William Law, at one time minister of Crimmond On the appointment of John Forbes by the Presbytery, *jure devoluto*, to Slains, 'his settlement was opposed by a multitude who prevented the edict being served in the church, and said they wanted no minister but Mr Law. . . . On the day fixed for the ordination certain agents, by going through pretended forms of law, as well as by the

the Church of Aberlour [1] and took violent possession thereof and Intruded therein, and continues so to do, not only excluding from it the Minister of the Established Church who is duly and orderly admitted thereto, But by force of armes in violent manner assaulting and beating ·and Invading the ministers of the presbytery of Aberlour when they came to setle and admitt the Legall Minister in that Church.

Mr. George Hay ordained by an Exauctorated Bishop but deposed for scandall and Immorality and thereafter banished Scotland by the Lords of Justiciary for diverse disorders and Irregularities has returned and Intruded on the paroch Church of Rathven [2] and exercises the office of the Holy Ministry there and has introduced the Liturgie of the Church of England into that paroch Church contrary to Law and does not so much as pray for her Majesty Queen Anne. This in name of the Commission of the General Assembly is subscribed By *Sic Subscribitur* Will: Mitchell, Moderator.[3]

---

violence of an armed mob, prevented the Presb. getting access to the church, the women affirming that " if it were not for better fellows, the Presbytery should be sent home with bloody breeks "' (*Fasti*, vol. iii. p. 613).

[1] George Lindsay, minister of Rothes, was presented to Aberlour by William Duff of Braco in April 1714, and 'admitted 12th May, at which time the Presbytery were mobbed by a party of non-jurants, who with their preacher had taken possession of the church, so that the settlement had to be made in the fields' This enables the date of the Particular Condescendance to be fixed as 1714 (*Fasti*, vol. iii p 217)

[2] According to the *Fasti*, vol. iii p 678, *John* Hay, who became minister of Rathven in 1669, was deprived at the Revolution In 1699 William Chalmers was presented by the Presbytery *jure devoluto*, but he only remained there till 1704 During all that time, and up to his death about 1712, this non-juror seems to have 'intruded' with more or less success He had a son *George*, served heir to him March 12, 1713.

[3] The Rev William Mitchell, one of the ministers of Edinburgh, was elected Moderator of the General Assembly on May 6, 1714 'He was a superior preacher, a fluent speaker, and, being perhaps the most wealthy minister of Scotland, had great influence at Court ' (*Fasti*, vol i p 29) He was the father of Sir Andrew Mitchell, minister at Berlin

PAPERS RELATING TO KINTYRE

INTRODUCTORY NOTE

FROM its march with Knapdale at Tarbert to its southern extremity the Mull, the peninsula of Kintyre, the *Epidium Promontorium* of ancient writers, is some forty miles long and, on an average, some eight miles broad. In the fifth century it was seized by the Dalriad Scots from Ireland, and later on it fell into the hands of the northern heathen who, under one name or another, were the pest of Scotland till their power was finally destroyed by Alexander III. Long before this, when Malcolm III. made an agreement with Magnus Barefoot under which the latter was to retain possession of all the isles that could be circumnavigated, it may be remembered that the Norse king was drawn in his galley over the narrow neck of land that separates East and West Lochs Tarbert, with the result that not merely did Kintyre remain for the time in the hands of Magnus, but so late as the seventeenth century, as Mr. Gregory points out,[1] it was still classed as one of the South Isles.

Early in the twelfth century Somerled seems to have cleared the Northmen out of Kintyre and to have incorporated the peninsula with his dominions. And this possibly explains how David I. was able in 1128 to grant to the canons of Holyrood one half of his tithe of the Kane, pleas, and gains of the Crown from Kentyr and Errogeill,[2] and to the monks of Dunfermline a few years later the half of his tithe from Ergaithel and Kentir.[3] On Somerled's

---

[1] *History of the Western Highlands and Islands*, p 14, note.
[2] *Cart. Liber Sanctae Crucis*, p 6. [3] *Regist de Dunferm*, p. 7.

death Kintyre passed to his son Reginald who, in a charter to the Abbey of Saddel, designed himself Rex Insularum dominus de Ergile et Kyntyre,[1] and through him to his descendants the Lords of Yla and Kintyre. By the middle of the thirteenth century Kintyre appears as one of the rural deaneries of the diocese of Argyll: and among the sheriffdoms erected by King John Balliol in 1292 is that of Kintyre, which comprised Bute and part of Cowal as well as the peninsula itself. From the fact that King Robert I. granted charters of lands in Kintyre to various of his supporters, it would seem that the lordship must at that time have been in the hands of the Crown; and after sundry grants and forfeitures, Kintyre along with half of Knapdale was in the year 1376 settled by Robert II. on John of Yla and his wife Margaret, the king's daughter, and their heirs. Donald, the eldest son of this marriage, succeeded his father as Lord of the Isles, while John the Tanister, his younger brother, received Yla and Kintyre to hold under him. From this John Mor Tanister, who married Marjorie Bisset, heiress of the Glens of Antrim, sprang the family known as Clan Ian Mhor of Yle, or Clan Donald of the South, of which the Chief was styled Macdonald of Dunyveg and the Glens.[2] In due time the lordship descended to Donald's grandson, John, Lord of the Isles and Earl of Ross, who was forfeited in 1475, and when he was restored next year the Earldom of Ross and the Lordships of Kintyre and Knapdale were

---

[1] *R. M S*, lib. xiv f. 408.

[2] Certain lands in Isla are described as 'of old pertaining to the Abacy of Derie' (*Highland Papers*, vol i. p 252) It was difficult to understand how these Scots lands had come to be possessed by an Irish abbey, but a quaint explanation is given in a memorandum in the Charter Room at Inveraray, dated 16th April 1659, regarding the lands of Maclean of Duart . 'As for that roume in Ila pertaining to the Abacie of Derie our Scheanachies or as Buchannane calls them Senetiones doe affirme that the same was mortified to the Abacie of Derie in Ireland by M'Donald of Ila ffor ane untymeous fart he did let goe. This I bot tell you by the way.'

expressly excluded from the restitution,[1] and remained in
the hands of the Crown.

In 1494 James IV. spent some time in Kintyre, and he
had hardly taken his departure when Dunaverty, where
he had left a garrison, was attacked and captured and its
governor hanged by Sir John Macdonald of Dunyveg. This
outbreak led to serious trouble for that family, who had
to take refuge in their Irish possessions. Shortly thereafter
the lordship, subject of course to the rights of various
vassals such as the Clan Ranaldbane or Macdonalds of
Largie, was placed in the hands of the Earl of Argyll as
chamberlain, whose accounts for the three years ending
28th July 1505, as well as a rental of the same date giving
the names of the individual holdings and tenants, are
still preserved.[2] It was also divided into two districts,
North and South Kintyre, and various grants of lands
and offices—permanent and temporary—many of them
probably being only confirmations of existing rights,
were made from time to time.

In 1540 the Lordship of the Isles with ' the twa Kintyris
with the castellis partening thereto and thare pertinents '
was by Act of Parliament annexed inalienably to the
Crown,[3] and in 1545 the services, *specialiter in resti-
tentia Veterum Anglie inimicorum* of James Macdonald
of Dunyveg and the Glens, whose father had become
reconciled to the Crown, were rewarded by a grant of
the extensive barony of Bar in North Kintyre, which on
his death in 1565 passed to his son Angus, who with
his son Sir James were prominent in the troubles of
their times.

In 1596 it was found necessary to arrange for an expedition to the Isles under Sir William Stewart of Houston,

---

[1] *R.M.S.*, July 15, 1476.
[2] *Exchequer Rolls*, xii. pp. 352-698.   [3] *Acts*, vol. ii. p. 361.

Commendator of Pittenweem, who received a commission of Lieutenancy and Justiciary. Proceeding to Kintyre the Lieutenant on 1st November 1596 held a court at which Angus Macdonald and others made their personal submission. The Record of this court, which is preserved in H.M. General Register House, is the first of the documents here printed, and, as will be seen, it contains a list of the tenants of Kintyre, of the lands occupied by them individually, and of the waste and unoccupied lands. A dispute between Angus Macdonald and his son Sir James resulted in the latter seizing the estates and deposing his father from the Chiefship, and following thereon he made certain proposals to the Government, with the object of himself and his people finally settling down peacefully and accepting the royal authority. These proposals were approved of by the Privy Council, but through the machinations of Argyll and Campbell of Calder, as Mr. Gregory thinks,[1] they came to nothing. Sir James, being seized by his father towards the end of 1603, was handed over to Argyll and then placed in Edinburgh Castle, where he was detained for many years.

In 1605 the Comptroller, David Murray, Lord Scone, proceeded to Kintyre, where on 3rd September he held a court similar to that held by Sir William Stewart nine years before. The Record of this court is the second of the documents printed. As Mr. Gregory points out,[2] the waste lands had considerably increased. In 1596, out of 139 merklands in North Kintyre, $36\frac{1}{2}$ were waste; and out of 205 merklands in South Kintyre, 45 were waste. In 1606, out of $151\frac{1}{2}$ merklands in North Kintyre, 62 were waste; and out of 203 merklands in South Kintyre, 51 were waste. In September of that year Angus Macdonald, who time and again had attempted to

---

[1] *History*, p 289. [2] *Ibid* , p. 308.

make an honourable settlement with regard to both Ila and Kintyre, submitted a final offer to the King, and this and the accompanying letter are also printed here. But again the hostile influence was too strong. And next year the Earl of Argyll, in implement of a contract dated 27th May 1607, obtained a feu charter dated 30th May 1607 of the lands of both North and South Kintyre, therein specified, which are said to have previously belonged to Angus M'Konnell of Dunyvaig, and to have been incorporated into the Lordship of Kintyre with Dunaverty as its chief messuage.

The inductive clause of this charter sets forth that the subjects of the grant had been for many years past possessed by unruly and barbarous persons destitute of the knowledge and fear of God, and of any reverence for the King or the laws of the realm, who maintained no civilisation among themselves[1] nor permitted the King's other subjects to trade with them save at the peril of their lives and goods; and it concludes with a provision that none of the lands thereby granted shall be set or disponed 'ad M'Laine nec M'Connell,' or any one of their names within the forbidden degrees of relationship to them, without the King's special licence. Argyll next got a grant of great part of the feu duties in settlement of claims which he had against the Crown.[2] Finally after various transactions the Lordship of Kintyre was disannexed from the Crown and settled on Argyll and the eldest son of his second marriage—afterwards Lord Kintyre and Earl of Irvine—with whom Lord Antrim in 1635 concluded an agreement for the repurchase of that part of the ancient patrimony of Clan Donald. But Lord Lorne—afterwards the Marquess of Argyll—intervened, and in the most high-handed manner the Privy Council set the transaction

[1] Cf. *post*, p. 113.
[2] Chiefly for his butchery of the Macgregors.

aside. In the long run Kintyre was acquired from his half-brother by Lord Lorne and finally incorporated with the possessions of MacCailein.[1]

---

[1] Vide *Scots Peerage*, vol. v. p. 23.

In view of all these facts and of the similar history of Isla it is little wonder that when Alaster MacCol Ciotach found his way into Kintyre he took a most thoroughgoing revenge on the oppressors of his race. 'Kintyre was left a desert, its few inhabitants became the prey of a fearful pestilence which followed in the train of all their other calamities. In this wilderness where a smoking chimney was scarcely to be seen, the lowlanders who had joined the standard of Argyle, were encouraged, after the war, to settle. Others came from the opposite mainland.'—*New Stat. Account*, vol. vii. p. 460.

PAPERS RELATING TO KINTYRE

I   [1596]

'Curia tenta per egregium et preclarum virum Do-
minum Gulielmum Stewart de Houstoun [1] militem
lieutenentem pro serenissimo domino nostro Rege
versus australes occidentales insulas et Hibernicas
partes hujus regni virtute commissionis sibi sub
magno sigillo prefati supremi Domini nostri Regis
desuper concessæ, apud caput lacus de Loch Kilkeren
in Keantyre, primo die mensis Novembris anno Domini j^m v^c lxxxxvj, curia legittime affirmata, ad-
judicatare Gulielmo Forrest.

'The quhilk day, in presens of the said Sir Williame
Stewart [2] of Houstoun, knycht, his Majesteis lieutenent
foirsaid, comperit Angus M'Conneill of Dunnavage and
Glenis with the remanent personis eftir nominat, present
occupyaris and possessouris of the landis respective and
particularlie underwrittin, and grantit and confessit that
ane pairte of the landis of South and North Keantyre war
occupyit and possessit be thame and ilkane of thame

---

[1] Printed from the original *Miscellaneous Exchequer Papers*, Portfolio 1 ,
H M General Register House

[2] According to Calderwood he commenced life as 'a cloutter of old shoes,'
but this statement is not accepted by Sir James Balfour Paul, who regards him
as a son of Thomas Stewart of Galston (*Scots Peerage*, vii. 64)   For some time
a soldier of fortune under the Prince of Orange, he returned to Scotland and
entered the service of James vi.   In 1583 he was made Commendator of
Pittenweem, and in 1590 he commanded the fleet that brought the King and his
bride from Denmark   In 1596 he had a commission of Lieutenancy in the
Highlands and Islands and in the course of his duties held the court of which
the record is here printed.

72

respective *pro rata* as eftir followis, and ane uther pairte thairof war lyand waist unoccupyit be thame or ony utheris ; viz. :—

The landis of North Keantyre

Farquhar Makcay and his subtenentis occupyaris of thrie merkland of the tuell merkland of Auchincros,[1] and the remanent extending to nyne merk land waist.

Donald Makcay occupyar of ane merkland of the fyve merkland of Bar, and the rest extending to four merkland waist.

Donald Makneill occupyar of ane merkland of the four merkland of Ballemullingis, the rest waist.

Certane pure tenentis occupyaris of twa merkland of the four merkland of Drumore, the uther twa merkland therof waist.

The thrie merkland of Eskelmore all waist.

The thrie merkland of Eskelbeg waist.

The twa merkland of Crosbeg occupyit be Johne Makcay.

Adame Makcay occupyar of the thrie merkland of Barieskmole.

The thrie merkland of Ballemanochis, callit in the rentell five merkland, waist.

James Makconneill occupyar of the aucht merkland of Smerbye.

Donald Makcay occupyar of the four merkland of Penneneir and Auldtirrie.

Donald Makmarkie occupyar of the thrie merkland of Laggen.

James Makconneill occupyar of thrie merkland of the

---

[1] Variants of the spelling of these place-names will be found in the Rental of 1605, printed *post*, pp 79 *et seq* , as well as in the charters to James Macdonald of April 21, 1545, and May 5, 1558 (*R M S*), and to Argyll, May 30, 1607 (*R M S*) A comparison of these different forms sometimes assists in the ascertainment of the true name of the place, notwithstanding the ingenious perversity of the lowland charter scribes

four merkland of Corpudzochan, and ane merkland therof waist.

Archebald Makgechane occupyar of twa merkland of the four merkland of Clangart, and the rest waist.

Gilbert Makfalac occupyar of twa merk land of the four merkland of Mermonogath, and uther twa waist.

The twa merkland of Auchtedewic waist.

Donald Makcay occupyar of the twa merkland of Glencardoch.

The thrie merkland of Balloch waist.

Donald Og Makstoker occupyar of xxs. land of the twa merkland of Kilmaloag, and the rest extending to vjs. viijd. land waist.

The Laird of Loup occupyar of the thrie merkland of Amote.

Johne Makcrewchie occupyar of the merkland of Garvald.

Gilbert Makstoker occupyar of the twa merkland of Scotodaill.

Johne Makcay occupyar of the fyve merk land of Mongastell.

The four merkland of Crubastell waist.

Angus Makconneill occupyar of the fyve merkland of Veach.

The Laird of Largie occupyar of the four merkland of Gortinvall.

Archebald M'Carlie occupyar of the twa merkland of Grenen.

The said Archebald occupyar of the twa merkland of Speresak.

The Erle of Argyle occupyar of the four merkland of Crosak, four merkland of Bellegronan and Maysreoch, and ar kirk landis.

Donald Makcay occupyar of the merk land of Blair.

Farquhar Makcay occupyar of the twa merk land of Arnekill.

The said Farquhar occupyar of the tua merkland of Kildonan Kirkland alsua.

Angus Makconneill occupyar of the landis eftir specefeit, bocht be him fa the Laird of Barskymming,[1] viz. :—

The thrie merkland of Dewpin.
The four merkland of Arcardill.
The twa merkland of Auchnasill.
The four merkland of Rannadaill.
The ane merkland of Kirknacrage.
Ane merkland of Kirknache.
Twa merkland of Kilmichaell.
Tua merkland of Stronovean.
Tua merkland of Auchroy.
Tua merkland of Tadowchreis.[2]

FOLLOWIS THE LANDIS OF SOUTH KEANTYRE

Rannald Makconneill, brother to the said Angus, occupyar of the four merkland of Bellegrogane and Craigoch.

The said Rannald occupyar of the fyve merkland of Lossett and Glenchain.

Angus M'Conneill occupyar of twa merkland of the four merkland of Knokeantmore, and the rest thairof waist.

Rannald Makalaster occupyar of the thrie merkland of Kilzechoane.

Donald Makfinlay occupyar of the twa merkland of Drumlanbill.

Cristeane Stewart occupyar of the twa merkland of Loch quhordill.

Rannald Makconneill lait occupyar of the fyve merkland of Tirieariois and Largabane, now waist.

Gilleis Makcochennell occupyar of the fyve schilling and xd. land of Bugill and Invergye.

Gillecallum more Makgowga occupar of ane half merkland of the twa merkland of Kilcobenach.

---

[1] Adam Reid of Barskimming in Kyle
[2] *Quære* the *Twa* dowchreis.

Kilde . . . llochan occupyar of ane uther half merkland thairof, the rest waist.

Gilcallummore M'Ilvenezie occupyar of ane merkland of the thric merkland of Claknahall.

Tavis Makfailan occupyar of ane uther merkland thaiiof, and the thrid waist.

Angus Makconneill and his spous occupyaris of twa merkland of the xvij merkland of Kilzeowman.

Donald Dow M'Neill and his tenentis occupyaris of ten merkland thairof, and the remanent extending to fyve merkland waist.

Angus Makconneill occupyar of ane merkland of Auchownastesak; the rest of the sevin merkland of Wegill, Antiquhorik, Kilbreid, Kynnachan, Auchownastesak and Ochterone, extending to sex merkland thairof waist.

The said Angus occupyar of the thrie pund land of Knokriochmore, Glenmugill and Ochterone, callit in the rentell v merkland.

Archebald M'Conneill occupyar of thrie merkland of the four merkland of Knokreochbeg, Arnaskeoch, Allabadowne.

Angus Dow occupyar of the uther merkland thairof.

The said Angus Makconneill occupyar of the tuell merkland of Kinloch.

James Makconneill occupyar of twa merkland of the four merkland of Kildallage, Knokquhirk and Auchnaquhonis, and uther twa meikland thanof waist.

Rannald Makalaster occupyar of twa merkland of the sex merkland of Ballatonay, Auchnacorvie and Ballabreid.

Gilliccallum M'Neill and his brother occupyar of uther twa meikland thairof, and the rest waist.

The said Angus M'Concill occupyar of the tuell merkland of Machiimore.

Hector Makalaster occupyar of the fyve merkland of Kildavie.

The twa merkland of Glenmuklok waist.

Angus M'Concill occupyar of thrie merkland of the fyve

merk vjs. viijd. land, callit be the present possessouris v merkland, of Poldowilling, and uther twa
merkland thairof waist.

Doncane of May occupyar of the thrie merkland of Glenda-
harvie.

Flaardoch Makgowgan occupyar of the merkland of
Garnagerach.

Archebald Makconneill occupyar of ane merkland of
Eredill.

The said Archebald occupyar of ane merkland of Socach.

Gilbert Makilvrenenich occupyar of the twa merkland of
Corsyn and Bairfairne.

Hector Makneill *alias* M'Illespie Vekachan occupyar of the
four merkland of Craig.

The said James M'Conneill occupyar of thrie merkland
of the four merkland of Kilmichaell and Auchinlek.

Hector Makneill occupyar of fyve merkland of the tuell
merkland of Carska, and the rest waist.

Angus M'Connell occupyar of the four merkland of Mule
of Keantyre.

Angus Maknachan occupyar of ane merkland of the twa
merkland of Keremenach.

Hew Makcochennach occupyar of ane half merkland
thairof, and ane uther half merkland waist.

The four merkland of Collolonfort, Ballavenen and Dalquhirnoch waist.

Angus M'Nachan occupyar of the merkland of Cardavay.

Gilleis M'Cochennan occupyar of ane merkland of the
twa merkland of Machribeg, ane uther waist.

Hector Makneill occupyar of the viijs. iiijd. land of Lepinbeg.

Angus M'Conneill occupyar of the viijs. iiijd. land of
Machriecastell.

Donald M'Varchis occupyar of the xxs. land of Keran-
more.

Niniane Stewart occupyar of the xxs. land of Glak.

Angus M'Conneill occupyar of half merkland of Legon-
tavart.

Murdoch M'Cochennoch occupyar of the twa merkland of
Dimidium De Lyell and Lepinstraith.

Archebald M'Conneill occupyar of four merkland of the aught merkland of Carcadule, Capritane, Gartunachan, Brakleid, Garclosken.

Hector M'Alaster occupyar of uther xxs. land of the saidis landis.

Johne M'Gacharne occupyar of uther xxs. land thairof.

Archebald M'Michaell occupyar of ane merkland thairof.

Douncane M'Cochennach occupyar of the four merkland vs. xd. land of Brunerikin, Amon, Drummerionach, Dalsmerie, Lagnandaw, Evencoulcalzeach.

Johne Makgacharne occupyar of the aucht merkland of Killellen, Pennagowin, Garclosken, Elrig, Arienskanchan.

The said Johne M'Gacharne occupyar of twa merkland of the tuell merkland of Auchnaglach, Lagnacrage, Keresower, Ballemannoch, Teronell, Dourglas, Glenranmuskilmore, Strone, and Gillenzadule.

Archebald M'Coneill occupyar of ane merkland thairof.

Angus M'Coneill occupyar of uther thrie merkland of the samin.

Douncane More Makchennach occupyar of ane merkland thairof.

Rannald M'Alaster Herper occupyar of twa merkland of the said tuell merkland.

And the said Cristeane Stewart occupyar of uther twa merkland thairof.

The twa merkland of Kilbaine waist.

Archebald M'Conneill occupyar of the merkland of Killequhattan.

The twa merkland of Dalnahanslek occupyit be Alaster M'Alester.

And the ane merkland of Cristilloch waist.

Angus Makconneill occupyar of the thrie merkland and ane half of Kilderowane, Knokistabill and Lanaquhanyc.

The Erle of Argyle occupyar of the viijs. viijd. land of Gartingobak, being kirkland.

Quhilkis personis and everie ane of thame being present

in proper persone offerit thair dewtefull obedience to the
said Sir William Stewart of Houstoun, knycht, levetennte
foirsaid in his majesteis name, and faithfullie promesit
to be ansuerabill to his Hienes lawis, and to observe
kepe and fulfill the samin, ilkane for thair awin pairtis
respective as becummis dewtefull and obedient subjectis,
and for the better keping and observeing Farquhar M'Cay,
Johne M'Gacharne and Hector M'Neill, thrie of the cheif
of thair clanis, faithfullie promittit band and obleist
thame and ilkane of thame to gif and delyver thair pledges
for observatione of gude ordour and dew obedience to his
Hienes amangis ilkane of thair awin clanis respective, to ✕
the said Sir Williame, lievtenent foirsaid, to be transportit
be him to the law cuntrey and thair to remaine during his
Majesteis will and pleasur ; upoun quhilkis all and sundrie
premisses Johne Stewart of Escok askit act and instrument
of me nottar publict underwrittin.   Extractum. Ita
est Robertus Lauder, notarius publicus ac ejusdem curie
scriba, testantibus meis signo et subscriptione.'

  Endorsed.—' Curia Wilhelmi Stuart, haldin in Kyntyr
primo die Novembris anno Domini, etc. lxxxxvj, Be the
quhilk it is easie to undirstand the present possessouris and
tenentis.'

II ¹   [1605]

' Curia   tenta   apud   Lacum   de   Loch   Kilcarran ²   in
     South Kintyre, super monticulo vocato Knokbae,³
     tertio die mensis Septembris anno Domini millesimo
     sexcentesimo quinto, per nobilem et potentem do-
     minum, Davidem, Dominum de Scone, supremi Domini
     nostri Regis computorum Rotulatorem et dicti do-
     mini Regis in hac parte locum tenentem infra bondas

---

¹ Printed from the original   *Miscellaneous Exchequer Papers*, Portfolio I.,
H M General Register House.
  ² The church of St Kiaran or Queran, who is said to have evangelised the
people of Kintyre in the sixth century. The loch bears his name, and the old
name of Campbeltown at its head is Cean-loch-chille-Chiaran.
  ³ Knock Bay is the name given by the constructors of the Ordnance Survey
map to an eminence in the outskirts of Campbeltown

et terras de South et North Kintyre et insulas
Hybeinicas regni Scotie, virtute commissionis sibi
desuper concessæ, curia legittime affirmata, adjudi-
catore Neill M'Camrois.

'The quhilk day in presens of the said nobill lord,
David, Lord of Scone,[1] Comptrollar and levetennent in that
part foirsaid, comperit personalie the personis eftir specefeit and grantit and confessit that his Hienes propir landis
of South and North Kintyre ar laborit and manuit as
particularlie followis, viz. :—

Tuelf merkland of Auchincrose : waist.

The nyne merk land of Bar : òccupiit be Johane M'Kay.

Ballemulingis Eister and Vestir, iiij merk land : quhairof
　　be Donald M'Neill ij merkland, and be Johne Stewart
　　the uther tua merk land.

Drummoir, iiij merk land : vaist.

Eskmelmoir, iij merkland : occupiit be Donald M'Kay.

Eskmelbeg, iij merkland : occupiit be Johnne M'Kay.

Corsbeg, ij merkland : occupiit be the said Johnne M'Kay.

Bareskmole, iij merkland : occupiit be Ferquard M'Kay.

Ballemanochis Over and Nethir, v. merkland : occupiit be
　　the said Johne M'Kay.

Smerby and Clakmoch, viij merkland : occupiit be Angus
　　Og M'Donald.

Pennenyre and Altincarroche, iiij merkland : occupiit be
　　Donald M'Kay.

Laggane, iij merkland : waist.

Drumgarroch, iiij merkland : occupiit be the said Angus
　　Og.

---

[1] David Murray of Gospertie, second son of Sir Andrew Murray of Balvaird.
In 1599 he was appointed Comptroller, in 1604 he was created Lord Scone, and
in 1608 the Abbacy of Scone was erected into a temporal lordship in his favour ;
a remarkable series of remainders being added in 1612   In 1621 he was created
Viscount of Stormont with a destination to the various heirs called in the charter
of 1612   He died in 1631.   In June 1605 he was directed 'to repair towards
Kintyre for ressaveing of the obedience of the principalls of the clannis within
the south Ilis and suirtie for payment of His Majesties mailles rentes and
dewties' (P C R , vii 59), and this document is the record of a court held by
him at Campbeltown on September 3, 1605

Corpidzochane, iiij merkland : occupiit be Duncane
    Reache M'Cauchane.
Clangart, iiij merkland : waist.
Mergmonogach, iiij merkland : occupiit be Gillespik
    M'Kouchane.
Auchtadowie, ij merkland : waist.
Glencardellis, ij merkland : occupiit be Johnne M'Kay.
Balloch, iij merkland : waist.
Kilmaloag, ij merkland : waist.
Amot, iij merk ½ merkland : occupiit be Nic Chirdow
    Colls dochtir.
Garvald, j merk land : occupiit be the said Nic . . .
    Scotodale, ij merkland : occupiit be Gilchryist
    M'Stoquhor.
Mongastell, v merk land : occupiit be Johnne M'Kay.
Crubcastell, iiij merk land : occupiit be the said Johnne.
Reache, v merk land : waist.
Gortinvaill, iiij merk land : occupiit be the Laird Largie.
Grenane, ij merk land : occupiit be Hector M'Alester.
Spercsak, ij merk land : occupiit be the said Hector.
Crosak, iiij merk land : occupiit be the said Hector.
Ballegregane and Mawisreoche, iij merkland : occupiit
    be Katherene Campbell.
Blarie, j merk land : occupiit be the Laird of Largie.
Dannonochane, ij merk land : waist.
Kildonane, ij merk land : waist.
Dowpein, iij merk land : waist.
Artardill, iiij merk land : waist.
Auchnasaill, ij merk land : vaist.
Rannadale, iiij merk land : waist.
Karnacrage and Kirknasche, ij merk land : waist.
Kilmichaell, ij merk land : waist.
Stronovean, ij merk land : waist.
Auchinra, ij merk land : waist.
The twa Dowreis, ij merk land : waist.

In South Kintyre

Ballegragane and Cragoch, iiij merk land : occupiit be
    Johne M'Neill.

Gloss

Losset and Glenhane, v merk land : occupiit be Angus Eloche M'Donald.

Knokeantmore, iiij merk viijs. iiijd. land : waist.

Kilquhowane, uj merk viijs. iiijd. land : occupiit be Duncane Omey.

Drumlaibill and Lochoidill, iiij merk land : Drumlanbill occupiit be Donald M'Kinlawoir, Lochordill be Johnne M'Kecherane.

Teirarrois and Laigavane, v merk land : occupiit be Alester Og M'Donald.

Pubill and Innergye, vs. xd. land : occupiit be Gilchreist M'Ilshannoch.

Kilcobenache, ij merk land : occupiit be Gilcallum M'Gowgane.

Blaknahall, iij merk land : occupiit be Gilcalum moir M'Millane.

Killownane, xvij merk land : waist.

Wagill, Auchtquhork, Kilbreid, Kinnachane, Auchnaslessen, and Ochtoron, vij merk ½ merk land : Off the quhilkis Wagill waist, the ij merk land of Auchiquhork occupiit be Gilcreist M'Kenric, Kilbreid waist, Kynnachane waist, Auchnalessen occupiit be John Molloche M'Kirley, Ochterone waist.

Knokreochmore, Glenmugill and Ouchterone, v merk ½ merk land : Off the quhilkis Knokreochmore and Ouchterane, iiij merkland and ½, occupiit be Angus Eloche ; Glenmugill occupiit be Charlis M'Kerchane.

Knokreochbeg, Ainaskauch, Allabodowie, iiij merk land : Off the quhilkis Knokreochbeg occupiit be Angus Eloche, Ainaskauch occupiit be Gillechalume M'Kerchir, and the half merk land of Alabodowie waist.

Kinlocha, xij merk land ; in Angus M'Donald's handis and occupiit be his hyndis.

Kildallage, Knokquhirk, Auchaquhony, iiij merk land : quhairof Kildallage occupiit be Duncane M'kinvay, Knokquhirk be Neill M'Gibbon, and Auchaquhonye be Andro M'Kechrane.

Ballanatoun, Auchnatorvic, Ballabraid, vj merkland :

quhairof Ballanetoun occupiit be Donald Oure M'Neill, Auchintoryie waist, Ballabraid occupiit be Gilcallum M'Neill.

Mauchramoir, xij merk land : occupiit be Angus M'Donald.

Kildavie and Glenmuklok, vij merkland : quhairof Kildavie occupiit be Neill M'Neill, Glenmuklok be Archibald M'Neill.

Poldomuling, v merk ½ merk land : waist.

Glenharyie, iij merk land : quhairof tua merk land occupiit equalie be Neill M'Neill and Lachland M'Quhurie, the thrid merk land thairof waist.

Garnageroche, j merkland : occupiit be Duncane M'Gilwrindie.

Aradill, j merkland : occupiit be Gillespik M'Neill.

Sorak, j merkland : waist.

Corfyne, and Bairfairne, ij merkland : quhairof Corfyne occupiit be Duncane M'Ilwrindie, and Bairfairne waist.

Craig, iiij merkland : occupiit be Angus Og.

Kilmachaell and Auchinlek, iiij merkland : vaist.

Carskay, xij merkland : occupiit be Hector M'Neill.

Mule of Kintyre, iiij merkland : occupiit be the said Hector.

Keremanach and Mekilloch, ij merkland : quhairof Keremanoch occupiit be Johne Dow M'Nachane, Mekilloch be Hew M'Schenoch.

Colelonfort, Ballavenane, Dalquhirnoch, iiij merk viijs. iiijd. land : quhairof John M'Olloche occupiis j merkland, Gillespik M'Kye j merk land, and Johne M'Farlane j merk land ; the rest waist.

Cardaway, j merkland : occupiit be Angus M'Nachthane.

Mauchrebeg, ij merkland : quhairof Gilbert M'Schenoache occupiis xxs. land, the rest waist.

Lepinbeg, viijs. iiijd. land : occupiit be Hector M'Neill.

Maucherecastell, viijs. iiijd. land : waist.

Keranmoir, xxs. land : waist.

Glak and Logointavart, ij merk land : quhairof Glak occupiit be Hector M'Alester, Logointavirt be Angus Omoylzereog.

Lyell and Lepinstorach, ij merk land : the ane half thairof occupiit be Duncane M'Schenoch, the uther half waist.

✳ Cattadull, Capritane, Gartinachin, Biakleid, Gartloskin, viij merk land : quhairof the iiij merkland of Cattadull waist, Capritane occupiit be Hector M'Alester, Gartinnachin waist, Brakleid occupeit be the said Hector, Gartcloskin occupiit be John M'Kecharne.

Brounrekin Amon, Drumterenach, Dalsmerill, Lagnadasa, Innerkewncallach, iiij merk iiijs. xd. land : occupiit be Duncane M'Ilshenoch.

Kelellane, Pennagovn, Garcloskin, Elrig, Arinskathar, viij merk land : quhairof Kelellan and Pennagown occupiit be Johne M'Eachrane, Garcloskin, Elrig and Arinskathar occupiit be Johne M'Kechrane.

Auchnaglach, Lagnacrage, Kerefour, Keremanach, Teirdonald, Dunglas, Glenranskilmoir, Strone, Glennadull, xij merkland : quherof Auchnaglach and Kerefour occupiit be Johne M'Kecherane, Lagnacrage waist, Keremanach occupiit be Johne M'Kecherane, Turdonald be the said John, Dunglas be Angus M'Donald, Glenraskilmoir be Katherene Campbell, Strone and Glennadull occupiit be Hector M'Alester.

Killewlane, ij merk land : quhairof vs. land occupiit be Evene M'Ewin, the rest waist.

Killequhattane, Dalnauchlesk, Crislauch, iiij merk land : quhairof Killequhattane waist, Dalnauchlesk and Chrislauch extending to ij merk land occupiit be Charlis M'Caichrane.

Kilderovane, Knokstabill, Lanaquhane, iij merk ½ merkland : occupiit be Hector M'Alester.

Gartingewoche, viijs. iiijd. land : occupiit be Cristiane Stewart.'

[On another page the following list of names is given.]

'Archebald M'Onald of Largy.   — Clan Donald iii. 582
Johne M'Kechran of Killallan.
Hectour M'Allester of Killerevan.

Johne M'Key in Mungastoun.
Donald M'Key in Pennevie.
Duncan M'Schenoch of Bruneregein.
Johne M'Kay in Smerby.
Neill M'Neill in Kildavie.
Johne M'Neill in Balgrogan.
Anguse M'Kechran in Croshall.
Donald M'Inlavaill in Drumlamber.
Donald Our M'Neill of Ballintone.
Alester Oug M'Donell of Terrareis.
Anguse Eylache of Knokreoche.
Duncan M'Ondoquhy Vane of Kildovie.
Gilespik M'Kerchan in Margmonanache.
Johne Bane M'Key in Bar.
Duncan M'Kechren in Corpulochan.
Gilleis M'Ilschenach in Machrebeg.
Ferquer M'Key in Barraskmull.
Donald M'Key of Ardincrosche.

> Witnesses, MR. ROBERT STEWART, minister,
> JOHNE STEWART of Rosland, and JOHNE STEWART
> of Eshok; ANDRO M'KECHRAN.

ALESTER M'ALLESTER of Dupin.'

Endorsed.—'Curia Domini de Scone in Kyntyr,
1605. Quhilk will give informatione of the present
possessouris of the landis.

[The following note is also written on the back.]

Alexander Makcloid de Donyvaig resignavit totas
et integras octo mercatas terrarum in dominio de
Trouternes una cum officio balliatus dicti dominii
20 Januarii 1539, in manus Jacobi Quinti, in the
buist.

In ane resignatioun maid be the Erle of Argyll 14
martii 1540 principale messuagium terrarum de
Ardnemurquhen is callit castrum et fortalicium de
Castlemeary, in the buist.'

III [1]

Offeris to be presentit to our maist gratious souerane and his hienes honorbill Counsall, in the name of Angus M'Donald of Dwnavaig, his freindis and followeris

First, with all humelite, I adheir to my former Offeris, maid and subscryuit with my hand, in presens of the Counsall, at Glasco, in the yeir of God 1^m vj^c and fyf yeir, and delyuerit to my Lord of Skone to haif bene schawin to His Maiestie; promesing to performe euery heid of the samin.

Secondlie, I offer my self to abyid the tryell of the lawis of His Ma^{tes} realme, twiching my obediens to his hienes and Consallis derectiones, in all poyntis; and keiping of all dewateis appertenyng to a loyall subiect, ewir sen His M^{te} past to mak residens within his hienes kingdom of Ingland.

Thridlie, seing I haif compleithe payit all bygane males of his hienes propper landis within Iyla and Kyntyir, posessit be me, heirtofoir, and hes obtenit His Ma^{tes} Comtrollerris discharge thairof, I offir, in lyk manir, in all tym cuming, during my lyftym, to mak thankfull payment of the full Rentall of the saidis landis, wnto the quhilkis I and my forrbeiris hes bene kyndle tenentis; and that termele and yerle, wnder the pane of tynsall of all kyndis of rycht, tytill or possessioune that I can cleame to ony landis within ony pant of His Ma^{tes} domminionis; his hienes respecting for the present the Wast landis of Iyla, quhill thai be pleneischit and manwrit.

Ferdle, I offir sufficient cautioune, within the Lawlandis, that I salbe obedient to the lawes of this His M^{tes} cuntre of Scotland; and to that effect, sall compeir befoir the Counsall of the said realme, vpone lauchfull premonitione, quhairsoewir the samin sall sit.

---

[1] *Denmylne MSS* in Advocates' Library

Fyftle, I offir to concur with thais quhomvnto it sall seme guid to (his) hines to gif Commissioune, with my haill freindis and followaris, and to set fordwart and asist sic reformatioune of the barbarite of thir cuntreis of the Wast and North Iyles of this His M^{us} kingdome of Scotland, as it sall pleas his hienes best to dewyse, be thir presentis, subscryvith with my hand, At Kilnachtane, in Iyla, the aucht of September 1606.

ANGUS M'DONALL of Dwnevaig.

IV [1]

Letter, Angus M'donall of Dwnwaig to the King

Sep. 10, 1606

PLEIS ZOUR EXCELLENT MA^{TIE}—It is knawin to zour Ma^{tels} honorabill Counsale, within zour hienes realme of North Britane, quhat hes bene my behaviour evir sen zour hienes past out of thir the North pairtis of zour Ma^{tels} dominioun; how many suttis, and how mony offeris of all dewiteis that it become a loyall subiect to his dred souerane, I haif maid to thair Lo.; and how that, efter I haid fullilie satisfeit and compleithe payit all byrun maillis addebtit be me to zour Ma^{tels} Comptroller, I obtenit his discharge thairupoun. I send with his lo. to haif bene presentit to zour Ma^{tle} certane speciall Offeris, subscryuit with my hand, befoir zour hienes Counsale in Glasgw, in the moneth of Junij 1605, of the quhilk I haif as zit receavit na ansuer nor quhat zour Ma^{tle} resoluis and derectis me to do; and being refusit of Licence to haif cum and presentit my self personalie befoir zour hienes, to haif maid my awin supplicatioun out of my awin mowth, I am enforceit to mak the samyn be a mediat persone, my Lord Bischop of the Iyles, quhome-by I haif gewin credeit to offer, in my name, to zour Ma^{tle} my lyfe and all that I may command, to be vsit as it sall pleise zour hienes direct; besciking zour

---

[1] *Denmylne MSS.* in Advocates' Library.

Matie, for the cause of God, to respect my aige and puir estait, and to lat me knaw zour hienes awin mynd, signet with zour Ma^{teis} awin hand ; and gif it mycht pleise zour Matie to continew me the possessioun of thais kyndlie rowmes, quhilkis my forbearis and I hes haid of zour Matie and zour hienes royall progenitouris, I sall nocht onlie paye the dewiteis and maillis vsit and wount thairfoir, bot also sall find sufficient souertie for obedience to zour Ma^{teis} lawis, in all poyntis, and in all tyme cuming ; or vthirwayis, that it mycht seim guid to zour Matie to let me kend how and quhairupoun I sall leive ; for it salbe knawin, I sall seik na vther refuge bot onlie zour Maties clemencie, nor na vther leiving bot that quhilk of zour Ma^{teis} princelie liberalitie it sall pleis zour hines bestow vpoun me ; as at mair lenth the beirar will informe zour Matie. And sua, I beseik God to bliss zour hienes with a long and prospeious ring.—Zour Maties maist humbill and obedient subicct,

ANGUS M'DONALL of Dwnwaig.

Iylaye, the tent of September 1606.

EXTRACTS FROM THE COLLECTION OF STATE PAPERS IN THE ADVOCATES' LIBRARY KNOWN AS THE DENMYLNE MSS.

INTRODUCTORY NOTE

Sir James Balfour of Denmylne and Kinnaird, author of the *Annales of Scotland*, and Lyon King of Arms from 1630 till 1654, was an indefatigable collector of manuscripts. Students of Scottish history are indebted to him for the preservation of a large amount of valuable material that in all probability would otherwise have perished. In particular he left behind him a large collection of papers relating to public affairs during the reigns of James VI. and Charles I., many of which appear to have belonged to the first Earl of Haddington, who was Lord Advocate from 1596 to 1612 and Secretary of State from 1612 to 1627, when he became Lord Privy Seal.

This collection, generally known as the Denmylne Collection, is the property of the Faculty of Advocates, who acquired it in 1678 for £150 sterling, a large sum in those days. Unlike some other writers on Scottish history, Mr. Gregory took the trouble to study these papers and even made a Calendar of most of them, which is also in the Advocates' Library. He further noted, excerpted, or transcribed such of the documents as related specially to the Western Highlands and Islands, and a volume containing this material belongs to the Society of Antiquaries.

To both these learned bodies the Society is indebted for their courtesy with regard to the present publication.

The last two chapters of Mr. Gregory's *History of the Western Highlands and Islands*, covering the period from 1603 to 1625, are based very largely on papers preserved in this Collection. These documents are also of great interest in themselves, as throwing light on the type of men by whom Scotland was governed, and their methods and motives. Certain of these documents have been printed already at various times and for different purposes. But, in deference to opinions which could not be disregarded, it has been thought proper to ignore that circumstance, especially as access to the printed copy is sometimes no easier than access to the original. Everything, accordingly, in the Denmylne Collection that Mr. Gregory regarded as bearing on the subject is now made available to the members of the Society.

A great amount of this material, it will be seen, deals with the final ruin of the clan Ian. Mhor. It would be an impertinence to attempt to tell again that story which Mr. Gregory has told once for all. But in order that the documents may be followed more readily certain facts should be kept in view.[1]

Isla, like Kintyre, had long been possessed by the Macdonalds and long been coveted by the Campbells. In the end of the sixteenth century Angus Macdonald of Dunyveg and his son and heir Sir James fell out, with the result that the latter was imprisoned in Edinburgh Castle.

Repeated attempts to settle matters with the Crown were frustrated by the influence of Argyll, who in May 1607 got a feudal title to Kintyre. Argyll seems to have been satisfied with this acquisition, but John Campbell of Calder, son of the laird who was shot at Knipoch,[2] was lusting after Isla, and the fact that his sister Margaret was the wife of Sir James Macdonald gave him a special advantage in the prosecution of his treacherous schemes. In December 1607 Sir James attempted unsuccessfully to escape from Edinburgh Castle. For this, after great

---

[1] *Vide ante*, pp 66 *et seq.*
[2] Vide *Highland Papers*, vol 1 pp 143 *et seq*

delay, he was brought to trial in May 1609 on a charge
of 'treasonable breaking of ward.' The proceedings were
characterised by scandalous irregularities, and he was
found guilty by a low country jury, with the unscrupulous
Ochiltree as Chancellor, and sentenced to death as a
traitor. The sentence, however, was not carried out and
he remained in prison. From his old father, who was
still alive, it is said that Calder obtained a renunciation of
his rights in Isla.[1]

In 1614 fresh trouble began in Isla, now regarded as
Crown property and leased to a brother of Lord Abercorn.
Dunyveg, which was held by a small garrison placed there
by the Bishop of the Isles, was seized by Ranald Mac Angus,
a natural son of Angus Macdonald, and then taken from
him by Angus Oig Macdonald, a younger brother of Sir
James. Calder then obtained a commission to attack the
so-called rebels, and vain attempts were made to implicate
Sir James in their doings. Angus Oig and some of his
leading followers, whose actings seem to have been largely
inspired by others including Lord Dunfermline the Chancellor, were induced to surrender. An elaborate inquiry
was held, in the course of which their innocence of any
guilty motive became apparent. But this was regarded
as of little importance by an Edinburgh jury, and they
were duly hanged on 8th July 1615.[2] Sir James made
another, and this time a successful, attempt to escape.
Argyll, much against his will, was brought up from
England and practically compelled to lead an expedition
against Isla. His presence stayed what, it seems, would
have developed into a well-deserved rising against the

[1] It is curious that only an abridgment is printed in the *Thanes of Cawdor*,
p 226, and that 'the original' cannot be found

[2] This seems to have made a public scandal, *vide* Calderwood's *History*,
vol. vii p 200 The names of the victims as given by Pitcairn, vol iii p. 364,
were Angus Oig M'Donald, Allaster M'Allaster, Angus M'Allaster, Allaster
M'Arliche, Johnne M'Condochie, and Johnne Gair M'Moylane.

Government, but his sole reward was having to spend some £7000 out of his own pocket in payment of hired troops. Calder duly got Isla, but it brought a curse on him and his family. Their mainland possessions in Argyll had all to be sold, and Isla followed later. His eldest son, the fiar of Calder, went mad, and only the capture of a Welsh heiress in 1688 prevented the sale of Calder itself.

The fate of Argyll was very strange. It has elsewhere been told how he and his brother, the orphan children of the sixth Earl and his wife, Agnes Keith, widow of the Regent Earl of Moray, narrowly escaped death at the hands of a group of conspirators including Glenorchy, Lochnell, and the Chancellor Thirlestane.[1] From an early age he was mixed up in public affairs which he handled with more energy than humanity or conscience; hence, it may be, his name Gruamach—the grim one. By his first wife, daughter of the Earl of Morton, he had several daughters, and one son, the well-known Marquess of Argyll, born a few months before his mother's death in May 1607. In 1610 he married Anne, daughter of Sir William Cornwallis of Brome, and by her had numerous children, of whom the eldest became Lord Kintyre and later Earl of Irvine.[2] After the acquisition of Kintyre Argyll seems to have been disposed to leave the Macdonalds in peace,[3] and it was with no great alacrity that he took command of the expedition against Isla.

When the King visited Scotland for the first time after

---

[1] Vide *Highland Papers*, vol. i. pp 143 *et seq.*   [2] *Vide ante*, p 70

[3] The following holograph letter, preserved at Inveraray, shows that his relations with the Earl of Tyrone and the Antrim Macdonalds were not unfriendly :

RIGHT HONOR. MY VERIE GOOD LO.—for as muche as I have mad a motion to zo[r] Lo/ of matchinge my sone and heire with zo[r] daughter and y[t] I receavid no resolute Aunswer therof All this while I thought good (in respect y[t] my sone in Lawe Sir Randall MakDonill) dwells sumewhat neirer that Koast then I do myselff to refer the further effectinge of theese Bussinnes to hym. And do desier

his succession to the English throne, Argyll, high in favour, carried the Crown at the State opening of Parliament on 17th June 1617.[1] Within a few months thereafter he obtained a royal licence to ' passe out of the countrie and to goe to the Well of Spa for his health.'

But he had more than his bodily health in view, and in due time it became known that, having found the Genevan doctrines of Andrew Melville and the Tudor ritual of the King alike unsatisfying, Argyll had given up everything he might have been supposed to prize and returned to the older faith.   Such a ' defection from the true religion ' could not pass unnoticed.[2]   Accordingly, on 15th November 1618, a royal proclamation was issued revoking his licence and ordering him to return and at once appear before the Council under pain of treason, and on 16th February 1619 ' Archibald Earle of Argile was with sound of trumpets and two or three heraults of armes openlie declared tratour and rebell at the Mercat Crosse of Edinburghe for not compeiring before the Lords of Secrit Counsell.'[3]   On 22nd November 1621, however, having made his peace with the King, he was ' by open proclamation at the Mercate Crosse of Edinburgh with sound of trumpet and Lyon Heralds declared the Kings frie

zo^r Lop to resolve me therof and in the meane tyme expectinge zo^r absolute awnswer by his meanes I comitt zo^r Lo to the devine protectione and with my kindest remembrance and best wishes to zo^r Sellffe and zo^r honor good Ladie, Rest, Zo^t Lo verie asured lowinge ffreind,   TIRONE.
   Dunganon, *the* 10th *of May* 1607.
         Dorso ' To the Right honor. my verie good Lo· the
                 Erll of Ardgeill in Scotland theesse,'
         and also endorsed in the 7th Earl's hand—' From Tirone '
   [1] At Holyrood, on Whitsunday, 8th June, ' The Chancelour, Secretare Hamilton, Sir George Hay, Clerk of Register, the Erle of Argale, the Bishops St Androes, Glasco, Rosse, Brechine, Dunblane, and sundrie others communicated kneeling not regarding either Christ's institution or the ordour of our Kirk ' (Calderwood, vol. vii p 247)
   [2] He added to his offence by entering the service of the King of Spain.
   [3] Calderwood, vol vii. p. 351.

liege.' But though he returned to England and lived till 1638, he never again set foot in Scotland, and his vast estates, of which the fee had been conveyed to his eldest son, were managed by a committee of Campbell lairds [1] until Lord Lorne attained majority in 1628.

By the kindness of the Lady Elspeth Campbell it has been possible to have as frontispiece to this volume a portrait of Argyll in a Spanish dress, decked however, it is interesting to know, with ribbons of his tartan.

The editor has done his best to arrange the various documents in chronological order, and a few notes have been added where it seemed they might be of use.

---

[1] Vide *P. C R.*, vol xi. pp. 437-9. One result was to put an end to the feud between Lochnell and Calder (*vide* Bond among the Barons of Argyll, *Thanes of Cawdor*, p 243)

DENMYLNE MSS.

1. Earl of Dunfermline [1] to the King

Edenburght, 7 *Januarii* 1607

In the Hielands the M^cgregours' affaires [2] lyis owir, partlie be the seasoun of the year, and partlie be my lord of Eigyle's [3] absence, whome we looke daylie for.

The Countrie of Atholl and adjacentis about it, throw the imbecillitie and weaknes of yis Earle, [4] and Intricat Estaite of that house, is now in warst rewll, and ordour of anye pairt of theese Countries, whilk was wount to be maist obedient of thame all. Bot your Ma^{tels} Secreit Counsall heir is presentlie on the adwysement how to reforme and put ordour to that pairt, whilk I hope shall be done schortlie to your hienes contentment. All the rest of the Hielands ar in sic ordour and obedience, as we heir naa complaint off thame nor of naa insolence in thame.

---

[1] Third son of George, sixth Lord Seton. Born 1555 A Lord of Session, 1588, as Lord Urquhart. Lord President, 1593 Chancellor, 1605. Created Lord Fyvie, 1597; Earl of Dunfermline, 1606. Died at Pinkie, 16th June 1622

[2] For an account of the infamous treatment of the Macgregors, *vide* Professor Masson's Introduction to the various volumes of the Register of the Privy Council, and in particular vol ix pp xxxiii *et seq*

[3] Archibald, seventh Earl of Argyll, born 1575, died 1638 He was known as Gilleasbuig Gruamach, a name sometimes given to his son the Marquess. For the story of the plot against him and his brother, vide *Highland Papers*, vol. i pp. 143 *et seq.*

[4] James Stewart, second Earl of Atholl of the Innermeath line. Born 1583, died 1626, when the earldom became extinct In 1629 it was created anew in favour of John Murray, eldest son of the second Earl of Tullibardine, and through his mother heir of line of John, fifth Earl, of the older family.

2. Lord Balmerinoch [1] to the King

Halyrudhous, xxj day of *Januar* 1607

Twisday nixt we haif the gentilmen of Athoill and other cuntreyis boidoᵣing thairto for setling these boundis, alsweill anent the brokin men of that cuntrey, as the Clangregor, who housoeuir thay ar become zoʳ Maiesteis Cosines ar litill better manert nor befoir.

3. Privy Council to the King

3 *March* 1607

MOIST GRATIOUS SOUERAYNE—Afoir the ressett of zoʳ Maiesteis lre [2] concerning the erll of Athoill, he had meanit him selff to zoʳ Maiesteis Counsell showing hou mony great and weghtie adois he had in handis tuicheing the estate of his house wherin he could tak no solide ordour during the tyme of his warde, the Counsaill knowing a parte thairof, and mony of the extremiteis wherunto he is redactit, thay transportit his warde fra the Castell to the burgh of Edinburgh upoun goode caution of xxᵐ merkis for his remaning and keiping warde thairin whill he be fred, this band sall ly abone his head whill the disordourit estate of Athoill be setled. Thair hes bene a preuey dealing be some of zoʳ Maiesteis Counsell anent the apprehensioun of Johnne Dow McGillichallum and Allaster his bruther, and zoʳ Maiesteis Chancellair [3] delt particularlie heirin wᵗ James Gordoun of Lesmoir. This gentilman in regaird of zoʳ Maiesteis obedyence and seruice by the earnist entreatie and solistatioun of zoʳ Maiesteis Chancellair tuke the seruice in hand and haueing maid mony purpoises for effectuating yairof wˡᵏˡˢ misgaif him; in end he lichted vpon the lymmaris upoun the   day of Februair last, and efter a lang and hett combatt and

---

[1] James Elphinston, son of Robert, third Lord Elphinstone He was made Secretary of State in 1598, and created Lord Balmerinoch in 1603 For the strange story of his disgrace, see *Scots Peerage*, vol i pp. 557 *et seq* He died 21st June 1612

[2] Printed in *P.C R*, vii p. 511.

[3] Lord Dunfermline.

slauchter of some fyve or foure of the principallis of thame, the said Allaster wes apprehendit, and Johnne, being veiy evill hurte, by mirknes of the nyght eschaiped. This Allaster wes the personall executo^r of all the murtho^{ris} contryved be him selff and his bruther, and hes bene ane of the moist notable and maisterfull lymmaris that hes bene in the heylandis thir mony yearis. Thair wes great intreaty and mony fair promises maid be his freyndis for his releiff, bot the gentilman his takair preferring zo^r Maiesteis seruice and his awne hono^r to thair offeris and to ony futur event hasaird or inconvenient w^{lk} doubtles he will undirly he hes p̃tit him heir within the tolbuith of Edinburgh, wher he is maid fast in the Irnis and salbe tane ordo^r with accordinglie, we hoip that his bruther sall not lang eschaip, and no goode meanis salbe omittit w^{lkis} may intrap him, and seing this gentilman hes so far advanceit him selff in zo^r Maiesteis service, and hes red the countrie of such a in^{r}full theif and lym̃air, we wilbe bald to re-comend him unto zo^r Maiesteis fauourable consideratioun and rememberance, wherby he and otheris may be .en-courageit to vndirtak the lyke seruice heirefter. The tyme of oure Parliament being now approcheing at the 18 of this instant we humelie requeist zo^r Maiestie to latt ws knaw zo^r heynes pleaso^r anent the cõtinuatioun of the same. And sua we pray God to grant unto zo^r Maiestie a lang and happy regãn and eteinall felicitie, frome zo^r Maiesteis burgh of Edinburgh the thrid of Marche 1607.

Zo^r Maiesteis moist humble and obedyent seruitouris,

MONTROISS. [1]

AL. CANCELL^s. [2]

LOTHIANE. [3]

JO. PRESTOUN, [4]   J. COKBURNE. [5]

HALYRUDHOUS. [6]   R. COKBURNE. [7]

---

[1] John, fourth Earl of Montrose   [2] Earl of Dunfermline.

[2] Robert Ker, second Earl of Lothian

[4] Sir John Preston of Penicuick, Lord President of the Court of Session.

[5] Sir John Cockburn of Ormiston, Lord Justice Clerk.

[6] John Bothwell, son of the Bishop of Orkney, created Lord Holyroodhouse 1607

[7] Sir Richard Cockburn of Clerkington, Lord Privy Seal.

4. Privy Council to the King

16 March 1607

Pleis zo[r] Moist Sacred Maiestie—Zo[r] Maiesteis Counsaill being cairfull to haif a cleir discouerie of the forme of Archibald McConeillis [1] eschaiping furth of the Castell of Dunbartane, and the constable of the said Castell and the laird of Ardincaple [2] being very instant in the urgeing of thair awne tryall for purgeing of thame selffis of the suspitioun whilk thay undirly in this mater, Ardincaple for his iustificatioun and cleiring him selff of that suspitioun as being vpoun the foirknowlege of the said Archibald's eschaip seing he wes transported over Clyde neir to his house, and be some of his seruandis, he without ony chargeis warrand or directioun exhibited heir befoir zo[r] Maiesteis Counsaill all his seruandis aganis whome thair wes ony presumptionis of suspitioun, who being very narrowlie examinat, we can find in thame no appeirance or suspitioun of thair foirknowlege or help to the said Archibaldis eschaip furth of the Castell, and no kynd of presumptioun aganis Ardincapill him selff. In one only named Robert Buntene we find some favour shawne to the said Archibald at his comeing to the ferry syde, by uttering of some foolishe speecheis to the ferryaris that thay mycht transporte him without hasaird. This Buntene is a young boy not capable of ony great fraude or policie, and altogidder ignorant what mycht be the event of suche doingis, alwayes we haif him vnder cautioun of 13 merkis to be ansuerable wheneuir he salbe callit for, and sua whateuir salbe zo[r] Maiesteis princelie censure of him, we sall see it accordinglie to ressaue executioun. Anent the Constablis parte we can learne nor try no thing aganis him of his consent or knowlege of that turne, and trewlie we presome safer of his awne credite and honnestie, that in regaird of the mony fauouris whilkis zo[r] Maiestie hes

---

[1] Archibald Macdonald of Gigha, a natural son of Angus Macdonald of Duniveg, who had been taken by Lord Scone as a hostage for his father's obedience.

[2] Macaulay of Ardincaple.

shawne unto him, he wald neuir prove sa vndewtifull and
disloyall.   Thair hes beene some negligence in his seruandis
who wer appointed to gaird the said Archibald in geving
over muche truist vnto him who wes worthy of no truist,
and in that the Constable acknowlegeis his error and humelie cravis zo^r Maiesteis pardoun for the same, and we will
be bald in all humilitie to be intercessors for him, and that
it wald pleis zo^r gratious Maiestie to relax him of his warde,
and we hoip that this his oversycht sall teiche him to be
moir circumspect in all tyme comeing, Allwayes remitting
this to zo^r Maiesteis gratious and fauourable consideratioun
and humelie craving pardoun of this o^r presumptioun we
pray God to grant unto zo^r Maiestie efter a lang and happy
regñn eternall felicitie, frome zo^r Maiesteis burgh of Edinburgh the 16 day of March 1607.—Zo^r Maiesteis Moist
humble and obedyent subiectis and seruitouiis,

MONTROISS
AL. CANCELL^s.

J. BALMERINO^k.   S. ROBERT MELUILL.[1]
           JO. PRESTOUN.   BLANTYRE.[2]

5. Privy Council to the King

Edinburgh the 26 of *Marche* 1607

PLEIS ZO^R MOIST SACRED MAIESTIE—According to zo^r
Maiesties directioun and līe of the xvj of this instant we
had befoir ws the Marques of Huntley [3] and conferrit with
him at lenth anent the busynes of the Ilis, and efter some
verball discourses past yairanent, we fand it meist and

---

[1] Sir Robert Melville of Burntisland

[2] Walter Stewart, created Lord Blantyre 1606

[3] George, sixth Earl and first Marquess of Huntly   For a full explanation of
'the busynes of the Ilis,' *vide* Gregory, *History of the Western Highlands and
Islands*, pp 313 *et seq*   Briefly stated, Huntly was to exterminate the native
population of the North Isles and get their lands in feu from the king   A dispute
that broke out between Huntly, who was a Catholic, and the extreme Presbyterians was the only thing that prevented this nefarious scheme from being
carried out   It however remains on record as an illustration of the methods
by which the benefits of Sassenach culture were introduced into the Highlands.

expedyent alsweill for formalitie as that a record micht be
keipit of oure procedingis with him, that some questionis
sould be givin to him in wryte and that he sould ansuer
yairunto be wryte, quhilk wes done. Thir questionis and
his ansueris and demandis yairupon with oure opinioun
anent the same demandis we haif send up to Maister
Alexander Hay who will importe the same vnto zo^r Maiestie
at lenth. We haif appointit the last of Aprile nixttocome
to the Marques with his awne consent for his personall
compeirance befoir ws to resaue oure ansuer and deter-
minatioun anent his demandis wherin we could do no
thing at this tyme without zo^r Maiesties awne allowance
and aduise. And thairfoir we moist humelie beseik zo^r
Maiestie to latt ws knaw hou far we sall go with the
Marques in thir his demandis, to the effect that at his nixt
dyet we may tak some solide conclusioun with him yairanent. And sua praying God to blisse zo^r Sacred Maiestie
with a lang and happy reignn we rest—Zour Maiesties
moist humble and obedyent subiectis and seruitouris,

MONTROISS,
AL. CANCELL^s,
D. SCONE.[1]

CÉS REGR̃I.[2]   A. WCHILTRIE.   BLANTYRE.
                 JO^s PRESTOUN.

Edinburgh, the 26 of Marche 1607.

6. Marquess of Huntly to the King

26th March 1607

PLEIS ZOUR MOST EXCELLENT MOST MICHTIE AND
IMPERIALL MAIESTIE—I haue stayit heir thir four or fyue
dayis bygaine with the Consall, in deliberatioun anent the
north Ilyis affairis, and in conclusioun thair desyr was,
that I suld mak ane offer quhilk thay wald direct unto zour
Most Excellent Matie befoir thay will giff me onie ansuer,

---

[1] *Vide ante*, p 80, note 1.
[2] Sir John Skene of Curriehill, Lord Clerk Register from 1594 to 1611.

quhilk I haue done according to the Consal's desyr and gif thair be onie thing in my offer quhilk zour Matie sall think onresonabill, I am content to resaue my iniunctions be zour Most Michtie Ma^{tis} awin discretioun beseiking zour Most Excellent Matie to considir the difficultis of this erand, and as I have euer fund zour Most Michtie Matie my fauorable and louing Maister, so now to considir of me as zour Most Excellent Ma^{tis} moie than supeinaturell wisdom plesis to dispos, to the quhilk I will halelie submitt my self, hauing feu freindis in this erand, saving the repos I haue in my loving Maister to quhois plesour I will altogidder submit my self, sua craving pardoun for this my baldnes eftir the kissing humblie of zoui Most Michtie Ma^{tis} hand, I will rest Zour Most Excellent Most Michtie and Imperiall Ma^{tis} humble subiect and Most affectionat seruiteur to the deith. HUNTLYE.

At Edinburgh this 26 of Marche.

7. Privy Council to the King

1st May 1607

MOIST SACRED SOUERAYNE—Vpoun the last of Apryle wch wes the dyet appointet to the Marques of Hunthe anent the affairis of the north Yllis, we had a lang dealing with him thairanent, wherein he hes gevin ws reasounable satisfactioun in all that wee demandit of him except onlie in the yearlie dewytie[1] vpoun w^{che} poynt he standis stiait and pretendis some difficultie, seing he hes tane the seruice in hand at his awne proper chargeis, and in the prosequutiouns thairof wilbe drevin to great expenss. It wes lang or he wald come to ony uther offer bot the auld dewytie, and to draw him on, we maid ane offer to him of the haill north Yllis except the Sky and the Lewis for ten thowsand pundis of yearlie rent w^{che} we thoght to be

---

[1] This haggling about the amount of the feu-duty hung up the matter until Huntly and the Presbyterians fell out, with the result that he was ordered to stay within eighteen miles of Elgin and undergo a course of sermons by their ministers

ansuerable in proportioun to the dewytie payit to the portionaris of the Lewis according to the computatioun of the landis in quantitie and qualitie, and in this offer we wald lykewayes haif used a reasounable mitigatioun yff he could haif bene induceit to haif maid ane offer accordinglie, bot for all that we could do with him he wald nevir exceed foure hundreth pundis Scottis in his offer and in this only . point we differ with him as moir particularlie zo^r Maiesteis secretarye will informe zo^r Sacred Maiestie to whome we haif send the autentick in write of o^r demandis and of the Marques offeris.

8. Bishop of the Isles to the King

17 *June* 1607

PLEASE zo^R SACREDE MA^TIE—As laitlie I caused present to zo^r hienes, according to my bund deutie the pñt estait of zo^r Ma^s west ylandis, Togidder with the causs of the in-ordinat leving of that pepill as I learned the same to be of treuth bothe be sicht and experience, So now heiring that zo^r Ma. was moved to doubt the veritie of sum asseitiones in that my lfẽ : albeit a litill tyme hes, and will try farther the vndoubted treuth of everie poynt yòf zit I maist humblie beseik zo^r Ma. that if zo^r hienes mistrust any thing writtin be me that it may please zo^r Ma. to lat the treuth of the samyne be tryed ather in zo^r hienes awin pñs, or ellis be sick cõmissionaris as sall please zo^r Ma. appoynt, before whome I think god willing being requyred to lat the treuth be knowne. And if it sall seme expedient to zo^r Ma. sall mak manifest ma causes of the pñt misordo^r of that peopill and the richt way by the which experience sall prove the same salbe maist easilie remeadit, And these folkis put to that pace and reformatioun which zo^r Ma. craves. As to the remede of my inhablit estait, I iefer it to that cairfull regaird, which zo^r Ma. hes evir had of all zo^r servandis and speälie of o^r calling, and to the humble sute maid to zo^r Ma. be my bretheren Praying the father of licht to mak the treuthe till appeir to zo^r Ma. in all thingis and to preserue zo^r Royall persoun from danger of bodie and

saule w^t the blissing of a long and prosperous Regñe.—Zo^r
Ma^s albeit onworthie zit maist addictit orato^r and servand,

AN: ISLES.[1]

Edinburgh, the xvij of Junij 1607.

9. Privy Council to the King

19 *June* 1607

PLEIS ZO^R SACRED MAIESTIE—We ressaued zo^r Maiesteis
lr̃e anent the affaires of the Yllis, and hes appointed the
xxiij of this instant to the Marques of Huntley for putting
of him to ane poynt anent the north Yllis, bot in that
poynt of the yearlie dewytie wherupoun we and he contra-
uertit zo^r Maiestie hes gevin ws no resolutioun. Always
seing zo^r Mat^{els} Comptrollair is now to be with zo^r heynes
we remitt that poynt to be resolued vpoun betuix zo^r
Matie and him. Anent the uest Yllis, thair is ane infeftment of few ferme past to the Erll of Ergyll of the landis
of Kintyre [2] and sett doun be the aduise of zo^r Maiesteis
ordinair offi^{rs} the advocate and clerk of reg̃^r according to
the prouisionis and restrictionis formarlie send up to zo^r
Maiestie. Thair hes been sindrie offeris [3] gevin in be Angus
McConeill and Sr James his sone this last wynter anent the
west Yllis and cautioun wes promeist for performance of
thair offeris, bot thay being remittit to deale with zo^r
Maiesteis Comptrollair and to gif him satisfactioun in the
suirtie and cautioun, thay failzeit in that poynt sua that
no certane conclusioun could be tane with thame, as mair

---

[1] The second son of John Knox of Ranfurly. Born in 1559, he became
minister of Lochwinnoch and afterwards of Paisley. In 1604 he had to do
penance in his own church for assaulting in court his opponent in a lawsuit.
In 1606 he was appointed Bishop of the Isles, and was largely employed in
public affairs. In 1611 he was made Bishop of Raphoe in Ireland, and held
both sees until 1619, when he resigned that of the Isles in favour of his son
Thomas. He died in 1633. He carried off from Iona to Raphoe two bells
which Charles I. ordered to be restored (vide *Collectanea de rebus Albanicis*,
p. 187).

[2] *Vide ante,* p. 70.

[3] *Vide ante,* pp. 86 *et seq.*

amplie zo^r Maiesteis Comptrollair will informe zo^r heynes,
as alsua of his particulair dealing with ye rest of the uest
Yllis, wherin we doubt not bot he will gif vnto zo^r Sacred
Maiestie contentment and satisfactioun.

10. Sir James Macdonald to the Duke of Lennox [1]

PLEIS YOUR GRACE—I am in verie greit missery, as this
beirar can tell. Your grace knawis I hawe depended vpon
your fawor, befoir I was put to this miserie; and now, I
wil beseik your grace to gett his Ma^{tis} power to taik ordour
with me, at your graceis cuming heir. I am willing to
axceptt quhatt his Ma^{te} wil bestow on me, ather in my
awin kyndly roume, or in oney vther pairtt of his King-
dwmes; and sall find causione for my obedience; quilk
I will beseik your grace to report to his Ma^{te}, and thatt
your grace will gett me thatt fawor as to be bainishid,
rather or I be in this miserie. As for my bastard brother,[2]
quha hes brokin your graceis ward, iff your grace taik
ane doing for me, and taik me in your awin hand, I sall
find the way he salbe putt in your graceis reverance, as he
was befoir. Beseiking your grace to remember my miserie,
and gett me libertie or banismentt. I rest on your graceis
faworable doing, quhatt I vrett anentt Archibald, Your
grace will hald it quyett till your grace cum hame.—Your
graces serwand duiring lyfe, S^R J. MACDONALL.

From Ed^r Castell, 27 Junij, 1607.
To my very gud Lord, my Lord Duik of Lennox.

11. Sir James Macdonald to the King

MY GRACIOUS SOVERAN—May it pleis your Maiestie to
apardoune my importunitie, being inforsid thairto, throw
the grett misery q^{lk} I aknawleg to hawe maist justly
deseruid, for my bypast offences towardis God and your

---

[1] Ludovick, second Duke of Lennox. He was Keeper of Dumbarton Castle.
[2] Archibald Macdonald of Gigha, *vide ante*, p. 99, note 1.

Matie : Zett my soueran, your Matie hes graciously forgiuein gretter offenceis ; zea, the giettest Treson zatt euer was deuysid aganst aney Prence, zour hienes hes forgiwein. For Chrystis caus, Sir, ance forgiue me my bypast offenceis, and with Godis grace I sall euer behawe my selff deutiffully heirefter ; and sall find causion to obey quhatt your Matie will injune to me ; beseiking that the Declaratioun of your Maties will may be sent to the Consall ; seing, without the same I can gett na ansuer of thair Loidschipis. Humblie kissing your Matie handis, I commit your Ma^{te} ewer to Godis protectione.—Your Maiesties maist humble and puir subiect to be imployid to dethe,　　Sᴿ J. Makdonall.

From Edinbruche Castell, 28 of Junj (1607).
To the King his maist excellent Maiestie.

12. Alexander Colquhoun of Luss to the King

23 *April* 1608

Pleas zour most Sacred Maiestie—I haue beine urgit be the Counsell to submitt with the M^cfarlanes my brotheris slauchter[1] and all uther slauchteris, murtheris. hairscheppis, theiftis, reiffis and oppressiounis, raising of fyre demolisching of my housis cwitting and destioying of woods and plainting committit be thame against me q^{lk} submissioune is now become in zour Maiesteis hands and being informit that my lord of Mar is to insist with zour Maiestie to pronunce ane decreit not onlie vpon criminall actiounis bot also vpon the civill actiounis q^r of I haue obteinit decreitis alreadie befoir the lordis of Sessioune extending to the sowme of lxxij thousand poindis money of North Britane I will maist humbillie beseik zour Maiestie to reserue my decreitis alreadie obteinit and quhat satisfactioune zour

---

[1] Through the treachery of a servant of his own name Sir Humphry Colquhoun was killed in the castle of Bannachra in 1592 There is a strange story that Sir Humphry's brother was concerned in the murder and afterwards hanged, but it seems to require confirmation (vide *The Chiefs of Colquhoun,* vol. i. pp 157 *et seq*).

Maiestie pleasis to decerne to me for the criminall actiounis I mane hauld me in content thairwith gife it be zour Maiesteis will that rebellis to zour Maiestie resaue that benefit for they ar oft and divers tymes at the horne for all the crymis above wrytine and sundrie vther crymis not mentionat unrelaxed as yet. Requeisting zour Majestie to tak in guid pairt this my humbill suit haiving nothing els to offer zour heynes for all zour undeserwit fawouris bot my most loyall hart q^{lk} sall never deword from the smallest of zour Maiesteis thochtis. This humbillie craifeing pardoune of this my presumptioun I pray God grant zour Maiestie efter ane lang and happie regne eternall felicitie.—Zour Maiesteis most humbille and loyaltie affectit subiect and serwand,

ALEXANDER COLQUHOUN
off Luss.

Rosdo, the xxiii day of Apryll 1608.

13. Privy Council to the King

21 *May* 1608

MOST SACRED SOUERANE—This conuentioun of zo^r Maiesteis Esteatis (albeit not sa frequent in nomber as we expectit) held the 20 of this instant, vnto whome the necessitie of this expeditioun for the Yllis, and the preparatioun maid be zo^r Sacred Matie of schipping and otherwayes for that seruice being propouned and urgeit with all instance and circumstanceis whilkis myght further the eirand the same abaid a lang and fasheous dispute, some obiecting the pouirtie and present burdynnis of the cuntrey, and some, other impedimentis tending to the delay of the seruice. In end thay resolued that thay wald serve zo^r Maiestie conforme to the proclamations and lawis of the cuntrey, and altogidder disassentit fra ony cotributioun or taxatioun for that seruice, wherupoun pñt directioun wes gevin to renew the proclamatioun, with designatioun of the same dayis and placeis of meiting contenit yairin, we haif lykewayes gevin directioun for

arreisting of the haill schippis on the coist syde of Fyfe
and otheris pairtis be noith, to attend the transporte of
zo^r Maiesteis forceis to the north Yllis, and for arreisting
of the schippis in the west to attend the transporte of the
forceis to the south Yllis, and in every vther thing w^{lk}
may further and advance the seruice we sall haif a speciall
cair and regaird. and fra tyme to tyme sall mak zo^r Maiestie
acquented w^t the progres of oure procedingis.

14. Privy Council to the King

25 May 1608

MOST SACRED SOUERANE—In respect of the difficulteis
quhilkis we fand at the lait conuentioun of zo^r Maiesteis
esteatis anent the prosequutioun of zo^r Maiesteis seruice
in the Yllis by suche meanis as we thoght to have bene
least grevous to the cuntrey, and most expedient for the
effectuating of the seruice, ws and some vtheris of zo^r
Maiesteis Counsell upon whome the burdyne of zo^r heynes
affaires doeth ly hes sensyne had some privat metingis
amangis o^r selffis for the furtherance and advancement of
that enand, and after divers conferenceis and reasoning
yairanent and upoun the possibillities of the effectuating
of that seruice to zo^r Maiesteis contentment and satisfactioun, ws according to the pñt necessitie, find it expedient that the burdyne of that haill seruice salbe layed
vpoun suche one persone as it sall pleis zo^r Sacred Maiestie
to mak chose of, who making his first randevous at Yla,
thair to attend zo^r Ma^{tels} schipping and forceis, may frome
that, coist the haill Yllis boith south and north, and becaus
the convening of the forceis of this kingdome according to
the proclamatioun is very uncertane, and not liklie to
assure zo^r Maiesteis seruice in that measure w^{lk} apperteyneth, and we being laith that zo^r Maiesteis lieutennent
upoun sa sclender a warrand sould hasaird his awne credite
or the fortoun of zo^r Maiesteis seruice, we haue thairfoir
ordanit a pñt levey to be maid of fyve hundreth men vnder
wageis for his gaird unto whome we haif appointit ten
thousand merkis for thair monethlie pay and transporte.

The payment wherof for the first moneth is very freelie and willinglie undirtane be zo^r Maiesteis comptrollair and thesaurair depute and for the secund moneth we sall mak sick provisioun as goodlie may be. We hoip that the fynnes of the absentis frome this seruice sall do that turne and moir, and we sall proceid aganis thame accordinglie. We haif ordanit the first meiting to be at Ila vpoun the first of July nixt, and the meiting of the northland forceis to be at Trouternes vpoun the xxiij of that moneth. It will pleis zo^r Sacred Maiestie to caus directioun to be gevin to the Capitanes of zo^r Maiesteis schippis and souldiouris who ar to attend this seruice, that thay rander thame selffis obedyent to zo^r Maiesteis Lieutennent, in every thing quhilk to the dignitie of his charge and place apperteyneth, and with the nixt pacquett to latt us know of zo^r Maiesteis chose for the Lieutennandrie.[1] In all otheiis particularis concerning this busynes zo^r Maiestie wilbe fullie certifeit be the Bischop of the Yllis who wes present with ws at all oure meitingis vnto whois sufficiencie remitting all thingis we end with oure humble praying vnto God to giant vnto zo^r Sacred Maiestie after a lang and happy reigñn eternall felicitie, frome zo^r Maiesteis burgh of Edinbuigh the 25 of Maij 1608.—Zo^r Maiesteis most humble and obedyent subiectis and seruitouris,   AL. CANCELL^s.

LOTHIANE.

A. UCHILTRIE.

HALYRUDHOUS.   J. BALMERINO^H.

BEWLEY, Comptroller.[2]   JO. PRESTOUN.   S. T. HAMILTON.[3]

---

[1] Andrew Stewart, Lord Ochiltree, was appointed, and held office for four years Having got into debt he sold his estates and dignity to his cousin, Sir James Stewart of Killeith, and was in 1619 created Lord Castle Stuart in the peerage of Ireland, where he had obtained a grant of forfeited lands

[2] Sir James Hay of Kingask succeeded Lord Scone as Comptroller On May 10, 1607, he received a grant for his life of the Priory of Beauly (*Reg. Mag Sig*), and thereafter is often designed Jacobus Dominus de Bewlie

[3] The well-known 'Tam o' the Cowgate' Born 1563 Lord Advocate, 1590-1612. Lord Clerk Register, and thereafter Secretary of State, 1612-1627 Created Lord Binning, 1613 Lord President of the Court of Session, 1616-1627, still remaining Secretary of State Earl of Melrose, 1619. Earl of Haddington instead of Earl of Melrose, 1627 Lord Privy Seal, 1627 Died 1637.

15. Privy Council to the King

May 27, 1608

MOST SACRED SOUERANE—This beirar, the Bischope of the Ilis, haueing the occasioun to repair to your Maiestie for some materis concerning the seruice in the Ilis, We haif committit vnto him the relatioun vnto your sacred Maiestie how far we have procedit in that busynes, and what course is tane for the furtherance and prosequution of that seruice, vnto whose sufficiencie remitting all thingis, We pray God to grant vnto your Maiestie, efter a long and happy reigne, eternall felicitie. From your Maiesteis burghe of Edinburghe, the 27 of May 1608.—Your Maiesteis most humble and obedient subiectis and seruitouris,

AL. CANCELL^s. ABERCORNE. J. BALMERINO^H. D. SCONE. BEWLY. HALYRUDHOUS. JO. PRESTOUN.

To the Kingis most excellent Matie.

16. Lord Wcheltrie to the King

May 27, 1608

MOST SACRED AND GRATIOUS SOUERAN—I ressavid your Ma^{teis} Lettir, with Alister Ogis Remissioune, and salbe cairfull to gif vnto your Matie full contentment and satisfactioune in euerie particular of the Letter. I haif reteinit the Remissioune in my handis, quhill I haiff ane certaintie of Alisteris conformitie ; quhairin I expect to find him ansuerable in some measour, to that great favour quhilk it hes plesit zour Matie to bestow wpone him. In all wtheris zour Ma^{teis} directionis, quhairin it sall pleis zour sacred Matie to burdene me, I sall haif ane speciall cair and regaird to approve my selff worthie of that trust quhilk zour hienes reposis in me ; having na wthir thing zit to acquyt zour hienes inestimable favouris, bot ane hart disposit, in all sinceritie, to discharge that dewtie quhilk

zour Matie expectis, and quhilk to my awin credit apper-
tenis, and to sacrifice my lyffe and all that I haiff, in the
executioune of all zour Ma^{tels} royall directionis. And sua,
recommending zour sacred Matie, with zour royall progenie, to the protectioune of God, I rest—Zo^r Ma^{tties} moist
humbill and obedient seruitour, A. WCHELTRIE.

Edinburgh, the xxvij of Maij 1608.
To the Kyngis moist excellent Matie.

17. Copy of the Lieutennentis Letter to the
    Counsall, to be send to Courte with Sir Alex-
    ander Hayis [1] Letter, &c.

Aug. 18, 1608

PLEIS ZOUR LORDSCHIPIS—I causit wey oure ankeris
and depairtit from Yla the 14 of this instant, at efter none,
and arryved at Dowart, in Mule, the 15 of the same
monethe; and that with giyte difficultie, in respect of the
greatest tempest of wedder and contrarie tyddis, quhairby
we wer put in great dangeir all that nycht; quhairthrow
I sailit downe ane of the mastis of my awne schippe. Att
oure out-comeing fiom Yla, we mett the Inglishe gallay,
with ane vther shipp, that caryis the munitioun and oidinance, the quhilk gallay, yf it haid not pleasit God to haif
givin hir that luke to anker in the Sound of Yla, sho could
not haif eschaipit saiff, in iespect of the giyte tyddis heir,
and hid gait to pas throw the quhilk sho appeiris to be
verie vnmeit: And finding hir nawise sufficienthe furneist
with victuall, to remaine heir to avait' on this service, yf
it war bot for the space of aucht dayis; and not being
certane of ony victuallis to come heir to furneish hir, bot
onlie, at my speciall requeist, Sir Williame St. Johnne, his
Maiesteis Admirall heir, hes tane vpoun him, out of his
awne furnitour, to supplie hir with viveris, quhill bak
adverteisment come from your ll.; and seing we have
no service in thir Ylandis that sho is meit for, and knowing

---

[1] Probably the Clerk Register (*vide post*, p. 121, note 1).

hir to be gryte expenssis to his M^{tie}, vpoun the avisement with the Admirall and remanent Capitanes of the Inglishe fleitt, and especialie with him wha is present Governour of hir, wha be painfull experience knawis, and hes declairit to ws, how difficle it is to keepe hir saiff, vncassin away, lett bee to do ony good office with hir, I haif thocht good to crave your ll. aduise, quhidder sho sal be direct bak agane to England, with all expedition, as we think all expedient— or yf sho sall be continewit heir—and to what vse, and how sho salbe furneist—for we knaw not.   As to the ship caryare of the batterie and instrumentis appertening thairto, albeit we think not meit to keepe the ship heir, bot remit hir bak with the gallay, for hir better preserva- tion, yit, for sundrie caussis tending to the forder and finall ending of this service, we think it expedient to keep the munition with the instrumentis, the quhilk I sall sie to be put in sic suritie, as I salbe answerable to his Matie and your ll.

Thir thingis I haif thoght good to commvnicat vnto zour ll., imparting vnto zour ll. oure opinioun heir, and craving your ll. forder resolutioun in the premisses, quhilk I think, God willing, to follow furth.   Vpoun the 16 of this instant, I directit Commissionaris to the House of Dowart, quhairin McClayne haveing his residence for the tyme, promesit to delyuer the House ; the quhilk he did vpoun the 17 of this instant.   I ressaveing the same, hes furneist with men and viveris that House to be keipit during his Ma^{teis} and zour ll. pleasour.   I haif proclamit Courte to be haldin, the xxiij of this instant, in Arrose of Mull, when I think, be Godis grace, to tak ordour with that Yland, in executioun of that pairt of my Commissioun, in distroying of lumfaddis, birlingis, and Hieland gallayis.

I find this ane gryte difficultye, that in respect of the great nomber of theis vashellis, quhilkis ar intertenyit vpoun the mayne-shoir, quhilkis ar so offensive to the Yllismen, that onles thay keepe the lyk counter with thame, thay can not eschaip thair oppressioun, nather can I justlie spoilzie thame thairof, vnles the lyk ordour be tane with these that ar vpoun the mayne-shoir, opposith to the North

and West Yllis ; and thairfoir, yf it wald pleis your ll.
to gif me lyk pouer and Commissioun, for the aboleishing
of sic vaschellis vpoun the mayne-shoir, as I haue with in
the Yllis, I sall do accordinglie with boith. The quhilk
Commissioun I expect, with diligence, into the quhilk
Commissioun, I wald desyre your ll. to include the intaking
and assedgeing and dismoleisheing of all sic Houssis vpoun
the mayne-schoir, apperteneing to ony Yllisman, or that
may be ayd or ressett to ony fugitiue rebell out of the Ylles.[1]

I will not trouble your ll. with farder Letteris quhill
mair occasioun be offerit ; bot, requesting zour ll. to
haist bak ansuer, becaus I can not depairt out of this
Yll, withoute ressett of the same, I rest.—Be zour ll. alwise
to be commandit,   A. VCHILTRIE.

Dowart, in Mull, 18 August 1608.

18. Bishop of the Isles to the King

17 *Sep.* 1608

PLEAS ZO^R SACREIT MA^{TE}—According to zo^r hiechnes
derectioun, as zo^r M^{tes} leutenēt haith laithe visitat yor
heohnes west Iyllandis whair also ye cheif mē of zo^r M^{tes}
north Isles did also meit his Lo. w^t such obediens to yais
zo^r heichnes lawes practisith be his Lo. as ye testemoneis
reportit will beir sufficiēt record, so haue I, being ewir in
cūpanie w^t his Lo. fay'fullie writtin ye trew histore of ye
speciall turnes of ony iportance wiche was done eũy day
of y^t Jurney and y^t to zo^r M^{teis} secretar for Scotland, yat
yairby he being warrādit to giwe zo^r Matie informatioun
of ye trewth zo^r heichnes may be inarmit aganis synisterous
reportes of o^r procedinges of ye w^{che} dyũss phaps may be
p^rsentit to zo^r M^{teis} secreit eares, as also wndirstand how
ease it is to zo^r M^{te} (w^t a lytill help of ye adwyss of sic as
hes bene ỹ and sene and considderit ye pñt estait of yais
folkis, now woid of ye trew knowlege of God, ignorāt of ye
mest pt of zo^r M^{teis} lawes and ỹ dewete towarttis ỹ dreid
soũane w^tout ciuilite or humaine societe, and zit wrā it

---

[1] These powers were granted to him by the Council on 1st September.

in ane servill feir of ye executioun of zo^r M^{tels} iustle cōceawit
wrath aganıs yā), out of ye deıpnes of zo^r M^{tts} heich wisdome to establısche and ınduce yam all w^{t}out hostelite or
openyg of zo^r hınes cofferıs to accept of such a soleit ordour
as may reduce yam to ane haıstc rcformatioun in na aıge
hereftcr to alter, ye wch sall be ıetenit and cōmıttit to
eternall memorc as ane of zo^r heıchnes notabıll workıs
ıncōparabıll w^t ye maıst sıngular actes of ye most famous
ancıēt Imprıo^{rls} of yc wıche yc most worthe could newir
attcınc to y^t hono^r, and sall testcfc zo^r M^{tels} wısdome and
actıoun to cxccıd also far yc most wyss and walıant practiss
of zo^r heıchncs nobıll progenıto^{rls} as zo^r heıchncs domı-
nıoncs ar ılargeıt bezond yaırıs,[1] nather can ye praıs nor
hono^r heırof be gcwın to ony ınstrumēt īployıt be zo^r M^{te}
ın thıs serueıce, albeıt boıth zo^r M^{tels} leutenēt and admirall
hes kythıt yaır curage, vısdome and ernıst effectıoun to
furthır thıs work, bot first to God, and yan to zo^r M^{tels}
self hıs anoȳtıt whom he hes ewır blıssıt, prosperıt and
brocht to anc happc cnd all zo^r heıchnes exploytcs w^{t}out
creweltc no^{t}w^{t}standıng of yc waıkncs of ye secound ınstru-
mētıs thaı followıng furth yc meancs that zo^r heıchnes hes
vsıt wyıslc and m̃cıfulle to derect, of yc wiche we all zo^r
M^{tels} subıectıs hes sene and cofortabıll cxpcrıēce   And sua
no^t doutıng bot zo^r Ma^{te} wıll follow fur^t yıs happe werk w^t
matur delıberatıoun I most cffectıoushe bescık zo^r hcıchnes
that seıng my ould aıge dayle crepıs on and be thır trubılsū
jurneys now semıs to mak grıtter haıst nor of befoır, and my
credeıt amāgıs thır folkıs, be the forme of yıs last actıoñ
practısclıt amāge tham s̄wwhat (as appcrıs) demınıschit,
that ıt my^t pleas zo^r M^{te} to appoȳt sum wther of yonger
aıgc, grıtter curagc, bcttır dıscretıoun and credeit ın thaıs
cūtreıs to thıs charge and that I may be pmıttıt̃ to ceıss
fra such vırısū trawcllıs and cnd ye remanēt of my dayes
ın ye exerceıs of sū poyntes of my callıng and ın specıall
ın prayıng to God yc father of o^r Lord Jesu Chryst to

---

[1] The Scots bıshops excelled even the courtıers ın theır adulatıon of the
kıng ‘ As they werc hıs creatures so they were oblıged to a great dependence
on hım, and werc thought guılty of gross and abject flattery to hım ’ (Burnet,
Hıstory of hıs Own Tıme, vol ı. p 19).

cōtinew w^t ws thais maniefauld blissingis spirituall and temporall wiche all ye ptes of zo^r heichnes dominiones enioyes be zo^r M^{tels} happe goūnamēt, the wich I beseik his dewyne M^{te} in his grit m̄cie to cōtinew long and prosperouslie w^t vs, and that our successo^{ris} may reioyss in ye lyk be ye futur rigne of zo^r heichnes royall piogene and that ewir to ye last cūing of ye grit Juge of ye world.—Ane of zo^r sacreit M^{tels} most onworthie subiectes,

AN: ISLES.

Ilintexa,[1] ye xvij of Septeber 1608.

19. Privy Council to the King

6 *Oct.* 1608

MOST SACRED SOUERANE—The Lord Vchiltrie zo^r Maiesteis Lieutennent over the ylandis of this kingdome haveing with a verie goode success returnit frome that expeditioun and making his appeirance befoir ws vpoun the fyft and saxt of this instant, he hes gevin vnto ws a full accompt of the whole course and progres of his procedingis in that seruice, the particularis wherof we haif send up in dew and autentik forme to zo^r Maiesteis secretare to be imparted and showne be him vnto zo^r heynes, that efter consideratioun therof zo^r Maiestie may returne vnto ws zo^r gratious will and pleasour what forder zo^r Maiestie will haif to be done in that mater, wherunto we sall conforme oure selffis and sua recommending zo^r Sacred Maiestie and zo^r royall progenie to godis divyne protectioun, we rest for euir.—Zo^r Maiesteis most humble and obedyent subiectis and seruitouris,

AL. CANCELL^s.

BUKCLUGHE.   BLANTYR.

JAMES HAY.   HALYRUDIIOUS.

Edinburgh, 6 October 1608.

---

[1] 'At the south coast of Ila there is ane iyle callit in Erische Tisgay, ane myle of lenth '—Dean Monro, cited *O. P S* , II. 1. 268.

20. Privy Council to the King

Oct. 6, 1608

MOST SACRED SOUERAYNE—This Nobleman, the Lord
Vchiltrie, 'whome it pleasit your heynes to prefer to the
charge of Leutennandrie of the Yllis of this your Maiesteis
kingdome, hes, with verie greate cair, pane, and travellis,
and with greate hasaird of his persone, broght that seruice
to ane goode perfectioun, by the entrie and exhibitioun
befoir ws of a noumer of the principallis and Chiftanes of
the Ylles ;[1] and by his awne promeis and Band, to mak
some otheris of thame, whome he hes not presentit, ansuerable and obedyent ; as mair particularlie he will informe
your sacred Matie. And sua, recommending him to your
Maiesteis gratious regaird and consideratioun, We pray
God to blisse your sacred Maiestie with all happynes, and
restis for evir.—Your Maiesteis most humble and obedyent
subiectis and seruitouris,

AL. CANCELL^{s}. ARGYLL. CRAFORD. BUKCLUGHE.
ABERCORNE. BLANTYRE.

Edinburgh, 6 October 1608.
To the Kingis most excellent Maiestie.

21. Privy Council to the King

Oct. 13, 1608

MOST SACRED SOUERANE—The beirar, the Bischop of
the Yllis, having the occasioun to repair towardis your
sacred Maiestie, we haif thoght meit to accompany him
with this our testimonie and approbatioun of his dewtiful
cariage and behaviour in your Maiesteis seruice, in the
Yllis, wherin he hes caryed him selff with verie goode
credite and reputatioun ; and is able, be his counsall and
advyse, (in respect of his awne credite and freindshippe
among the Yllismen,) to do vnto your Maiestie goode

---

[1] At the instigation of Bishop Knox, Lord Ochiltree invited a number of the
chiefs on board his vessel to dine and hear a sermon by that ecclesiastic, and
then kidnapped them.

seruice thair. And sua, recommending him vnto zour
sacred Maiestie, and most huimelie beseiking your heynes
to heir him, in suche thingis as he will propone, anent the
prosequutioun of this seruice, We pray God to blisse your
sacred Maiestie with all happynes and felicitie, and restis
for ever.—Your Maiesteis most humble and obedyent
subiectis and seruitouris,

AL. CANCELL⁵. ROSS.[1] TORPHECIN. BUKCLUGHE.
HALYRUDHOUS. CL⁵ REG^{RI}. A. ELPHINSTON.[2]
S. T. HAMILTON. JO. PRESTOUN.

Edinburgh, 13 October, 1608.
To the Kingis most excellent Maiestie.

22. Earl of Dunfermline to the King

Edin., 8 *July* 1609

MAIST SACRED SOUERANE—I haue no forder for the
present to aduerteis your highnes concerning the Estaitt
of this your Majesties Kingdome. Bot yat yis last Coun
sall daye the 6 of this monethe the Erle of Ergylle caussed
present the heades of twa notable malefactours in the
hielands whoe had done manye ewill turnes and wrangis
yir yeares bygayne. I spair to truble your highnes with
onpleasand, onworthie and ongodlie naymes.[3] Bot I have
written the same to Sr Alexander Haye.

23. Alexander Colquhoun of Luss to the King

13 *Nov.* 1609

MOST GRATIOUS SOVERAIGNE—May it pleas zour most
Sacred Maiestie I oftymes compleaned of the insolence
and heavye oppressioune committed vpoun me my ten-

---

[1] David Lindsay, Bishop of Ross
[2] The Master of Elphinstone, nephew of Lord Balmerinoch.
[3] This suggests Milton's lines in defence of the title *Tetrachordon*
　　　　'Why is it harder Sirs than Gordon,
　　　　Colkitto, or Macdonnel, or Galasp?'

nentis and lands be the Clanegregour, and have beine
forced to be silent this tyme bygaine Hopeing that some
tyme thair sould beine ane end thairof Bot now finding
my selfe disapoynted and thame entered to thair former
coursses Have taine occasioun to acquent zour Sacred
Maiestie thairwith Beseiking zour Maiestie to haue pitie
and compassioune vpon ws zour Maiesties obedient subjectis and remanent pwire pepille quha sufferis and to
provyd tymous remeid thairin, and that zour Maiestie may
be the better informed in the particularis I haue acquent
zour Maiesties Secretare thairin To quhois sufficiency
referring the rest and craveing pardoune for importuneing
zour Maiestie I leive in all humanitie in zour Maiesties
most sacred handis.—Zour Sacred Maiesties most humble
and obedient subiect,

ALEXANDER COLQUHOUN
off Luss.

Rosdo, the 13 day of November 1609.

24. Earl of Argyll to the King

5 May [1610]

SIR—According to your Matie Commandement, I derected
my brother[1] to Kintyre for expelling the rebels wch wer then
tocht to be thair, and rather to neglect all my awin par-
ticuliers then the laest point of your Maties seruice, wch he
did, and I wilbe ansuerable to your Matie that quhen the
lyk occatione beis offered he schabe reddy to do his best
for the repressing of any rebellione in thois perts : As for
my going to Scotland, your Matie knaws the cheif occatione
of my stay and what can mak me hable vhen I am thair
to do you seruice, wch I recommend to your Maties princely
consideratione, Sence w^tout that I am rather hable to go
home, to leive at home, nor to do your Matie any seruice
vhen I am thair : I humble beseach your Matie to call to
mynd how willing I haif beine both to spend my tyme and
estait in your Maties seruice and that it would Ples your

---

[1] Colin Campbell of Lundie

Matie to think my willingnes as mouch as euir according to my pouer, and it now rests in the performance of your Matie royall promeis to mak my pouer as good as euir wch salbe holie imployed in gifin your Matie testemonie that I am, Your Maties most humble and obedient subject,

ARGYLL.

The 5 of May.

25. Privy Council to the King

6 *June* 1610

MOST GRATIOUS AND SACRED SOUERANE—ffor satisfactioun of zo^r Maiesteis directioun send vnto ws wherby zo^r Maiestie desyris to be resolved of all suche mater of scruple and doubt w^{che} we haif in that commissioun soght be the Maister of Tullibairdin, and what we hold ather vnreasounable or vnfitting to be grantit thairin, togidder with oure reasouns for euerye one of the same, we haif of new revised and examined the said Commissioun, and in the particulair pointis and headis thairof following, we find thir scruplis and doubtis. First ane ample criminall iurisdictioun over the boundis and landis of diuers baronis and law byding subiectis, who and thair haill tennentis and scruandis ar ansuerable and obedyent to iustice, the lyke whairof hes not bene in vse to be grantit heir bot hes bene refuisit to the Duke of Lennox, the Marques of Huntlie, the erll of Angus, and vther noblemen who soght the same, and thay made to be content with a simple power of iusticiarie within their awne boundis allanlaie. Nixt the conseruatorie of zo^r Maiesteis haill forrestis within the saidis boundis, whairof as we are informit some personis pretendis hiritable title and right and aucht to be hard for thair interes. Thridlie the royall and souerane pouer of iusticeairis w^{lk ls} thir mony yeiris bigane hes not bene hard 'of in this Kingdome, and ar not vsuall in the persone of a subiect, bot onlie proper to zo^r Maiesteis heich iustice.

ffourthe the haill eschettis of the courtis and airis w[lk is] ar never disponit bot in some heich point of seruice for repris- ing of ane oppin and avould rebellioun twichcing the haill body of the estate. ffyfthe ane limitatioun of all the souerane Courtis of the Kingdom with ane expres pro- hibitioun that no exemptioun, discharge nor suspensioun sall pas aganis him in ony point of his commissioun. This is a very grite noualtie very preiudiciall to zo[r] Ma[tels] sub- iectis, who at all tymes, as thay haif mater of greif or iust caus of suspitioun aganis ony iudge that thay ar euer conforted with the ordinarie and lauchfull remeidis of law be suspensioun or aduocatioun. Saxtle the command- ment of all the castellis, housis and strenthis within the boundis of his commissioun for ressett of him and his companie, for halding of his courtis and keeping of his prisonnaris thairin. In w[che] point thair is mony of zo[r] Maiesteis subiectis who will pretend verie iust caus of greif and discontentment yf thay salbe dispossest of thair housis and the same convertit to Jayllis and prisonis. And last, this commissioun is for terme of lyffe, wheras vther comis- sionis grantit heirtofoir ar for some short space allanarlie, Thir ar the scruplis and doubtis w[lk is] we find in this com- missioun, and we haif heirwith send up the same commis- sioun to zo[r] Maiestie to the effect that zo[r] Maiestie vpoun consideratioun of thir particulair heidis thairof may returne vnto ws zo[r] will and pleasour thairanent whairvnto we sall conforme orselffis, and so recommending zo[r] Maiestie to godis divyne protectioun we rest for euer, Zo[r] Maiesteis most humble and obedyent subiectis and scruitouris,

AL. CANCELL[S].   SANCTANDROIS.[1]   GLASGOW.[2]
JO. PRESTOUN.   BLANTYRE.   S. J. COKBURNE.
                                      S. R. COKBURNE.

Edinburgh the saxt of Junij 1610.

---

[1] George Gledstanes, Archbishop of St. Andrews.
[2] John Spotswood, Archbishop of Glasgow.

26. Sir Alex. Hay [1] to ——

dated Edin. 3ᵈ *Sept.* [1610]

You haif hard no doubt of the piratte ship takin by
Neill M^ccloyde of the Leuis.[2] The caice is altered when
the brokin hielanderis are become the persaquuto^ris of
pirattis. Yit they still observe our forme albeit it carye
not muche honestie yit it is not lease hazairde. This
english captane wanting men desyred some supplie from
Neill, and he willinglie yeildit to it. Neill is feasted
aboorde of him and will not be so vnthankfull bot will
repay him w^t a bankett on land. The cap^ne & his c̄opany
for most pairt being all invited, whatevir there faire wes,
the desert wes soure. Whither it wes that they refuised
to pay there rakneing or that Neill held thame to be
heretickis & so thoght thame not worthie to be keipt
promise to, for Neill is thoght to be of the romishe faithe
or that now by there deliuery, he thoght to gett his pardoun,
he deteynis thame, hes putt of his owne men in the ship and
hathe sent advertisment to the counsell wherevpoun my L.
Dounbar [3] hath directed Patrick Greiss w^t a ship to bring
hir aboute. By the reporte of the mesinger w^che come
from Neill It is affirmed that the pirate had that same
intentioun aganis Neill, bot the other hes tane the first
start, It wes right sick lippes, sick latuce. I think the
Clangrego^r culd wishe Bishope and Wairde and all the
rest of the pirattis in Breadealbane so that they might
find meanis of a pardoun. It is reported that the ship
hathe some cutshoneill, sugar and barbarye hyides and
xxvj peicis of iroun and many muskettis. If his Ma^tte
wald be pleased in regaird of the service done to direct
Neill to the pairtes of Virginia and to direct a staite of

---

[1] Son of Alexander Hay of Easter Kennet. A Clerk of Session till 1608, when
he was appointed Joint Secretary along with Lord Balmerinoch. In 1610 he
became a Lord of Session and in 1612 Clerk Register, having exchanged offices
with Sir T. Hamilton, afterwards Lord Binning and Earl of Haddington. He
died in 1616.

[2] Vide *Highland Papers*, vol. ii. pp. 63, 278.

[3] George Home, created Earl of Dunbar 1605. Died 1611.

inheritance to be gevin to him there, I think o^r countrey
heir suld be best rid of him.   There wald be no suche
danger there as of his being in Iyireland, for albeit bothe
the speiches be barbarous yit I hope he sall neide ane
interpreto^r betuix him and the savaiges.

27. Sir T. Hamilton to the King

Edin., 14 *Januar* [1612]

The Counsall ressaued your Maiesties letter concerning
Robert Abroches [1] remission and protection which vpon
hope of your Maties gratious permission thay have delayed
to performe till be thair direction to me your Matie may be
informed be my letter that Robin Abroch is reported to
have bene the most bludie & violent murthourar and
oppressour of all that damned race and most terrible to
all the honest men of the countrie who now ressauing
fauour aboue all vthers of his kin being dispensed from
compeirance before the counsall to mensweare his name
and from finding caution for his compeirance before the
counsall whanever he sall be charged vnder competent
paynes which hes bene the ordour prescryved to all the
rest of that clan without exceptioun.   The fauour granted
to him gevis him louse renzies, discurages these who stands
in feir of his barbarous oppression and may move vther
brokin men to stand out till thay get the lyke condicions
and perhaps tempt some who stand alreddie bund to the
peace to lope furth whill thay obteane the lyke fredome
and immunitie from all ordour and obedience.   And thairfore the Counsall most humblie craives that your Matie
may allow thame to vrge Robin Abroch to obserue the
comon ordour prescryved to all vthers of his clan and
obeyed inviolablie be such as obteaned remissions.   Bot if
your Maiestie be resolved to the contrare vpon significa-

---

[1] A distinguished and gallant gentleman of the Macgregors, who had secured
the protection of Lord Melrose, and sometimes took the name of Ramsay after
his own name was proscribed

tion of your determined pleasour thay will most reddehe
obey your royall commandementis, and do intend for his
present saiftie to grant him ane protection whill the 15
day of May provyding he forbeare to repaire to the schirefdomes of Dumberten, Stirling, Perth and Innernes. Thairfore I most humblie beseik your Matie to returne the signi-
fication of your gude pleasour so sone as convenienthe may
be in thir pourposes. In expectation whairof I beseik
God to prolong your lyfe preserue your health increase
your Ma^{ttes} prosperitics and accompleis your wished con-
tentmentis. Edin^h, this 14 Januar — Your most sacred
Maiestics most humble faithfull and bund scruand,

S. Th. Hamilton.

28. Privy Council to the King

18 *Sept.* 1612

Pleis zoure Sacred Maiestie—The erll of Ergyle compeiring this day befoir zoure Maiesteis counsaill he exhibite
ellevin of that nomber of the Clangrego^r resting vpoun
him be his formair accompt who hes changeit thair names
and found cautioun conforme to the ordoure he hes a
warrand grantit to him for his repair towardis zour
Maiestie according to zour Maiesteis pleasour and directioun
signifeit vnto us by zoure Maiesteis lfe of the sevint of
this instant and he hes nominat the laird of Lundy his
bruther to haue a cair of the proscquutioun of that seruice
till his returne, who hes vndirtane the chairge with pro-
missis to do dis indevoir to bring the same to some setled
perfectioun. We haif had sindrie conferenceis anent the
bairnis of the Clangrego^r, and hes consultit and advisit
heirvpoun with the landisloidis whose aduise and opinioun
is, that, that string sall not be tuitcheit nor no motioun
maid thairof quhill the seruice now in handis aganis the
men be first setled & broght to ane end, at w^{che} tyme
the executioun of everie sutche course as salbe then
resolued vpoun aganis the bairnis may with the lesse
difficultie be effectuat. This is all that hes bene done

with him at this meiting. So with oure hairty prayeris
vnto God, recommending zoure Maiestie to godis divyne
protectioun we rest Zo^r Maiesteis most humble and
obedient subiectis and seruitouris,

AL. CANCELL^s.
ALEX. HAY.

Edinburgh, 18 Sep^{ber} 1612.

29. Lord Ochiltree to the King

(Without date)

PLEAS YOUR MOST EXCELLENT MA^{TIE}—Haiving from
tyme to tyme this four yeares bypast impashed your
Sacred eares withe the great straitts and extremyteis
whervnto I am dicarin vpon occasioune of your Ma^{tles}
ymployment and service which I undertook and performed in the Iylles.[1] And notwithstanding of your
Ma^{tels} severall precepts and warrandes direct for ansuer-
ing me of ane pairt therof notheles I have from tyme to
tyme bene delayed and so forced to pay the enteress of the
wholl mony that I wes ingadgit for.

This S^r is my present estate and conditioune proceiding
as I acknowledge from my own misfortune seing I am
the only man who appeirandlie shall perishe by doing
your Ma^{tle} good seruice.

And that your Ma^{tle} wold be also pleised to give command
to these of your highnes counsell heir present to tak notice
and revise the particular accompts of my debursments
in the accompleishment of that service.

30 [2]

14 *January* 1613

Wpoun the xiiij day of Januar, The Marqueis of
Hamiltoun according to his Ma^{tels} directioun wes

---

[1] Lieutenant of the Western Isles, 1608-1611.

[2] This and many other items with no heading appear to be memoranda of
what happened at meetings of the Council.

admittit vpoun Counsell and the same day the captane
of Clanronnald gave his appeirance befoir the Counsell
and exhibite w^t him Neill McNeill sone to [Ruari]
McNeill of Barra quha is challengit be Aball Dynnere of
Burdeoux as guiltie of robborie and slauchter cõmittit
vpoun him at the yle of Barra This McNeill being twyse
befoir wairdit in the tolbuthe of Edinburghe for the same
caus and no proces nor actioun intented aganis him and
Aball Dynnere his pro^{rls} being this day hard, haveing
nothing to say against him bot ane simple and a naikit
accusatioun qrof McNeill be his solempe aith purgit himself. The Counsell hes tane cautioun of him for his exhibitioun befoir theme vnder the pane of ten thousand
m̃kis for redres and satisfactioun of quhatsũeuer decreit
and sentence salbe recovered aganis him befoir the Judge
competent betuixt and the first of August nixt.

His Maiesteis missive conc̃nĩg Robert Abroch wes
p̃tit and red in counsell Bot becaus he culd not find
cautioun for his dewtifull behavio^r in tyme cũĩg and for
his remanĩg furthe of the boundis q^r formerlie he cõmittit
his insolences, the Counsell hes superseide the expeiding
of his remissioun till the knawlege of his Ma^{teis} pleaso^r and
in ye meintyme they haue grantit vnto him ane protectioun to be vntroubled q^{ll} the xv day of Maij nixt
w^t promeis that he sall not hant within the boundis
abouewttin q^{ll} that day and he sall compeir befoir the
counsell gif he sall happin to be dischairgit afoir that day.

The Laird of Lundie brother to the erle of Argyle being
to repair to court to confer w^t his brother anent the seruice
of the Clangrigo^r as he pretendis. He hes nõit the Laird
of Laweris to have the charge of that seruice till his returne and vpoun Laueris acceptatioun of the charge
Lundie is to haue a licence for his upcũing.

31

26 *January* [1613]

Vpoun a petitioun gevin to the Counsell in name
of the lairdes of Glenvrquhy and Luss the inhabitantis

of Dunbartane and Coline Campbell of Laweres [1] Com-
plaineing that the Clangrigor who war guyltie of the
✗ boucharic and slauchter comittit at Glenfrone and of the
fyre rysing, slauchteres and depredatiounes comittit vpoun
Glennvrqulue, Luss and Colleine Campbell of Laweres
did now begin to flock togidder in cõpanies and to go in
armes athort the cuntrey iniuring his maiesties subiectis
quhair thay may be maisteres. The Counsall w^the vniforme consent without onie kynd of contradictioun hes past
anc act and proclamatioun [2] Prohibiting and dischairge-
ing all and sindrie persounes of the Clangrigo^r who wer
present at the comitting of the crymes abouew̃tin In
ony caise to weir ony kynd of armo^r Bot anc poyntless
knyff to cutt yair meatt wnder the paine of death and this
proclamatioun contemes anc warrand and chairge to all
officeres, stewartis, justices of peace and vtheres magis-
trattis to tak and apprehend all suche persounes of the
Ciangrigo^r whom thai sall find weirand ony armo^r and to
present thame to iustice.

32. Glenurchy to the King

2d Feb. 1613

PLEIS ZO^R EXCELLENT MA^TIE—Zo^r Heighnes l̃res writtin
in fauo^r of Robert Abbroche McGrego^r now calling him self
Ramsay I haue ressaueit, Q^rby I am willit to repossesse him
in quhatsoeuer landis he haith rycht vnto w^tout truble
or plea in law. It is of treuthe that he did possess certane
landis belonging to me without ony rycht or titill at all,
zea so far aganis my consent that withe remembrance of
my verie grit loiss I sall repent I had suche tennent, and
quhen he as one of the cheif & speceall ringleadaris of his
viperous clan, did nocht cõtent thame selfis to wrong me
by the moist barbarous oppressing of my tennentis but had
also ovirrwne ane grit pairt of thre or foure S^refdomeis;

---

[1] A mistake for Aberuchill He was a brother of Sir James Campbell of Lawers

[2] *Privy Council Register*, iv. 539

than the generale greif of sa mony dewtefull subiectis maid
the exterminioun of this damnable raice of people to be
resolueit wpone, as moist expedient & necessary for zo^r
Ma^{tels} peace and obedience and the suretye of zo^r heighnes
dewtefull subiectis duelling in thais pairtis, w^{che} work
since it tuik beginig haithe bene euir chairgable to zo^r
Matie, panefull to the cūtrie and w^t my particular very
grit hurt and skay^t, haveing had besydis many former
loises w^{h}in les nor thais xviij monethis twa hundrethe merk
land waistit and spoiled be that clan cōducted by this sam
man now recommendit. My tennentis thair wyfis & zoung
childrine wnmercefullie murthoured, and sick of thame as
eschaipit the sworde, in regaird thair houses wer all brūt,
being left in the oppin air, boithe the aigit and zounger sort
wer killit w^t colde. It may perhapis by some be supponit
that this seruice is at sum gud poynt, bot quhen all, boithe
noble men, barrounis and gentilmen who haithe moist
intcress in this work wer cōveyned, than it wes amang
thame resolved and by thame to zo^r Ma^{tels} counsall proponed and thair also allowit of, That w^{t}out transplantatioun of this clan no quyetnes to thais boundis culd be
expected, So as this manis repossessioun to any landis w^{che}
by strong hand he held foirmeilie without any rycht at all
Implyis a derect ranversing of quhateuir was intendit for
the gude of that seruice. The particular harme and inconvenience q^{r}of being wnfelt no dout to thais who hes
bene so eirnest solicitoris in the behalf of this man. So ar
thay als far mistakin in thair wndtaking for his gud
behavio^r in tyme cūing. In regaird thair is no dout at all,
bot quhen he findis him self of new strenthned withe a
fresche grouth of this wnhappic weid, q^{r}of thair be of
X male kynd sum̃ xvj^{xx} of new aryseing, lyke encuche he will
put who promises in his behalf to ane personall actioun
for thair releif.

And becaus hard experience haithe maid me more sensible
nor wtheris and my dewtie to zo^r Matie doith enforce me
to cōceale no thing of my knawledg heirin : I hauc thairfoir presumed to acquēt zo^r heighnes withe the treuthe
assureing zo^r Matie one my credit that gif the ringleadaris

X 320?

of this clan sall haue the libertie to dwell and reside in
thair former possessiounis this wndircotting wonde sall
be found heireftir moire incurable, Alwayes for my awin
pairt haueing lyfe and whoile estait euir reddic at zoʳ
Maiesteis dispoiseing, I moist humblie tak my leif. Praying god almychtie to contenew long zour heighnes happie
and Prosperous Reigne and Restis.—Zoʳ Maiesteis most
humble and obbedient Sʳuitoure,

                              DUNCAN CAMPBELL
                              of Glenurquhay.

    Edinbruche, the 2 of ffebruarij 1613.

33. Counsall materes

11 *March* 1613

Mᶜcleud of Hereiss hes gottin ane licence to repair to
court to visite his Maᵗˡᵉ. He pretendis to haue no vther
earand bot to kiss his Maᵗᵉˡˢ handis zit some ar of opinione

that the drift of his earand is outher to seik ane rewaird
for the exhibitione of Neill Mᶜcleud or then to procure
some fauoʳ and grace to Neill at his Maᵗᵉˡˢ handis.[1]

34. Sir Tho. Hamilton to the King

Edʳ, the 7 of *Apʳ* [1613]

Neill Makcloyde [2] died at his execution verie christianlie
And Makcloyde Hereis hes tane veyage to court onlie
desirous of your Maᵗˡᵉˢ gracious countenance.

---

[1] Vide *Highland Papers*, vol. ii. p. 278
[2] His chief, if not his only, offence was defending himself and his people from
the Fife filibusters who were attempting to seize the Lewis.

35. Sir Gideon Murray [1] 'To my verie luving freind James Douglas attending his Maiestie for dispatching the Scotts affairs at Court'

8 *Apr.* 1613

S^R—I haif sent you heir inclosit Neill M^ccloud his conuictioun to be schawin gene the Kingis Maiestie inquyre for it. Ze may onlie tell that I sent you it. This wther inclosit is frome Sr Wm Hart wch ze sall ressave heirwith And so having no wther bussines whairwith to trouble yow for the present I tak my leiue with the remēbrance of my looving dewtie and will remaine Your luving freind to be cōmandit, S. G. MURRAY.

Edinbur^t, the 8th of Apryle 1613.

36

28 *April* 1613

The commissioun is past conforme to his Maiesteis directioun for heiring and discussing of the suspentioun to be grantit vpoun the fynes of the recettaris of the Clangrego^r and the lordis of Sessioun ar dischargit of all granting of ony such suspensiouns.

Directioun is gevin for staying of that infeftment grantit to the Laird of Lawers of the landis of Moverne & vtheris landis formarlie ptenīg to M^cclayn conforme to his Ma^{tels} warrand send doun for that effect.[2]

---

[1] His career is somewhat interesting Originally parish minister of Auchterless he had to give up the Church in consequence of a murder which he committed, escaping punishment through the influence of the notorious Countess of Arran. He then became factor on the Buccleuch estates, and attracting the attention of the king and of his disreputable favourite Robert Carr, afterwards Earl of Somerset, he was made Treasurer Depute in 1612 In 1620 he was accused of malversation, but died in curious circumstances before his trial took place. In 1601 his children by Margaret Pentland, the daughter of a miller, were declared legitimate, and he was ordained to marry Margaret *in facie ecclesiae.* The eldest son Patrick was in 1643 created Lord Elibank.

[2] Fear of a rising on the part of the Macleans apparently put a stop to this attempted theft of Morvaren, *vide* Gregory, *History*, p. 348.

The Laird of Lundy who hes the charge and burding
of the seruice aganis the Clangrego^r in the absens of the
erle of Ergyle his brother haveing desyrit of the counsall
that they wald assigne to him ane day for geving of ane
accompt of the proceidingis in that seruice sen the last
accompt maid be the earle. The counsall hes assignit
vnto him the xv day of Junij nixt and hes wicittin to the
landis lordis of the Clangrego^r to keip that day for heiring
of the said accompt maid.

The Lord Vchiltre hes bene lykwayis at lenth hard vpoun
that mater of his accompts & expenses in his office of
livetennandrie over the Yles. He standis preceis vpoun
the articleis of his compt and thinkis that he gat wrange
in that act of counsell allowing vnto him x^mlib. in satisfactioun of his haill accompts in that seruice and imployment. The Counsell in lyk maner standis be thair awne
act and will enter in no vther conditioun wth him.

Alex^r M^cclewd brother to M^cclewd of Hereis hes apprehendit laitlie four of the principall rebellis of the Lewis
& chargis ar direct aganis him for exhibiting [them]
befoir the Counsell.

37. Counsall matteris

xx° *Maij* 1613

The Lord Vchiltie hes bein sindrie tymes hard vpoun
his compts, and this day wes at lenthe hard, bot the
auditouiis of the excheq^r and he ar not lyk to agrie. They
differ vpoun thrie substantiall poyntis, the nomber and
transporte of his companyis, thair pay, and his awin interteynment. Thair wes sum actis of counsall past when
that seiuice wes first vndertane, and the audito^{ris} will not
compt w^t him bot according to these actis viz. anent the
nomber of his men of weare and thair pay whilk be ane act
wes appoyntit to be v^c men w^t allowance of ten thousand
mkis for thair monethlie pay and transport, besydes ij^m
mkis whilk the lordis be way of consideratioun allowit to
him be ane vther act for transport of his companyis and
thair baggage, his compt beris vj^c men and far grittar

allowance bothe for thair pay and transport nor wes set doun be the actis.

Anent his awin chairges and interteynment, seing thair wes no recorde maid at the vndertaiking of the seruice anent that poynt, nor nothing spokin thairof, The auditouris thinkis that they haue no warrand to compt wich him vpoun that article. Bot standis to the conditioun of the first act anent the ten thousand merkis of monethlie allowance whiche they interpretc to be in satisfactioun of all chairges.

Thair is ane vther questioun anent the keiping of the hous of Dunnyvaig, the expenses whairof he hes set to ane verie grit sowme. The auditoᴿⁱˢ will compt wᵗ him vpoun that article, and hes gevin directione to the resauearis to try be the rollis of the excheqʳ what allowances hes bein tane for keiping of that hous in the preceiding comptis of the former theʳ and comptrolleris, and accordinglie they will haue consideratioun of that article so far as may stand wᵗ modestie and discretioun.

38. Counsall Maters

8 *Junij* 1613

My Lord Vchiltrie hes beine at lenthe hard vpoun his accomptis and the excheqʳ could go no fordar with him be way of compt nor according to the warrandis and actis of counsale maide and sett down at the undᵗtaking of this seruice wherby the noumbers of men of warre ordained to be listed for that seruice. Theare allowance and pay and the charges of there transporte is particularlie sett doun and according to thir actis thay haue compted with him and put him to an poynte allowing wnto him that xᵐ libis sett doun be act of counsall, In contentatioun of his haill charges in that seruice. Thay haue lykvyse gevin him allowance for the hous of Dvnyveg for fyifteine monethis eftir the date of that act of ten thousand pundis whairin the thesaurar is to give him satisfactioun, he is not weell contented with this forme of compting. The excheq[r] hes wryttin to his Ma. in his favour.

That lr̃e send doun in fauoures of S[r] Randall M[c]soirll [1] wes presented and hard this day and his Ma. directioun ordained to be obeyed bot M[c]soirll mon be heir in persoun anent the perfyteing of his securities and geveing of satisfactioun anent his awn parte and the conditiounes to be fulfilled be him.

39

xvij *Junij* 1613

The erll of Ergyll come heir this day in the efternoone, he is to meete the morne with the landislordis of the Clangreg[ris] and to confer and ressone with thame anent that seruice w[che] he hes in handis aganis the Clangregouris and vpoun fryday or mononday nixt he is to gif his accompt how far is proceidit in that seruice sen the last accompt maid be him in the monethe of July bygane.

40

octavo July 1613

The Erle of Ergyle compeiring personallye before the counsall Hes made an free and willing offer to his Maiestye off the sowme of tuentie tua pundis ten schillingis out of euerye hundrethe pund of the fynnes of the recepters of the Clangregour, whilk shalbe intrometted withe be him.

Mackcloyd of Hereis [2] gave his compeerance this day before the counsall and presented the lettirs wrettin be his Maiestye in his fauoures. The counsall accepted verye well of him, hes made him a iustice of peace within his awn boundis promeist him fauourable iustice in all his laufull adoes, and hes vtherwayes encureaged him to continowe in his promeised obedience to his Ma.

The most parte off the landislords of the Clangregour

---

[1] Second son of Sorley Buy Macdonald, created Earl of Antrim.
[2] Sir Rorie.

who should have taine the Bairnes of the Clangregour aff
the laird of Lawers handis conforme to the act of the xxiij
of Junij last hes failzeid in that poynte, and therefore
chairges ar direct againes thame for payment to Lawerss
of the soume of tuentie markis out of euerye merk land
perteining to thame and formerly possest be the Clangregour.

41

29 *July* 1613

There hes bene dyuerss meteings held with the lands-
lordis of the Clangrego[r] anent that sowme whilk wes pro-
mitted to haif bene payed to his Ma. for making of theire
landis peacyeable, and thay haif bene delt wth both in
privat and publict to haif gevin to the Kings maiestie
satisfaction in that mater, bot in no caise could thay be
moved to do ony thing therin; And this 29 of July being
appoynted for geving of sentence against thame, Thay
then come to there defenses, And first thay obiected
against the validitie of the act as being made without the
presence of a full nomber of the counsall, the act nowyse
being registrate nor the ordinar clerk present at the making
therof, Secundly that the consent of a few nomber of
thame being only fyve, wherof Glenvrquhie wes one and
protested againes the act, could nowyse obleiss nor bind
the rest, who were saxteine in nomber of the best rank and
qualitie of the saids landislordis. The counsall haveing
advysed heirvpon, it wes fundis be the voites of the most
pairte, That this act in the forme and tennour as it wes
consauit could nowyse bind nor obleiss the rest of the
landislordis to the observation therof, And so this mater
restis without ony hoipe that his Maiestie sall come speede
this way.

42. Sir Rorie M[c]Leod to the King

11 *Aug.* 1613

MOST GRACIOUS SOUERAIGNE—Quhairas it pleasit zo[r]
Gracious Majestie to wreit doun heir with me to the Chan-

cellar, Thesaurar, and remanent Lordis of zo^r hienes privie counsall to pas ane gift of nonentrie to me of sum of my landis quhairintill my grandfather was infeft : According thairto I causit forme ane signature and presentit thairwith zo^r hienes letter of recommendatioun in my fauo^{ris} Alwayes I am refuisit thairof vpoun that, that Sr Gedeone Murray now p̃nt The^{sr} wald first acquent zo^r hienes thairwith. Seing he was to go to court to zo^r Matie in respect quhairof I haif takine that boldnes to wreit to zo^r hienes and let zo^r Matie be acquentit thairwith to the effect zo^r Matie may give command be zo^r awin mouthe to the said Sr Gedeone to pas the samī. Seing it is alwayes equitable and dew to me of the law the feu deuteis of thais landis being alreddie payit heir in checker of all zeires and termis bygane. As also to craive zo^r Maties fauo^r to give command to the said Sr Gedeone to assist me in vther my necessar and lauchfull effaires as occasioun sall offer befoir zo^r hienes privie counsall heir. Sua my humble deutie and seruice euer remembrit to zo^r Matie w^t all humilitie and reuerence. Committis zo^r Matie most hertilie to godis protectioun.—Zo^r Majesteis most humble seruand,

S. R. MACLEOD.

Edinburgh, xj August 1613.

43

Vpoun the xiij of August Allester McAllester being in Straithspey (the laird of Grantis cuntrey) accumpanyit onlie wth one man, and going to visite his wyff who had hir ordinarie residence in Straithdone, is apprehendit be the laird of Grant bot his man escaped.

The same day the laird of Grant send out ane company of men to haue taikin Duncan M^cV^ceandowy, who having in his cūpany fyve M^cgrego^{ris} is vnbeset be Grant his men, he and four of his men escapethe, the fyft being a poore fellow and gevin be the landislordis to be a threscher in a barne is hurt and taikin.

Duncane himselff fled to the Erle of Enzee wth whome he is p̃ntlie in company.

44

Decimo quinto Septembris 1613

According to his Maiesteis directioun chargis ar direct
aganis the laird of Grant, his wyff, bruther and vtheris
keeparis of Allaster M^callester M^grego^r for delyuerie of
him to one of the gaird, who is directit to resaue him and
bring him heir, and the erll of Murray is appointit to send
three or foure men to assist the gaird in bringing of the said
M^callester heir.

The counsell hes writtin to the erll of Enzee to send
Duncane v^ceanduy heir. At thair comeing thay wilbe
keept conforme to his Maiesteis directioun.

His Maiesteis directioun so wyislie and gravelie sett doun
in that particulair concernīg M^ckintoshe wilbe preceislie
followit oute and obeyit be the counsall in euerie poynte.

45

Vltimo Novembris 1613

There hes bene dyuerse metteinges with the erle of
Ergyle and the landis lordis of the Clangregour, anent this
last accompt maid be the erle vpon the accomplishement
of that seruice, and what course wes most fitt and expedient to be taine with the bairnes who wer apprehended
be the Laird of Laweris, and the landislordis wer deeplie
sworne to declare the treuthe of that whiche rested in the
accomplischment of that seruice, and this being the appoynted day for making of the accomptis, and for heereing
of the obiectiones proponed be the landislordes againes the
samen, the erle gave in a roll conteeneing the names of
these who rested vpon him at his last accompt made in the
monethe of Junij last being threttie persones in nomber
or therby, this nomber he hes reduced to tuelf persones who
ar to be declared fugitiues and outlawes and accordinglie
to be prosequited with fyre and sword, and proclamationes
ar to be decreet againes the ressettares of thame, besydes
this nomber, thair is tua persones in the handes of the laird

of Grant, and one in the erle of Enzees handes, againes
whome charges ar derect for there exhibition, and charges
ar to be direct againes the erle of Perth and the Lord
Modeitic for the exhibition of Robert Abroche and
Gregour gar M^cphadrick vic conill, who as zet not fund
caution nor gevin there obedience.

There hes bene dyuerse conferences anent the bairnes
and sindrie ouertures hes beine proponed to the landislordis
theranent, whervnto thay culd not agrie, sua that the first
course whiche wes agreed vpon in the monethe of Junij last
anent the distribution of the bairnes, amonges the landislordes according to the proportion of there mark landes
wes thoght meete to be followed oute.   The few nomber
of the landislordes who consented to the contribution of
lx^{ll} oute of the merk land finding that this course anent
the distribution of the bairnis amongis the haill landislordis
broght a double trouble vpon theme making thame subiect
both to the payment of the contribution and to the intertainment of the bairnes, whair as thay who dissassented
fra the contribution being the greitest nomber and of best
rank, wer only subiect to the intertainment of the bairnes.
Thay therfor not only protested againes the payment of
the contribution vnles thay weic fied of the bairnes, bot
with that thay made offer to ressaue the bairnes with condition to be free of the contribution.   The Counsall haueing
aduysed vpon this propositioun and finding that with
reason thay could lay no burdyne of the bairnes vpon these
who consented to the contribution, seeing there consent
was conditionall to be free of all forder truble and burdyne
of that race, and considering therwithall that thay wer
bot a few nomber who consented, and that there pairtis of
the contribution wes of lytle availl, thay therefore thoght
mete to tak hold of this proposition and offer and pro-
ponned the same to the haill landislordis who wer pñt, who
hes consented thereunto vpon thir conditiones to witt that
the bairnes shalbe equalie distributed amonges thame
according to the proportion of there merklandes, that they
shalbe subiect to keepe thame and to mak thame furth-
cumand and ansuerable when euir thay shalbe called for

whill they be of the aige of xviij yeeres at which tyme thay
shall exhibite thame to the counsell to be thane tane ordour
with as shalbe thoght meete, vnder suche a pecuniall
paine as shalbe aggreed vpon ansuerable to the rank and
qualitie of euerye bairne, yf the bairne shall happin to
eschaip frome his keepar, the ressatter of the bairne shall
not only be haldin to releve the landislord who had the
keeping of him all paine and danger that he may incurr
throughe his eschaiping, bot lykwyse salbe subiect to suche
ane arbitrall censure and punishment as the counsell shall
inflict vpon thame ; the bairne so eschaiping being within
xiiij yeeres of aige shalbe scourged and brunt on the cheek[1]
for the first eschaip, and for the nixt eschaip shalbe hanged,
and yf he be past the aige of xiiij yeeres he shalbe hanged
for the first eschaip, and proclamatiounes ar to be direct
and published heervpon.

The Clerk of Registrar[2] and the lord Killsyithe[3] ar to meete
with the landislordis and be thair aduyse to mak a catol-
logue and roll of the haill bairnes, and accordingly to mak
a distribution of thame, and to sett a sowme vpon euerye
bairne according to the whiche sowme the keepares shalbe
ansuerable for thame.

The first question proponed be the landislordis vpon the
poynt of accomplischement of the seruice wes the deceis of
some of the cautionaris for the Clangregour wharby thay
wer in oppinion that the cautionar being dead, the pairtie
for whome caution wes fundin wes free, In this poynte
thay ressauit satisfaction in respect of ane act of parliament beiring that all cautionares tane for the good reule
and quyetnes of the heylandis and bordoris shall obleis the
aires of the cautionares alsweell as the cautionar him self.

The nixt obiection proponed be thame wes againes in
insufficiencye of some tua or three of the cautionaris,
In this poynte thay wer satisfied by derection gevin for
renewing of these cautionis.

---

[1] Argyll had already received from the Privy Council the privilege of brand-
ing 'all the wyffis with ane key upoun the face' (*P.C.R.*, ix. p. 179).

[2] Sir Alexander Hay.

[3] Sir William Livingston of Kilsyth, a Lord of Session, 1609-1627, when he died.

Thirdlie thay obiected againes the erle of Ergyle as not being a goode caution, to this it was ansuered that the erle wes the best cautioner thay could gett, seeing he wes ansuerable and obedyent to the law, and more able to reteane these for whome he wes caution vnder obedyance nor ony vther cautioner wes.

Fourthly thay vrged transplantatioun of all these who had fund caution. This wes thoght most vnreasonable, as being a meane to brek thame all louse and to bring there cautionares in trouble and danger, seeing the most pairte of there cautionaris hes thame on there owne landes, and would not haue bene caution for thame, yf thay had knowne of any suche motion anent thair transplantation.

46

Secundo Decembris 1613

The marqueis of Huntlye being written for to come heer for geveing of his aduyse and oppinion, anent the forme of proceeding againes Allane mak eane duy,[1] he compeered be Knokaspek and Bucky his seruandes excuiseing himself be his letter by reason, that presently he wes somewhat disceased, his seruandes gaue vnto the counsell, conteaneing the forme of the cõmissiones proclamationes and charges whilkes he craved againes Allane and his complisches, bot becaus sindrye questiones resulted vpon some particular heades of these articles, The Counsell being loath, rashly to resolue thervpon, thay haue appoynted the erle of Cassilles, the bishop of Caithnes, the thesaurer depute, aduocat, Kilsyithe and Meedope [2] to conveane the morn at afternone, and to confer, reason andaduyse vpon the saides articles, and to consider of euery question, doubt or inconvenient that may result, be moved or followed thervpon and to reporte to the counsell the nixt counsell day what is there aduyse and oppinion thairanent, how far shalbe

---

[1] Cameron of Lochiel, *vide* Gregory, *History*, p 342.
[2] Sir Andrew Drummond of Medhope, a Lord of Session, 1608-1619, when he died.

proceeded in that busyness, and what cōmissiones, proclamationes or charges shalbe granted thervpon, aduerteisment shalbe send therof with the nixt pacquet.

47

Nono Decembris 1613

The counsell hes past ane ample cōmission of Justiciarie
to the Marquess of Huntlie, the erle of Enzee his sone, the
lairdes of Clunye, Lesmore, Bucky and some otheres
barrones and gentlemen of the said Marquis his kyn and
frendship for the persute of Allane mak eane duy and his
rebellious complishes. In this cōmission powar is granted
vnto thame to beare weare and vse hagbutes and pistol-
lettis the tyme of there goeing from there own housis to
execute this cōmission and in the tyme that thay ar
actualy in the execution of that seruice, and in there returning home fra the seruice to there own housis, and with this
speciall prouision and condition that thay shall not beare
weare nor vse the saides hagbutes and pistollettes againes
nane of his Maiesties lauchfull and good subiectis.

Proclamationes ar past and exped chargeing all and
sindrie Erlis, Lordes, barrones, landed gentlemen, and
substantious yeomen within the schirefdomes of Invernes
and Cromertye, and within the countryes of Sutherland,
Caithnes and Stranaver, within Perthshire aboue Dunkeld, and within Ergyle and Tarbett, to ryse, concurr,
fortifye and assist the cōmissionares in euery thing tending
to the execution of that cōmissioun and to conveane and
meete at such dayes tymes and placeis, and with sa mony
dayes victuales and prouision as thay shalbe aduerteised
be new proclamatioun, missiue, letter or otherwyse and
in this proclamation it is specialye provyded that nane
shalbe subiect to this concurrance bot within the shiref-
dome wher thay duell, and that erlis and lordis shall
nawyse be subiect to concurr bot when the Marqueis of
Huntlye or the erle of Enzee his sone ar present in persone
at this seruice.

Proclamationes ar derect prohibiting the ressett, suphe and intercōmounīg with the rebelles, thir furnissing of thame with meat, drink, victualis, pulder, bullat, armour or any other thing comfortable and necessar vnto thame, the taking of there goodes and geare in keepeing or the concealing or hoording of the same vnder the pane to be repute haldin and esteemed as arte and partakares with the rebelles in all there wicked deedes and all these who standis vnder bandes of frendship with Allane or charged to renvnce and discharge the samen.

Proclamationes ar derect conteaneing a promeis of pardoun to whatsomeuer persone or persones presenthe standing vnder the danger of the lawes for ony capitall crymes not being treasonable who will tak, apprehend; present to Justice or slay the said Allane and there is a pryce of a thousand pundes sett vpon the head of the said Allane, fyue hundrethe pundes vpoun the heades of tua of his chiftanes and ane hundreth pundes vpon the heades of euerye one of the rest of his followares to be payed be the Marqueis to ony lawfull subiectes who will tak, apprehend, present to iustice or slay thame.

Charges ar derect againes these who hes the custodie and keepeing of Allanes eldest sone [1] for exhibition of him before the counsell, To the effect that now in his minoritie some course may be taine anent his education and keepeing wherthrow he follow not the unhappye coursis of his father.

Charges ar derect againes a nomber of barrounes, gentlemen and otheres who ar suspect to be fauorablie inclyned and disposit to Allane, chaigeing thame to find caution acted in the bookes of secrete counsell not to ressett, suphe nor intercomoun with him nor his rebellious cōplishes vnder certane pecunyall paines mentionat and conteaned in the saides charges.

Derection is gevin that no suspension nor relaxatioun be granted to Allane nor nane of his rebellious complisches whill first thay entir there persones in waird within the tolbuith of Edinburgh.

---

[1] John, the young Lochiel, father of the famous Sir Ewen Dubh.

48

27 *January* 1614

This day being appoynted to the Lord Madertie[1] for exhibitione of Allane m^ceanduyis sone being in his handis, he be his lfĕ excuised his not compeirance be reasone of his seiknes, whairvpoun the Counsall hes assignit vnto him the fyifteine day of Februare nixt, outher to bring or send the boy heir, And he is fund to be ansueirable for him in the mean tyme.

49

29 *Aprilis* 1614

The house of Dvnyveg in Yla being possessed and keeped be the Bishop of the Yles his brother and two or three servandes the same house has bene of late surprysed and tane be one Ronnald oig alledyeand to be bastard sone to vmq^le Angus M^cconeill of Dvnyveg, whom the said Angus did neuer in his tyme acknowledge to be his sone. This Ronnald being a vagabound fellow without ony certane residence come latelie to Yla, and finding the house to be but slenderlie keeped resolued to surpryse and tak the same, and for this effect he and his complices being four or fyue in nomber retered thame selues to ane wood neare by the house whair they made some ledderes, and with thame one day airlie in the morning thay clam the vtter wall, keeped thame selues obscure whill the yettis wer oppined, and then they took the house, and patt the bishopes folkes oute thereof, The reporte whereof comeing to young Angus M^cconeill[2] laufull brother to Sr James, who wes within sex myles of the house for the tyme, he immediatlie according to the countrie fassioun send the fyre crose athorte the countrey warning all the countrey people who wer affected to his maiesties obedience to ryse and concur with him in the recourie of the house, And so he

---

[1] James Drummond, one of the king's companions at the time of the Gowrie 'Conspiracy.' Created Lord Maddertie in 1609.

[2] Hereafter referred to as Angus Oig.

with such assistawnce as come to him inclosed the house.
Thay within held good for sex dayes being well prouyded
with pulder, lunt and bullott whereof thay fand good
store in the house, and thay wer prodigall eneughe in
bestowing the same vpon the Beseagares. Bot in end per-
ceaueing that thay war not able to keepe the house thay
in the night eshued at a bak yett in a litle boat with sex
oares which lay at the castle, And took with thame such
goodes as thay fand in the house. Angus followed thame
but what farther hes fallin oute is not as zet come to the
counselles knowledge. Sr James Mcconcill is the Counselles
informar of all this busynes, and as he sayes, his brother
hes offerred to delyuer the house bak againe to the Bishopes
seruandes who refuised to ressaue the same. The counsell
haueing hard at lenth Sr James discourse made in this
earand, and looking shortlie to heere from the erle of
Ergyle or els frome the bishope the constant and certane
truthe of all this mater, They haue reserued all delibera-
tion heerin till thay heere from the said bishope or erle.

50. Privy Council to the King

2 *June* 1614

MOST GRATIOUS SOUERANE,—Thair wes a petitioun gevin
in this day to zo^r Maiesteis Counsaill in the name of S^r
James Mcconeill proporting that thir tuelff yeiris bigane he
had sustenit grite trouble distresse and misirie by his strait
imprisonment in the Castellis of Blaknes and Edinburgh
whair he hes beene this lang tyme keept in unis, And his
desire wes that he might be fred and relevit of his warde
and sufferrit to remane with his freindis in ony pairt of
zo^r Maiesteis dominionis, quhill it sould pleas god to pñt
some occasioun quhairby zo^r Maiestie might imploy him
in zo^r Ma^{tels} seruice And he did offer cautioun for his
personall compeirance befoir the Counsell quhenevir he
sould be chargeit, and for his not repairing to Kintyre nor
Yla, without zo^r Maiesteis licence vnder suche soumes as
sould be inioyned vnto him, his petitioun being harde and
considderit be ws, and we remembering that thair wes a

decreit and sentence of forfaltor standing aganis the said
Sr James for certane crymes of treasoun committit be him
quhairof he wes convict in iudgement,[1] And knoweing of
no favour, grace nor pardoun as yitt showne be zo^r Maiestie
to him, we wer thairfoir spairing to grant the desyre of
his petitioun quhill first we vnderstoode zo^r Maiesteis
gratious will and pleasour thairanent And wheneuir zo^r
Maiestie salbe pleasit to gif significatioun vnto ws what
zo^r Maiestie will haif to be done in that mater, we sall in
all reuerence conforme or selffis thairvnto, And so praying
god to blisse zo^r Maiestie with a long and happie reignn
we rest, zo^r Maiesteis most humble and obedyent subiectis
and seruitouris,

AL. CANCELL^s.   OLIPHĂT.
BINNING.[2]
JO. PRESTOUN.   ALEX^r HAY. KILSAYTH.
SIR A. DRUMMOND.   S. G. MURRAY.

Edinburgh, 2 Junij 1614.

51

Nono Junij 1614

Whereas Anguis oig m^{c}coneill brother to Sr James
M^{c}coneill did recouer the house of Dunnyveg from Ronnald
oig m^{c}allester [3] who surprysed and tooke the same frome
the bishop of the Yles servandes who hade the charge of
the keeping therof, in the moneth of March last, And the
said Angus pretending that the respecte and regarde of
his maiesties obedience and seruice moved him to enter-
pryse the recouerie of the said houss with the hazarde and
perrell of his lyff, and that he wold be readdy and willing
to delyuer the same outher to the bishop or to suche otheres
as the counsell sould appointe to ressaue the same, Sensyne enformation hes come heere from the bishop, that
the surpryse and taking of the house be Ronnald proceeded

---

[1] In 1609. *Vide ante*, p. 92.
[2] Sir Thomas Hamilton was created Lord Binning, 19th November 1613.
[3] A mistake for M'Angus.

from the said Angus, and by speciall cōmand, warrand and
direction from him, And that he fearing that the said
Ronnald wold discover that mater, hes now latelie slane
his foure men, and tane him self prisonar, And that the
said Angus hes not onlye refuised to delyuer the house to
the bishope, he being him self in Yla readdy to resaue the
same, bot hes furnished the said house with men, victuelles,
poulder, bullet and other warre lyk provision, of purpose
and extention to keepe the said house as ane house of
warre against his Matie and his authoritie, This enformation being made to the counsale vpon the eight of this
instant, and thay apprehending that no suche mater could
haue fallen oute withoute the said Sr James his privie
knowledge and allowance, Thay therefore directed the
captane of the guarde with the clerk of counsale to the
Castle of Edinburghe with a warrand to the constable to
lay Sr James in the yrones and to keepe him close prisonar,
and thay had alsua direction to iype [1] Sr James persone and
cofferres and to entromett with the whole letteres and
wrytes thay could find vpon his persone or in his cofferres,
This direction being with all diligence execute, and a
nomber of letteres and writtes being fundin vpon his
person and in his cofferres, as alsua some letteres being
gotten which he had written that same day and directed
to his mother and brother, And all thir writtes being
sighted and narrowlie remarked, there could nothing be
fundin in ony one of thame which might breede ony kynd
of suspition or imputation agains Sr James, but by some
of his lr̃es wiitten to his brother, it wes cleare and evidente
that he counselled and advysed his brother, to conteane
him self in all obedience to his maiestie to forbeare all
occasiones which might be offensiue to his maiestie, and
to mak the house foorthcomand according as his maiestie
or the counsale wold cōmand, And there alsua one letter
gotten directed from Angus oig to the counsale, by the
whiche he pretended to haue done good seruice to his
maiestie in recouerie of the house, and said that he made

---

[1] Search.

offer thereof to the bishopes brother who refuised the same, And that he wes yett willing to delyuer the same according as the counsale should direct and cōmand he ressaueing one approbation of his seruice in recovering of the house from Ronnald Mᶜallester.

Thir letteres with the bishopes enformation being at lenth hard and considered, This course following is tane, to trye yf Angus will rander his obedyence, to witt, letteres and charges ar direct against Angus Oig and the remanent keepares of the house, for randering and delyverie of the same to the said bishope within sex houres after the charge vnder the paine of horning, And yf he refuise and go to the horne, Ane cōmission is exped to the bishope for persute and asseageing of the house with fyre and swerde. And letteres ar direct againest his maiesties subiectes in the boundes nixt adiacent to concurre and assist with the bishope in the execution of the cōmission.

Charges ar alsua direct againes Angus for delyuerie of Ronnald Mᶜallestar to the bishope, to the effect he may be broght heere to his tryall, examination and punishement.

52

Tertio Augusti 1614

Thair compeired this day befoir the Counsall, Mᶜclane, Donald Gorme, Mᶜcleude of Hereis, MᶜKynnoun and Mᶜclane of Lochbuye, nane vther of the principall Ilismen being absent, bot the captane of Clanronald, who wes heir some tua monethis ago, Thir men who wer pñtt hes ratifeit and approven the formair bandis, actis and constitutiounis maid and agreit vnto be thame in the sex hundrethe and nyne zeir of god quhen the bischope of the Ylles as his Maᵗᶦᵉˢ cōmissionair wes amanges theme at Icolmekle,[1] they have acted them selfis to compeir befoir the Counsall anes euery zeir in July vnder gritt panes They haue also actit themselffis to keip his Maᵗᶦᵉˢ peace, to follow thair actionis aganis vtheris be the ordinair course of law and not to resist the executioune of ony decreittis

---

[1] At that time the well-known Statutes of Iona were enacted.

or sentences that salbe recouerit aganis theme, They haue nommate domicilis within the burghe of Edinburghe whairat they sall be chairged in all tyme cūing And they ar ordanit still to remane in this burghe whill they be fred.

Mᶜcleude of Hereis is cōmitted to waird within the Castell of Edinburghe for not exhibitione of some of the rebellis of the Lewis, who ar provin to haue bein ressett in his boundis.

The xxiij of this instant is appoynted for heiring of the accompt of the seruice aganis the Clangregoʳ, and the erle of Ergyle and haill landislordis ar wreittin for to be heir that day.

53

24 Augusti 1614

The bishope of the Yles is now at Yla, There wes one directed by the counsale to accompany him to Ila, and to bring frome him a speedie answere anent the obedience he ressaued there.   This man is looked for to be heere one of thir two or three dayes.

The whole Ylesmen hes beene heere and ar demitted vnder band for their compeirance euerye yeere heereafter in the moneth of July befor the counsale.

54. Copie of my letter[1] to the Bischop of the Iles

8 Sept. 1614

My verie honorable good Lord—I haue presentlie ressaued frome your Lo. footeman your Lo. letter of the fourt of September from Brodick signifieing your Lo. messages to the rebelles of Duniveg, the offer to thame of his Maiesties remission and there tryall of the sufficiencie therof and not the les there delay to giue there obedience till your Lo. go to Ila which now your Lo. is prepareing to do: I am verie sorie of the progres and succes of that busynes which ap-

---

[1] Where there is a reference to 'my letter' or 'letter to me,' it may be assumed that the person using the phrase is Lord Binning himself.

peares to be miscarryed not without your Lo. oversight,
for, when his Maiesties cōmissiō wes according to your Lo.
desyre to yow by the counsale and suche remission exped
to the rebelles as your Lo. requyred, your Lo. vndertook
and faithfullie promeised to the thesaurar depute and me
that your Lo. should go in person with all possible diligence
to Ila being confident to find readdy obedyance of the
rebelles there, and after your Lo. parteing from ws we delt
with your Lo. sone to haist after your Lo. to latt your Lo.
know that we had perswaded the earle of Caithnes [1] to
promeis so sone as he had performed his vndertaken
cōmission to tak fordward his shippes, shouldiouris and
canones to asseage and batter the house of Duniveg, yf
your Lo. should mak ws speedie adverteismēt of there delay
or disobediance of your charges as his Maiesties cōmissionar,
for which purpose we wrote verie particular to your Lo.
by Duncan Campbell whom we send expreslie to your Lo.
commanding him and requesting your Lo. that he should
not returne to ws whill he had accompanyeed your Lo.
to Ila, and vpoun the sight of the event of your trauelles
might haue reported to ws by your Lo. letters and his
owne sight the certantie of thinges your Lo. send whom
bak to ws from Bute, with your letter bearing faithfull promese that his jornay should not be necessar, Bot that your
Lo. should go presentlie then fordward and return ws good
and speedy contentment, Whereby finding our selues far
disapoynted of our exspectatioun, of new we derected
Duncan Campbell vpon the 29 of August with our letteres
which was thoght should haue fund your Lo. in Ila and
haue agane this tyme reported the estate of your proceedinges, But now finding that your Lo. is still in Arrane and
begining to mak your preparationis as for ane seruice to
begin we haue good cause to regrate the inexcusable losse
of so good tyme as the season of the yeare w^{che} brings on
vnmendable difficulties and is lyklie to mak the earle of
Caithnes vnhable to do the seruice and so to giue your Lo.
lesse incuragement and such advantage to the rebelles as

---

[1] George Sinclair, fifth Earl of Caithness.

may mak his Maiesties houss which wes lossed by default of your keepars to be deteaned by the rebelles whill the nixt sommer : it beeng more probable that your Lo. imploying of the cuntrey people to inclose the houss shall giue thame vexation, nor bring difficulties or necessitie of ouergeveing the house to the rebelles, to whom your Lo. hes besyd the aduantage of there former preparation of victualis given occasion by this delay of tyme to furnish thame selues with new cornes, Neuertheles I haue delyuered to your seruand the warrand and direction in wryt which your Lo. craues to Donald Gorme and shall with extreame diligence cause exped all that your [Lo.] can reasonable require for furtharance of your vndertaken charge in his Maties seruice. I pray your Lo. consider of our burding according to the weaght thereof and imploy your judgment, frendes and powai geven your Lo. by his Maiesties cōmission for the speedy and ductiefull performance thereof for your owne credite and his Maiesties honour and contentment of whose gratious consideratioun of good seruices no man knowes better the assureance and experiance then your Lo. self. So hopeing vndoubtedlie that your Lo. will stryve with care and diligence to amend bypast negligence and wisheing your Lo. happie success in this and all vther your affaires I rest,

Your Lo. assured frend to be cōmanded.

Edr, aught of September 1614.

Your Lo. man hes not had cause to stay heere ane hour vpon his answer and hes ressaued money for his charges.

55. Lord Binning to his brother, Mr Patrick Hamilton [1]

15 Sept. 1614

The Bischop of the Iles hes protracted long tyme verie vnproffitablie whairof he now persaues the errour and regraitis it be ane letter which we ressaved from him

---

[1] Afterwards Sir Patrick Hamilton of Little Preston.

yesternight whairby he promeises now to go fordward to
Ila Bot verie vnseasonablie, becaus the cuntrie people
be whoes assistance he might haue expected to haue straited
the rebels ar now so busied with thair harvest that thay
will rather aduenture to disobey the proclamation nor losse
the cornes whairvpon thay and thair families must leive
whill this tyme twelmonth. Alwayes we have granted
him all the warrandis the requyres and sall omit nothing
that is in oure power to aduance his seruice and incourage
him thairin albeit I mixed my last ansueir to him with
sum bitternes becaus his inexcusable delayes had greatlie
preiudged his Ma^tties seruice.—Your loving brother,

BINNING.

Ed^r, 15 September.

To my beloued brother
    Maister Patrick Hamilton
          at Court.

56. Copie of the Contract betuix the Bishop of the Iles and Angus Og and his complices

22 Sept. 1614

At the Castell of Dynnievaig the [twenty-second] day of
September the zeir of God j^m vj^c and fourtene yeiris it is aggreit and endit betuix ye pairties wnderwryttin, to wit, betuix
the right hono^ll Angus Oig McDonald, Ronald McJames
M^cdonald, his vncle Colene gillespie M^cdonald, Ronald
M^csorle and   on the ane pairt and the reverend father
in God Andro, bischop of the Yllis, his Maiesties cõmissionar
and stewart of the west and north ylles of Scotland vpoun
the vther pairt That is to say fforsameikill as the saidis
Angus Oig and Ronald McJames and the rest of thair
freindis and followaris hes beine lyik as thay remaine verie
desyrous that the said reverend father sould kyth his
constant fauo^r and freindschip toward thame by his dilligence in dealing for a sufficient securitie to thame of his
Maiesties landes in the yll of Yla thay payand thairfore
suche yeirlie dewtie as accordis of ressoun As alswa that

the said reverend father sould sett to the said Angus Oig
his haill churche landis whairever vmq^le Angus M^cconeill of
Dynnevaig his father died in possessioun As alswa the
said Ronald McJames all and haill theiss landis set to him
of before be the said reverend father and to Colene Gillespie
M^cdonald and Ronald M^csorle all and sindrie the kirke
landis whilk they haue alreddie in tak of the said reverend
father and that for the same yeirlie dewties alreddie
speït in thair takis and suche enties ressonable as sall be
aggreit vpoun be the saidis pairties, and for fulfilling of
the piemissis be the said reverend father the saidis Angus
Oig M^cdonald and Ronald McJames cravit pladges to be
delyverit to thameat Losset the tuentie twa of this September last vnto the whilk thair earnest sute and for certantie to
thame of the faithfull keiping and observing of the articles
and heades efter speït The said reverend father delyuerit
vnto thame his nephew Johnne Knox of Rampherlie and
his eldest sone Maister Thomas Knox to be intertenyit and
keipit be thame in honest and good estait ay and whill the
dilligence of the said reuerend father in satisfeing of the
said Angus Oig and Ronald McJames thair desyre abouc-
wryttin to be maid notorius and knawin to thame be the
sight and discretioun of Donald Gorme of Slaite and
Sir Awlay McCawlay of Ardincaple and thairfore the said
reverend father bindis and obleissis him to do his vtter
dilligence and indevore to procure and obtene to the said
Angus Oig M^cdonald ane sevin year tak of all and haill his
Maiesties proper landis within the yll of Yla, in possessioun
of the whilk Sir Ronald M^csorle of Dunluse is for the
present and that for the yeirlie maill of aucht thowsand
merkis to be payed be the said Angus Oig in his Maiesties
cheker yeirlie As alswa Secundlie sall resigne and delyuer
to the said Angus Oig M^cdonald the houss and castell of
Dynnevaig with the whole rightis and giftis whilk the said
reverend father hes of the samē and gevin be his Maiestie
to him, the said reverend father obteining his Maiesties
licence to do ye samen, and thridlie sall set in tak and
assidatioun to ye said Angus Oig all and singular these
churche landis and speciallie the twentie fywe merk land

whilk was possest be vmq^le Angus M^cconeill his father and now be Ronald M^csorle and that for the samē dewties speīt in the said vmq^ll Angus his tak and suche ressonable entres as the said reuerend father and the said Angus Oig sall aggrie vpoun be the advyse of freindis and feirdlie sall gif vnto the said Ronald McJames a sufficient lrē of tak for the space of sevin yeiris in lyik maner of all and singular his sevintene merk vj^ll viij^d kirk land pñtlie possest be him and that vpoun the samen conditioun of entres and yeirlie dewtie mentionat and speīt in his foresaid tak and as the said Ronald McJames payed of before to the reverend father And fyftlie sall set to the said Colene Gillespie M^cdonald and Ronald M^csorle ane sufficient lrē of tak of all and singular the churche landis possest be thame and speciallie the xvj^ll viij^d land of Radadell pertening to the said reverend father for the space and vpoun the conditiounes abouewryttin And saxtlie, the said reverend father bindis and obleissis him selff be the faithe and trewth of his bodie to do his vtter dilligence and indevore to procure and obtene to the said Angus Oig, Ronald McJames, Colene Gillespie, Ronald M^csorle and the remanent of his kyn, freindis and followaris whose names he sall gif vp in wryte a sufficient remissioun wnder the great seall of all crymes and wrongis and suche vther offences criminall and civell as they haue comittit before the day and dait of the samē and finallie sall stand thair good freind in all thingis and to further whatsumever thair bussines or earrandis sall occur according to equitie and iustice And that so far as his dilligence and credit sall extend to ffor the [which] caus the said Angus Oig M^cdonald, Ronald McJames, Colene Gillespie, Ronald M^csorle   bindis and obleissis thame be the faith and trewthe of thair bodies wnder the pane of perpetuall periurie and defamatioun for ewer to interteny and keip saiff frome all danger or skaith within ye boundis of the Castle of Dynnevaig or suche other places being competent for honest men to lieue into The said Johnne Knox of Rampherlie and Maister Thomas Knox vpoun thair awin expenssis and to suffer thame haive a competent number of servandis to serve thame dureing the space of the said reverend father his dilligence in performing at the leist in doing his indevore to performe the heidis abouewrytten; The whilkis being performed [by] the said reuerend father the said Angus and remanent persones foresaidis bindis and obleissis thame selffis to delyver the said Johnne Knox of Rampherlie and Maister Thomas Knox to ye said reverend father haill and sound, vntrublit in body or goodis be thame or onie of thame or onie vtheris whome they may stop or lat directlie or indirectlie, And in caice the said reuerend father his credeit extend nocht to performe all is abovewryttin, in that caice they bind and obleissis thame selffis nochtwithstanding, to delyuer the said Johnne Knox of Rampherlie and Mr Thomas Knox to the said reverend father Provyding bothe his dilligence and indevore be tryed to haue beine done to ye vttermost he could do be the sicht and discretioun of Donald Goime of Slait and Sr Awlay M^{c}awlay of Ardincaple : Bot also efter his dilligence being tryed as said is, to pay to the said Angus Oig M^{c}donald sic sowmes of silwer for ransoum and redelyuerie of the saidis plaidges as sall be aggreit vpoun betuix the saidis pairteis. And finallie, the said Angus Oig and remanent forsaidis persones bindis and obleissis thame selffis to refound and pay to the said reverend father sic soumes of money as he sall be fund to haue debursed in expenssis and giftis for procureing of ye takis of his Maiesties landis and remissioun abovewryttin, And that be the sicht and discretioun of Donald Gorme of Sleat and Sr Awlay M^{c}awlay of Ardincaple ; in witnes whairof baith ye saidis pairties hes subscryvit thir presentis with yair handis, day, zeir and place foresaid befoic thir witnessis, Alex^r M^{c}donald of Largie ; Donald M^{c}allester, tutor of Loup ; Donald oig M^{c}ronald buy, Maister Johnne Vas, servito^r to the said reverend father ; Maister Patrik McLachlan, minister, Killating [1] ; and Hector McKawiss of Kembuss. [2] Sic sub^r Angus Oig M^{c}doneill ; An: Illis ; Alex^r M^{c}donald of Largie, witnes ; Hector McKawiss, witnes ;

---

[1] *Quære*, Kilchoman.   [2] Kenobus.

Maister Patrik McLauchlane, minister, witnes; Mr. Johne Wass, witnes.

57. Copie of the letter ressaued from the Bischop of the Iles the penulti of Sept. at nyne at night

MY SPECIALL GOODE LORD—Receaving frome my lord Secretare ane velie byiting lr̃e laying the weytt of the taking of the house of Dunavaig vpoun the negligence of my keiparis theirof, and the long keiping theirof be the rebellis vpoun my sleuthe whilk semed to proceid ather of some of my vnfreindis informatione of his Lo., or els of his Lo. consait of me, whilk I neuer merited I preased als cairfullie as my might or credit micht extend to (albeit I wanttit both place purse and credit neidfull to haue affectuatit suche ane carand) to releive my self of that imputatioune and with all diligence I tuik my jurney toward the Yles prouydit with suche furnito^r and small cumpany of men as I micht with suche haist procure. And thinking my nūber too small to venture in conference or plotting with rebellis I send sex of the best of my cumpany weill acquented with theme to theme with the remissione thinking that according to thair oathe and promeise be wrytt and vpoun the ressett theirof they suld haue deliuered the house whilk they returned ansuer with some of my seruandis to me that they suld be reddie to do within tua houris eftir they had advysit and being resoluit whidder the remissione wes sufficient or no as I wrait to your Lo. of befoir vpoun the whilk promeise I sent ouer my seruandis the secund tyme and I rested still in Arrane thinking they suld haue kepit their promeise but they returnit the secund ansuer to me that they culd not delyuer that house bot to my self being personall p̃utt and to ressaue ane sufficient assurance be wreat of my freindschipe in all tyme cūing And theirfoir leist they suld haue excused their rebellione in respect of my crayning to come that far vnto theme And leist that your Lo. suld haue layed ane new burden vpoun my sleuthe

in respect of the neglect of that seruice And that feiring
the treacherie of these rebellis I prouydit suche cūpany as
ather my credit amangst my freindship or of any money
whilk I might procure to convoy me thair.   The haruest
wes so great ane impediment that the nightbouris in the
Iles and the Yles men themselfis so cairles in this seruice
that for the most pairt all men refuised me and in
speciall Mᶜlen and Mᶜcleude of Hereis sua that I culd obtene
no nomber to go thairwith except thrie scoir and ten personis of the whiche their wes fyiftie weageit souldiouris
and twentie followeris ot the Laird of Ardincaple, my nevoy
the laird of Ranfurlie, and my self.   With these I landit
in Ila the 19 of this instant being assuredlie informit that
Donald Gorme of Slait and the land of Hardincaple whome
I had send befoir my self yet agane to the house to mitigat
the rebellis humoᵣⁱˢ pacife and move theme without delay
to obey the charge.   I wes also defyed be word and wreat
that the tennentis of the countrey wald concur with me
and that the best half of the Clandonalde of that Ile would
assist me to the whilk effect some of theme mett me be
the way and convoyit me to Ilay and remanit with me
night and day whill the 21 day at aucht houris in the
mornīg who depairting then fiome me and Hardencaple
and Donald Gorme comeing to me and gaue up cōmonīg
and vtter refusell to delyuer the house any maner of
way and immediathe after theme the greittest nomber of
the name of the Clandonald of that Yle both of the taikeris
of that house and suche as medlit not with it befoir come
togidder to the nomber of ane hundret men in armes and
mae   And ley betuixt ws and our boittis whilkis they
immediathe brake all to the nomber of four boittis and
spoyled the haill guidis thairroutof by our knawlege affirmīg
that they come onlie to confer with me and pak vp materis
be the aduyse and intercessione of Donald Gorme and the
laird of Hardencaple whill the 22 day about aucht of the
clok when they resortit to theme ane vther hundrethe and
mae pairtlie of the cuntrey men and pairtlie of their owin
accustomit followaris And so having ws cut of frome our
boittis they directed a threating to ws that they wald

put ws all to the edge of the sword without exceptione or
els it behovit ws to deliver suche of our nomber to theme
as they wald chuse vnto the whilk for eschewing of bluid
and greittare inconvenientis it behovit me to yeild and
so to chuse out of our cumpany my nevoy the laird of
Ranfurlie and my sone Mr Thomas whome they have
taiken with theme to the Castell of Dunavaig whairby your
lo. may perceaue how traitourouslie I haue bein oft defaissit
be that pestiferous clan, how hard my caice is many wayis
and in what trouble my freindis ar cumin be my cair to
serue the Kingis Maiestie both in keiping that house and
in preasing to recouer vpoun litle or none of his Maties
charges whiche I dout not as his hienes so your Lo. will sie
remedit and that with all diligence vtherwise I am vndone.
Nather can I depairt frome this yle whill I sie some com-
fortabill way for the relief of their captives as moir particularlie I haue givin informatioune to the bearer. Besciking your Lo. to grant yr.to whilk salbe no wayes preiudiciall
to his Ma^{ttes} or your Lo. intentione in that particulare what-
euer it be his Ma^{tte} recouered the bishop of Darayis house
and his wyf whose house and castell wes taikin be Odochortie [1]
and recompensed the skaithe, his hienes wairit expenses
vpoun the recoucrie of the house of Dunavaig when it wes
taikin frome my lord of Scone who had for the keiping
theirof ane thousand mk sterling a year. I hoip your Lo.
will not sie me and my freindis wrak whilk referring to
your conscienabill discietione and beseiking god to bliss
your lo. I rest—(Subscryuit), zour lo. affectionat servand,

An. Iles.

Frome Yley the xxiij of September 1614

They have biggit ane new forthe in ane logh whiche they
haue mäit and victulat. Angus og their captane affirmis
in the heiring of my manie witnesses, that he gat directione frome the erle of Argyle [2] to keip still the house and

---

[1] Sir Cahir O'Dogherty. In consequence of the behaviour of an English
ruffian named Paulet, Governor of Derry, he attacked and burned that town,
including the palace of Bishop Montgomery.

[2] For similar statements, *vide post*, p 216.

that he suld procure hım theırfoır the haıll landis of Yley
and house of Dunavage to hımself.

　　　　　　　　Dırect to my verıe specıall goode lordis
　　　　　　　　My Lord Bınnīg, Secretare, and
　　　　　　　　My lord thesaurer of Scotland.

58. Lord Binning to his brother Mr Patrick Hamilton

28 *Sept.* 1614

BROTHER—The bearer heırof Archıbald Cambell [1] having
tane earnıst trauellıs to moue the Laırd of Cadell to consent
to accept the few of Ila vpon condıcıons far aboue any
thing that ony responsall man of qualıtıe dıd euer to my
knowledge offer for ıt, he hes also persuaded Cadell to
vndertake the recouerıe of Dvneveg ıf be his owıne forces
and at his prıvat chaırges he beıng furneıssed of canon,
pouder and bullet be hıs Ma[tıes] gracıous acknouledgement
efter the seruice be well accomplcısed as the depute
thesaurer, the aduocat and I haue wrıttin breıflıe to my
lord Chamberlane [2] whaırwıtlı I haue thought fite to acquent
you to the effect you may gıue your freındlıe concurrence
to thıs gentılman ın hıs affaires becaus I know him well
affected to hıs Maıestıes seruıce. It pleased my lord
Chamberlane to recommend to me the aduancement of
the Iles whaırof I am ıgnorant except so much as I may
learne be ınformatıon of these who know the true estate
of these countries whaırın I know not any to be more
trusted nor the bearer　And thaırfore ıf you vnderstand
my lord Chamberlane to persıst ın that resolutıon ıt wıll
be fit that his Lo. dırect thıs gentılman to relate the true
estate of these cuntries to hıs Lo. and the best meanes
to reduce thame to peace, cıuılıtıe and proffeıt and thaır-
efter what my lord sall be pleased to command me I sall

---

[1] Often desıgned of Glencarradale. He was a younger brother of Sır James
of Lawers and Colın of Aberuchıll　He was made Commendator of the Prıory
of Strathfillan, and was also baılıe of Kıntyre under Argyll.　He was employed
ın the persecutıon of the Macgregors, and appears often ın the documents now
prınted.

[2] Robert Carr, Earl of Somerset (cf. p　176).

most willinglie obey it. Referring all farder to your nixt
aduerteisment I commit yow to God. Ed^r, the 28 Sept.
—Your loving brother, BINNING.

59. Privy Council to the King

1st Oct. 1614

MOST GRATIOUS SOUERANE—Scn the aduerteisment
laitlie send vnto zo^r maiestie anent the affairis of Ila with
the copie of the letter send vnto ws frome the Bischop of
the Illis whairin he conceded some credite and truste to
Bryce Simple bearair of his lr̃e, we convenit and mett
day with suche otheris of zo^r maiesties counsell as in this
vacant tyme could be had and at lenthe hard the gentilman
vpoun that credite and truste conceedite vnto him, who
reportis vnto ws, That the conditioun craved be the
rebellis is, That thay may haif ane nynetene zeir tak of
Ila maid be zo^r Maiestic tó the Bischop in thair fauouris
for the zeirlie payment of aucht thowsand merkis, and
thay offer to find cautioun to the bischop for the thankfull
payment of the said sowme. This being a mater tuicheing
zo^r Maiestie so neirlie in honnour, and whairof the pre-
parative is so pernitious and dangerous in consequence
and example, we wald nouther allow nor refuse the same
bot hes reserved the same to zo^r Maiesteis awne princelie
consideratioun. We haif had some conference with the
Laird of Cadell how this rebellioun may be supprest yf
so it sall pleis zo^r maiestie to follow oute that course and
we did lay to his charge yf he wald vndirtak ony burdyne
thairin, At the first he seamed to propone some impedimentis, as namelie the miscontentment w^che perhaps some
noblemen wald apprehend yf he wer preferrit in that
seruice to thame, thay being more able to prosequute the
same in suche substantious maner as is requisite nor he,
And nixt the dangeir whairin the bischoppis pledgeis wald
be yf ony suche hostile course wer followit oute aganis
the rebellis, And in end he is come to this, That yf it sall
pleas zo^r Sacred Maiestie to lay ony suche burdyne vpoun
him, he, to testifie his goode affectioun to zo^r Maiesteis

seruice, will willinglie vndirtak the same, he being onlie
furneist with some cannonis and with twa cannonaris,
and other twa expert men for battering of housis, And
that he sall mak a sufficient pouer and force of his awne
for prosequuting of the seruice, and who salbe able to
command the haill Ile, except the Castell, and that he
sall do his best endevoiris to recouer the Castell, bot yf
the seruice salbe of ony lang continewance by halding oute
of the Castell and so sall require the abiding of his forceis
a lang space togidder.　In this poynte he pretendis some
difficultyis as yf the seruice must be followit oute be zo^r
Matie.　This being the effect of oure conference w^t him,
we do humelie pñt the same to zo^r Ma^{teis} princelie consideratioun.　And so praying god lang to preserve zo^r
Maiestie in helthe and felicitie we rest Zo^r Maiesteis most
humble and obedyent subiectis and seruitouris,

AL. CANCELL^s.
BINNING.
OLIPHANT.

Edinburgh, the first of October 1614.

60

Quinto Octobris 1614

There wes a petition geven in to the counsell in name
of Sr George Hamiltoun [1] proporting that he beeng takkis-
man of Yla and oblished to his Maiestie in a certane yeerlie
ductie for the same, and beeng lykwyse burdened with
the payment of his Maiesties taxation for the said yle,
That now the tennentes and inhabitantes of that yle,
in respect of the present rebellion there, hes refuised other
to mak him payment of his Maiesties duetyes, or yett of
the taxatioun, and therefore his desyre wes that he might
haue had a cõmission to go there with a force of his Maiesties
subiectis in armes for vplifting of his Maiesties dueties and
of the taxation.　This petition beeng hard and considered,

---

[1] Brother of the first Earl of Abercorn.　According to Calder's doer, James
Mowat, the tack was really for behoof of Sir Randal MacSorlie (*Thanes of
Cawdor*, p. 225).

the counsell hes forborne to grant the same whill his Maiesties will and pleasour be knowne.

61. Sir Alex. Hay to —— [1]

6 *Octob.* 1614

S^r—in this vacatione tyme haveing some reasoun of more privat reteiring In regaird of my laite visitatioun in the loise of my bedfellow, I tooke occasioun to review some of the olde recordis in the regrē and by collationeing of former things w^t this present tyme, I haif deprehndit my M^r to haif ressawed a greitt prejudice, for it hathe bein evir in my tyme muche mervelled how the landis in the west pairtes of this kingdome suld haif bein so high retoured, and the landis in the northe pairtes and in the choicest pairtes of o^r countrey, as fyife and Lothiane to be so far vndervallowit, heirvpoun I haif begune w^t a shyire or tuo, comptrolleing there bypast retouris w^t the present and findes the oddes so greitt as his Ma^{tle} in tyme past hes bein very far interest in his proffeitt for not in wairde landis only bot in blensh also endureing the tyme of the nonentrye the K. Ma^{tle} gettis the retoured dewtye yeirlye and this is a speciall poynte wherew^t the shereffis yeirlye in the exchecker ar burdeyned in there accomptes. Now whereas his Ma^{tle} in tyme past for fourtie pundis hathe gottin only ten pundis, and sometymes skairse foure pundis, this in many small particularis wald turne to no meane prejudice, The reasoun how this hathe befallin is cleaire to haif bein done in his Ma^{tles} owne minoritye and in the less aige of his mother of blissed memorye And lyike aneugh most of them haif done it of ignorance, for tuo yeiris befoir pinkye feild to wit in 1545, the toun of Ed^r wes by o^r neighbo^ris brunte and then many menis parl^{ar} evidentis and the most pt of all regñs bot some few w^{che} wer in the castle, wer all conswimed, So that sensyne every man preswimeing that nothing wes extant to controll them, they retoured their landis at pleasour and so vnder-

---

[1] It is unfortunate that there is nothing to show to whom this shrewd and pungent letter was addressed.

valewed them as skairse they keiped the sixt pt of the proportioun of there former reto^res, Now my controlment sall procceide vpoun goode warrantis of there owne retor^ls from the tyme of flowdoun to pinkye, Now as for the compassing of the busynes it hathe in it self no difficultye at all, being so cleare that no wryter boye will putt questioun in it, Bot it tuiches many and the greitt ones moste, who howevir they haif gottin there landis frielye of his Maties predicesso^rls yit ar they loathe according to o^r Scottishe proverbe to give him kaile of his owne peittis, And every one cryis still to haif from the crowne, bot veiy few ar willing to returne any thing back to it, Alwayes for the prosequuteing of the busynes, the more quyett the mater be keipt for some space, it wilbe the easier compassed, There neideth nather Parliament nor assemblye or convention of estaites, it sall not requyre recommendatioun ather to sessioun or counsell generall or particular, Bot if his Matie do allow that I suld proceide in it, I will break this Iyce where it is thinnest, and will procwire some cleare decisiouns aganis some of my owne freindis in the Northe, And so peice and peice bring it furdward in severall corneris of the countrey, where there salbe leist resistance and the greitt ones salbe then ashaimed to oppose. I haue cõicatt this mater as yet to no fleshe alyive bot vnto his Maties Advocatt, becaus I neid not the concurrance of any other at first in it. And as his Maiestie desyres any otheris to know of it, it will no^t be the worse to spaire it vntill the turne be ryiper, As for my owne pairt I mak no exceptioun of any persoun in this busynes, Nather do I propone to my self any prospect of rewairde, if the busynes do frayme weill for his Maties proffeitt so as his Matie may find that I a weill willed dewtifull servant, I haif obteyned my intent. I haif written this particular vnto yow to be impairted to his Matie and that I may vnderstand back againe of his Maties pleasour whither I suld proceide or surcease, As for the reasonis wherefore I wald haif the mater so muche keipt vp, no questioun the knowledge of it wilbe the crosseing of it, and heirof at some other tyme if his Matie so requyre it I can giue more p^{lar} remonstrance. Bot there is one thing that wald be adverted into, that when as this mater sall breake furth, it may that some propone as a grounde of a swite at co^{rte} to haif the byrunes of the vndervalewing, Bot his Matie must be pleased to reserve this to be dischairged by way of gratuitye to the whole subiectis generallye, they amending the erro^{ris} of all there reto^{ris}, whereby his highnes sall haif his owne And the subiectis must acknowledge to haif ressaived very greitt favo^{re}. Eftir you haif côicatt the mater with his Matie vpoun the first goode occasioun I hoipe you will certifie me of his pleasour, There is no nobleman nor gentleman in the countrey bot makis his best vse of his charto^r kist And I think there is muche reasoun that these who servis his Matie suld sie and endevo^r to help where the crowne hathe bein hurte, So till next occasioun I tak my leave and Restis, Yo^{ris} at Y. S.

ALEX^R HAY.

Ed^r, 6 Octob.

62. Bishop of the Isles to John Murray of the Bed chamber [1]

Oct. 11, 1614

RYCHT WERSCHEPFULL AND LOWING COUSING—As being gritûlie grewit I wryt to zow befoir bescking zow to deall w^t his M^{tie} for his heichnes wyss derectione to be sent to ye Consall what manir my frendis schall be relewit, so now cûing to Edinburgh to wirk sumwhat farder in that erand I must also intret zow zit to hauld hand to that wark and if my serwand hes no^t as zit receawit his dispatche that ye wald further him thairto. All ye trubill that is done to me and my freindis is becauss of Archebauld Cãbellis diligẽs to procure ye Iyll of Iyla to ye lard of Cadell, of ye wiche thai ar certãle informit, the wiche if it tak effect will breid grit trubill in ye Iylles far moir nor all ye fyn and dewite of ye Iyles of Scotland will efford thir many zeris and in ye

X

---

[1] John Murray of Lochmaben, son of Sir Charles Murray of Cockpool, created Viscount of Annan, June 2, 1623, and Earl of Annandale, March 18, 1624.

mean tym be the wrak of my freindis, nather cā I or any
mā who knowes ye estait of that cūtre think it ather good
or profitabill to his M^te or this cūtre to mak that nā [1]
gritter in ye Iyles nor thai ar alredie, nor zit to rut out one
pestiferous clan and plant in one lytill bettir, seing his M^te
hes good occasione now with lytill expenss to mak a new
plantatioun of honest mē in that Iyland answerabill to
that of Vlstir in Iyrland lying wpon ye nixt schoir w^t ye
wiche Iyla haith dayle cōmerss.   The way how this mycht
be done is athir be a lytill police of ye wiche I hawe gewin
information to my Lord Secietar and thesurer deput,
Bot becauss it is to difficill to belewe thais pipill, I wold
hawe a sycht of forces wiche wolde effiay tham and mowe
tham to keip cōditione, and thir foices wold be ptle col-
lectit out of sundre townez wpone ye west cost of Scotland
and ptle of sū ould sogeo^ris out of Iyrland and it war ten
out of cūry one of ye four garisones led by Sr Richard
Handfurd, Capitane Stewart, Capitane Ciawfuid and Captane Wachane, togidder w^t a cānonc w^t powdir and billet
out of Darre and thais to be send o^r wndir cōduct of S^r
Rodolph Binglay w^t a derectione frome his M^te to my lord
depute to this effect ye wiche being send heir I wold carie
thā and hest tham to Iyla out of Darrie, to meit so many
as sould be derect out of Scotland to meit thā, for I think
200 wold serwe the twrne, or if it wold pleas his M^te to
derect one of his schippes to ye west cost of Scotland to this
serwice, it wold hestele tak effect if scho haid any good
munitione in hir, and sū wther sogeo^ris of ye wiche ye sycht
onle wold effrey the rebellis at the lest so far as to mowe
tham to keip conditione, the cōditione to be maid to tham
schall mak to tham no surās of any pt of his M^teis fawo^r
for zei know albeit I must alwayes deall for the relewe out
of thais vilanes handis of my narrest freindis, zit I am
nowayes oblist to do tham grit good, who hes kyitht tham
self to have nathir feir of god, cair of thair dew obediens
to thair souane king nor zit fayth or trewth to thair nycht-
bo^r bot referring all to his M^teis wyss and royall resolutione
I onle request zow to remēbir his heichnes of this my

---

[1] That name, viz Campbell.

fwlische adwyss wiche I be vofull experiēs hes lernit according to ye natur of ye pipill I hawe ado with to be the best in my jugement. I hawe also to remēbir zow that sum of Bruchtone's pipill viz. his wyf good sones and brether accusit me for delyvere of that mater out of myn handis and ye evidēts I wod be glaid to receaue zo^r warrād thairfoir, ye wche albeit it was promeist to me by ye laird of Lochinvar vndir his hand I hawe not receauit ye samī as zit. Thair is also a Scotisch knaw whom (wpon wrang ïformatione) I admittit to ye ministere in Iyrland who wpon instigatione of Sr Henrie Fullort and Capitan Cowe hes cū in to court and vpon sinisterous ïformatioun hes procurit a grit brek of all ye ordo^r I establischit in my diocess thair.[1] They call ye mā Mr Robert Benneit, he dependis wpon my Lord Roxbrugh, bot he is weill known to the Lard Lochinvar, of quhom zow schall receawe farder adûteismēt w^t Sr Jo^n Stewartt schortle to cū to court And so I beseik ye eternall god to bliss zow and all zo^{rls} for by his graice I schall dwring lyve rest.—Zo^r awin to be comandit in Ch. Jes., AN: ISLES.

Edinbrughe, ye xi of October 1614.

I hawe writtin to his M^{te} that I hawe send my informatione and adwyss how to follow furth this serwice to zow to be imptit to his heichnes, &c.

63. The same to the same

23 Oct. 1614

RY^r WERSCHEPFULL AND WORTHE SIR—I dout no^t but zo^r W. will excuse my to homle bouldnes importwnȳg you with so many frivolus letteris tending all to one end, because of ye necessite of my crand, wiche is the relewe of my nerrest frendis wiche I p^{r}fer to my awin lyve, albeit I hawe hard nothing as zit fra my serwand Bryce Sempill zit I heir that his Ma^{tle} haith takin a cours soleit and substantious for ye recoūing of ye houss in Iyla and keiping of that Iyll vndir obediens heireftir, My sut now w^{che} I

---

[1] Raphoe.

bescik zo^r w. to piopone to his M^{te} is, to wndirstand, seing that boith Inglische and Scotische ar to be thair, and thair also (if it pleas god) I must be, what schalbe my credcit amāgis tham especiale what cōditiones it schall pleas his M^{te} to giwe liberte to his heichnes lewtenēt to grant to ye rebellis for ye relewe of my freindis takin vndir trest in his M^{tes} serwice and detenit now in irones, no^tw^tstanding of promiss maid to me in ye cōtrar. S^r far beit from me ewer to entir vndir cōdition or trust w^t that falss generatioun and bludie pipill, zit I must first, for ye relewe of my freindis out of ye irones and thaireftir out of ther handis if it can be possibill, for ye pñt be thair slawe and promeiss to do, and do what I hawe credeit to do, as thai derect me. Bot zit by ye grace of god, schall newir promeiss nor press to do any thing in thair fawo^{ris} that may offend his M^{te} or twiche his heichnes in hono^r or piofeit. And thairfoir albeit I past to this last jurney towartis Iyla wthir wayes nor his M^{te} derectit the cōsall to send me, becauss ther Lo. was bisseit in ye effairis of Orknay and ptlie leanyng to ye oithes and promisses of ye rebellis and ptle deceawit be thois who was w^t me and promised to haue bene my gard, I com in ye dāger of thais most rigorous vilanes who vset and zit vses thair victoie vere tyrānicale aganis thois who newir offendit tham in word nor deid, zit I hoip to do his M^{te} good serwice, as I hawe done warie laithe boith in Iyrland and Scotland of ye wiche his heichnes will heir or it be long. And swa my trust is that his M^{te} will be gratiousle pleased to wryt to his heichnes cōsall heir what credeit I schall hawe w^t ye levtenēt in Iyla at this tym, as also what cōditiones may be grantit to ye rebellis for delyvere of ye captyvis, thay ar many vayes to o^rthraw ye holl generatione, no^tw^tstanding that sum what be zeldit to sum of tham for ye eschewing of ye dāger of ye mēs lyvs who ar in ther handis. Thair is certane offeris maid by Sr James M^cdonald wiche it behovit me to p^rsent to ye cōsall who cōmandit me to send vp the samī to his M^{te} wiche pleas zow reccawe heir inclosit and to pñt ye samī if yow think good to his heichnes ; The thre quhom he offeris to delyver ar ye auctoris of all ye rebellion in Iyla, They ar many

vther mē heir who thinkis that ye pformyng of thir offeris
war ane ware ease way to satisfe his M^{te} for ye cōtempt,
and purge ye land of that pipill, bot referring all to his heichnes princele derectiones and zo^r awin discretione I beseik
god to bliss and prospir zow and zo^{ris} for by his graice I
schall remaine.—zo^r awin to be cōmandit,

An: Isles.

Edinburgh, 23 Octob. 1614.

64. Sir James M^{c}donald his offeris

1614 *about Oct^r*

First I offer (if it might pleass his Matie of his clemencie
to give to me Ilay) I would pay eight thowsand m̄kis yearlie
therefoir and find sufficient cautioun of lordis and barounes
for good paymēt, and obedience be my selfe and all the
Clannis that shall dwell there, and cravis but a sevin
yeare tak to try me.

Secondlie I offer, if his Matie pleass to hold Ilay in his
awin hand, to mak it worth ten thousand merkis yearlie
to his Matie, and to transport my selfe, my brethir and my
kin to Ireland, or to whatsumewir other place his Matie
will appoynt ws, and his highnes to give ws one yearis
ductie or rent of Ilay, or to by land wth, And in
the meintyme I shall go wth the Bishop of the Iles,
and shall god willing athir get the house and his pledgis
without any chairges to his Matie or than returne heir
to myne owne waird within fourtie dayis. Provyding
if I get this done I have assurance of his Matie and cōsall
that my self and my brother shall get leave to go·p̄ntlie
thereaft^r wth my Lord Bishop to courte and get a kiss of
his Matie hand, and my cautiounars shall remaine bound
for me, that I and my brother shall returne bak heir to
his Maties cōsall to abyid such order as it shall pleas his
highnes to inioyne to ws, and I shall leive my sone heir as
pledge for my performance in all, and for satisfactioun
to his Matie and cōsall I shall bring Ronald m^{c}allast^r who
first took the house and Ronald m^{c}donald vallich to suffer
for there fault, and Coll m^{c}gillaspie to be keipt in irnes

× Colla Ciotach?   v. p. 149, 150, 151, 188, p. 203

during his Ma^{tles} pleas^{r}. My cautiounars shal be the
Erle of Tullibairne, My Lord Burlie, Sr Ronald m^{c}sorle,
Johne Campbell of Cadell,[1] Malcum Toshe [2] and the Laird
of Grant, every one for fyve thowsand merkis, and my
sone to die if I faill.

And last I offer w^{th}out any condition of land or money,.
that if it may please his Ma^{tle} to give me libertie vpon
such suretie by cautionaris as I am able to pforme, or
pledgis, I shall transport my self, and my brother and
kin out of all his Ma^{tles} dominiounes, having his Maties
lr̄e of recōmendation to the estaittis of Holland, and
libertie to tak vp m̄e, if we be imployit, with his Ma^{tles}
frie pardoun for all byganes.

65

26 *October* 1614

Thair being a cōmissioune of liftenendrie past to the
Laird of Caddel [3] vpoun the tuantie tua of this instant for
suppressing of the rebellion in Ila with suche vthers lrez̄
and chearges as he thocht fitte for the furtherence of this
seruice, and he hauing vnder teane to be in Ila accom-
panyed with ane thousand persones betuix and the tent
of Nouember now approching, the cōmissioun is renewit
according to his maiesties directioun p̄ntit this day in
counsall in the psone of the erle of Argyll, and in his
absence furth of the cuntrey in the persone of the said
Laird of Caddell, and quhairas it wes craved that the concurrance of the inhabitantes within the sherefdomes of
Argill, Tarbett, Dumbartoun, Air and Irwing might be
had in this scruice, and some questioune being moved vpon
this poynt be the counsall efter lang reasoning thairanent,
it was fund zat suche a generall concurrence of sa mony
shyres wes altogither neidles and vnnecessare and tendit
rather to vexatioun and trouble of his maiesties subiectis

---

[1] Sir James was married to Margaret Campbell, sister of Calder.
[2] The Laird of Mackintosh.
[3] Calder's instructions, which were not copied by Mr. Gregory, are printed in
P.C.R, vol x. p 716, and his commission, *ibid*, p. 720.

then to the goode of the seruice And thairfoir this concurrence is onlie restrictit to the shyres of Argyll and
Tarbett, seeing Caddell had vnderteane the seruice with
the concurrence of these tua shyres allenerlie, and the
wairning to be maid vnto them is ordeanit to be vpoun
aucht dayes.

Proclamatiounes [1] ar derect that non resett the rebellis
nor furneis them with wictuallis, pouder, bullet nor no
vther thing comfortable to them.

Proclamatiounes ar lykwayise derect promissing pardoun
to ony one of the pledges, and to suche vtheres of the
rebellis as will leave Angus oig, come to the lieutenent
and pñt to him ane of the associats of this rebellioñ of as
goode rank as them selfes. And touching Angus Oig him
self he hes promeis of pardoun vpõ conditioun of redelyuerie
of the tua pledgeis with two of his associatis according to
the directioun of his Maiesties lfë.

Proclamatiounes ar also derectit that nane within Ila
beare, weare, nor use hagbuttis nor pistolettis in ony tyme
cuming.

Anent the discharge of having and keiping within the
Ile of galayis and birlingis, that poynt was thocht vnreasonable becaus it is vnderstand that diuers within the
Ile ar obleist be thair infeftmentis to hauc galayes and
birlingis.[2]

And touching the prohibitioun craved that non of the
inhabitantis and tenentis of Ila, thair guidis or geir be
resett be ony of his maiesties subiectis, This poynt was
also thocht vnreasonable becaus it war no reasone to preiudge theme of the comon benefite of frie subjectis and
to hauld theme vnder suche a thraldome and bondage.

Anent the bringing of the cheife and principall Ilandares
to the burgh of Edinburgh or some vther pairt of the
incuntrey quhill this rebellioñ be suppressit, Thair was
no necessitie fund in this poynte, becaus all thir people ar
vnder band for thair goode behavioure and for thair com-

[1] Precursors of the Orders in Council under D O R A , 1914-1919.
[2] Vide *Highland Papers*, vol. ii pp. 235 *et seq.*

peirence anes eueric zeir befoir the counsall in the moneth
of July.

Anent the dischearge craved to be past to Sr Ranald
M^csoirll of this zeires rent of Ila and the lyk dischearge to
be gevin be him to the tennentes of that quhiche is deu
be theme vnto him,[1] Thair could no thing be done in this
particulare without his consent, for quhoweuer his maiestie
may dischearge him of that quhiche is addebtit be him to
his maiestie, he can not be straitit to dischearge the
tennentis bot at his awine pleasoure, And touching his not
reparing to Ila Thair is no caus of his going thair, And
gif he wald presume to go thair whiche is not looked for
his maiesties lieutennentis will be able to cōmand him,
and to mak him conformable.

And quharas it is thocht that the Bischop of the Iles
his pñt cōnsell and assistance with the lieutennent may
do goode to the seruice, he is ordanit with his awin conssent
to go thair ; and the counsall hes wreiñ to the Lieutennent
to accept of him and to vse his aduise and opinioñ accordinglie, And becaus the bischope feared that this proclama-
tioune conteining the promeis of pardoñ to the rebellis
might draw some inconvenient vpoñ his sonne and nephew
and raise suche a suspition amongis the rebellis them
selfes as wold mak them to distruste one ane other and so
to enter in some disparat course againes the pledgeis. The
cōnsell hes wreiñ to the Lieutennent to be werie war and
circumspect in yis matei, And to conceale the proclama- •
tioune quhill he find the occasioñ that it may worke the
awine effect without dangeir to the pledgeis.

66

October 1614 [2]

It hes Pleased zour Matie to commande me That quhen
zour Mat^{eis} counsell hes causit piocleame suche actis and

---

[1] Vide *History*, p 347.

[2] The internal evidence suggests Archibald Campbell as the writer (*vide ante*,
p 156 and *post*, pp 177 *et seq*).

proclamasionis as zour Ma^{tle} hes commandit to be meade
That then I sall appoint w^t ye Laird of Cadell q^t nūber of
men sall be requiseit for him to teake w^t him to Illa. As
lykuayis to causs Cadell appoint w^t ye cuntrie peiple quho
ar w^tin zour Ma^{tles} schirrefdome contenit w^tin zour Ma^{tels}
proclamasionis. The present tyme and in q^t nummeris
he will haue yame to cum to him And that ye bottis and
galleis be in reddines.

To appoint that viueris be in reddines for zour Ma^{tles}
soldioris yat ar to cum from Irland.

To desair Cadell before my going to Irlande To vse all
ye meins he can ffor inteaking ye houss of Dunavege in
Illa and to indouore him selff in inteaking ye same houss
so long as I sall be in Irland bringing zour Ma^{tels} forsis from
thens to Illa. At least yat he pmit not ye rebels to furnische yame selffis any more w^t viueris.

That w^t all diligens I go to Irlande and bring w^t me from
zour Ma^{tels} depute such necessaris for zour Ma^{tels} seruice as
zour Matie hes commandit him to haue in reddines And
heaving cum w^t yame to Illa yat I remaine yair attending
zour Ma^{tels} seruice And yat I sall teake notisch q^t pouder
and bullett sall be spent at zour Ma^{tels} seruice yat zour
Matie may kno yairby q^t cheargis zour Matie sall be at.

That zour Matie giues leicens iff any of zour Ma^{tels} rebels
quho ar now w^tin ye houss of Dunavege in Illa or yair
freindis can be apprehendit yat thay may be gevin bake
ageane to those quho sall be in ye houss Provayding they
rander the too pleagis quhich they now heave and no
wtheruayis.

That gif yair be any ma actis or proclamasionis necessar
for advansing zour Ma^{tels} seruice that zour Matie may be
pleased to command zour Ma^{tels} counsell as they sall ressaue informasion they may cause piocleame ye same.

Albeit zour Matie hes commandit zour Ma^{tels} depute of
Irland to send onlie too hunder soldiaris to zour Ma^{tels}
seruice in Illa that it may pleis zour Matie to giue me leicens
to desair zour Ma^{tels} depute in zour Ma^{tels} name to send
on or too hunder soldioris ma then zour Matie hes alreddie
commandit I being eabell to giue zour Matie a sufficiēt

reasone for ye sending a gieater nummer then zour Matie did first command.

67. Earl of Dunfermline to 'To the right Hono^{bl} my weilbeloued Cousing Mr Murray in his Sac. Maiesties bedchalmer'

17 *Nov.* 1614.

. Off the affaires off Ila and that mutinerie thair, wee heir na farder worde zit sence the B. of the Iles went frome this ; I send yiow heirwith suim lettirs fra my lady Eglin-toun[1] to y^{r} bedfallow[2] quhome to I also desire to be recommendit, and sua wissing yiow all happines Restis, yiour louing cousing, to be comandit,

DUNFERMELJNE.

Ed^{r}, 17 Nou^{r} 1614.

68. The same to the same

9 *Dec.* 1614

RIGHT HONO^{BL} AND WEILBELOUED COUSING—I haue not writtin to yiow this whyle, because I had na subiect off moment to impairt to yiow ; at the present, I haue this aduertisment to mak to yow, to be imparted to our Maist Gracious Souerane, sence thir rebellis off Yla besidis the inuading and possessing thame selfis with his Maties houss of Duniwagge, presumed also maist treasonablie to tak the Bischioppe off the Isles sonne, and the Laird of Ranfurlie his cheiff, to be as pledgis to thame, to haue quhat condicions thay pleased requiie, onderstanding weill his Ma. Royalle minde nocht habill to condescend to entir in onye condicions with sic peopill, and knowing also weill his heighnes forces ouer sufficient to dantoun all the pride of sic barbarous limmers, as his Ma. had send

---

[1] Anna, daughter of Alexander, first Earl of Linlithgow.
[2] Elizabeth, daughter of John Shaw of Breich.

his directions, quhilk ar still going fordwart, sufficient to·
bring all thair to his will ; considering neiuertheless still,
that the parrell of these gentilmen, albeit too rakleslie
cassin in that danger, could nocht be bot uerye onpleasand
to his Gracious Matie, as it wald also haue tuiched this
haill estaitt and us all in honour, if thay had gottin onye
skaith, I was maist cairfull for thair releiff, and thairfore
fand out ane man off my awin, quha had guid Irish, and
on his ondertaking upon suim auld acquentance he had
with Angus Ogg McDonald quha is the cheiff off all thir
outlawis, that he thocht he wald be habill to persuade
him to deliuer to me the said gentilmen free, I directed
him about the beginning off Nouember to goe thair, gaue
him na write off mine with him nor powar to gif to these
men onye promeis frome me, off onye particulair condicion,
bot gif he could on guid rasons and appeirance off guid
generally alluire thame to the deliurie and friedome off
the gentilman, I promist to him self honest rewarde off
his Matie.   He went thair with greate difficulties of wadder
and otherwayis, and in end and conclusioun, dealt sa
with these rebellis as he has broght hame frie the twa
gentilmen (quhairoff I thank God) butt onye promeis or
condicion, farder thay send to me with him the keyis off
the houss with this worde, thay will be content to deliuer
the houss to onye I sall pleis send thair to resaue and keip
it, with onye cumpanie thairfore, on this onlye desire off
thairis that thay may haue free libertie to haue access ather
to his Ma. or to his counsall to declair thair awin pairtis,
and quhow thay ar fallin or casin in this troubill, that
say thair sould be found leitill falt in thame, and mair in
others.   The consideration off this I remitt to his Sac.
Maties Royall wisdome, i will no^t meddill in the like off
that butt speciall warrand and directioun his Ma. knawis
I professed eiuer ignorance in all Irische Cabale.[1]

   I hoipe his Ma. will think thir gentilmennis releiff guid
seruice, The bischioppes sonne has said to me, thay bosted
thame eiuer gif onye seige came frome his Ma. to that

---

[1] This appearance of the word prior to the existence of the famous ministry is
interesting.

houss thay suld be sett out ouir the wals to kep the first
shoittis ; the gentilman quha has bein my moyenner and
doar of this seruice is ane Ross man called George Grahame,
i promiss to him gif he sould bring me hame the prisonnaris as he has done for his chargis and recompense at
leist ane thousand markis scottis, and quhat farder rewairde
sould pleis his Ma. allow on him, I will not brake my condition to him, bot sall satisfie him before this be at ziow,
and sendis ziow thairfore heirwith ane precept to be signed
be his Ma. maist gracious hand to comand the threasurar
depute heir to rander me that meikill siluer, nane will think
it euill bestowed, or the men had nocht bein releiued for
his Ma. and estaitis entres and honour, I wald rather haue
parelled the loss off ten thousand off my awin.[1]   His Ma.
may remembir be sic priuie moyennis for small soumis I
had Ihone dow McAlaster the greatest limmer and brokin
man in all the north, and his brother baith putt out the
ane execute in this toun, the other with twa of his marrowis
brunt in ane houss because they wald not rander, for
this I gaue thrie thousand markis.   Ane other, Mcgillie
worike, I had broght in to this toun and execute, ane stark
theiff and captane of theifis, a Barrabbus insignis latro,
trubled all Cabroch and braa off Mar, for him I gaue ane
thousand markis, quhilk soumis be his Ma. comand was
rembursed to me be my lord Dumbar and Sr Jhone Arnott,
like as I haue his Ma. generall comand to threasaururis to
deburse at my desire onye sic soumis upon sic occasions
bot I think meitest haue his Ma. speciall allowance for
the seruice in eurie particular : I will omit na thing to
doe his Ma. guid seruice.   All this I remitt to yiour imparting to his Sac. Ma. at guid tyme and opportunitie.
God preserue his Ma.   Sua wissing yiow all weill, restis,
ziour maist affectionat Cousing to be comandit,

                                                DUNFERMELJNE.

frome Edr, 9 Decr 1614.

Thair is laitlie cuimed to this toun suim worde off suim

---

[1] Not merely did Grahame get the money; but the Chancellor had the
assurance to ask and receive repayment from the Treasury.

late slaughter cõmitted in the Isles, in the Ile off Jura on
his Ma. guid subjectis quhairoff I remitt to my L. Secre-
tairis and Sr Gedeonis relatioun, for thay ar mair particularlie aduertist off the same.

69. Sir Rorie Macleod to the King

7 *Jany.* 1615

MOST GRACIOUS AND SACRED SOVERANE—Since it hes
bene the good pleasour of god by zour maiesteis most
prudent and happie govcrnament, And to zour maiesteis
immortall prais and commendatioune with the exceiding
grit comfort of all zour faithfull subiectis to bliss this zour
maiesteis kingdome with ane vniversall peace and quietnes
throughout all the nukis and cornaris yairof especiallie in
the yllis and heylandis Swa that now ye hoip and expecta-
tioune of iustice makis all men to seik redres of these
wrangis whairin thir mony zeiris bygane through the in-
iquitie of the tyme thay háif bene silent So it is that I
and my predicessorls being heretable tenentis to zour
Maiestie and zour predicessouris of the landis of Slait
Northvust and uyeris landis ly and in the north yllis, quhairin
we war heretablie infeft be zour Maiesteis worthie goodsir
of famous memorie efter his perfyte aige, The clandonald
quho efter the daith of zour Maiesteis said goodsyr wer
of gritest power force and freindschip in the yllis did most
violentlie detrude my forbearis furth of oure saidis landis
with grit slauchter of diverss of thame, especiallie of my
father brethir and vther kynnismen, And by fyre and
suord mantenit thair violent possessioune aganis my forbearis and myself sen syne.   And I having now enterit my
self as air to my father brethir in the saidis landis, and
being infeft and seasit thairintill, and zour maiestie being
lykwayis gratiouslie pleasit at my laite being with zour
maiestie, To dispone vnto me the nonentrie of the saidis
landis, I haive thairvpone intentit actiounis befoir zour
maiesteis sessioune for recoverie of my possessioune and
richt of ye saidis landis, In the quhilk actioune I am lyke

to sustene some preiudeice by ye practezeis and dealing
of my adversair pairtie, Donald Gorme of Slaitt, quho
taking hald of yat act of parliament, quhairby ye inhabitantis of the yllis war ordanit to exhibeit and produce
thair infeftmentis befoir zour maiesteis chekker To the
effect the tenor and conditiounes thairof micht haue bene
knawin to thame, The said Donald vpon my alledgit
failzie in that poynt of the exhibitioune of my infeftmentis allenerlie, intendis to furneis actioune and pley
aganis me   And vpone that onlie caus to detene and
withhald fra me my lauchfull heretage, Althocht it be of
trewth that I and all my predicessoris haif euir constantlie
profest zour maiesteis obedience, And did nevir kyth in
counsall actioune or hostilitie with ony of ye rebellis of
the yllis aganis zour maiestie, Lykas I my self, in ye
fourscoir sextene yeir of god gaif my compeirance befoir
zour maiesteis counsall, and at that tyme fand cautioune
for my conformitie in all tymes thairefter, And I thairvpone simplie apprehending that the said act of parliament could nawayes stryke aganis me quho wes a lauchfull
subiect, Bot that the samene wes maid and devysit aganis
ye rebellis and brokin men of ye yllis, In ye quhilk nomber
I disdanit to rank my self, I ignoranthe and not vpone
contempt failled in that poynt of the productioune of my
infeftmentes, quhilkis I could not produce the tyme of
ye making of ye said act In respect the said Donald
Gorhame stud than infeft in the saidis landis haldin of
zour maiestie and continowit in ye violent possessioune of
the samene lykas he zit does, And I am bot laithe servit
and retourit air to my said father brether in ye saidis
landis, Quhairin I am certane that it is not zour maiesteis
meaning that any advantage sall be tane of me bot that
I sall haif iustice aganis ye said Donald. Notwithstanding thairof or of ony obiectioune that can be moved aganis
me thairvpone The said act of parliament being onlie
maid to draw the brokin Ilismen to obedience and not to
snair simple ignorant and lauchfull subiectis, In con-
sideratioune quhairof I am bauld in all submissioune and
reverence to haive my recource vnto zour sacred Maiestie·

as the fontane fra quhome all zour distressit subiectis
ressavis confort And in all humilitie to beseik zour
Maiestie to wryte in my favouris to zour Maiesteis sessioune,
willing thame to proceid and minister iustice vnto me
aganis ye said Donald and vtheris violent possesso^{ris} of
my landis and heretage notwithstanding of ye said act
of parliament and ye not productioune of my infeftmentis,
or ony thing that may result or follow yairvpone. And
so craiving pardone for this my presumptioune Humblie
praying god lang to preserve zour Maiestie in zour blissit
governament that we zour poore subiectis may in tyme
of oure distress haiv our recourse to zour Maiestie I rest
Zour most humble and obedient servito^r,

S. R. MACLEOID.

Ed^r, 7 Januarij 1615.

70. L. Gordon and James Mowat's [1] information to his Matie

PLEIS YOUR MAIESTIE—Eftir ane Inhibitioun was
scruit agaynst McKintoshe his teynds, at my lord Gordoun
his instance, And he was requyrit to giue teynding as
ordour of law prouyds, My Lord Gordoune send on of his
scruands with tuo notars and thrie witnessis to the lands
of Collodin perteyning to the said McKintoshe and thair
be werteue of a decreit obteyned be my lord befoir the
Lords of sessioun, conteynand a seuen zeirs spulze of
the teynds of the saids lands; To haife poyndit for the
byrun spulzeis, But McKintoshe send and haid lying await
about the number of aught or ten scoir men armit with
guns, pistolats, bous, suords and axis. All of them bend
their bous and guns and wiolentlie deforssit and boistit to
haife kilt the saids seruande and witness gife they suld sett
thair foot wpon ther ground and manyfastlie misregairdit
the lords decreit, and reallit out that they did not cair
for any decreit or letters that culd cum from your Matie.
This they did the aught day of Septemb^r and tuentye tua

---

[1] This James Mowat was a Writer to the Signet in Edinburgh, and doer for
many north country people, including Mackintosh and Calder.

day of September last, in moir usurping maneir nor can
be schouin your Matie. McKintoshe did yis moir to haif the
cuntrey and your Ma^teis peace brockin nor for ony wther
respeck, as may be euidentlie knowin he ressone my lord
Gordoun wsit means to apoynt seuen seuerall trystis sence
your Matie was in Scotland for agreing that mater and
submissiouns wer pend and subscryuit be aither of pairteis
and freinds, but McKintoshe not being willing the mater
suld pack wp freindlie, fand means to break euerye on of
ye meittings on day or tuo befoir thay suld haife mett, and
hes drawin all the broikin heigh land men to him, seik as
Robert Abrach on of the Clangrigor with wthers of his
acomplecees that ar your Ma^tees rebells to be his suldeours
and keeps them in his houss of Collodin for the sayme
effeck, And gifs it out yat the most pairt of ye heigh land
men in Scotland will tak his pairt, and will be glaid to
fynd any occatioun of a break, becaus they say they haife
not threuen sence your Ma^tee maid the cuntrey so peaceable. Heirfoir My Lord humblie intreats your Matie
wreit to the Cunsall of Scotland to punishe McKintoshe
and his complecees for his rebellioun and misregairding
your Ma^tees laus, and that McKintoshe may be maid to
present yees rebells quhom he keips as suldeours that
they may be taikin ordo^r with for the better obseruing
your Ma^tees peace and preuenting of gryter inconuenienwse.

Ye next Cunsall day in Scotland is wpon Wedinsday
ye tuentye of yis month.

71. Sir J. Campbell [1] 'To my most honored and noble lord the errlle of Sommersett Lord chamerlin of England'

8 *Feby*. [1615]

Most honored—I haive herew^t sent to zo^r hono^r a
trew acompt of all that hes proceidit in his Maiesties
serice in Illa. As to the charges his Maiestie hes beine
at in sending of the cannon frome Ireland I haue a just

---

[1] The signature is that of Campbell of Calder.

recking yairof to bring to zo^r H. the which is not werrie much. I hoip yair salbe small dificultie in macking the rest of the Iyllis profitable to his Matie. The cours his Matie and zo^r H. hes taikin wth this Ille maiks all the Illanderis werrie afrayit so hoiping yat zo^r honor wilbe myndfull of my pains and chargis taikin in his hienes service as I salbe ewer redie to adwenture my self wherin I can be abill to serve zo^r honor, I rest, Your honoris humble and obedient serwant,   S. J. CAMPBELL.

Dunwege, the 8 of Feb.

72. Account referred to [1]

Pleis zo^r Lo. to heir ane accompt of his Ma^{ttes} serwice sence my going to Deirling. I cam to Dirling on the tuentie of November where I stayit whill the fourt of December attending the shipping of two cannons and one culwring wth wtheris necessaris belonging to his hienes serwice. My Lord, I cannot omitt to remēber zo^r Lo. of the gryt cair my Lord Depwtie of Ireland did taik in dispaching with all diligence such thingis as was commitit to his charge.

On the fowrt of December Sr Oliwer Lambert[2] commander of his Ma^{ttes} Iyrish forces shipit in his Ma^{ttes} ship callit the *Phœnix* accompaniet with the *Moone*, one of his Ma^{ttes} pinages, a hoay wherein the Ordince wer and a Scottis bark wth wittallis they cam to Aldersleit neir to Knok- X fergus where they ankerit and Sr Oliwer Lambert went to Knokfergus where he stayit thrie or fouie dayis attending sum timber necessar for the Ordince and in shiping a hundereth and fyftie soldioris wha war appoyntit to gard the cannon.

On the threttin of December at night they weyght anker and did taik saill towardis Illa.

On the fourtein day abowt two of the klok in the efternō

---

[1] This account is evidently by Archibald Campbell of Glencarradale (cf *ante*, p. 156, note 1, and *post*, p 183, note 2) The MS. also seems to have been written by the same person that wrote No 66

[2] His son was created Earl of Cavan

thei cam to ane anker in the sownd of Illa at the whit foir
land of Jwra, I expectit to haue hard of the Livtenant's [1]
being in Illa attending the cuming of the cannon, bot for
two dayis I culd not haue occassioun to meit wth any to
demand newes of.

On the sextem day Donald gygay [2] commander of the
Ille of iura cam aboord wheie I was in the *Phœnix* who
shew me that the liwtenant haid beine for the space of
fowitein dayis in two litell Iyllis neire to the castell of
Dunywege and yat he haid retwrnit bot two dayis befoir
oure cuming.

Lyk wayis he shew me that the liwtenant remanit at
Duntroun prowyding wittallis and wold be redie to returne
to Illa so soone as he wer aduertised of the cūing of his
Maties shipis. I derectit away a letter to the liwtenant
shewing him of o^r cuming.

On the twentie two day of December the liwtenant re-
twinit me ane answere and writ to Sr Oliuer Lambeit
desyiing him to hawe a littell patience and he should be
wth him wth all possible diligence.

Sum of the men of Iura and of Illa wha cam in to speik
wth me ieportit that a litell befoire the liwtenantis cuming
 towards Illa yair cam one callit <u>Grahame</u> to the castell of
Dunywege wha shew the rebels that he was derectit be
my Lord Chancler to receawe frome them the pledges and
the hous and for his warrant he alledget to haive instructionis vnder my Loid Chanclens hand, for obedience
wherof the rebelles haid randerit wp the pledgis and the
castell and yat yis Grahame haid maid Angus Oge constable
of the Castell.

Hawing not hard frome the liwtenant how fare he haid
proceidit wth the rebellis I schew Sr Oliwer Lambert of the
report I haid hard wherby Sr Oliuer tuik occasioun to writ
and sumond the iebelles to rander the hous ; The copie of
Sr Oliwer Lambertis letter I hawe herewth send to zo^r Lo.
and the iebelles answer to Sr Oliwer.

Sr Oliwer being desyrous to wnderstand the strenth of

[1] Sir John Campbell of Calder
[2] Donald Gigach MacIain

the Castell and to hawe a wiew of yair aledgit warrant frome the Chanclere sent Captain Parkins to report to him the trew estait of boith, the copie of Sr Oliweris secund letter wth the copie of Grahamis aledgit instructionis [1] I hawe herew^th sent to yor Lo.

Efter yat I haid seine the copie of Grahamis instructiouns I shew Sr Oliwer Lambart that in my opinioun all yat past betuixt Grahamis and the rebelles was dewisit by Grahame himself for releif of the pledgis.

What gryt chargis Grahamis dealing hes putt his Matie to, and what gryt paynis his doingis hes bred to those who follovit his Maties service I lieve the report yairof to a beter tyme.

On the fyft of Januar the liwtenant met with Sr Oliver Lambert at the whit foirland of Jura, being fowrtein or fyftein dayis afoir stayit by contiarie wynds and wehemēt stormes, such as Captane Buttone, caiptane of his Maties ship calit the *Phœnix*, a worthie gentelman na thing inferior in knowledge of sea fearing matteris to any in his Maties dominions, afirmis that he newer endurit the lyk nor vas newer in a moir dangerous place.

On the sext of Januar the Liwtenant landit in Illa and immediathe yairefter sumond the countrie peopil nixt agiscent to geve yair compeirance and to prowyd horsis for his Maties yrishe commanderis and souldiouris.

Sr Oliuer Lambert at his meting wth the livtenant shew him that he behowit to hawe beivis for his souldio^ris and yat he haid not broight no mony wth him for witling of his souldio^ris.

The liwtenant causit prowyd thretie fyue beifis weeklie for his Maties yrishe forces which yei haid dwhe gewin to them.

At the Liwtenant first landing in Illa he was bot two hundereth men, on the nixt day yairefter yair cam to him sewin scoir men. On the nynt of Januar the Liwtenant derectit Mr Donald Campbell and me w^t aught scoir men to march befoir him to the castell of Dunywege and if any

---

[1] These four documents follow.

of the rebelles wer in the fieldes, to peisew them, the which we did.

The Liwtenant hawing prowydit horsis for his Ma^tles yiishe compañes wha landit in Illa the nixt day efter the Liwtenant landit in Illa, the liwtenāt and yei marchit togidder on the nynt of Januarj to Portinellan.

On the tent of Januarj the liwtcnant and the yrishe compames marchit to the Lagan sum fowre myll from the castell.

On the elevint of Januarj they marchit to Baleneill which is within a myll of the castell.

On the twelfth of Januar the liwtcnant marchit wth his awin compames to the Balenachtan which is wth in half a myll to the castell wher Mr Donald Campbell and I haid remaynit too dayis befoir.

His Ma^tles yrishe forces stayit at Balenneill in regaird yair was no lodging wher the liwtenant remaynit.

On the fyfteen day of Januar the hoay wth the rest of the shipis that attendit the service saifing onlic his Ma^tles awin ship the *Phœnix* cam to the Ill of Tixa [1] which is w^thin a myll and ane half to Dunywege wher foir the space of too or thrie dayis ye indwrit a most wehement storme.

On the aughtein day of Januar the pillats wha wer sent be caiptan Bwttone to wnderstand if yair was any saif ryding at the Iyll of Tixa for his Ma^tles ship, went back to him and shew him yair opinioun of the rod.

On the twentie day of Januar the liwtenant himself went in his gallay wth a number of boitts and onlodnit the hoy and the wther shipis of the shoat, pouder and timber and such wther necessaris as belongit to the Ordince and all yair pickaxis, shoollis, watellis for the sogeris, cabinis, and deall boordis to build housis for his Maties yrishe commanderis.

On the twentie ane the liwtenants' boatts attendit as thei did befoir one the twentie and in the night fowre of the rebellis stoll away out of the castell of Dunywege wha war receawit be the liwtennant according to the tennor of his hicnes proclamatioun.

---

[1] *Vide ante*, p 115, note

On the xxj of Januar Rannald Ma^cJames [1] who haid taikin in the Illa and fort of Lochgwrme did rander the same to the liwtenant and his promeist to do serwice against the rest of the rebelles in regaird wherof the liwtenant hes asswrit him and his sone of his Maiesties favore. Rannald Ma^cSorle v^c Donill Ballie, Johne Ma^cdonill Baillie and Sorrlle Ma^calaster v^c donill bailie hes randerit yem self and promeist to do serwice conforme to the act of Cowncell for yair remissioun.

On the 22 day of Januar the livtenant vent and Sr Olipher Lambart for weiwing a place for landing of the Ordinces the whiche wes fund owt werrie happillie althogh sum what vnder the danger of the castell.

On the 18 day of Januar the *Phœnix* his Maties ship came to the Illa of Tixa hawing indwrit ye Wedinsday before no les danger by the extremite of the storme yan all hir worth, and hawing castin anker neir to ye said Ill of Tixa she indwrit for thrie dayis a most wehement storme so y^t if yair haid not bene a better rode fund owt by caiptane Buttin's painfull cair and diligence than the rod of Illantixa is, of all necessitie his Maties ship behowit to hawe bene dismissit, bot he espyit a place callit the Lodomes where his Maties ship lyis wthout any danger.

On the 23 day of Januar caiptan Buttone did man his awin boat and ane vther ship boat and causit the hoay to be broight to the place apoyntit for landing of ye cannon. The hoy hawing come wnder the shoat of the castell whiche of all necessitie sho behowit to do ; the rebelles did tak y^r advantage and powrit out a great many shoate one the twa boats that wer abringing in the hoay bot no harme was done, praisit be god.

On the 25 day of Januar the culwring and cannō were landit.

On the 27 day of Januar the vther cannon wes landit where the livtenant and all his people did labo^r as they did the day befoir in bringing yame ashoare and the same day in ye efternone ane of the cannons being a drawing frome

---

[1] Uncle to Sir James and Angus Oig Macdonald.

the shoare towardes the place where the platforme was to
be maid thei broght the cannon wthin shoat of the Castell
whairof the rebelles taiking thair adwantage powrit owt a
great many shoat amongst ws where Caiptane Crafwrd a
worthie gentelman was shoat in the small of the lege and
w^tin fyve or sex dayes efter had his lege cut of be the knie
and w^tin twa ho^{rls} thairefter he diet. Thair was lykwayes
at the same tyme one of the livtenants company was shoate
in the bodie and leifit bot a few dayis. The wther cannon
and culwring being brocht wp and plantit neir to the plate-
forme, all o^r companies being lykwayis intrinchit in the
moist commodious pairts round abowt the castell so as
yair was no hoip for the rebelles to eshaipe the land.

The plateformis being finishit the ordinces were broicht
and placit one the first of frebr^r, in the morning the cannons
and culwring played hawing shoate many shoates. The
rebelles sent vp a boy w^t a lettir in a clofin stik to ye liwtenant desyring him that he wald send down sum of his
freindis to parlę wth yame : he retwrnit yair berar and
desyrit to tell Angus, if he wold not cum to him where he
ves on promeis of his saif returne, he should hawe non
of his freindis to parle wth him. The mess^r went not
sooner back to the rebelles when yei sent him to the livtenant back agayn wth ane wther letter desyring him that
he wold cum and meit wth Angus in the midway betwixt
the Castell and where he campit, he retwrnit the mess^r and
told him as he did before ; All this tyme the cannon and
culwring plaid, saf onlie so long as the berrar was in his
cūing and going. About sex of the clok at night Angus
wryt to the liwtenant ane wther lettir desyring him yat he
wold in ye nixt morning the secund of feb^r send to him
Sr Thomas Philiphis and Archiabald Campbell and he
him self wold cum wth them to the livtenāt where he was.
The livtenant adwysit wth Sr Olipher Lambert what answer
he should mack to him. It was thoight expedient that yei
should go and meit wth him and wth all the liwtenant shew
the mess^r yat he wold protract no tyme bot the cannons
should play still, saf onlie q^{ll} Sr Thomas Philipis and Ar^d
Campbell ware in bringing of Angus to the liwtenant ; be

yis tyme the rebelles ware greathe discouragit be the effect
of the battrie yat was the first day and fearing yat yei wold
adventwre yame selfis to go away be sea the luiftenant did
strenthin his gward which he keipt on yame by sea the
nights preceiding and derectit M[r] Donald Campbell [1] w[th]
sum wther speciall gentellmen to watch the rebelles by sea
that night, and caiptan Button wha hes beine a willing
indeworrer of him self to forder the service did all that
night watche the rebelles in his longe boat.

The 2 of feb[r] in the morning efter many shoats of the
cannon and culvring the Luiftenant sent S[r] Thomas Philips
and my self [2] to bring Angus to him as apoyntit the day
befoir wha came wth S[r] Thomas Philips to the Luiftenant.

The Luiftenant hawing demandit Angus of sindiie
particullaris in presence of S[r] Oliwer Lambart, S[r] Thomas
Philips and Caiptan Button, Angus told the luiftenant
how he haid at the desyre of my Lord Chancler randerit
wp the pledgis and the Castell to one callit Grahame and
yat Grahame haid commandit him to keip the Castell for
the Kyng. The luiftenant lett Angus wnderstand by
many good reassouns yat Grahame as the luiftenant
wnderstood haid no suche power no derectionis and yat
he thoight werrilhe yat Grahame haid deceavit him. At
lenth Angus returnit back to his assoaciats and promeist
presenthe to come him self and so many as wald fallow
him and rander them self in his Ma[ties] will. The luiftenant
sent wth Angus two gentelmen to conduct him back frome
the Castell : Angus na sooner cam to the castell then he
retwrnit, the two that were sent wth him desyring them to
shew the luiftenant that on no coditio wald he iander him
self. Than the ordince was plyed which haid not shoat
above sum sevin or aught shot when Agus sent to the
luiftenant desyring ane wther parle : the luiftenant refuisit to answer him bot commandit me to assure him that
the luiftenant wold heir no moir of his delayis ; abowt

---

[1] Of Barbreck, Lochow : afterwards Sir Donald Campbell of Ardnamurchan.

[2] This identifies the writer as Archibald Campbell of Glencarradale (*vide
ante*, p 156)

fyve of klok in the ewning Āgus sent to me a mess^r desyring that I wold crave the luiftenant's promeis that the luiftenant at his Maties handis. The whiche I shew to the luiftenant wha ansrit me that he wald mak no promeis to any of the rebells nether wald he remember any privat quarrell of his awin against Angus bot so far as his place wald command him. All this tyme the cannon and culwring played on the Castell and the messinger being on his way to the Castell and āgus not abill to wthstand the scage any longer was cum furthe owt of the Castell where all that wer abowt might sie him and in ye midway Āgus being cuming to rander him self, the mess^r met wth him and tald him as I hawe w'ttin.

Āgus hawing cum to the luiftenant betwixt fyve and sex a klok at night wth sum wther of the principall of the rebelles thei knilit all befoir the luiftenant in presence of all that wer thaire and told yei wer cum in all humilite to rander them self in his Maties will wthout any conditiō: lykwayes he told the luiftenāt that sum of the rebelles wha war in the Castell haid desyrit him to ask if the luiftenant wald be pleasit to assuire them that yair lyfis should be saif wntill yei werre broight afoire the cōsell; the luiftenant sent me to Sr Oliwer Lambert to let him know of this message: in the mean tyme the luiftenant derectit his boatts to ly watching ye rebelles if yei should steill away be sea as he did ewerie night befoire Bot the cūing in of Angus almost wnder clood of night and the message he broight frome the rest of the rebellis as lykwayis Sr Oliwer Lambart hawing assuirit the luiftenant so shone as it wer dark he wold send his companyis to lodge wnder the wallis of the Castell the which whill I was my self wth Sr Oliwer Lambart shewing him the message that Āgus had broight frome the rest of the rebellis Sr Oliwer was prowyding his companyes to go to the Castell and stayed onlie to let yame hawe a littell meatt for yei had laborit werie hard all the day befoir. Thos that werre attending the boattis knowing of all this it maid sum of them the moire neglegent hoiping yat yei should hawe littell or no thing ado I had no sooner taikin leave of Sr Oliwer Lam-

bert being on my way towards the liwtenant when ye
rebellis wshit owt in a boat whiche yei haid fittit for ye
purpos. Sum of the luiftenant's men that watchit for
yem by sea did geive them a woille of shoat and lenchit owt
yair boatis and followed them which ye rebellis ansrit w^th
yair shoats so as the luiftenant and Sr Oliwer Lambart and
all yat war one the shoare might sie the luiftenant's boattes
and ye rebellis boate gif fyre to wthers a longe tyme ; a
rock lykwayis neire to the Castell wherone yair was plantit
a nūber of muskiteris did geue ye rebellis at thair wshing
owt a woille of shoat. The rebellis boat being moire swift
then the boats yat were apoyntit to wache them that night
did ower rowe them and the rebelles boatte being sum
what onthight althoghe werrie swift yei were forcit to
drawe to the narrest shoire yei culd cum att and landit in
the Od of Illa where yair boate wes sunk ; the luiftenant
sent pñtlie efter yame in ewerie corner of the cuntrie and
causit brek all the boatts of the Ille so as yei can not
eshaipe.

One the 3 of feb^r the luiftenant did hold ane Justice
court where yaire were of the rebellis that war taikin
in the Castell of Dwnywege fowrteine Angus Oge him
self and Alaster Ma^ckarlye one of the ringlederis and two
messingeris that ar privie to all the rebellis proceidingis
ar to be sent to the counsell, yair to be examinit. I wnderstand by Agnus yat he hes not beine the first dewysser of
this treassoun. I leaue to writ any moire of this wntill a
better tyme : yair ar sex wha war aprehendit in the Ille
and fort of Lochgwrme to be execut. One the sext of
feb^r thair ware sex of the rebellis that went owt of the
Castell one the boat, aprehendit and executt : yair is onlie
at the writting heirof fowre of the name of Clandonald as
yet on aprehendit, yair ar nyne or tenn of wther clannis
wha war yair associats as yet onaprehendit, yei ar seprat
and the fowre Ma^cdonaldis ar be them selfis and the rest
of the wther clanns ar ewerie ane be them selfis. Sence
my cuming heir I fand owt a number of images whiche I
hawe caussit to be bruntt : the religioun that the cuntrie
pepill hes heir amongst them is Popishe for yair is newer

a minister in the wholle Ille except wan poore man that the bishop did leaue heir.[1] I wnderstand be the luiftenant yat he hes just cause to complein of those wha war commandit to assist him be the proclamatioun.

Dwring the seivice thair is nether boat nor bark come frome Scotland wth any furnishing no^t w^{t}standing of all derectionis that the counsell gaue for ye same.

This is the trew accompt of all that hes as zet proceidit in his Maties serwice.   S. J. CAMPBELL.[2]

73. The copie of Sr Oliver Lambart's first letter to the Rebellis

[*December* 1614]

The Kyng our most gracious Maister hes sent me wth his forces out of Irland his royall ships and cannons to chastis such his subjects as ar rewolted frome yair obedience and holdis ye Castell of Dunywege againis his peace and dignitie I thoight good befoir I landit and put my self and souldiers to farder trouble to summond you in his Maties name to surrander ye said Castell to me for his Matie and to send yor resolutions be one man of accompt that yow in my word and credite fairlie returne and fairlie come and yor ansuer I expect the first of Janwarij.

74. The Copie Angus Oge's first letter to Sir Oliver Lambert

[14 *December* 1614]

MY HONORABILL GOOD LORD—I have receavet your Letter, and hes vnderstand be your meaning, that ze wuld hawe me to rander this Hous to yow into the Kyngs name. My Lord, as to that, if I had not receavit ane better

---

[1] The destruction of all the old-time aids to devotion gave special satisfaction, not merely to the hypothetical 'rascal multitude,' but also to their leaders who in fanaticism much exceeded Knox and the original Reformers (vide *Highland Papers*, vol. ii. p. 40, note 2, p 65, note 2)

[2] The same signature as that to No. 71.

Warrand frome my Lord Chancler and Counsell of Scotland
to rander thame this Hous of Dunywege, I wald obey your
lo. or any wther subiect, hawing his Maiesteis Warrand.
My lord, if ze doubt of this, send me zour awin Secrctar,
or ame wther that can reid, and I shall let him sie my
Warrand frome the Counsell, desyring me to keip this
Castell, wnto the tyme that his Ma^{tles} wil be
declairit to me. The quhilk my Warrand sall testifie.
And if yow will trouble me, efter I hawe obeyit his highnes
will, be yow assurit that I sall complayne to his Ma^{tels}
Counsell. Not troubling zour lo. any forder, comitts yow
to God. Frome Dunywege, the 14 of this instant month.
And if ze will send any of zour awin men, ze sall hawe frie
passage to pas and repas to and fro —Your friend, to your
deserwing,   ANGUS OG MA^CDONALL.

75. The copie of Sr Oliwer Lambertis secund letter to the rebellis

That his Ma^{tles} should derect his forces, his cannons and
his prowissioun at this tyme of the yeir and put him self at
so gryt a charge wnto a place that is alredie in his Sub-
jectioun can not but be much doubtit by me and being
loth to spend any longer tyme in yis place if y^t ze wryt be
trew I send this my Serwant both to reid yor warrant and
to bring me a trew coppie yairof wnder yor hand which I
expect presentlie and the saif returne of this berar, fiome
the whit forland the 16 of Decembris.

76. The copie of Grahamis aledgit instructionis

God save the King.
Memorandum of the Chancleris derectioun to be obeyit.

First, to speir at ye Caiptanes of Dunywege whome yei
hawe to warrand them frome ye forces of the Kyng of
Britane's power and all thes nationes wha ar chargit not
only to tak ye Castell bot to aprehend them whiter yei go.
Secundlie, to desyr the said Caiptanes in the counsellis
name and myn to randar zow the prisoneris and hous and

ıf yeı be loth to twın with the hous that zow mak ane of yaır awın chosıng Caıptane tıll the Kyng's wıll and counsell cõe tıll them, thıs ıf yeı do without any serimonies I promeıs you be word yat ye Counsell and I sall work at ye Kyng's hand to forder any thıng resaonabıll theı wald and sall end zow or any wther to court for that effect.

Thrıdlıe, ıf the saıd Caıptanes or any of yaır freındıs hes any petıtıons to the Kıng or Counsell for let them send the same wıth zow and ze sall hawe ane ansuer back agayne yanof shortlıe, and the Counsell shall do for yem yaırın.

Fowrtlıe, ıf yeı hawe done any mısorder that yeı wald hawe remıssıoun or suspentıoun or relaxatıoun brıng wıth zow the ınformatıoun and yeı salbe grantıt Swa that yeı obey zow ın oᵣ name qˡᵏ we ar assurıt yeı will.

Fyftlıc, let yame knawe qᵗ gryt expenss the kyng was dryvın to be the Seıge of Kırkway,[1] what gryt anger he conceawıt for ye same and how mercıeles all was execut. And ıf yeı hald furthe tıll yeı be bot chargıt wıth ye lyoun,[2] no remeıd ıs for yame and all yaır kınred ın Scotland, And ıf yaır kın ın Iyrland gıf yame bot cowntenence yeı salbe wterlıe wrackıt.

Sextlıe, ıf yeı obey ws ın yoᵣ persoune we sall not onlıe laboᵣ at hıs Maᵗᵗˡᵉˢ handıs for yaır pardoune bot for yaır possessıounis at the Kıngıs hand Swa that yeı pay for the same as salbe modefıct and fynd Catıoune for ye same.

Sewıntlıe, ıf ye wıll bed my self be Catıoun for yem wnder sıck Condıtıouns as I hawe shawın you, I wıll not faıl to do the same and wıll laboᵣ for them all yat I may. Sa wıshıng god zoᵣ hapıe jorney.   2 Novembrıs.

Thıs ıs the trew copıe of the chanclerıs warrand receawıt frome George Grahame yat day I delywerıt possessıoun of yıs Castell to yame ın the Kyngıs· behalf : wıtnes of our handıs the 17 of December 1614.

Angus Oge Maᶜdonald,
Coll Maᶜgillespik.

---

[1] In 1614 the Earl of Caıthness was wıth dıfficultv prevented from destıoyıng the Cathedral church of St. Magnuˢ.

[2] For a specımen of Letters of Treason addressed to Lyon ın 1674, vıde *Highland Papers*, vol ı p. 263

77. Earl of Dunfermline to John Murray of the Bedchamber

From Ed^r, 24 *feb^r* 1615

Richt Hon^{ll} Cousing all that I haue to write to ziow is that wee haue no mater off moment to write off frome this, nor be apeirance wee will haue na subject off aduertisement till the prisonaris frome Ila be heir to be tried and examinat.

78. Bishop of Argyll to the King

24 *Feb.* 1615

MOST GRATIOUSS SOUERANE—Cōsiddering zo^r M. royall and indeserued fauo^r in euecting me to that honorable estat of episcopall societie within this Kingdome far besyd other thocht or appetite : and inrespect thairoff thinking not onlie still to exorne ye place committed vnto me, bot more and more to interceid at ye most highe for lenth and happines of zo^r M. dayis, it behouethe me in regaird of bodilie infirmitie to craue pardone that heirby I supple that personall homage addebtit to zo^r M. for so grit benefeit : least I sould seime ather ignorant or forgetfull thairby giveing zo^r M. occasione to repent that gratiouss munificencie. Heirwithe it wald pleass zo^r sacred Matie remember that ye pairtis of zo^r M. kingdome cōmitted to my spirituall o^{r}sicht being so barbarous, that without seuer animaduersione thay can not be cohibite from thair wonted souage behauio^r : Nather can this be so cōuenientle done as by the presence of the erle of Argyll : quha at my last assemble not onle gave to me, in secreit, exceiding gude piove of his religione, baking the same w^t no worss knawledge : bot, in publict, offerit (vnder zo^r M.) to cawss all obedience be givein to discipline, churches to be bullid, and violent detineris of ministeris gleibis and māsis thairoff dispossessed : in all quhiche, as his L. was required, he did performe : And thairfore seing it wald be bothe confortable to my charge, and helpfull to his awin decaying state : quhairunto I trust zo^r M. will rather inclyne nor that he (throwe staying at court and necessitie vrgeing) become ane dehonestamēt to zo^r M. this kingdome, and honorable place that thair into bothe be birthe and office he bruikis, I humlie requeist zo^r M. in 'regairde heiroff, ather to direct him to his awin cuntrie, or confyne him w^tin the samin.

Craueing pardone for this my boldnes, and cōmitting to Johne Murray relatione of sum particular anent my self, and agane beseiking ye almi^{tie} God for zo^r M. happines heir and honor I wess remaneing euer—zo^r M. most humill servand,   AN: LISMOREN.[1]

Edinb^r, 24 feb. 1615.

79. Earl of Dunfermline to the King

16 *March* 1615

MAIST SACRED SOUERAJNE—I can nawayes sufficientlie declaire vnto yiour Matie the greatte contentment I haiff ressaued be yiour maist prencelie letter of the first of this instant, albeit the same conteyne ane challenge and accusatioun[2] of great owirsight and onworthie dealing in me gif I had sua proceidit in George Grhaymes trafique, for the Laird of Ramfurdhe and Bischope of the Iles his sonnis libertie, as the informatioun and articles geivin to yiour Matie as proceiding from me beiris. Whereanent to cleir and resolue yiour maist gracious Matie at ane worde, As yiour Highnes declairis in yiour awin letter ; Zee could nocht esteéme theese articles to be other nor fals and suppositicious of thair awin inventioun, Whairin I haue fund greate joye, yat zio^r Matie sould sua cleirlie tak vp and consaue the sinceritie of my mynde, I certifie yiour Sacred Matie on my faithe, honour, and on that deutie of treuthe

---

[1] ' Andrew Boyd, Parson of Eaglesham, natural son of Thomas Lord Boyd, was preferred to this see *anno* 1613. . . He died 22nd December 1636, aged 70.' —Keith's *Scottish Bishops*, p 291.

[2] By this time some report of the trickery of Lord Dunfermline and his emissary had apparently reached the King

and fidelitie I aucht to yiour Maiestie, I gaue nather theese directiouns or articles to George Grhayme whercoff yiour Matie send me copie, nor nayne other directioun or article at all ather be woord or wreitt, other nor this simpill directioun be tung allanerlie (for I refused to giff him ony writt, in regaird all dealing was onlie betuix him and me) to use all laufull meanes he could be anye good addresse or dexteritie, to releive the twa gentilmen prissoners, whilk giff he could be anye meanis attayne to, I promeist to be his debtour, and sua soone as he sould present to me the saidis prissoners or sure aduerteisment and testificat of thair freedome and libertie I sould deliuer to him reallie ane thousand merkis for his charges and recompense; farder he had nather directioun, article, nor promeis of me : And this I obserued maist preceislie to him, for sua soone as he returned hayme, I maid him instant payment of the soume promeist; whilk ziour Matie hes sensyne maist Royallie caussed zio^r Thesaurer heir restore againe to me, The wtter veritie of this I hope yiour Matie shall haue weiie good opportunitie and occasioun to try at this present instant, because I onderstand the said George Grhayme is presenthie ather at Court or at Londoun, ffor he went thair from this 20 dayis sence ; Be the Laird of Urchill I think zour Matie may easilie haiff inquisitioun of him, and mak him be examinat heir upon ; And giff he say anye farder or otherwayes contrair to this my declaratioun, as I think he shall nocht, yiour Matie may cause him be send hayme, for I think Angus Oig shall be heir schoirtlie, presented be Cadell, And be thair confronting wee shall find out the haill veritie. Besides that gif he wald alledge he had anye sic directioun from me he should schaw my hand writte whilk he will newir be habill to doe, nor of nayne apperteynis to me in onye degrie or respect ; and this I hope shall satisfie ziour Sacred Maties height and judicious conceptioun for my purgatioun of any sic imputatioun ; I war ane onworthie man, et me ipso judice, woorthie of all rigorous punischement, gif I had committed sua lourde ane faulte againe a Prence his honour and dignitie, after sua lang apprentisage and

trajnmg vp in ziour Sacred Maiesties schoolle of honour,
in sua mony and sua honorabill chargis and imploymentis,
As hes oft pleased ziour Maiestie honour me withe, And
whairin I thank God and ziour Highnes clemencie and
fauourabill interpretatioun I haue hithertill euir gevin
ziour Matie reasonabill contentment and satisfactioun.
This man not mak me forziett nor omitt my deutie in all
humilitie and thankfulnes of hairte to acknowledge ziour
Sacred Maties greater bountifulnes and gracious dispositioun in granting to my Nepuieu (whome I may now, be
ziour Sacred Ma^tels fauour and permissioun, stile Erle of
Eglintoun) that honour and dignitie whilk sua manye of
his predicessours enjoyed and whairbye thai haue done
to ziour Ma^tels maist nobill progenitours good and accept-
abill seruice I hope in God zio^r Matie shall find him prowe
nather onwoorthie nor oncapabill of ziour Royall fauour,
As ziour Highnes may haiffe occasioun to employe him.
Sua wischeing to ziour Highnes from the King of all Kings
a long and Prosperous Regne withe the submisse kisse of
ziour Royall hand, Restis, z^r maist Sacred Maiesties maist
humbill and obedient Subject and Servitour,

DUNFERMELJNE.

Edinburght, 16 Martij 1615.

80. Earl of Dunfermline to —— [1]

30 *April* 1615

Suim thing y^r Lo. has writtin to me 19 Aprile be his
Ma. cōmand anent suim examinatioun off George Grahame,
quha procuired the releiff of B. Iles sonne and Ramfurlie
frome the rebellis off Ila; I haue writtin lang sence to his
Ma. in ane letter off my awin, quhilk was deliured be Jhone
Murray all my entress and pairt in that mannis proceidingis, and all that was betuix him and me, and farder
will neuer be found off me in treuth quhairin I think I
did als guid seruice for his Ma. honour and countries as
euer I could be habill to doe, The said George Grahame

---

[1] It would seem that Lord Fentoun, afterwards Earl of Kellie, may have been
the person (cf *post*, p. 303).

had neuer farder warrand off me worde nor write bot
my naked promeis of ane thousand marke to him self be
my worde in case he releieved safelie the twa prisonars, I
think he sall neuer say farder, if he say I sall prove him
fals, if he has gone onye farder it has bein on his awin
or suim other mannis warrand nor myne, latt him and
thame ansuer thairfore on thair parrell. I think certanlie I haue mair cause to rejoice and glory in all that
I did in that nor rew the same, and sua I persuade my self
his sacred Ma. thinkis also off me, quhat euer onye wald
say or mantein in the contrair, I sall euer be cairfull of
his Ma. honour and guid seruice en despit des enuientis ;
Nocht hauing farder for the present bot to wiss ziow all
happines and contentement, restis, y^r lo. maist affectionat
to serue yiow,   DUNFERMELJNE.

frome Ed^r, Ult° Aprilis 1615.

81. Angus Oig his first depositioun recognosceit this 23 of Maij 1615

Angus oig M^cdonald his depositioun as efter followis

Deponis that in Marche 1614 the Castell of Dunyvaig
wes keipit be Ro^t M^cgilchrist, Jonet Hamiltoun spous to
Patrick Knox and his dochter.

Depones lykwyse that about the last of Marche foirsaid
Ronnald Oig M^calester of lait callit Ronnald Oig M^cagnus,
bastard sone to vmq^{ll} Angus McDonald come in the nicht
and brocht with him ane ledder on the w^{che} he him self
Gilecalom M^cgilemole Donald onnavenye and ——— M^cilveny
his brother and ——— M^clachlan come vp to the draw brig
of the Invirbahan [1] of the Castell and all the nicht ludgeit

---

[1] Jamieson's *Dictionary* gives Inver as a variant for inner. But it may also
be suggested that it is merely a copyist's mistake. In either view Invirbahan is
the inner bahan or bawn. 'Gr. and Gael. babhun (pron. bawn), originally an
earthwork strengthened with stakes surrounding a castle or house in Ireland ;
hence any similar enclosed place whether designed as a fortification or as
an enclosure for cattle.'—*Imperial Dictionary*.

thame selffis in ane grite quantitie of hedder that lay in the said bahan : on the nixt moirning the said Ronnald and his complices finding the zettis of the Castell oppin, Johnne Hairt and Johnne Mwire being past furth in thair awne busynes he enterit in the Castell with his complices with [1] [*sic*, ? where] Robert M^cgilchrist and Patrik Knox wyff and his dochter was and perforce thrust yame out of the Castell and maid him self maister thairof.

Depones lykwyse that Coall M^cgillespik accumpaneid with ten or xii of the Clandonald wer directit be the said Angus Oig about the sext or sevint of Aprile to tak in the said Castell of Dunyveig frome the said Ronnald oig alledgeit bastard to vmq^{ll} Angus M^cdonald and his foir-said compliceis and that the said Coall M^cgillespik with his associatis beseidgeit the Castell and for iust feir the said Ronnald oig bastard to Angus with his compliceis staw away in the nicht out of the said Castell and the said Coall M^cgillespik and his associatis enterit in the same quha immediatlie acquentit the deponner with thair proceidingis. The deponer deponis that he enterit not in the Castell of Dunyveig quhill aucht dayis before beltane last, bot desyrit Coall M^cgillespik to keip the house and that he him self wald dwell in Aroiss foure myllis distant frome the Castell. Depones lykwyse that Ronnald Oig alledgeit bastard sone to the said Angus wes tuentie dayis in Ila before the deponer apprehendit him efter that he had stollin out of the house of Dunyvaig and haueing found him in the O of Ilay with his foirsaid complices the said Ronnald Oig wes taikin and the vther foure wha war with him war slane at the same tyme.

Depones lykwyse that haueing brocht the said Ronnald Oig to the Castell of Dunyvaig and put him in irins yair, the said deponer sent Alaster M^charleych to the said Ronnald Oig desyreing him to lat the deponer knaw wha wes the aduyser of the said Ronnald to tak the house of Dunyvaig or be quhais meanis he hoipit to be suppleit of his wantis, promitting to the said Ronnald his lyff gif he

---

[1] It would seem that *with* should be *where*.

wald acquent the said Angus quha wes the advyseris and directairis of him to tak in the house of Dunyvaig.

The deponer depones that the said Ronnald Oig being demandit vpoun his grite oath to tell the treuth of this mater deponit in pñce of the said Angus Oig, Coll M^cgillespik, Allaster M^ckerliche and Catherine Campbell, spous to the said Angus, that the said Ronnald had bene at the bischop of Rapho [1] a litle before his comeing to Ila, and haueing receavit frome him a warrand to tak meit and drink frome the tennentis in Ilay, quhair he come thairefter to Down-lipis pertening to Sr Ronnald M^csorle, and haueing come out of Ireland he mett with Donald Gorme bastard sone to Sr James M^cdonald quha schew him that he hard the Ile of Ila wes to be gevin away be his Maiestie and that his freindis was to be turnit out of the same, desyreing thair-fore that the said Ronnald Oig wald go and tak in the house of Dunyvaig seeing it was the onlie strenth of the Ile, promitting to the said Ronnald mony good conditionis and that he wald be his mantenair and defender in that actioun.

Lykewyse the said Angus deponis that quhen the said Ronnald oig wes apprehendit he had ane lfẽ w^{che} he tooke out of his sleif and raive and beit it with his teithe, and being demandit be the said Angus what a lfẽ it wes, he deponit it wes ane lfẽ not to be seene and of na grite importance Ronnald desyrit not to haif it seene.

Lykwyse the said deponer depones that in May last the bischop of the Yllis sent to him Allaster M^ckynie and Mr Dougall Campbell desyreing the deponer to rander to him the Castell of Dunyvaig and efter they had cõmonit a long tyme of the conditionis for randrie of the house it was concludit that the bischop sould obtene ane remis-sioun to the deponer and his complices and the bischop thair efter to haif the Castell.

Lykwyse the deponer deponis that Donald Gorme sone to the said Sr James come to the Castell of Dunyvaig about Lambes last accumpaneid with sevin or aucht of

---

[1] *Vide ante*, p. 104, note 1.

the Clan allaster and offered to the said Angus his seruice,
and efter that he had stayit a schorte space, the deponer
deponis thair come ane lr̃e frome the bischop of the Illis
to the said Donald Gorme desyreing him to repair to the
bischop the w^{che} he did at Brodik in Arane, deponis lykwyse
that he demandit the said Donald Gorme quhat warrand
he had to direct Ronnald Oig to tak in the house of Dunyvaig, quha ansuerit that he had nothing for him bot
becaus he hard that the Ile of Ila wes to be disponit be
his Matie to vtheris than his freindis and deponis lykwyse
that he had detenit the said Donald Gorme captiue vnles
that the bischop had writtin for him, deponis lykwys that
in harvest last the bischop sent M^ckanzie and M^cdonchie
bane messinger in Bwit to him with ane remissioun vnder
the grite seale and that the said M^cdonchie ban did reid
the copie of the remissioun, the w^{che} bwir that Angus
sould within xxiiij ho^{ris} rander the Castell efter the recept
thairof vtherwyse the remissioun to be null, deponis
lykwyse that the caus quhairfore he refuisit the remissioun
[was] becaus he could not in sa schorte a space w^tin xxiiij
ho^{ris} get him self, his people and thair cariage transportit,
deponis in lyke maner that about Hallowmes last the
bischop of the Iles sent Donald Gorme and Ardincaple
with a messinger to him for randering of the Castell of
Dunyvaig, he ansuerit that gif the bischop sall bring him
ane sufficient remissioun he wald willinglie rander the
Castell, deponis that within foure or fyve dayis thairefter
the bischop of the Yllis come to Portasiqz[1] in Ila place whair
Donald Gorme and M^ccaulay mett him with thair message
w^{che} thay had receavit frome the deponer, and thair the
nixt nicht thairefter Ronnald McJames and Coll McGillespik
and yair complices did ly about the bischopis house and
on the nixt moirning thairefter the boitis being brokin
that come with the bischop be Ronnald McJames the
deponer come whair the bischop wes and efter sindrie
messageis sent betuix yame, he desyrit the bischop to
deliuer him the Laird of Ramfurdlie and his sone M^r

---

[1] Portaskaig

Thomas Knox as pledgeis that the bischop sould do his best endevoiris to get the deponer ane sufficient remissioun.

Lykwyse the deponer deponis that nather himself nor any vther be his knowledge wes of intentioun to haif troublit the bischop in ony sorte at that tyme when the pledges wer taikin frome him bot that the taking of the pledgeis proceidit of ane suddane anger w^che he consauit becaus of the bischop his taking of Donald Gorme.

Forder the deponers deponis that he him selff knew no thing of ony trouble that wes betuix the bischop and his freindis quhill he wes advertised be Ronnald McJames and Coll M^cgillespik. Sic subscribitur Angus Oig M^cdonald, Alex^r M^cdougall, witnes, W. Campbell, witnes, Colene Campbell, witnes.

82. Angus Oig his secund depositioun recognosceit this 23 day of May 1615.

Angus oig M^cdonald his depositioun

The deponer deponis that vpoun the day of Nouember 1614 zeiris Donald M^calaster vrie dwelland in the Aros in Ila come to him to the house of Dunyvaig tymouslie in moirning before he did ryse out of his bed and tauld him that thair wes ane callit George Grahame a servand of the Chancellairis at the zett quha desirit the said deponer to come out and speik with him w^che sa soone as the said deponer hard he maid all the haist he could to array him selff to go out w^che haueing done he went out immediatlie and mett with the said George Grahame and haueing saluted utheris the deponer demandis of the said George frome whence did he come, wha sent him thair, and what wes his eirand, George ansuer to the deponer wes that he wes come out of Ed^r directit with a warrand frome the Chanceller and the rest of the Counsell to desyre the Castell of Dunyvaig and pledgeis to be randerit to him.

Lykewyse the deponer deponis that the said George Grahame told him that thair wes ane lyoun herauld[1] directit

---

[1] Robert Winram, Ila Herald (*vide post*, p. 207).

to chairge the house and gif the deponer wald appoint
with him before the comeing of the herauld, that he sould
not onlie stay the herauld bot he sould also stay his Maiesteis
lieutennent wha wes comeing to besedge the house.

The deponer deponis that he inquired of the said George
quhat conditionis of peace wald be gevin him gif so be
that he sould obey the Chancellairis and counsaillis desyre,
to the w^{che} the said George ansuerit that he sould haif
a remissioun to him selff and all his followaiiis.

As lykewyse that the Chancellair sould be his freind and
travell so fer as his creditt could extend to acquie him
ane richt of the lands of Ila, as lykewyse that the Chanceller sould tak his defence in all his lauchfull adois, and
in toakin of his favo^r wald be cautioun for him to his
Maiestie and his counsaill for his obedience in tyme
comeing.

Farder the said deponer demandit quhat certantie he
sould haif that the Chancellair sould performe these conditionis that wes offered be him, to the w^{che} the said George
ansuerit, that to verifie that the Chancellair wes of ane
vpricht mynd to performe all these conditionis offered,
the Chanceller wald be content that the Castell sould be
keepit be some of the deponeris awne men whill ayther the
said George or some vther whome the Chanceller pleasit
to mak choise of war sent to his Maiestie wha sould mak
the deponer certanelie advertised of his Maisteis intentioun anent the delyuerie of the said Castell of Dunyvaig,
as lykwyse what micht be wrocht at his Maiesteis handis
anent a richt of the landis of Illa in fauo^{ris} of the said
deponer.

The deponer after a dayis conference with the said
George in pñce of Duncane Campbell of Dannay, Donald
and Coline Campbellis his sones and mony vtheris witnesses
delyuerit the pledgeis w^{che} he had, to witt, the Laird of
Ramfurdlie and Mr Thomas Knox togidder with the Castell
of Dunyvaig and keyis thairof to the said George in name
of the Chanceller and remanent of his Maiesteis counsaill
of Scotland, w^{che} keyis the said George as haueing power
of the Chancellair and remanent of his Maiesteis counsell

to place any man constable in the said Castell of Dunyvaig ✗
w^{che} the said George sould think expedient delyuerit bak
to the said deponer, apoynting the said deponer to be a
constable him selff cōmanding the said deponer not to
rander the Castell to ony man quhill the said George send
new adverteisment bak to the deponer frome the Chancellair and remanent of his Maiesteis counsell of Scotland.

Lykwyse deponis that he in presence of the Laird of
Ramfurdlie and Mr. Thomas Knox, said to the said George
that he wes affrayit that the keiping of the Castell micht
breid some trouble to him heirefter, thairefore he requeistit
the said George to tak the keiping of the Castell him selff,
his familie and all his followairis out of it, to the w^{che} the
said George ansuerit that his warrant bwir no moir bot
to mak ane of the deponeris awne men capitane of the
said Castell.

As lykwyse althocht he had a warrant to posses the
Castell him selff, he had not at that tyme a sufficient nomber
of men for keiping of it,[1] thairfore desyrit the deponer to
keip it him selff and to gif it ouer to no man quhill his
nixt adverteisment.

Lykewyse it wes demandit be the said deponer at the
said George gif his Maiesteis Lieutennent came before the
Chancellairis adverteisment cam bak, whether or no sould
he delyuer the Castell to his Maiesteis Lieutennent. the
deponer deponis that the said George ansuer wes that he
wes to go immediatlie out of that where his Maiesteis
Lieutennent wes, that he had a wairant to stay his
Maiesteis Lieutennent frome comeing fordwart and gif
so be that the Lieutennent or ony vther wald come to
demand the Castell to miskene yame obsoluthe quhill the
said George sould adverteiss the deponer of new.

Lykewyse the deponer deponis that when the Lieutennent wes about the Castell of Dunyvaig, Allaster
McKerlech wha is presenthe in waird cam out of Kintyre

---

[1] In the reddendo of the Charter of his lands the Captain of Dunstaffnage
was bound to supply only 'sex homines probos et decentes cum armatis et
armis licitis pro guerris et custodia dicti castri et sufficien. ostiarium et vigilem
ad numerum in toto octo personarum in tempore pacis.'

in the nycht be boit to the house of Dunyvaig, wha brocht
with him to the deponer twa lr̃ez ane frome Hector Mᶜcaijs
desyreing the deponer to receave a lr̃e fra George Grahame
to the deponer and schawing that him selff had receavit
ane vther lr̃e fra the said George Grahame be the whiche
he wes informit that the Chancellair wes the deponeris
good freind and that the deponeris adois wer liklie to
frame weele. The vther lr̃e frome George Grahame
schawing that the bischop of the Yllis sone, Mʳ Thomas
Knox, wes gone to courte and that the Chancellair had
sent directionis with the said Mʳ Thomas anent the
deponeris busynes, thairfore desyrit the deponer to be of
good curage and not to gif ouer the house till his comeing
assureing the deponer that he sould be at him with a
particulair ansuer of all his adois betuixt and Candilmes
at the farthest.

I the said Angus Oig Mᶜdonald testifeis this my foirsaid
depositioun writtin be Johnne Inglische, seruitoʳ to Sʳ
Johnne Campbell of Caddell, knycht, to be iust and trew
in all pointis as is abouewrittin, be this my subscriptioun
at Dunyvaig the nynetene of Marche 1615 before thir
witnesses Alexʳ MᶜDowgall brother germane to the Laird
of Rara, Williame and Coline Campbellis, seruitoʳⁱˢ to Sʳ
Johnne Campbell of Calder, knycht, and Johnne Inglische,
writter of the premisses. Sic subscribitur Angus oig
Mᶜdonald ; Alexʳ MᶜDougal, witnes ; W. Campbell, witnes ;
Coline Campbell, witnes.

83. The King to Lord Binning [1]

Hauing by reason of the arriuall of Archibalde Campbelle
had occasion of further conference with George Grahame
since the dispatch of a letter directed to yow oʳ secretary
concerning him, wee have founde the said Archibalde and
him in such contrarietie and direct opposition in their
reportts as we have thought good to sende the said Grahame

---

[1] This seems to be a draft or copy and is obviously addressed to Lord
Binning, ' yow oʳ secretary.'

to yow (to whose offices it principallie belongeth to trie the verity in the like cases) willing you withoute fauo^r feede or respecte of any person whatsoeuer as yee will aunswere to ws, so exactlie to try and examyne him as by zo^r carefull diligence not onlie the treuth may be founde oute but wee also may be certified of all particularityes necessarie, and because we haue reserued the tryall of some particulare pointes to o^r selfe, wch are speciallie to be learned of some gentlemen who are shortelie to be here, wee haue thought good to require yow cheefelie to insiste in the tryall and cleering of these articles here enclosed.

And because he onlie confesseth a parte of the fifth of these articles, and all the rest he obstinatelie denyeth, notwithstanding that there be vehement presumptionis against him, it is most necessarie that he not onlie be confronted with Angus Og, but also with such others of the principalles of the Clandonale as may giue any light in the busines in hand, and their asseuerations diligentlie conferred and exactlie compared together, for wch effecte it is our speciall pleaso^r that with all convenient expedition, yee cause the said Angus Og, his wife, his father in law, and the specialles of the reste be brought to Ed^r and there surelie and conuenientlie lodged, that not onlie they may be keepte secrete frome the companie and conference of all others but that as occasion shall require yee haue them fitlie brought before you.

And whereas the said Angus hath promised to reueale an important secrete vpon some greate one[1] if he may haue assurance of his life : that mater wolde prouidentlie and sparinglie be dealt in, otherwise the said Angus will haue to greate aduantage, who although he shoulde malicioushe calumniate any greate man and succumbe in the probation, yet were assured of his life, yee are therefor to deale with him eyther to gette it oute of him withoute conditions or then that he sette it doune vnder his hand in a close letter and directe it to vs, but if he will do neyther of both withoute the said assurance. yee are to advertise

---

[1] In Mr. Gregory's opinion the reference is to Argyll (*History*, p. 365, note 2)

vs thereof together with yor oune opinion how far the
discoverie or neglecte of that mater may importe or concerne o^r seruice, to the ende that wee hauing seene it may
returne o^r pleaso^r and dispose of him according as wee
shall thinke the cause to require.

84. Petitionis to be desyret of his Matie [1]

ffirst that his Matie may be pleaset to caus Agnus M^cconill
be brought befor his Maiestie quhairby ye devyseris of ye
treasoune cōmittit be him may be made knowen to his
Matie as lykwyse that his Matie may know by Agnus how
fare George Grame went on withe him.

That his Matie may be pleaset to ordain thos quha wentt
not to his hines service in Yla according to ye proclama-
tione to be fynet and the fynes to come to his hines
Thesaurer.

That his Matie may be pleaset to grant remissiones to
Ranald McJames and his sone for giueing vp ye yle and
fort of Lochgurme in Ila. [2]

That his Matie may be pleaset to grant a remissione to
Ranald M^csorle quha presentet Donald Baine M^cfinlay
alias Torke quho was ane cheefe actor of the slauchter
cōmittit in Jura, and on y^t keipt ye fort of Lochegorme
and was at taking of ye Bischope of Yles and his sone.

That his Maiestie may be pleaset to grant a remissione
to Sorle M^calaster on that keipt ye hous of Dunieweig, and
quhen ye act of fawour was proclaimet to thes quho wald
leaue ye rebellis im̄ediatlie yairefter he left ye rebellis and
came to the louetenent: he hes lykwyse presentet Angus
M^calaster to the Luiftenent on y^t went away w^t Colle
M^cgillespick and ye said Agnus M^calester is to be presentet
before ye counsell.

That his Maiestie may be pleaset to appoint quhat
ordour salbe taken withe Angus Oig his twa sones, Colle

---

[1] This seems to be a memorandum prepared by Lord Binning.
[2] This was done on 31st January 1615.

M^cgillespick his twa sones, and Archibald Dow M^cconill his sone.

To desyr of his Maiestie y^t thes quho came to ye service be werteu of the proclaimatioune and wald not stay withe ye luiftenent vnles he wald giue yame yair charges y^t they be fynet and yair fynes to come to his hines Thesaurer.

To desyre lykwyse of his Matie y^t some of ye awoulet receateris of ye rebellis may be punishet as his Matie selfe think expedient.

To desyre his Maiestie caus writt a left to the Deputtie of Irland desyring him to caus apprehend Sr James M^cconill his bastard sone quho is w^t ye lord Burlie in Irland.

To desyr of his Matie a remissione to ye Laird of Caddell.

To desyr a warrant from his Maiestie to Sr Judeon Murray [to] giue Laweris ye fynes according to his Matie and my lord chalmerlanis former warrantis.

Item to speak to his Maiestie anent Duncane M^cfarlane.

To desair his Matie yat yair may be a lr̃e writtin to ye depute of Irland commanding him yat Sir Ronald M^csorle be discheargit to go to Illa during zour Maties seruice yair.

That zour Matie may be pleased to appoint q^t ordour zour Matie will haue teakin w^t the rest of ye Illes.

That zour Matie may be pleased to command ye Bischope of ye Illes to causs plant ye kirkis of Illa w^t ministeris.[1]

That zour Matie may be pleased to caus writt a lr̃e of thankis to the Bischope of Meath and to Sr Hew Mongomrie and to ye M^r of zour Ma^{teis} monisioun in Irland for yair keare teakin in advansing zour Ma^{teis} seruice.

85. Copie of Hector M^ccawis depositioun tane the 23 of Maij 1615

At Edinburgh the xxiii day of Maij 1615, in p̃nce of my Lord of Binning, secretair, the thesaurair depute and aduocat.

Hector M^ccaus in Ila sworne and demandit yf he knawis Ronnald Oig M^cangus, deponis he knawis him,

---

[1] In obvious reference to *ante*, p. 186.

bot knawis not who counsallit or persuadit him to tak the house of Dunnyvaig, bot be reporte that Donald Gorme bastard sone to Sr James M^cdonald wes the persuadair of Ronnald to tak the house.

Deponis that George Grahame come to the house of Dunnyvaig vpoun ane satterday and vpoun the morne thairefter being sonday Angus Oig send for the deponner to come to him bot he come not quhill the mononday at w^{lk} tyme the deponner vnderstoode by Angus reporte that George Grahame wes come thair be directioun frome my Lord Chancellair to deale with Angus for delyuerie of the house and pledgeis to him, and that his Lop. promeist to be thair freind, and to procure ane remissioun to him w^t ane right to him and his freindis of thair landis in Ila, and that his Lp. wald ryde to courte yf neede wer for that effect, and deponis that Angus delyuerit the pledgeis and the keyis of the house to George Grahame in my Lord Chancellairis name and that be commoun aggreement of the said Angus and of the remanent personis being w^tin the house the said George delyuerit the keyis bak agane to Coill M^cgillespek who wes ordanit to haif the keeping of the house till my lord Chancellairis farder pleasoure wer knawne, and deponis that at Angus command this deponnair write ane lr̃e in Angus name to my lord Chancellor showing his lp. how far he had gone w^t George Grahame in these materis, and that this lr̃e wes delyuerit to the said George to be caryed to his lp.

Deponis forder that he this deponner at Angus command come with the pledgeis in George Grahame's company to Dynnvne, and that George desirit the deponner to stay at Glasg^w till he send him ane ansuer of the chancellaris lr̃e and sayis that he stayed in Glasg^w vpoun this ansuer till Newersmes,[1] and vpoun new aduertisment frome George Grahame he stayed still in Glasg^w till Fasteinsevin,[2] bot past home wthout ony ansuer except the lr̃e w^{lk} is p̃duceit. Sic subscribitur Hector M^ccaus.

---

[1] New Year's Day.

[2] The evening preceding the first day of the Lenten fast. In England it is called Shrove Tuesday.

The copie of the lr̃e

Hector M^ccaus I pray you be heir in Edinburgh anes or the xx day of this moneth vther wayes go zo^r way home, my Lord can tell you of my Lord Chancellaris goode will in all thingis, and siclike he can informe zow of all my p̃cedingis in the Clandonaldis weelefair. So in haist fair-weele restis—Zo^{ris} and the Clandonaldis freindis and agentis will this tyme trye, bot the stur is grite now,

GRAHAME of Eryne.

I pray you be heir w^t diligence or zow will not find me. The pacquett is not come from Courte quhairin the Clandonaldis petitioun is to come.

86. At Edinburgh the 23 day of Maij 1615 in p̃nce of my Lord Secretair, Thesaurer depute and aduocat

Allaster McCarliche sworne and examinat quhither he wes with Angus Oig M^cdonald at ye persute and taking of Ronnald M^cangus callit bastard sone to vmquhill Angus M^cdonald of Dunyvaig, Grantis that he wes at the taking of the said Ronnald and that he saw Ronnald tak a lr̃e q^{lk} he had vpoun him and put it in his mouth and ryve it in peceis, and the deponner haueing earnesthe delt with Ronnald to get knowledge of the contentis of the lr̃e, he could get no knowledge of the same.

Being demandit gif he wes in the house of Dunyvaig when George Grahame come thair, declaris that he wes absent, and come bak when the pledgeis wer reddy to be deliuerit to George, and he hard the conference betuix Angus oig and George in the heich chalmer of the Castell, quhair George declairit to Angus that he wes send thair be my Lord Chancellor, to get the pledgeis deliuerit and the house randerit to him, and that my Lord Chanceller

promeist to deale with the Kingis Maiestie to procure ane
remissioun to the said Angus and his complices, and to
get yame ane richt of thair landis, and that his L. wald
be cautionair for the said Angus, deponis he saw the
warrand w^{lk} George Giahame deliuerit to Angus, and
that the said George affermed that the warrand wes writtin
and subscriuit be my Lord Chanceller, and he saw George
deliuer the warrand to Angus and the deponer takis it
vpoun his saluatioun that the house of Dunyvaig wald
haif bene deliuerit to the Laird of Caddell wer not
George Grahame's dealeing with Angus oig and his
complices.

Deponis that during the tyme of the assedge the deponer
haueing past fra the Castell to Kintyre in his comeing bak
agane to the Castell he saw Neill M^{c}ky deliuer ane lr̃e
of George Grahame's to ane M^{c}phersone to cary to Angus
and this M^{c}phersone come frome Kintyre in the boit with
the depouner to the Castell of Dunyvaig and thair deliuerit
the lr̃e to Angus, and the deponer hard Angus say that
the contentis of the lr̃e wer, that Angus sould brooke and
keepe still the thing he had whill the said George send him
new adverteisment, and that my Lord Chancelair had
writtin in his fau^{oris} to courte and that his busynes was
lyke to go weill.

Deponis that Angus oig send the deponner to Ronnald
M^{c}angus to demand of him by whose perswasioun or directioun he tooke the house and that Ronnald said to the
deponner that Donald Gorme bastard sone to Sr James
M^{c}donald wes the peiswader and moveair of him to tak
the house, and denyis that euir he demandit of Donald
Gorme gif he wes the perswadair of Ronnald, althocht he
met sindrie tymes thairefter with him in the Castell and
had mony occasionis of conference and speiche with him.
Sic sub^i ALEXANDER M^{c}ALLASTER.[1]

---

[1] 'The Lordis allowis to Angus Oig M'Donald XIIIs. 4d. daylie and to
Allaster M'Allaster M'Tarlich Xs. daylie and to Angus M'Eachan M'Allaster
VIs VIIId daylie and to ilk ane of the uther three prisoneris committit to warde
in the Tolbuithe of Edinburgh Vs. daylie, 24 May 1615' (*P. C. R.*, x. p 330).

87. Copy of George Grahame's lre to Hector McNeill of Tayneis, quhilk lre being produceit and showne to George he acknoulegeit to be his awne lre writtin with his awne hand

Right honourable S^r my most hairtlie dewytie rememberit, as for zo^r kyndnes I will not counter the same w^t ony complementis, becaus thay ar no sure piops of trew freindship, as for newis yow sall haif thame and my opinioun in yor voyage, yow sall vnderstand that I haif ressauit the Castell of Dunnyvaig and hes broght the keyis with me, and hes maid ane cap^ne till my returning bak agane q^lk wilbe quhen god, the King and counsaill pleisis, I haif heir the gentlemen wardo^ris who wer tane thair, I reporte of yow to that gentleman that w^lk I hoip sall wyne yow goode freindship anes or you die, I haif spokin the Lieutennēt and desirit him to stay till my bak comeing or to go with me vp to Courte, and I sould tak the burdyne of his returning on me, bot he will not stay, yitt he will do no thing in the Ile till I send him worde frome the Counsell, also I pray yow, yf yow go ouer be war of yor self and be trew to the gentlemen of the Ile, ffor I protest to yow I find thame weele disposit, yf I had spokin you I had tauld you more of my mynd, quhilk mynd sall studie to do you pleasour and seruice in the least of yor adois q^rin my persone or goodis may availl. So in the best of my affectioun I most hairtilie bid you fairweele restis zo^r assured freind to pouer, Grahame of Eryne. I ressauit the tua lrez quhilkis I directit to Craignes w^lk yow did send doun, for thay wer not delyuerit.

88. Copie of the depositionis of Robert Winrahame and Katherene Campbell tane the **23** day of May 1615

At Edinburgh in presence of my Lord Secretair, Thesaurer depute and aduocat

Robert Winrahame, Ila herauld, sworne, deponis that

he being vpoun his voyage towardis Ila for chairgeing of
the Castell of Dunyvaig to be randerit, and haveing in
his company the prior of Ardchattan, thay mett with
Duncane Campbell of Danna and George Grahame in the
Ile of Jura, quhair the prior spak with thame, and tauld
the deponner that thay wald go with thame to Ila, and
concur with the deponer and do the best officeis they
could for recouerie of the house, and depones that contrair to thair promeis thay eschewit the deponeris company and past away in the nicht, sua that the deponner
mett not with the said George Grahame quhill vpoun
sonday thairefter within fyve myllis of the house of
Dunyvaig in Ila the deponner is of opinioun that George
had bene at the place of Dunyvaig the nicht befoie, and
deponnes that when he mett with George Grahame the said
George aduisit the deponer to stay and not to go fordwart
to the house becaus it wes the sabboth day, saying vnto
the deponner, that the counsaill wald be offendit with him
gif he past fordwart in that cirand, to quhome the deponner
ansuerit I am imployit in his Maties seruice and will do
that q^{lk} is concredite vnto me, bot gif zow haif ony cōmis-
sioun.or warrand to stay me, I will obey, and the said
George in ane anger replyit and sayd I wilbe better hard
with the counsaill nor you wilbe, and gif you go fordwart
at this tyme you sall spill the haill eirand, and thair wilbe
mekle blood spilt, and yor folye wilbe the wyte of it, and
the prior of Ardchattan heiring the said George vnseamelie
langwage, he withdrew him and fand fault with him, and
than George w^t Duncane of Danna come to the deponner
and promeist that vpoun the morne thay wald accumpany
the deponner to the Castell, and they trystit to meit the
deponner about daylicht bot thay keipit no^t the tryist,
the deponer with the prior haueing awaitit vpoun yame
quhill xi ho^{ris} afore none at q^{lk} tyme the deponer advisit
the said prior to go foidwart for he looked for litle good
of George Grahame, quhairvpoun the deponner with the
prior come fordwart vpoun foote towardis the Castell,
the wind being contrair to yame sua that thay could not
go be sea, and haueing approcheit the Castell within twa

myllis, the said George Grahame and Duncane Campbell
followit and ouertooke the deponner vpoun horsbak, and
lichtit frome thair horse, and the deponner desyrit and
cõmandit yame in his Maiesteis name to stay w^t him and
to assist him in his Maiesteis seruice, and to defend him
frome harame, bot thay disdaneing that chairge past
directlie fra the deponner towardis the Castell, and to the
company who had isheit out thairof being fourty personis
in nomber as the deponer thinkis and thay wer in thrie
companyis, quhairof Angus Oig M^{c}donnald had one company, Coill M^{c}gillespik ane vther company, and the thrid
company stayed about the Castell, and concerning the
rest, he referris him to his executioun and indorsatioun
vpoun the bak of his lrēz. Sic subscribitur R. Wynrahame.

Katherine Campbell hir depositioun

Katherine Campbell [1] spous to Angus oig M^{c}donald
sworne and demandit quhat directioun hir housband
gaif to Duncan Campbell of Danna when he came to Ed^r
after the taking of the bischop of the Iles his pledgeis,
depones that scho knowis no thing of hir faderis being in
Edinburgh at that tyme, and that hir father neuir reveillit to hir that he had bene in Edinburgh and depones
that afore euir scho saw George Grahame hir husband and
George had aggreit vpoun the conditionis of deliuerie of
the pledgeis and deponeis that hir father haueing come to
the Castell of Dunyvaig with George Grahame, scho wes
offendit with hir fader becaus he come in George company
and refuisit to latt him haif entrie within the Castell and
directit him to ane cottoun neirby and sent some prouisioun out of the Castell to him, and deponis that vpoun
the morne thairefter sho mett with hir fader vpoun the
craigis ewest to the Castell and that hir fader tauld to
hir that the Laird of Caddell wes to come as lieutennent
frome the king to persew the house, and scho apprehending

---

[1] Daughter of Campbell of Danna.

that the warrand q^{lk} George Grahame producit in name of my Lord Chancellcr wes mair availlable than ony cōmissioun or warrand the Laird had. That the haill company within the house consentit to hir opinioun in that poynte, and deponis that quhen the herauld come to chairge the housc the said George his opinioun and aduise wes that some men micht be send out of the house, to advise the herauld to stay, and gif he wald not be stayed, to force him to stay.

Demandit gif ony lr͂ez come to hir housband frw George Grahame efter the Castell wes inclosit be the Laird of Caddell, deponis that scho remembcris that in that tyme thair come ane lr͂ez frome George Grahame to hir husband adviscing him to keepe the house and noway to rander the same quhill he ressauit advertisement frome the Lord Chanceller at the leist to keepe it quhill Fasteinsevin and deponis that George Grahame delyuerit this lre to Neill McKay, and that Neill delyuerit the lr͂e to M^cphersane who deliuerit the same to hir husband.

Declaris that the lr͂e q^{lk} Sr Olipher Lambert send to hir husband wes immediatlie directit and send be hir husband to George Grahame be Neill McKay and that no ansuer wes send bak be George bot that q^{lk} scho deponit in hir former depositioun.

Demandit quhat could haue movit hir husband to truste George Grahame his word mair nor his Maiesteis cōmissioun grantit to the Laird of Caddell and to Sr Olipher Lambert whome thay saw assisted with the kingis forceis of Scotland and Ireland and with his Maiesteis schippis, cannoun and mvnitioun, and chairges to the detenairis to delyver the house in the Kingis name, q^{lk} thay refuisit, and truisted George Grahame's worde better nor thair warrandis, Ansuer, that George Grahame declairit to hir husband in pñce of all the rest of the men that wer in the house of Dunyvaig and in hir awne heiring, that Archibald Campbell haueing informit his Maicstie that the haill houssis in the Ile of Ila being brint and distroyit, the goodis reft and slane and the poore inhabitantis so beggerit be the violence of the Clandonald as thair wes no cloathis

left vpoun thame, bot the Ile all uterlie distroyit and
layed waist, that thairby he movit the Kingis Maiestie to so
grite angir that in his wraith he had gevin his cōmissioun
to the Laird of Caddell and Sr Olipher Lambert to persew
yame within the house, bot gif thay wald deliver to the
said George Grahame the house and pledgeis that my
Lord Chancellair wald do for thame and be cautioun for
thame, and gif neid wer wald go to courte and travell
in thair effairis, or gif he could not haif lasure to go, that
he wald direct the said George to go to courte to deale
for thame and to procure vnto yame ane remissioun for
bigaines, and suirtie of y^r awne antient possessionis for
payment of the auld dewtie.

Deponis that Donald Gorme bastard sone to Sr James
McDonald was the speciall persone that perswadit Ronnald
M^{c}angus to tak the house of Dunyvaig, and the deponer
hard that Donald Gorme and Ronnald M^{c}angus wer vpoun
this conference in Irland in Sr Ronnald M^{c}sorlis boundis,
bot declairis vpoun hir grite aith that scho neuir hard that
Sr Ronnald wes preuey to these materis, and sayis that
Ronnald wes keepit in ye irenis q^{ll} he confest who movit
him to tak the house.

Demandit, seing hir husband wes so curious to vndirstand of Ronnald Oig by quhais aduise and perswasioun
he wes movit to tak the house, and seing Ronnald confest
that Donald Gorme wes the perswader of him to tak it,
quhairfore wes he not als curious to vndirstand and try
of Donald Gorme vpoun what occasioun he had movit
Ronnald to tak the house, and quhat freindseip and assistance expectit in that eirand, deponis that hir husband
delt with Donald in that mater bot Ronnald [*sic* Donald ?]
refuisit and denyit that euir he had gevin ony aduise to
Ronnald thairin. Sic subscribitur Katherine Campbell.

Anent the cōmissioun send be Malcolme McNeill to hir
husband w^t eune M^{c}writtie, sho is conforme to hir husbandis
depositioun in that poynte and knowis no thing thairof,
bot be hir husbandis reporte and declaratioun maid to
hir, and anent the lfē send be Hector McNeill to hir husband
sho knowis no thing bot be hir husbandis reporte.

89. At Edinburgh the xxiii day of Maij 1615 in
pñce of my Lord of Binning, secretair, the
thesaurair depute and aduocat

Angus Oig Mᶜdonald being deiplie sworne and demandit
yf the tua depositionis formarlie maid be him, and quhilkis
wer produceit and showne vnto him and red in his pñce
wer trew as they ar writtin, sett doun and subscryuit be
him, deponis that he acknowlegeis the depositionis to be his
awne depositionis and that thay ar trew, and he abydis
be the same in euery pointe.

Demandit yf he wes vpoun the counsell foirknoulege,
plott or devise of the first intaking of the Castell of Dunn-
vaig be Ronnald Oig Mᶜangus callit his bastard bruther,
denyis the same.

Demandit how he can cleir him self of that mater seeing
the house wes tane in be his awne bastard bruther, and
recouerit agane be him self wᵗ litle or no pane or travell,
and·seeing he had slayne foure of the said Ronnald his
company who wer wᵗ him in the house, feareing that thay
sould haif discouerit and reveillit his awne dealing with
Ronnald in that mater, and had reservit the said Donald
alyve and sufferit him to eschaip after xv dayis imprisonment, and sccing his awne behaviour and cariage sensyne
in keeping and deterring the house aganis his Maᵗᵉˡˢ lieutennent, argues his guyltynes of the first surprise and
taking of the house deponis as of befoir that he knew
nothing of Ronnaldis doingis in that mater and that
Ronnald had no advise, counsell, nor directioun frome
him to tak in the house.

Demandit yf he askit of Ronnald be whose directioun he
tooke in the house, deponis that he askit that questioun
of Ronald who ansuerit to him that Donald Gorme bastard
sone to Sʳ James Mᶜdonald wes the intysair of him to tak
in the house.

Demandit yf he inquirit at Donald Gorme yf he had
gevin ony suche advise or directioun to Ronnald, deponis
that he speirit that questioun at Donald Gorme who confest

to him that he had aduysit the said Ronnald to tak in the
house, and grantis that the said Donald wes in the house
with the deponner comeing and ganging at his pleasour
fra the tyme that the house wes recouerit fra Ronnald
M^cangus vntill the day that his Ma^{teis} remissioun wes pñtit
to, the deponner and his companie and refuisit be thame.

Deponis that when the deponner hard that the Kingis
Ma^{teis} herauld wes comeing to charge the house, George
Grahame wes pñt with the deponner at the house, and the
deponner askit of George what wes fittest to be done, to
whome George ansuerit yf the herauld see my face he dar
not come fordwart to charge the house, I will go to him
and stay him, and sayis that George past agaitward a
litle space towardis the herauld, and then come bak and
desirit to be accompanyit with three or foure men, wher-
upoun Coill McGillespik w^t some three or foure otheris
past with the said George to the herauld, and the deponner
hard that thair wes some evill language betuix thame,
and deponis that George Grahame advisit the deponner
to send foure men to a hill neirby to await vpoun the
herauld and to stay him to come fordwart, and yf he wald
not be stayit to slay him, bot the deponner mislykit his
advise and counsell in that poynte, and deponis that
Allastir M^cinvoir and Donald M^callaster wrek wer pñt
and hard thir speecheis betuix the deponner and George
Grahame anent the herauld.

Deponis that the said George Grahame come to the
deponner vpoun ane satterday in the moirning and desirit
the deponner in my lord Chancellaris name to rander the
house to him, and he tauld to the deponner, that yf he
refuisit to rander the house, that the herauld wald come
and charge him to rander the same, bot he said that the
herauld wes not imployit nor directit in that earand be
his Ma^{teis} counsell, bot be the laird of Caddell, for the
laird wald gett als mony herauldis for money as he pleasit
to imploy in suche charges,[1] and deponis forder that the

---

[1] The venality of the seventeenth-century English heralds in genealogical matters
was notorious. But it may be doubted whether in Scotland heralds could be
hired as here suggested.

said George said to the deponner, that yf he randerit not
the house to him, thair wald come forceis oute of Irland
to persew the house, bot he said that thir forceis wald not
be directit be the Kingis Maiestie, bot that they wald be
gottin be the moyen and procurement of the laird of
Caddell and of Archibald Campbell, and that Archibald
wes directit for that effect to Irland, and George said
forder to the deponner that he had a warrand bothe to
stay the lieutennent and the forceis frome Yrland.

Demandit yf George Grahame affermed to the deponner
and his complices that the instructionis w[lk]is he shew to
thame wer vnder my lord Chancellaris hand ansueris that
George affermed the same and produceit the saidis instructionis writtin as the said George affermed w[t] my lard
Chancellaris hand.

Demandit yf the said George desirit the deponner and
his complices to keepe and detene the house till he returnit w[t] my lord Chancellaris directioun to him or till
he send him new worde, ansueris that the said George
desirit the deponner to do sua.

Demandit yf the said George said to the deponner that
he had a wairand to stay the lieutennent to come fordwart,
and to stay his Ma[tels] forceis and cannoun to come frome
Irland, ansueris, that George said to the deponner, that
he had a warrand to stay the lieutennent, and yf he, to
witt the said George gatt obedyence that the counsaill
vpoun his reporte of the obedience gevin to him wald
write to Irland and stay the haill preparatioun maid for
this earand and discharge his Ma[tels] lieutennent and
armey to come to Ila.

Demandit quhidder yf after the Laird of Caddell had in-
cloisit the house of Dunnyvaig the said George write ane
lře to the deponner willing him not to gif ouer the house
till he come bak to the deponner and broght him ansuer
of all his affairis ; Ansueris that the said George Grahame
write ane lře of that tenno[r] q[lk] boore alsua that my lord
Chancellair had send vp the deponnaris petitioun in a
pacquett writtin with the bischop of the Ilis sone, and
sayis that this lře wes delyuerit be George Grahame to

Neil McKay poist who gaif it to Mcphersone and Mcphersone delyuerit the same to the deponner belevis that his awne wyffe, allaster Mccarlyt and Hector Mccaus hard the lře red.

Demandit yf he send to George Grahame the lře that Sr Olipher Lambert send to him, chargeing him in the Kingis name to rander the house of Dunnyvaig, Grantis the same, and that he write ane lře of his awne to my Lord Chancellor declaireing that he haueing delyuerit the house to George Grahame in his Lops. name he lippynnit not to haif bene troublit after this maner, and thairfoir desirit my lord outher to tak the house af his hand, or to send him directioun what he sould do anent the delyuerie of the same.

Demandit what ansuer he gatt of this lře, deponis that gatt no ansuer frome my Lord Chancellair, bot that Neill McKay haueing caryed Sr Olipher Lambertis lře and the deponnaris lře to the Chanceller and haueing delyuerit the same to George Grahame, he broght bak frome George to the deponner the said George lře befoir mentionat wlk Mcphersone hes away with him.

Demandit what commissionis or lřez he ressauit frome his brother Sr James befoir the intaking of the house of Dunnyvaig or during the keeping thairof, Ansueris that all that he ressauit contenit perswasionis to rander the house to thame who wer directit be his Maiestie to ressaue the same.

Demandit yf George Grahame wes permittit to see thair prouisionis of victuall and poulder and how lang he stayed in thair company within the house of Dunnyvaig, Ansueris that he stayed bot ane night disionit wt the deponner the nixt day, and that he nowayes saw thair poulder nor quantitie thairof, becaus it wes lockit in ane kist quhairof the deponnaris wyffe had the key, and that thay had no more bot tua barreills of poulder ather of thame cōtening xii stane of poulder and some litle poulder wlk the soiouris had in thair poulder baggis, Grantis that thay wer reasonablie prouidit with victuallis suche as beiff, maill, butter and cheis, and had no drink bot watter.

Demandit vpoun his grite oathe yf he knawis that ony grite[1] man in this kingdome hes had ony purpois or dealing in the materis of Ila, or concerning the same in ony poynte, deponis that he being duelland in Arross in the last sommer after the intaking of the house, and being accustomat sometymes for his recreatioun to tak a hacquebute and to shoite at foullis, and being one day vpoun the feildis with his hacquebute in his hand, he persavis ane boit approtcheing neir the shoir, and the deponner past to the shoir syde to see who wes in the boit, and thair wes within her Ewne M^cwrittie who duellis in Giga ane auld man of lx yeiris, and the deponner haueing askit of him what newis he had, quhairfra he wes come, and yf the erll of Ergyle wes gone oute of Kintyre, the said Ewne ansuerit, that the erll wes gone oute of Kintyre, and that the said Ewne his earand thair wes to the deponner, and he said to the deponner that Malcolme McNeill vncle to Hector McNeill of Tawneishe had directit the said Ewne to the deponnair to tell him that he being in Kintyre with the erll of Ergyll, he hard some conference and speeche in the erlis house and company anent the taking, detenning and delyuerie of the house of Dunnyvaig, and he hard the erll say, that he wes feared that this deponner and his freindis wald gif ouer the house, and yf thay did it, and gaif ouer the house, that it wald turne to thair vtter wrak, and the said Malcolme haueing askit of the erll yf he might reveill that to the deponner, the erll ansuerit that he might without skaithe or periell reveill the same, and said that he had purpoislie spokin these wordis to the effect the same might be reveillit and tauld to the deponner and that the erll desirit the said Malcolme, outher to go in psone, or then to direct some trustie freind to reveill and tell this to the deponner.

Deponis forder that about ane moneth afoir the Erll of Ergyll his last comeing to Kintyre, Hector McNeill in Carskeigh in Kintyre, send ane l^{re} to the deponner w^t Donald M^cconnoyll in Ila, desiring the deponner to appoint

---

[1] *Vide ante,* p 201.

some tryist and meeting w^t him in the Ile of Cara [1] quhair
thay might confer togidder, ffor he had some message fra
the Erll of Ergyll to the deponner w^{lk} he wald reveill and
showe to him at meeting, and the deponner returnit bak
ansuer w^t the said Donald and appointit the tyme and
place of thair meeting to be in the Ile of Cara, and the
deponner at the appointit tyme for the tryist send ane
boit to the Ile to see yf Hector had keept tryist, bot Hector
come not thair, and the deponner hes not seene him sensyne nor hes had no intelligence w^t him be worde, write
nor messege sensyne.   Sic subscribitur Angus og M^{c}donald.

90. Archibald Campbell [2] to Lord Binning

(Received 29 *May* 1615)

RIGHT HONORABELL—As I writt to zour lo. from the
Wode of Meffen,[3] Sir James M^{c}coneill and McRanald [4] went
by that way ; and, as I was informed, he had stayed Wednisday night and Thursday in Murthlie. So I, heaving
riddin Wednisday night and Thursday all day, I wachit
at Murthlie all that night, bot thay maid no stay thair :
Bot McRanald sent a man of his for a zoung boy of his
awin that he had in Murthlie, and convoyed him with him.
On Wodnisday, at night, they were in a pure man's house
in Strabrane ; and on Thursday, at night, thay wer in
the East end of Ranoch, quhair I might haue bene sex
houris before thame, gif I had bene sartane of thair, way.
The Erle of Atholl was advertised by the Erle of Mar, and
he followed thame.   And on Fryday, in the morning, com
in sight of thame ; bot my lordis men had run so far, and
his spayis that went before him so wnprovedent, that Sir
Jeames and his companie wer advertised be Strowan [5] his
wyf, quho is McRanald his dochter. They wer forssed

---

[1] A small island off Kintyre immediately south of Gigha.
[2] Brother of Lawers (cf. *ante*, p. 156, note 1).
[3] Methven, near Perth.
[4] Allaster M'Ranald of Keppoch.
[5] Robertson of Strowan.

to leive thair horssis and clothes, and teake thame to the wodis. The Erle of Atholl apprehendit Sir Jeames his man, that was with him in the Castell, and quho stayed efter him in the Castell that morning he brake ward, and too men of McRanaldis; bot my lord tels me he dismust thame all. My lord, so far as I culd learne, the Earle was exceiding willing in this persute, bot thair was sum wronge done him, that I believe his lo. as zit knows not of. Those that I send to be before thame ar not as zit returned, nor no word from thame. I hope in God zour lo. sall heir that thay haue mett; for thay can hardlie pas by thame. The Erle of Atholl assuris me that thair cam a compane of men to meit McRanald. My lord, if thay wer bot too hunder men and ane honest commander on the feildis, they wer not cabell to do any thing be land; nor could thay haue tyme to mowe any to follow thame: Bot in treuth, if thay be permittit, they will no dout grow stronge. Sir Jeames man that the Erle of Atholl apprehendit, told, that thay resoluit to burne Cadell his landis of Mukarne [1]; and that he thoght a grait many Illenderis ver on thair course. My lord, so schune as I heir from those I derectit eftir thame, and that I kno quhat course Sir Jeames teakis first in hand, or quhich way he teakis him to the seie, I will, God willing, returne; not douting bot my lord Thesaurer will haue some considerasioun of my peans, as I sall be reddie at all occasions to adventur my self in his Maties scruice; I rest—Zour lo. ewer to serue zow,

AR. CAMPBELL.

From the Furd of Lyon this Setterday
at xij houris of that day.

I pray your lo. adverteise Cadell, that he may send word to his men of Mackarney, to be war of the rebels.

To the right honorabell, and my speseall good lord
My Lord of Binning, Secreter, &c.

---

[1] Muckairn pertained to the Abbot of Iona before the Reformation.

91. Sir James Macdonald [1] to the Earl of Caithnes

MY VERIE HONOURABLE GUD [LORD]—Feiring that your lo., to whose fauor I am so much ob[l]ishid, suld not mistaik the caus of this my last offence, in braicking of Ward, I have beine this bauld to vrytt to your lo. the only mosion quhilk, I protest to God, maid me to braik Ward. It is trew, my lord, thatt the Laird of Calder said to honest men, wha can beir record, thatt how soever my pairt was anent Donnoveg, zett he had ane Wariand past be his Ma^tes hand, quhilkis the Consall saw nott, to command the Consall, presently efter the sicht of thatt Warrand, to putt me to exsecutioun; and how lyttill resone I had to trust my lyfe to Calder, your lo. self and vthers of the Counsall knawis; for, be his misreport, he did all he culd to have perallid my lyfe. And this trewly was the caus I fled with my avin lyfe, and for no mistrust I had in his Ma^tes clemence, or in the Consallis fawor; nor zett, for oney feir I had off oney thing thay culd try aganes me, anentt Dunoveg; for as I said when I was in ward, I will say now; God is my vittnes, my pairtt, ever, anent the taiking or keiping of Dunoveg aganes his Ma^te, hes beine ever most honest and lyall; and efter all just tryall, I will defy my onfreindis prive vtherwayis. And sence the braik of Waird I maid with the Lord Maxvell, by my exspectatione, to this night I brak Ward last, be God him self, I was never privie nor a consenter to aney Plott aganes his Ma^te or my cuntre, I mein his Ma^tes dominions. And now, seing my braik of Ward was nott, as God is my judge, for no desyre of Rebelion, nor no vther desing, bott only for saiftie of my avin puir lyfe, I will most humblé beseik your lo. speik such as is your freindis in Consall, thatt his Ma^te micht be moveid, nott to tak no heste or violent curse aganis me, onto the tyme thatt thair lo^s will heir my

---

[1] Apprehending with good reason that through the machinations of Calder, his own brother-in-law, his life was in danger, Sir James Macdonald had succeeded in escaping from Edinburgh Castle in the end of May. For his own justification he wrote to several persons of importance letters which are here printed.

Peticione.   And give your lo. will gett me that fawor that my Peticion salbe hard, and thatt oney whom I sall send with my Letters to zour lo. sall not be trubled ; and I being advertesid by your lo., I will, be your lo[ls] advyse do aney thing thatt may best satisfie his Ma[tie] and Consall ; my lyfe, and the lyfis of these thatt helpid to saif my lyfe being saiff.—So, with the rememberance of my humble deute, I rest, Your lo[ls] puir freind euer to serve yow,

S[R] J. MAKDONALL.

To my verie honourable gud lord, my Lord Erle of Caitthnes.

92. The same to the Earl of Tullibardin

MY VERIE HONORABLE GUD LORD—Treuly the tyme hes beine, when I wald never a luiked thatt your father sone suld persew me so hardly of my lyfe ; for I protest I was never so hardly followed ; and was so neir tane, thatt your lo. self, and sum few with you, was within thre pair to me. Bot I am much oblist to zour lo. for in faith ze maid me to be ane better fuitt-man, in one hour, nor I thocht to hawe beine in ane zeir.   Allwayis, seing itt was his Ma[tes] service your lo. did, I forgiwe you with my hartt ; and I wish att God, my self had the place to serve his Ma[te], quhilk in my hartt I sall ever do.   And this offence quhilk I have now committitt, I protest to God, is nott for desyre of trubles or Rebellion, nether for oney mistrust I had in his Ma[tes] clemencé, or his honourable Consall, nor zett throw feir of aney thing thatt can be tryed aganes me, anent thatt crand of Dwnoveg ; bot as God knawis, my braiking Ward was only for the saifté of my lyfe, for it is sertan, and I will gett veré honest wittnessis, to whom the Laird of Calder said itt, thatt he had ane Warrand from his Ma[te], quhilk the Consall never sawe, for to put me to present exsecutione, efter the presenting of thatt Warrand ; so thatt my lyffe was in Calder's will ; and how lytill resone I had to trust to Calder, pairt of the Consall self knawis ; for not only all vther vrganis he did me, he vrett both to his Ma[te], and vthers att Court and in Consall,

shawing, I was giltie both of the taiking and keiping of
Dunoveg, that thairby my lyfe micht be tane. Bott now
that the warld may se his mailish, whan I am, as I hop in
God, out of his denger, I will say to zour lo., as I sall ansver
to God, I am and was ever as inosent of the taiking or
keiping of Dvnveg aganes his Ma^te as zour lo. is ; and when
all is tryid, I defy my onfreindis to try vtherwayis, be oney
just tryell. And thairfoir, seing, efter such long miseré, and
the loss of all my kyndly lands,[1] I bott only fled with my
awin lyfe, I hop the Consall will evin pité me. And I
beseik your lo. to be my freind, so far as ze may, without
offence to his Ma^te ; only, in moveing your freinds in
Consall nott to be over hesté, att ze desyre of my onfreindis,
to tak oney violent cursis aganes me, whairbé thay may
gett preferment, and cairis nott what may follow, in
exspence to his Ma^te, or truble in the cuntré ; quhilk sall
nott be neidfull : For, give your lo. will gett me an assurance, that his Ma^te honourable Consall will heir the same,
I will give in such ane humble Peticione to thair lo^s in
fullfilling his Ma^tes will, and thair lo^s in aney thing posebill
to me ; my lyfe and liberté being only reservid : And
give his Ma^te dispence with my lyfe, and offences, sall mak
gud suirté to truble no man, by ordour off law. So luiking
for your lo^s ansuer, be the Barron Rid's meins,[2] commiting
your lo. in God's protextion, I rest, Your lo^is assuired
freind to command, S. J. MAKDONALL.

Junij 2.

To my verie honourable gud lord, my lord Erle off
Tullibairne.

93. The same to the Bishop of the Isles

MY VERIE GUD LORD—I doutt nott bott, or now, your
lo. hes hard of my braiking of Ward ; and the only caus
quhilk maid me ventour the same, quhilk, as God knawis,
was for no vther caus bott only for the saifte of my lyfe,

---

[1] *E.g.* Kintyre and Isla.
[2] Robertson of Straloch alias Reid (Ruadh).

quhilk the Laird of Calder said was in his will only. All-wayis, prais to God, I am out of Calder's denger; and zett, give be oney meines I may have his Ma^tes gracius pardon to my self and these gentill men that asisted me, I will latt your lo. se his Ma^te commodite sall novayis be impaired, the pace of the contrie sall novayis be trublid, nor his Ma^te putt to no chargis, be giveing imployment to the Cambellis, wha crawis ever to fish in drwmly watters; and thairfoir, I pray your lo. deill with his Ma^te and Consall, for a continewatioun of oney violent curse to be tane be his Ma^te aganis me, ontill yow may gett one of your avin to cum to me; and with thatt man, or with your lo. self, give I know how to sie you, I sall send such Offers as I hop sall content his Ma^te and Consall. So, as my trest is and was ever in your lo., I pray you vryt to me, what I may luik for? As for that erand of Dwnveg, God is my vittnes, I am inosent thairof; and I pray your lo. try that erand, as geve I war in ward; and I trest ze will find my pairtt honest.—So, luiking zour lo. ansver, I committ you to God; and rest, Your lo^is ever att command,

Sr J. MAKDONALL.

Junij 3.

I pray your lo. gett me Lisence to send ane man or boy with my Letters to your lo.

To my verie gud Lord, my lord Bishop off the Iyllis and Rapho.[1]

94. The same to the Privy Council

MY VERIE HONOURABLE GUD LORDS—Pleis zour lo^s, my offence in braiking ward suld mak me loth to presume to vrytt vnto zour lo^s, zett, feiring the mosioun quhilk maid me to eschep suld be otherwayis thocht be zour lo^s nor the trewth of my intencion, I am this bauld to deleaitt wnto zour lo^s the only caus quhilk maid me to braik ward; and this is itt. The Laird of Calder said to twa sewerall honest gentillmen, thatt how soever my tryall past anent

---

[1] *Vide ante*, p. 104, note I.

the erand of Dwnoveg, zett he had ane Warand, in his
avin kciping, past be his Ma^te quhilk the Consall novayis
did sie, commanding, immediatly efter the presenting
thairof to putt me to exsecutione, butt farther proses [1];
and so, my lyfe as it war gevin be his Ma^te over in the
hands of him wha had not only medlid with my kyndly
lands, my frends lyfes, and withall the only man who re-
portid warst of my self, to haue gottin my lyfe with my
lands, the only feir thairof maid me flie with my lyfe, and
no desire of Rebelion; nether aney mistrust I had of his
Ma^tes clemencie, nor of your lo^s favor; nether wald I
braik ward for oney thing (they) culd try aganes me, anent
the erand of Dunoveg; for God is my vittness I am
mosent thairof. And I beseik zour lo^s try the same, as
giwe I war in ward to be accusid, and I trest your lo^s sall
find my pairt, in all that buissines, honest and loyall.
And now I will, in all humilyté, beseik zour lo^s to pité my
cace, and grant me thatt fauor as to suffer me to send in
ane humble Peticione to zour lo^s, be the quhilk I hop to
give such satisfaction to his Ma^te and zour lo^s as I may
best, to satisfe his Ma^tes will and your lo^s in all thingis, my
avin lyfe and these wha hes assisted me being saiffe. And,
in the meintyme praye your lo^s most humblé, befoir I
be hard, not to wis oney wiolent curse aganes me, ether
to putt his Ma^te to exspenceis, and me to disparatione.
So, beseiking the grett God to move his Ma^tes hartt and
your lo^s to pité me, according to the intencione I have to
be ane paceable man, with the assuirance of my lyfe;
only luiking your lo^s will latt me knaw what fawor I may
luik for, commiting your lo^s in Gods proteStione, I humbly
taks my live, and rests, Your lo^s humble servitour,

S^R J. MAKDONALL.

Junij 3.

To my verie honourable gud Lords, my Lord Chancellar
    of Scotland, and the remenent of his Ma^tes honour-
    able Privie Consall.

---

[1] No doubt in respect of the old sentence of 1609 (*vide ante*, p 92)

95. The same to the Earl of Crawford

My verie honorable gud Lord—It may be zour lo.
think it streng thatt I obscuirid my intencioun of braiking
Ward, fra your lo. in regair of our luif and familiarité; zett
I hop your lo. will exscuis me. For the reveilling thairof to
your lo. micht do zou hairme, being whan ze ar, and no
furtherance to my intencione. Allwayis, as God sall
judge my saul, my braiking ward was nott throw aney
mistrust I had in his Ma^tis clemencé, nor in the Consalls
fawor, nor zett for feir of oney thing culd try aganes me,
anent thatt treson of Dunoveg; bott the only thing which
moued me was only thatt I was credably informid, be
honest men, thatt Calder said it to (thame), thatt howso-
ever the crand of Dunoveg zed, he had ane Warand past be
his Ma^te thatt com never in the Consallis sicht, commanding
to put me to exsecutione, immediatly efter the presenting
thairof. Your lo. self and M^cintois micht heir James
Movat [1] say this; bott my authors ar better nor James.
Allwayis, as I said aft to zour lo. self, when I was in ward,
I will now say; thatt as God sall judge my saule, I was
nevir airt nor pairt of the taking or keiping of Dunoveg
aganes his Ma^te, nor of no vther plaitt, sence the braik of
ward that I maid with the Lord Maxvel till now, and give
efter such long miscré of imprisonment, lose of lands, and
kin, my braiking ward for the saifté of my lyfe, be thocht
be ze sensuir of my onfrendis, such ane offence as will not
be pardonid, I most tak pacience; for I am better now,
prais to God, nor as I was; and I will, as long as I live,
pray for his Ma^te long and prosperus regne. Zett, seing
give I be crost now, it cumis moir be my onfreinds nor be
his Ma^te, albeitt I will never preis to liue long in his Ma^tes
dominions, by his hienes ovin will, altho I micht; I wow
to God, or I liwe the contré, I, and moir nor I, sall ether
lose our lyfes, or than I sall, God willing, liwe ane rememberance to my onfreinds; I mein only sik of the Cambellis

---

[1] Calder's doer (*vide ante*, p. 175, note 1)

as wilbe my onfreinds, thatt itt salbe hard of when both
they and I is deid and gone ! I hop, to thair small com-
modité : Bott I had rather gett liwe to live in pace, and
find gud suirté for my obedience and gud ordour. I wish
to God, with his Ma^{tes} contentment, zour lo. war ane fré
man, both for your avin weill and the weill of zour freindis ;
and seing itt lyis in your avin hand, better be fré nor liwe
thair with sik crosis as I knaw men will have in thatt
place. I heir maney of the Keipers of thatt Castell ar
putt in ward, for my braik ; bott, as God sall judge me,
thair was nane of the keipers of thatt Castell that ever I
thocht to mak privé to my desing. I protest to God, I
love the gud Constable and all thatt is thair. I haitt none
of thame ; bott I culd nott bott love my self befor. Thair
is nane withhn thatt Castell to whom I am adebted, that
salbe oney wayis intrest be me, if God grant me his Ma^{tes}
pace. I desyre Petie Gilcrist keip my stare.[1] Remember on
our last discourse, thatt same nicht I braik ward, anent
Margarett.[2] Sik newis as may nott be thocht offencesive,
I pray your lo. vrytt to me. My Lord Tuillibairne and
the men of Atholl, on that Fryday, after I brak waird,
persewid me so hardly, thatt I was almost tane. We lost
our hors, and all our clais. His lo. maid me to gett mair
speid on fuitt, in one hour, nor I thocht to have gottin in
ane zeir, give sik sudent medesin had nott bein aplyid to
me. Liewing to truble your lo. with longer discurse,
wishing zow ever all happines, I rest, Your lo^s avin euer
to command,   S^R J. Makdonall.

I pray your lo. as ze do vther thingis, lovse my mvntour [3]
fra Pettfindie, for 48 lib ; and get my buiks fra him, and
fra Elizabeth Gib. Sho hes twa buiks. Commend me to
Christiene. When your lo. vrytis to me, send itt to my
Lord Tullibairne' to be sent to me. For sum of your lo^s

---

[1] Or stane, probably an ornament
[2] His wife, Margaret Campbell, sister of Calder. At his trial in 1609 she sat
beside him when he was deserted by all others, including actually his counsel,
Mr John Russell, Advocate.
[3] Watch   Fr. *montre*.

avin particullar, I wald glaidly sé your man William Rattra, or oney of zours; the erand tuichis only zour self.

To my verie honourable gud lord, my lord Erle of Crawfuird.

96

Octauo Junij 1615

Information and aduertesment beeng send from the citie of Glasgow that Coill Makgillespik with four score broken hieland men assisted with a bark and some birlinges had taken the seas and lay betweene the coastes of Scotland and Yreland awaiting the opportunitie and meanes to robbe his Maiesties subiectes in there course betweene the two kingdomes, and that they had alreddie melled with a ship of Glasgow, had slayne some of the equippage and made pryse of her loadning; the counsale heervpone wrote to the borrowes of Air, Glasgow, Irving, Renfrew and Dunbartane willing them to send there cōmissionares heir, instructed to giue there aduyse and oppinion to the counsall, how thir rebelles might be suppressed, what shippes they thought fittest to be imployed in that earrand, what nomber of soioures was requisite for the seruice, and what there pay, charges and expenses would extend to, and what burden they would vndertak thame selues in this mater, seeing the same did most neirlie and propperlie concerne thame at there compeereance before the counsale. They first gaue ane generall answere that the mater concerned the whole estate and borrowes alswell as thame, and that they could tak no dooing therein be thame selues, Bot they beeng vrged to answere particularlye to the heades of the missiue send to thame from the counsall, thay gaue in there answere in wrotte,[1] whitch beeng redd and considdered by the counsale they thoght meete that his Maiestie should be acquented therewith, and the same is heerewith send vpe to be showene to his Maiestie.

---

[1] The next document, No. 97.

The Larde of Lundy, brother to the erle of Ergyle wes lykwyse send for, to resolue the counsall what burdyn he wold vndertak in his brotheres absence to keepe his boundes and countryis frie of the rebelles of Ila especialie of Sir James M^cdonald and his complices, Lundy excoosed him selue as haueing no charge from his brother in these affaires, and that he could do no forder but to wrote to his brotheres balyees to do there dewtees in persute of the rebelles yf they come in his boundes. This beeng thoght no good answere whereby the earle of Ergyles boundes might be assuired from ayding of the rebelles or that the rebelles might be persewed yf they come there, therefore the counsale homelie entreates his Maiestie to speak with the earle of Ergyle in this bussines, and to move him other to come home to attend and keepe his owne boundes and countrey, or then to lay the burden thereof on some speciall gentlman of powar, credite and frendship who will vndertake to the counsall to be ansuerable for his whole boundes.

The Larde of Caddell hes vndertaken to be answerable for Ilae, in such forme and maner as the remanent landeslordes of the Ylles, ar haldin to answere for there boundes, and yf the rebelles come there, he sayes he sall not complaine nor crave no assistance from his Maiestie nor his counsale whill first he prove his owne powar and forces againes thame. And tuitching the Castle of Dunyveg he vndertakes to be answerable for the sure keeping thereof.

There wes a petition [1] geven in to the counsall in name of certane barrones and gentlemen cautioneres and creditoures for the erle of Ergyll complaneing of the gryte distress and trouble whitche they vnderly for his caus not only by the want of there owne proper moneyes lent and advanced by thame to him for non payment whairof he is denvnced and regrate at the horne Bot they ar compelled as cautioneres for him to pay greate sowmes of money and therefore the desyre of there petition wes that his Maiestie might be pleased to send him home to tak ordour in his

---

[1] No. 98.

owne affaires and to releeve thame of there distress and
trouble for his caus. This petition beeng hard by the
counsall, they thoght meete to send the same vp to his
Maiestie to the effect his Maiestie may do therein as he
shall think good.

The counsale hes wrotten to the erle of Ergyll his
bailyees to haive a care of the keepeing of his countreyes
till the earle's home comeing.

97. Ansueris gevin in be the burrowis of the west cuntrey to the missiue bill send to theme from his Maiesties counsall

It is ansuered be the cōmissionaris of the west burrowis
with aduise of the right honourabill the Lairdis of Lundie
and Caddell, to the headis of the missiue writtin to the
saidis burrowis anent thair aduise how the rebellione of Coill
Mᶜillespie Mᶜdonald and his associates salbe repressed.

First it is thought be theme that his Maiestie and Counsall
wald cause reik furthe [1] ane of his Maiesties shippis and ane
pynnage weill equippaged and furneist in all necessairis
to cum and attend in the west seas viz. in Loch Kerrane,
Lochryand and Alderfleit, or sik vther pairtis as may
be thocht maist meit, and whair they may haif best
occasione for the seruice to ryde and attend vpoun the
rebellis And that the principall gentilmen, and vthers
of the Inlandis be cōmandit to attend whair his Maiesties
shippe and pynnage reddy with tua gallayis and thair
birlingis to await on the commandiment and directione
of the Commissionare direct frome his Maiestie and
counsall as they salbe appoyntit and directed be him in
this seruice.

Nixt that euerie gentilman of the ylis and these who
duellis in the mayne shoir whair the rebellis hantis be
cōmandit to keip thair landis and boundis frie fra ony
ressett, support, supplie or intertenement of the rebellis

---

[1] Fit out.

directly or indirectlye, and to keip and hald theme af shoir within thair awin boundis and landis.

As for ansueir tuitcheing the saidis burrowis help in the west, they declair they pay thair haill custumes and impoistis of all thair wairis out and in[1] and in respect of thair pouertye and inhabilitye hoipis his Matie and counsall will not impoise ony burding on theme in particulare by the rest of the haill kingdome.

And when it sall pleis your Lo. to conclude what number salbe thought fitt for this persute, and how many salbe thought expedient to be leviat out of the erle of Arygle's boundis, Pleis zor Lo. cause direct zour Lo. lr̃es for Kintyre, to Archibald Campbell, chalmerlane and baillie of Kintyir; ffor the boundis of Cowall, to the Laird of Ardkinglas, baillie thairof; ffor the boundis of Argyle, to the Laird of Auchinbrek, or, in his absence to the Laird of Barbrek, baillies thairof; and for the boundis of Lorne, to the Laird of Coull, baillie of Lorne. This is the best course to be taikin till the erle of Argyle be present himself, or that he lay the burding heirof on sum speciall freindis wha wilbe ansueirabill to his Maiestie and yor Lo. thairanent.

98[2]

My Lordis of secreit counsall—vnto zor Lo. humlie meanis and shawis we your servitoris Sr Ard Stirling of Keir, knyt, Johne Scrymgeor of Dudope, knyt, constabill of Dundie, Sr James Foulis of Colingtoun, Colonell Bartilmo Balfour, Johne Hamiltoun, Andro Creiche, Adame Rae, Wm Dik, Mr Johne Dempster, Robert Ainot of Ferny, James Nesmyt, Clement Russell, That whair we out of our affectione to Archibald erle of Ergyle haif not onlie advanceit and furneist vnto him diuerse greit sowmes of money of our awin proper geir bot with that we haif ingaaged our selffis as cautionaris for him in greit sowmes,

---

[1] I e export and import duties
[2] This is the petition referred to, ante, p. 227.

ffor the whilkis and for the payment of our awin proper
debtis, he and certane baronis and gentlemen of his kin
ar bundin and oblist vnto ws, and we having this long
tyme bygane to our greit hurt and inconvenient abiddin
the saidis erles laisour with great patience euer expecting
that in regaird of his awin hono[r] he wald haif done his
dewtie vnto ws ; in end finding no purpois nor intentione
in him nather to pay ws our awin sowmes nor to relcif ws
of our ingagement for him, we wer constraynit to vse the
ordiner remcid of his Maicsties lawis accustomit in lyk
caiccs and to denūce him and his cautionaris to the horne
whairat thay haif remanit this long tyme bygane as they
do zit vnrelaxit, and now the said erle to his farder discredit and to our hurt hes withdiawin him sclff furthe of
this cuntrey toward court whair he remaynis at his
pleasure leaving ws to compt at home with his creditouris
and the baronis and gentlemen of his kin wha standis
oblist to ws for him, hes not onlie given out in playne
speiches that they mynd neuer to pay ane peñy of his
debt seing they haue burdingis aneuche of thair awin
whilkis they mon prefer to his, bot with that they haif
in defraud of ws maid privie dispositionis and assignationis
of thair haill estaitis and fortownis cutting ws thairby
short of all reall exccutione aganis thair landis or guidis
and to frustrat ws of all personall exccutione aganis their
bodyis, they ar vpoun thair preparatione lykuise to depairt the cuntrey and to preiudge ws of all we can lay to
thair charge, whilk being a motiue of verie bad example
that we who ar peciabill and lawfull subiectis ansueirabill
and obedient to the lawis ; sould by suche forme of doing
be frustrat bothe of our awin geir and of our relcif of our
ingagement and that the said erle and his frends who ar
rebellis and at the horne and aluise senseles and cairles of
the greit distresses, trouble and wrak which we vndirly
for that cause sould liue and peace and suretye at court
without controlement, we haif thairfoir thought meit to
gif notice thairof vnto yo[r] Lo. and humlie to requeist zo[r]
Lo. to recōmend ws to our sacred souerane, that his
Maiestie wald be gratiouslie pleasit to send hame the said

erle heir to Scotland to tak ordo^r in his awin affairis and
to releif ws of our ingagementis for him and to pay ws
that whairvnto he standis obleist to ws and zo^r Lo. ansueir
humlie we beseik.

99. Copie of my letter to the Erle of Tullibairdin

13 *Junij* 1615

MY VERIE HONO^{BLK} GOOD LORD—I receaved this morning
zo^r Lo. packett, and after reeding your Lo. owne letter,
I declared to my Lord Chann^r what lers your Lo. had
sent to me. His Lo. conveyned the Archbishope of S^t
androis and the Lordis president, deputy thesaurer and
Clarke of register and in their presence opned and red the
lers[1] sent be Sr James M^conell to your Lo. self, the Earle
of Crawford, Bishope of the Iles and Earle of Cathenes,
the substance of the lers are for the most part uniforme
so as the copic of his letter to your Lo. self will informe
your Lo. that he intendis to excuse his breatche of warde
for feare of his life, offering all obedience yf he can have
saiftie and libertie, intending to send ane petition to the
counsell to be sent be their addresse to his Matie, Since
he protestis so solemnelie and with greate oathes that he
is innocent of the taiking and halding of Duneveg I am
sorie that he is so vnhappie as to have broken waird, for
he had great experience of his Maties clemencie who after
his conviction of treason for many odious crymes did
surcease all rigour and give thereby hope to Sir James
rather to hope for marcie nor to take any desperate
resolution, yf any such petition had come to the counsellis handis as without offence might have bene presented
to his Matie they wald haue sent it to courte. Bot his
lfes are out of purpose, I am sorie that he hes aggreged
his Maties wraith be his breatch of warde, and that hauing
cōmitted that heighnous offence it was not his happines
to go furth of his Maties dominions from whence he might
haue more convenientlic made offer of his humiliation,

---

[1] *Vide ante*, pp 219 *et seq.*

but so long as he remaynes within his Ma^{tles} dominionis
and hes societie and dealing with rebellis and broken men
I can not expect that his petitions can be receaved be his
Ma^{tle}, vnles he wold do such notable service aganis some
prin^{ll} rebellis as might perswade his Ma^{tle} to think him
wourthie of mercie. My Lord Chann^r hes promised to
superseid your Lo. actions till your coming here at the
tyme appoynted. Your bill is past for delay that your Lo.
may [be] called before breeves be directed at the instance
of your partie. The counsell acknowledgeis your Lo. good
discretion in the sending of thir lers, and are confident
that your Lo. will continew carefull and diligent in everie
thing that may concerne his Ma^{tles} service or good of the
countrie. So wishing your Lo. all happines I rest.—
Your Lo. affectionat freind at comand,   BINNING.

Ed^r, 13 Junij.

100. At Edinburgh the xiiij of Junij 1615 in pñce of my Lordis Secretair, thesaurair depute and advocate

George Grahame solemnclie sworne and demandit yf he
had directioun to go to Ila to travell for releif of the bischop
of the Iles his pledges, Grantis that he had suche a directioun, and that in his going to Ila, he mett w^t the Laird
of Cadell and Coline Campbell bruther to the Laird of
Lawers in Innerara and that he tauld Coline that he wes
bowne to Ila to travell for releif of the pledgeis, and that
he said to Coline, that he wald glaidlie meete with the
Lard of Cadell to craue his aduise and opinioun in that
mater for he wald be loathe that ony of his travellis sould
be ony latt or hinder to the Lairdis doingis and that
Coline allowit of his speecheis and promeist to send for
the Laird to confer with him in that mater, wherupoun
Coline send for the Laird who come to Innerara the
secund night after.
      Demandit yf he shew ony warrand or comissioun to the
Laird of Cadell or to Coline Campbell for his dealing in that

busynes, denyis that he shew his warrand to the laird of Cadell, and grantis that he shew his warrand to Coline Campbell, and that the warrand wes writtin with the deponnair's owne hand, Grantis alsua that he shew the warrand to Duncane Campbell of Danna and denyis that he saw or spak with the Laird of Lundie at this tyme.

Demandit yf he shew his instructionis to the rebellis of Ila, deponis that he onlie shew thame to Angus Oig M^cdonald, thair being nane pñt bot they twa, and the deponner said to Angus that it wes onlie a memorandum of his awne, and that he maid no mention of my Lord Chancellair in these instructionis, or that they wer his Lр̃s instructionis or subscryuit w^t his hand.

Demandit yf he desirit the rebellis to keepe the house aganis the Lieutennēt till thay gatt a warrand frome my Lord Chancellair, denyis the same vpoun his grite oathe.

Demandit yf he assuirit the rebellis that he had a wairand to stay the Lieutennent and his Ma^tles forces and cannoun to come from Ireland, denyis the same, and sayes that he onlie said to thame, that he wald go to the Lieutennent and trye his mynd, and yf the Lieutennent wald not stay that he sould send thame warde, and deponis that he send thame worde that the Lieutennent wald not stay, bot come fordwart.

Demandit yf he write a lr̃e to the rebellis quhen the Lieutennent was lyand aboute the house willing thame to keepe the house quhill he send thame worde of his affairis, denyis that he wryte ony such lr̃e to thae at that tyme, Grantis that he wryte ane lr̃e to Duncane Campbell of Danna about that tyme desiring him to deale with the keepairs of the house willing thame to go away, becaus he saw no appeirance of releif for thame, bot that his Maiestie wes havelie incensit aganis thame, and he write this lr̃e after that Angus Oig had writtin his lr̃e to my Lord Chancellair with Sr Olipher Lambertis lr̃e.

Grantis that he write ane lr̃e to Angus when he vnderstoode the Castell wes inclosit and batterit, the copie whairof he promises to produce.

Denyis that my Lord Chan^r send ony ansuer bak to Angus, or that the deponnair him selff send ony lr̃e bot onlie that lr̃e w^{lk} he write to Duncane of Danna.

Denyis that at onie tyme he spak with Sr James M^{c}donald afoir his going to Ila, or that he had ony message frome him, or ony dealing w^t him in that bussynes.

Grantis that when he come frome Ila, and p̃ntit him selff befoir the counsell, he said that the Castell of Dunnyvaig wes the strongest house that euir he saw, and that it wes victualled for ane yeir and that thair was a Spanish pype full of poulder in it.

Denyis that he said to Duncane of Danna that his instructionis wer writtin w^t my Lord Chancellaris hand, bot that he said thay wer writtin be the deponner him self.

Demandit yf he delt w^t Coline Cãpbell willing him to deale w^t the Laird of Cadell to sell Ila to my Lord Chancellair, denyis that he had ony suche speecheis w^t Coline concerning my Lord Chan^r bot sayis that he conferrit w^t Coline to deale w^t the Laird for selling of Ila to the deponner him selff and he wald gif Cadell x^m merkis for his bargane and he wald gif to Coline j^m lib. for making of the bargane.

Demandit yf at his returne from Dunnyvaig he delt w^t the laird of Cadell to go bak, for he, to witt this deponner had endit the turne, denyis that he delt with Cadell in that mater, saying it had bene a presumptioun in him to have delt in so heigh a poynte, bot grantis that in a conference he had with Cadell he aduisit him to be war, and not to go fordwart, vnles he was assuirit of the cannoun and of goode forces, for otherwayes he might ressaue bothe skaithe and shame.

Demandit after quhat maner the instructionis writtin be him wer subscryuit, deponis that he subscryuit the same with the worde Cathedrall according to his ordinair custome to write in euery memorandum the place quhair he subscryves the same, and deponis that he declairit the contentis of the articlis to the bischop of the Iles, who recommendit to the deponner the cairfull doing of the bussynes. Sic subscribitur Grahame of Eryne.

101. Memorandum anent George Grahame

That George Grahame denyis that ye instrucsionis quhich he left w^t Agnes M^{c}coneill in Ila wer subscryuit be ye Lord Cancellar or ye Lord Burlie and yat ye lyke instrucsionis wer not gewin him be ye lord Cancellar for his wairant nor yat ye Cancellar did not allow him to offer those condisionis to ye rebels.

Lykuayis he denyis that he did deliver those instrucsionis to Coline Campbell of Abervrq^{ll} [1] in Inderraruy nor yat these instrucsionis had no subscripsioun at yame, and yat they wer not subscryuit be ye lord Cancellar nar be ye lord Burlie neather counterfitt be him selff, and yat Lundy nor Cadell and wther too gentill men did sie yame.

Denyis lykuayis that he affermed to ye rebels that those instrucsions wer wnder ye Cancellaris hand.

Denyis lykuayis yat he desired the rebels to keipe the house from ye louetennent wntill he returned w^t ye Cancellar his derecsionis.

Denyis lykuayis that he assured ye rebels yat he had a warrant to stay his Ma^{tels} louctennent and his Ma^{tels} cannown from cumming to Illa.

Denyis lykuayis that he writt any lr̃e to ye rebels q^{ll} ye louetennent was about ye houss desiring yame not to giue ower ye houss wntill he cam and broght to yame ane ansuer of all yair bissness.

Denyis that he insistit w^t Cadell to returne from ye service assuring Cadell yat he had endit yat seruice be ye Lord Cancellar his derecsionis, and yat he delt w^t none of Cadell his freindis to go bake frome ye seruice.

Confessis yat ye rebels sent to him Sr Oliuer Lambertis lr̃e writtin to yame commanding yame to rander ye kastell and yat he schew yat lr̃e to ye Lord Canceller, bot denyis any ansuer send bake to ye rebels, nor condesends not to q^t end ye rebels sent to him this lr̃e to be schawin ye Lord Cancellar.

To be demandit of George Grahame gif he said to Coline

---

[1] Brother of Lawers and of Archibald Campbell of Glencarradale.

Campbell yat not onlie was ye instrucsionis subscryuit be ye Lord Cancellar, bot lykuayis yay wer all writtin with ye Cancellaris own hand.

To demand of lum gif Sr Jeames M^{c}coneill knew of his going to Illa, and gif he had any derecsionis from Sr Jeames.

To demand of George Grahame gif he said to ye counsell yat ye houss was wnvinsibell, and yat he knew Cadell was not eabell to teake it in, and yat ye rebels had greit punschouns full of powder, and greit store of wittels This he did to moue ye counsell to recall Cadell from ye seruice. In tokin of this ye Secret [Council] reiectit hun opinlie and callit lum ane leud leier.

To demand of him gif he delt w^t Coline Campbell dsiring lum to mowe Cadell to sell Illa to the Cancellar, offering hum x^m fñke Skottis, and to the said Coline ane thousand $\hbar$ for his peans and offred to hauc teakin ye said Coline to ye Cancellar, ye quhich Coline refused : this he did efter he cam from Illa.

To demand of him gif he did not assuir Doncane Campbell of Dennay Agnes M^{c}conell his father in law yat went w^t him to Illa that those instrucsionis wer all subscryuit be ye Lord Cancellar.

102. At Edinburgh the xvj day of Junij 1615 in presence of my Lordis Secretair, thesaurair depute and advocat

George Grahame solemnelie sworne and demandit quhair he mett first with the prior of Ardchattane and Robeit Wynrahame in his going to Yla, deponis that his first meeting with thame wes in Ila.

Demandit for quhat cause he left Duncane Campbell of Danna in the yle of Jura that nicht that the prior and herauld come thair, deponis that vpoun occasioun of the convoy of ane man of Angus Oigis whome he recounterit thair, he gatt ane schorte, easie and reddy passage to Ila.

Demandit what was his first conferrence with Angus Oig when he come to Ila, deponis that he come to Yla to

Angus Oig vpoun ane settirday, and that he delt with
Angus to deliuer the house and pledgeis to him in the
Kingis name and the Chancellairis name, and at the first
Angus seamed to refuise to rander saying that it wes not
the Kingis bot the bischoppis of the Yllis that intendit
thair trouble, and efter lang conferrence Angus in end
become moir tractible and craved of the deponner quhat
course he sould tak for his releif, for he said that he tooke not
that house of his awne accord, bot wes enducit thairto be
the erll of Ergyle,[1] and that he wald iustifie this with his
swerd aganis the erll, and deponis that this deponner tooke
oute of his pockett some articlis q^{lkls} he deliuerit to Angus
to reid, and desyrit him to mak choise of ony of these
articlis and he wald deale with the Chancellair and the
counsaill in his favo^r.

Demandit what aduise he gaif to Angus quhen Angus
proponit to him quhat he sould do anent the house gif the
lieutennent come thair afore my Lord Chancello^r send bak
worde, deponnes that he aduisit Angus to deliuer the house
to the Laird of Caddell his Maiesteis lieutennent and to
deliuer the pledgeis to the deponer, and Angus ansuerit he
had rather bene slayne or he delyuerit the house to ony
Campbell levand, bot gif the deponner wald tak the house
he wald deliuer it to him.

Demandit quhat conferrence he had with Angus anent
his Maiesteis herauld, ansuer, that he aduisit Angus to gif
obedience to the herauld, and denyis that he counsallit
outher to stay or slay the herauld.

Denyis that he aduisit the herauld to stay and not go
fordwart or that he said to the herauld that he had a
warrand frome the counsall to stay the lieutennent.

Denyis alsua that he said to the prior of Ardchattan that
the house wald nowther be randerit to the Lieutennent, to
the pryor nar the herauld and denyis that he vsit ony
minassing or threatning speitcheis aganis the prio^r or the
herauld.

Demandit gif he saw Coill M^{c}gillespik misvse the

---

[1] *Vide ante*, p. 155, note 2.

herauld, ansuer, that the depouneris servand tauld to the deponner that Coill had abusit the herauld.

Denyis alsua that he said to Duncane Campbell, that gif the house and pledgeis wer deliuerit to this deponner, that he had warrand to stay all the preparations and forceis that wer maid for this seruice or that he maid ony mentioun of the passing or staying of Caddellis· infeftmēt.

Demandit whome he maid keipair of the house of Dunyvaig when the same wes deliuerit to him, deponis that Angus Oig deliuerit the keyis of the house to the deponner, saying that he deliuerit the same in the Kingis name, and the deponner deliuerit the keyis to Angus, and denyis that he gaif yame ony aduise or counsell to hald out aganis the lieutennēt.

Demandit gif he said to Angus Oig that the instructionis shawne be him to Angus wer my Lord Chancelloris instructionis writtin euerie word with his awne hand, denyis the same bot sayis that he tauld Angus that thay wer notis of his awne and that he desyrit Angus to aduise vpoun these notis, and the deponner wald travell in his fauoͬ anent yame with the counsaill.

Demandit gif he schew the instructionis to Duncan Campbell of Danna, deponnis that he schew yame to Duncane in Innerrara and that he tauld Duncane that thay wer writtin with a kynd of sand qͬwith noblemen writtis thair lꝛez and denyis that euir he named the Chancelloris name to Duncane Campbell.

Grantis that the instructionis producit and schawne vnto him ar the same instructionis that he schew to Duncane of Danna.

Grantis that he write ane lꝛe oute of this toun about the tent of December to Hector Mᶜcawis and that the contentis of the lꝛe wer ane reprooff to Hector that he had betrayit the honnest men that lyppynnit in him, and that he come not fordwart to this toun to get ansuer of the petitionis qͭᵏⁱˢ he brocht frome Angus Oig.

Grantis alsua that he write ane lꝛe to Hector McNeill ane nycht or twa after he come out of Yla, in Duncane of Danna's house, and that the contentis of the lꝛe wes

a lr̃e of courtesie and thankis for his good interteny-
ment.

Grantis that efter the house wes inclosit he write onlie
ane lr̃e to Angus and na ma lr̃ez, the copie of the q^{lk} lr̃e he
producit.

Duncane Campbell of Danna confronted with George
Grahame, the said Duncane in his pñce constantlie affirmed
that George said to him, gif he gat the house and pledgeis
delyuerit to him, that he had a warrand to stay the Lieutennent and his Maiesteis forceis to come fordwart and
that my Lord Chancello^r wald stay the appending of the
grite seale to Caddellis infeftment, Sayis forder that
George stayed the herauld to vse the charges aganis the
house, Sayes forder that the said George [shewed] to the
deponner his instructionis and said to the deponner that
[they were in] my Lord Chancello^{ris} hand write, and he wes
angrie with the deponner becaus he seamed to mistruste
the instructionis saying, what tak zou for a traytor, and
Duncane sayis vpoun his grite aith in George pñce that
the instructionis producit ar not the instructionis q^{lkis}
George schew to the deponner, the contrair of q^{lkis} premisses wes affirmed be George.

Coline Campbell of Abirvrquhill sworne, Grantis that he
wes in Innerrara quhen George Grahame come yair, and
that George tauld the deponner that he [was] going to Yla
to deale for deliuerie of the house and pledgeis, and the
deponner dissuadit George to go fordwart vnles he spak
with the Lieutennent who come to Innerrara and spak
with George Grahame, and the Laird asking of George
quhair he wes going, George tauld him that he wes going to
Yla to deale for the house and pledgeis, and the laird
haueing tauld him that the chairge of that seruice lay
vpoun him and that George could haue no doing thairin,
George ansuerit, that he had a way to effectuat that turne,
whairvpoun the laird and he contestit in termes, and
sinderit not kyndlie, and the deponner staying behind in the

chalmer with George Grahame, the deponner enterit with
him and proponnit vnto him the difficulteis q^{lk} he wald
find in that mater becaus the Lieutennent had stayit all
passageis, and eftei diuerss discourses betuix yame, in end
George said to the deponner, quhat think zou that I am
come heir w^{t}out a warrand, I am not sic a foole, I will lat
zou sie my warrand gif zou will keip secrite whairvpoun
George tooke out of his pockett a papper writtin on baith
sydis and dehuerit [it] to the deponner, and did seame to
the deponner that it wes subscryuit be my Lord Chancello^r,
and George Grahame affermed to the deponner that thay
wer my Lord Chancello^{ris} instructionis, and this deponner
took yame to the Lard of Lundy and latt him sie and reid
yame, and the deponner grantis that he coppeit the instructionis, and that George Grahame red thame to him
quhen he coppeit yame, deponis alsua that the same instructionis wer subscryuit be the Lord of Burley as appeirit
to the deponner and his depositioun wes maid be the said
Coline in the said George pñce and audience.

George Grahame confrontcd with the said Coline, the
said George denyis that he said to Coline that the instructionis wer my Lord Chancello^{ris} instructionis and artichs,
and that he said no farder to Coline, bot thir wardis following to witt, he that devisit the artichs subscryuit thame,
the contrair q^{r}of wes affermed be the said Coline, the said
George lykewyse denyit that the instructionis q^{lkis} he
schew to Coline boore the subscriptionis of the Lord Chan-
cello^r or Lord of Burley, the contrair q^{r}of Coline affermed
vpoun his grite aith, to witt, that the instructionis boore
bothe thair subscriptionis verie cleirlie and verie lyke thair
subscriptionis.

The instructionis [1] being producit and schawne vnto
Coline, and he demandit gif thay wer the instructionis
q^{lkis} the said George schew to him, the said Coline affermed
constantlie that thay ar not the instructionis q^{lkis} George
schew to him, the contrair q^{r}of wes affermed be George

---

[1] *Vide ante*, p 187.

that thay ar the verie same subscriptionis q^{lkls} he schew to Coline.

The said George demandit vpoun his grite aith gif after he ressauit the pledgeis he desyrit the Lieutennent to stay and not to go to Yla q^{ll} he, to witt, this deponner come bak frome Ed^r denyis the same and denyis alsua that he desyrit the Lieutennent to go with him to courtt, or that the Lieutennent promeist to him, that he sould do no thing in the Yle q^{ll} he send him bak woord frome the counsell.

Demandit gif he write to ony personis desyring yame to be trew to the gentilmen of the Yle the deponner rememberis not of the same.

Grantis that he write to Hector M^{c}cawis that the Clandonaldis petitioun wes send vp to courte.

The said George Graham rememberis him selff that he had tua of the saidis articlis and instructionis, bot knawis not q^{lk} of the twa he schew to Coline Campbell, and sayis confidentlie that nane of yame boare the subscriptionis of my Lord Chancello^r and the Lord of Burley and being demandit gif thay were subscryuit lyke the subscriptionis of the Chancello^r and Lord of Burley, denyis the same.

In witnes of the truth of the premisses the saidis George Grahame, Duncane Campbell and Coline Campbell euery ane for thair awne pairtis hes ratifeit thair depositionis by thair subscriptionis following. Sic sub^r GRAHAME of Eryne, C. CAMPBELL of Abirvrquhill, D. C., Danna.

103. Sir Rorie McLeod to Lord Binning

Dated 18 *June* 1615

MY LORD—My homble dewtye after all reverence and seruice remembered, in the begining of Apryll I left Ed^r and passed till Glasgo to viste my barnes who ar at the shoole there, where I remained the space of fyifteinth dayes, and thereafter I passed till Striviling and going in to the toun I mett my lord Fleming comeing out of the toun, who had a ledd coursho^r besyd and I rydand on a other coursho[r], both the courshours brailes togidder, and I wes forced to leave and fall af my horss, where I brack two ribbes in my syd and lay for the space of xv[th] dayes in Perth vnder the cure of phisik, and thereafter I reteired to my owne countrey. And in the meantyme of my absence Coill Makgillespik and his companie come to the north Illes, and stoppet the first night at the yle of Camis, and thereafter passed derectlie to North Wyest Donald Gorme his landis, where he wes reseat, his men enterteaned, and Makintoshie's dochtar, Donald Gorme's wyff, beeng for the tyme in that countrey, togidder with young Donald Gorme, Makkenyees good brother, send to the said Coill beeng scant of viueres, four horse load of meat, in the whitche there wes two swyne, on salted and one vnsalted, and the said Coill and his companie wes perswaded, moved and requested by the saide Donald Gorme's wyff and young Donald and clann Neill vaine the speciall tenents of north Wyest to pass to a yle of myne called Hirta,[1] a day and a night sailing from the rest of the north yles far out in the ocean sea, and to that effect derected two of the tenents of north Wyest to be there guyd and pylat there for they wer vnknowen thame selues there, and coming to the ylle they slew all the beastiall of the ylle both kowes and horses and sheepe and took away all the spoolyee of the yle, onlie reserved the lyves of the en- habitants thereof. And when all wes done they returned to North Wyest againe, where they randered there guyde and pyllats agane, and gave to the inhabitants thereof all and whole the spoyle of my yle, and afore my comeing to the yles the saide Coill Makgillespik passed away south to Ila againe. Now sence I persave Sir James hes brocken warde, and come to Lochquhaber, and out of that come to Moror and Knoddort, where he took per force a young youth, the secund sone of Glengarrie on-a-worse,[2] and keepes him still in custodie ; and the Captanes sone, a son of Donald M[c]Allan M[c]Ean, Captain of the Clan-Ronald.

---

[1] Now better known as St. Kilda.
[2] Unawares.

And thereafter, come to Sleat, to Donald Gorme's bounds, where he gott a bigg boat, with oares, saile, and tailkleing ; and intercomoned at lenth with Donald Gorme there ; and a nomber of Donald Gorme's folkes of Sleat, called Clann Tarlich, is gone with him. And thereafter, passed till the Yle of Egga, where he mett Coill and his companyee, to-gidder with his base sone, and a sone of Sir James Maksorle of the Route.[1] And they ar in nomber, as I leine, tuelfue or thretteinth score, at the present tyme. And whidder they go South or North I can not tell, at the witteing heerof. It is my advyse to your lo. and Counsall, that your lo. derect a ample command and chaige, till all and sindrie the Superioures of the Yles, till convocat thame selues in armes, with a full Commission till everie one of ws, till persew the said rebelles, by sea and land, with fyre and sword, in this form, in thrie severall armyes and companyees. That is, Makclaine of Doward and Makcleane of Lochbuy in a companye and armie ; Donald Gorme and the Captane of Clann Ronald in a other armie ; and I, the Lairde of Coill and Mackynnoun and my Lord of Kyntaile's forces, in a other companyee ; and lett euerie one of thir armies endeavoire thameselues in his Ma[ties] seruice ; and he that doeth best therein, have the greatest honour, and prefer-ment, and reward of his Ma[tie] and Counsall. And becaus the said Sir James and his companyee hes taken thamselues to the sea, in two barkes and sindrie other boates, it were expedyent that your lo. and Counsell would send me ane Commissioun and powar to embark any ship I can appre-hend, in thir Iles, to the better persute of thame in thir Iles ; otherwise, your lo. and Counsell till furnishe out two or three shippes, well provyded, to thir Iles ; and derect one of thame to me, that I and they may concure to-gedder, in his hughnes seruice. And I desyre the Iles Superiours to be devyded in three ffactions, for this caus. Sir James and the rebelles of the Clanndonald ar of kynn, blood, and alia to Donald Gorme and to the Captane of Clann Ronald ; and Sir James and his rebelles ar deedlie

---

[1] The Route is one of the divisions of Antrim.

enemies to Mackclene and his name, and they will never
aggree in a companyee and armee. And as for me, your
lo. knowes verie well that I have geven a proof of my
obedience and seruice to his Matie and Counsell allreddye,
in taking, and apprehending, and delyuering my own
name and blood,[1] the rebellis of the Lews ; and in making
these landis peaceable to his Matie. Lett the rest do the
lyk seruice now to his Matie, and it is verie well knowen
to his Maiestie and Nobilitie of Scotland, that my hous
neuer rebelled, nor yett shall rebell. But as it hes
beene ay subject to his Maties will sa shall I contenew
God willing to my lyves end and shall endevor my
selue with all possible force and powar till persew these
rebells and all other rebells that shall rebell againes his
highnes authoritie, yea if it wer my father, brother or
sone, ffor blissed be god and his Matie I have whereon to
leeve his Maiesties peacyable subiect, whilk I will not
losse for my lyve and all the world, and if yor Lo. thinkis
it is expedyent, I care not supose zo^r Lo. present this my
letter to the counsall. I receaved my cõmission concerning
Coill Makgillespik on Witsounday afore I com home and
after that Coill wes away till Ilae, I requeast zo^r Lo. in
hombilitie and homlienes till aduertese me of all occurrent
newes, I end geveing zo^r Lo. to god's most holie tuition.—
Zo^r lo. homble seruito^r at powar,

Sir Rorie Makcleud.

Dunvegane, 18th of June 1615.

104

Vicesimo Junij 1615

This day in the forenoone, there wes a meeteing of the
counsalle, and there wes present the marques of Hamilton,
the erles of Mar, Caithnes, Lynlithgow, besydes the whole
officears of the estate, and such others of the counsale as
ar ordinarie and daylie attendantes. They mett at eyght

---

[1] He seems to have resembled his better known kinsman Neil Macleod of
Assynt.

of the cloak in the forenoone, and satt whill tuelue. At there first meetinge the Chancellar produced two missiue letters wrotten from his Maiestie, the one to his lordships selue wherby his Maiestie recommended vnto him the care of conveancing of the counsale, and the proponing and resolueing vpoun such courses wherby this appeereing rebellion of some of the Clanndonald may be prevented and supprest, and the other letter derected to the whole counsale, wherby his Maiestie hes verie gravelie sett doun his Maiesties owne oppinion concerning the sade rebellion, and what course his Maiestie thinkis fittest to be followed thereintill. Thir letteres beeng redd and considdered there wes many propositiones and oueitoures made thereupon, and by what meanis that seruice might be best effectuate to his Maiesties honour and contentment, and after long debeateing of mater and heereing of the obiectiones and impedimentes that wer proponed therein, in end with vniforme aduyse, oppinion and consent, the course and ordor following is aggreed vpon and sett doun.

In the first considderatioun beeng had of the nomber of the rebelles who ar estimate to be three hundrethe men or thereaboute, it wes thoght that no feware could adventare and vndertak the persute of thame then fyve hundreth men and that this persute behooved to be by sea, with galayes, birlingis and such lyk veshelles of this birth or there abouttes and that they should be provyded and derected alswell to persew the rebelles by sea, and to follow and persew thame on land in caise thay should happin to come on land, and that there randevous and meeteing shalbe in some pairte of Lochquhaber whitche is the midds betweene the north and west yles, and there to joyne thame selues togidder and with there galayes and birlingis to go to the sea, and neuer to leave of the persute of the traitoures whill they be apprehended or expelled the countrey.

This company and nomber of fyve hundreth men, is appoynted to be furnished and sett oute with there galayes, birlinges, and veshelles, and with there whole furnitoure of warre and with fourtie dayes prouision and victuales by the persones following, to witt, by the erlle of Ergyle and his frendes for there landes in the yles and continent two hundreth and fyftie men ; by Makelane and his frendes to witt, the Lairdes of Coill, Lochbuy and Makkynnoun, ane hundreth men ; by Makeleud of Herrese fyftie men; by Donald Goime tuentye fyve men ; and by the tutor of Kyntaile, tuentie fyve men, and there is proclamationes and charges ordained to be derected againest thame, and particular missiues wrotten to euerie one of thame to haue the particular nombers designed and appoynted to thame in reddynes with all there furnitour and prouisioun at the place and tyme of meeting sett doun vnto thame, and in there missiues there is some twitche geven that none of there kyndlic possessionis shal be sett ouer there heades [1] yf so be they will appróve there affection to his Maiesties obedyence in this seruice.

And byeaus thir forces will not be holden vnder obedyence and cōmandement and consequenthe will do lytle goode in this seruice vnles some person of qualitie be authorized with cōmission and authoritie to conduct, derect and gouerne thame, therefore it is thoght meete seeing the erle of Ergyle (who is the specyall person of powar and frendship in the Heighelandes) is now absent, that his brother the Lairde of Lundy shalbe burdaned with this charge, and that he shall have some consideration oute of his Maiesties cofferes for his charges (yf he can not be induced vpon no other condition to embrace the seruice) and he is wrotten for to be heere for this effect vpon the morne at night or the nixt day following airlie in the morning at whitche tyme this mater wilbe setled.

The whole landislordes in the yles ar wrotten to, to keepe there owine boundes and countreyes free of thir rebelles, and to persew thame with fyre and sword yf they shall happen to come there, and the setting foorth of the particular nombers of men appoynted to euery one of thame will liberat thame and there countreyes from all forder seruice by sea, and outwith there owne boundes,

---

[1] This practice of thus treating large parts of the Highlands and Islands as Crown lands by reason of some alleged forfeiture on the part of a chief was responsible for much of the trouble in these regions

and they wilbe no forder astrictit bot to keepe there owene boundes free of the rebelles.

The Marques of Huntlye hes gotten a verye ample Commission for persute of the Rebelles, especialie of Macronnald,[1] and his sone, who ar his owne tennentes; and the Counsale hes wrotten vnto him to send his sone the Erle of Enyee, with diligence, to Lochquhaber,—to persew the rebelles, to tak, demolishe, and destroy Macronnaldes housses, to meddle with his whole goodes, and with the goodes of such as did ressett and supplie Sir James Makdonald and Makrounald, and not to come out of that countrie, whill he assuire the countrey to be keeped vnder his Maiesties obedience.

There is a Proclamation sett oute againes Sir James Makdonald and his son, Coill Macgillespik, and some otheres of the principall ringleadares in this rebellion; conteaneing a reward to any such persone or persones as will tak or slay[2] onie of thame; to witt, for Sir James McDonald there is a promese of fyve thousand pundis; for Makronnald and his sone, Coill Makgillespik, fyve thousand markes a peece; and for some others of the rebellis, thrie thousand markes. And there is a promese of pardon proclamed to such of the rebells thame selues, as will tak, and exhibite, or slay onie of there owene companie, being of a better rank and qualitie nor thame selues.

Sir James Makdonnald and Makronnald, in there going towardes the Iles, took a sone and a servand of the Larde of Glengarries; information whereof being made to Young Glengarrye, he, with such forces as he could mak vpon the suddane, followed thame to the sea syd, and in a conflictt betweene thame, he hes taken two of the principallis of Makronnaldes companie; ffor whose releef Makronnald offerred delyuerie off Glengarryes sone; bot Glengarrie refuised to delyuer his two prisoners, and hes promesed to exhibit thame heere within ten dayes.

Donald Gorme and the Captane of Clannronnald hes

---

[1] Macronnald is Macdonald of Keppoch.

[2] Such incitements to murder on the part of the Government were not uncommon.

by there writtinges promesed to continew in there obedience, and to do the best of there endevoures in the persute of the rebelles.

And concerning that poynt of his Maiestie letter, beareing that the granting of a infeftment to James now Lord Ochiltree [1] of the captane of Clannronnaldes landes hes moved him to joyne with the rebelles in this rebellion [2]; trew it is that there is no suche infeftment as zitt past to the Lord Vchiltree and all that proceidit in that bussyness wes this, to witt, there [was] a contract past betweene the sade Lorde and one who pretended right to the captanes landes, anent the heritable disposition of the saides landes to the saide lord, and he thereupon desyred a new infeftment to be exped to him of the same, Bot yo[r] Maiesties deputie thesaurar foreseeing that such kynd of infeftmentes might enterupt the course whitche wes then and is zitt in handes for reduceing of the yllesmen to obedyence, he refuised the passing of that infeftment afore his Maiesties warrand come doun for that effect, and there is nothing done therein sensyne, and the captane hes not nather entendes to joyne with the rebelles so far as is zett hard, But he promeisis all dewtiefull obedyence, and to persew the rebelles with his whole powar and forces.

105
22 *Junij* 1615

Thair hes bene diverss metingis of the counsall anent this appiring rebellioun of S[r] James M[c]conell and vpoun the 20 of yis instant yei spent ye most pairt of y[t] day vpoun ye bissines and diverss proposiounes and ovirto[ris] being maid y[r] anent. In end it wes resoulit, etc.

He [Lundy] cam heir this 22 day of Junij and yis mat[r] being proponit vnto him w[t] mony persuasiue argumentis to embrace ye service he profest him self very willing to do all his indevo[ris] in his Maties service bot anent the vndir-

---

[1] Previously Sir James Stewart of Killeith (*vide ante*, p. 109, note).

[2] *Vide ante*, p. 129, for a similar attempt at robbery, also unsuccessful, on the part of Campbell of Lawers.

taking of yis particular service and prosequutioun y^{r}of w^t suche force as wes agreable w^t his Maties honour and weill of the cuntrey, he proponit many difficulties, impedimentis and impossibilities to effectuat ye same in his awne persone speciallie the absence of his brother without whose speäll directioun, at the lest without the directioun of his ballies and chalmerlancs, his cuntrey people wald not ryse. The counsale being loathe to ressaue yis ansuer and refusall, they desyrit him to aduyse w^t suche of his brother freindis as wer in yis toun and to gif in afternone suche ourtouris in writt as wer fittest in y^r judgement for the furtherance of this service.

In ye efternone he comperit w^t ye lairdis of Caddell, Auchinbrek and Lawiris w^t ye Capitane of Craignesche and Coline Campbell, brother to Lawiris and gaue in sume ovirto^{ris} in writt the substance q^{r}of tendit to yis course and ardo^r following q^{lk} wes agriet vpoun be ye counsale.

The laird of Auchinbrek as ballie of ye erldome of Argyle is authorized w^t cōmissioun and strait charge and directioun is gevin vnto him to levey tua hundreth able men out of Argyle provydit w^t galayis, birlingis and all weirlyke prouisioun and w^t xl dayis victuallis and provisioun for defence of the cuntrey and persute of ye rebellis be sea and land frome ye marche of Lorne southwart to Kintyre and cōmissioun and directioun is gevin to the laird of Ardkinglass, ballie of Cowell to levey ane hundreth men out of Cowell provydit and furnist in maner forsaid to attend and be reddy to joyne w^t Auchinbrek as he salbe advertist and directit be him.

The lyke cōmissioun is gevin to the Laird of Lochinzell, chalmeilane of Lorne to levey ane hundreth and fyfty men out of Lorne and Glenuiquhy prouydit and furnist in maner forsaid for persute of the rebellis be sea and land betuix Morverne and the merche of Kintyre and the Laird of Cadell hes promist that all his men in these boundis vnder the charge of his brother Mr Donald[1] salbe redy to joyne w^t Lochinzell in yis service.

---

[1] Mr Donald Campbell of Barbreck Lochow—afterwards Sir Donald Campbell of Ardnamurchan—a natural brother of Calder.

The lyke cōmissioun and directioun is to send to Mᶜclayne to list out of his boundis tua hundreth men provydit and furnist in maner forsaid for persute of the rebellis be sea and land betuix the iow of Ardnamurchine and the niche of Lorne and Mᶜclayne is to be assistit wᵗ ye lairdis of Coll, Lochbuy and Mᶜkynnoun wha ar his awin freindis and lyis in his boundis.

Within yir boundis particularlie abovewrittin ar cōprehendit the haill south and west Iles and gif yir cōmissionaris do yʳ dewtyis the rebellis wilbe forcit to leaue all these Iles or yen to ye oppin seaes.

Gif they go to the seaes and leaue ye Iles His Maᵗˡᵉˢ ship and pinnace wilbe redy to persew yame and for the defence of the north Iles and persute of the rebellis yʳ, this ordoʳ is tane.

First for Lochquhabir qˡᵏ is the narrest bound to ye north pairt of ye west Iles, the erle of Enzie is authorized wᵗ commissioun to levey ane hundreᵗ men out of Lochquhabir provydit and furnist as is aforsaid for persute of ye rebellis be sea and land and keping of Lochquhabir frie of yame.

The lyke cōmissiones and directiones ar gevin to ye Capitane of Clanranald, Mᶜcleude of Heress and Donald Gorme for listing euery one of thame ij^c men wᵗin yʳ boundis to the effect forsaid.

And becaus the Lewes is dispeopled [1] sua yᵗ no man can be listed yʳ the tutor of Kintaill is writtin to that he haue a cair of ye keping of ye cuntrey.

The Marques of Hamiltoun and the shereff of Bute is lykewyis writtin to for keping of ye Iles of Arrane and Bute frie frome ressait, supplie and ayding of the rebellis and ather of yir Iles ar to joyne wᵗ ye vther in ye persute of ye rebellis gif ye necessitie sall so requyre and according as yei salbe adueitist the one frome ye vther.

All thir preparationes and forces ar appoynted to be in redynes agane ye sext of July now approching wᵗ ane monethis victuallis and provisioun.

_____

[1] A result of the civilising efforts of the Fife adventurers (vide *Highland Papers*, vol ii pp 270 *et seq*).

Particular missiues ar directit to euery one of yir cōmissionaris proporting how yat his Matie and his counsale out of y^r assurance of ye fidelitie and senceritie of the cōmissionaris in his Ma^tties servicc hes maid choise of thame and honorit yame w^t zir cōmissiones and y^rfore willing yame to accept ye same and deutifullie to execute ye same and yei ar ordanit be ye missiues to keepe correspondence wth ye capitane of his Ma^tties schip and anys euery oulk to aduertise ye counsale w^t ye progres of y^r procedingis and w^t ye courses of ye rebellis.

Thair is charges also direct aganis yame for accepting of ye cōmissiones wnder ye pane of treassone and y^r is a proclamatioun direct for concurrance to be gevin vnto yame in ye cōmon forme.

Thair is a proclamatioun sett oute aganis Sr James and his cōplices cōtening the rewaird following to ony persone or persones that will tak, apprehend, exhibite or slay yame or ony of yame, to wit, for Sr James, fyve thousand pund, for M^crannald and his sone and Coill M^cgillespik ✗ v^m m̄kis the peece, for gillichallum M^crorie M^ccleude and ⚡. ✗ Ronnald Oig M^cangus iij^m m̄kis ye peece w^t a promise of pardoun for all bygane faultis to ony persone or personis that will tak and exhibit or slay ony of the rebellis being of better rank and qualitie nor yame selffis.

Becaus y^r is sindry persones that accidentlie hes intercomonit w^t ye rebellis and not vpoun ony treasonable purpose or cours and some vthiris hes bene forceit to acumpany yame and to go w^t yame aganis y^r will who now being in fear of ye lawis will rather mak choise to remane wth ye rebellis yen to cum in whairas gif yei wer sure to be vnchallengit for y^r bygane intercomoning and going w^t yame they wald now leaue yame. Thairfore thair is a proclamatioun maid contenīg a pardon to all suche persones as accidentlie hes cōmittit no cryme in y^r cumpany provyding that within ten dayis efter ye publicatioun of ye proclamatioun they leaue ye rebellis and joyne not w^t yame y^refter and yat yei address yame selffis to one of ye cōmissionaris forsaidis and gif notice vnto him that yei haue left ye rebellis; thair is exceptit oute of yis pro-

* Son of Rorie Og, bastard son of Rorie
Macleod of Lewis v. Highland Papers Vol. II
56, 64, 263, 276-7, 279 & n.

clamatioun Sr James M^cdonald, M^crannald and his sone
and all these who assisted Sr James in his brek of waird,
Coill M^cgillespik and all these who assisted him in ye
rebellioun of Ilac.

Thair is a proclamatioun to be publist at Glasgo, Air,
Renfrew and Dumbartane prohibiting ye selling of ony
poulder, bullet, or armo^r bot to suche persones as wilbe
ansuerable vpoun ye perrell of y^r lyves, and will find cautioun that no pairt y^rof sall come to the vse of ye rebellis.

The Lairdis of Lundy and Cadell being so far ingadgit
for ye erle of Argyle as yei dar not vndirtak oi seiuice or
frelie hant in ye cuntrey for fear of trouble [1] thairfore yei
earnistlie delt wth ye cõsale that yei micht haue licence
to go to court to deall wth ye erle of Argyle for y^r releiff
and gif yei come no speid of him to meane yame selffis to
his Matie the counsale hes grantit yame licence and yei
haue actit yame selffis to returne and pñt yame selffis
befoie ye counsale vpoun ye xx day of July nixt q^lk
wilbe about ye expyring of ye tyme of yis seruice and
y^rfoie yei wald be haisted hame to ye effect yat at ye
expyring of yis pñt service some new couise may be tane
to hald ye service fordward

The Cap^ne of Clanrannald and Donald Gorme hes promist
to continew in y^r obedience and to persew ye rebellis wt
y^r haill forces.

The infeftment craved be James now Lord Ochiltrie of
ye Cap^ne of Clanrannaldis landis wes not granted nor
exped vnto him ffor it being pñted to ye depute thesaurer
and some questioun being betuix ye said lord and him
anent ye patronage of certane kirkis q^lkis he had includit
in y^t infeftment, the the^r wald not exped the same till it
wer reformed, and in ye meane tyme afore ye infeftment
wes writtin ouir His Maties warrand cam doun for staying
of the same, and so it restis zit stayed and vnexped.

The Cap^ne neuir joyned w^t ye rebellis bot promises all
dew obedience and altho M^crannald trayned ye cap^nes
sone out of yis toun who is a young boy of ye age of xiiij

---

[1] For fear of proceedings being taken against them by creditors.

zeiris and wes heir at ye schoole the Cap^{ne} refuisis to tak his sone agane w^{th}out a wr̃and frome ye counsale.

The laird of Auchinbrek one of ye crle of Argyllis distrest cau^{rls} being wardit in yis toun for some of ye erles debtes the cōsale vpoun necessitie of yis seruice hes fred him of his waird and hes tane himself actit for his re-entrie q^{n} he salbe chargit vpoun xv dayis warnīg.

The rebellis in yair going towardis ye Iles having tane ane sone and ane seruand of ye laird of Glengarreyis they wer followit and persewit be zoung Glengarrie and suche forces as he could mak vpoun ye suddane to the shoir syde foiranent Slait and in a conflict betuix yame Glengarrie tuik tua of ye prin^{llis} of M^crannaldis men ffor whose releiff delyverie wes offerit of Glengarryis sone and seruand Bot Glengarrie refuisit ye interchange w^{th}out ye counsallis w'rand and having come heir and imparted yis mater to ye counsale they haue ordinit him to exhibit his tua prissoneris q^{lk} he hes promist to do w^{th}in ten dayes.

106. Earl of Tullibardine to Lord Binning

MY VERRIE HONOURABILL GOOD LORD—I haue ressawit McAllane McEan, Capitane of the Clan Ronald, his ansuer of my Letter, quhairby I perceaue that he is nocht previe to Sir James his brekking of Waird, and is resoluit nocht to mell with thair courssis, ffor Sir James and McRonnald did all that thai culd, be messages, to haue met with him, vpone pretence to haue delyverit him his sone ; bot he onnawyis wald have ony midling with thame, nor wald nocht ressaue his sone, becaus he wes in thair cumpany, without ane Warrand of zour lo^s of the Counsell. Bot I heir that sensyne, quhan Sir James tuik the sea, he send him frome him. Sir James at his passing out of Lochabber, wes onlie accumpaneit with fourtene men and boyis, and McRonnald followit him with sextene men and boyis. They past out that to McEan of Ardnamurchais cuntrie ; quhair I heir that McEan him selff, with all his cumpany with him ; att the leist, thair is an great pairte of thame. He gat sum boittis thair, and past thairfra, langis the coist ;

bot he culd haue no landing, nather in McAllane McEane his cuntrie, Mcclewd Hereis, nor Donald Gormis cuntrie ; ffor thai pat forcis on all the sea-poirtis, to stop his landing ; and I think thei had maid sum onset on him, if thair boittis had not bene all sunk of befoir, for feir of supprysing thame.

I heir he landit into the Iles of Rowme and Eg, quhair Coull McGillespie did meit him with ane cumpany of hagbutteris, about the number of sewin scoir of men. Thair forme of meiting, as I heir, wes this. Sir James and his cumpany stude in ane plaice be thame selffis, quhair the wther with his cumpany went round about him, onis ; and at the nixt going about, salutit him with thair wolly of schoittis ; and continowit sua schuitting and iniuring of him, for the spaice of half ane hour ; and thairefter com to him everie man, particularlie, chapping handis. Wpone the morne, thai conuenit all the haill bestiall, horse, and ky, to one plaice, quhilk thei thocht to haue slayne haill ; bot, vpone better aduysement, thei slew onlie ane number of ky, for meat, quhilk thei caryit immediatlie to thair boittis ; and thairefter tuik the sea, to the number of Thre hunder men, of all. Cole brocht him tua crearis, with sum wthir boittis that Sir James him self gat in Ardmurche, and supprysit in wthir pairtis. It is thocht that thei haue tane thair woyage to Ilay ; and if the cuntrie be vpone thair gaird, as thai suld, I think thai sall nocht proffeit mekill. The occasioun of my mannis stay ; it wes long befoir he could get tryell quhair McAllane McEan wes ; for he wes bussie, in gewing of ordour, that Sir James suld nocht land on any of his Isles ; and abscuring him selff, that thei suld nocht get him. I vnderstand he hes send him Letteres to the Counsell, quhilk I think zour lo. knawis of befoir now. I will request zour lo. to lat me vnderstand, quhat directioun is cumit zit frome his Matie, concerning Sir James Mcconeill, and quhat conclusioun zour los of Counsell hes taiken thairanent. Sua, hawing na farder at this present, committis zour lo. to the protectioun of God ; and restis, Zour lo. euir assuirit freind and seruant,   TULLIBARDINE.

Perthe, the 24 of Junii, 1615.

I vnderstand Glengarrie is presenthe in Ed^r, and is trublit be my Lord Lowatt in some actionis betuix thame. I wald request zour lo. to be his freind and to forder him hame ouir ; for I mynd to meit with him, in his by-cuming, and sall lay him rycht to any thing that concernis his Ma^{teis} seruice, to my power. And becaus he is dealler betuix me and McAllane McEane, Capitane of the Clan Ronnald, pleas zour lo. wret to me, quhat particular ze wald haue me to lay to thair chairge ; and I sall do the best.

The pretext that Sir James M^cconeill and McRonnald myndit to haue vsit, to haue peisuadit McAllane McEane and Glengarry to haue taikin thair pairte, in this auld actioun that my Lord Lowat hes aganis thame, and the taking of McAllane McEanes landis ouir his head be Sir James Steuart.[1] In my opinnioun, zour lo^s of the Counsall suld do weill to delay the discussing of thir debaittis for ane quhyle till thir wther materis of Sir James war setlit.

107. Hector McNeill of Thyneis[2] to Lord Binning

26 *June* 1615

MY LORD—Zo^r Lo. accepting so weill of my last newis of the eyll^{is} hes imboldonit mee now, with moist expedition to foirsee zo^r Lo. of this lait accidence fallen out, for the xxiijth of yis instant. Sr James M^cdoneill landit in Yllay and cam onperceaved near Doneweage and be traine of a craftie fellow of the contree, ye Constable of ye Castell be name Alex^r M^cdowgall brother to Raraye[3] was broght furth be yes fellow and fyw soldio^r wth him and cw̄ing a litle space frome Castell war sett upon be S^r Ja^{es} and Coill M^cgillesp^t and all yair companie. The gentle man spying yem maid for ye house and is slaine and thrie of

---

[1] *Vide ante*, p 248

[2] On the death of Neill MacNeil, who sold Gigha in 1554 to Macdonald of Duniveg for 1500 merks, Neill MacNeil vic Eachan of Taynish became Chief. His descendants reacquired Gigha.

[3] The Macdougals of Raray in Glen Euchar are said to be the oldest cadets of the House of Lorne.

his companie, the house taine and the pryo[r] [1] and his twa
sonnes quha war w[th]in ye houss, but ar now at libertie
be S[r] Ja[es]. Calder his haill companie is c$\bar{w}$ frome eyllay.
S[r] Ja[es] was four nightis in ane little yllan callit Collinsaye
and slew ane numir of merttis, he hes maid ane strenth
in it upon ane fresh wattir loch in ane eyllane. Yair is no
apeirence bot ane vthir wrake for ye haill suith eyll[ls]
except svm heistie remeid be founde, for the morne they
dewyd theam self. S[r] Ja[es] cwmes to Juray and Coill cwmes
to the little eyllan yat I posses, ffor the q[lkls] I byde twa
extremities for yir rebellis persewes my lyff and guidis
and my Lord of Meidope be rigo[r] of law : In thir twa
extremities, I moist mein me to zo[r] Lo. fawo[r] that for
ony serwice or pleiso[r] I can do yat zo[r] Lo. hawe sume
compation on my p$\tilde{n}$tt affaire. Because ye perticular war
longs$\bar{u}$ to wreit I hawe appoyntit ane of my advocatis
Adam Cwninghame to confer zo[r] Lo. at lenth yat zo[r] Lo.
may find remeid yat I be not trubillit be war and law at
anes. This I refer to zo[r] Lo. and my puir serwice to zo[r]
disposition moist humblie remembered and my baldnes
excuised I shall ewir rest—Zo[r] lo[rls] moist humble and
reddie to serwe zou to death,

H. MAKNEILL of thyneis.

Zis in heist for expeditione ye newis ar certtane and
fallin out on setterday at morne xxiiij of yis instant.

Roist yis 26 at night.

[Postscript]

MY LORD—S[r] Ja[es] is about iiij[c] men all north eyll[ls] men.
At ye taking of ye houes, thrie of his war slaine, in spe[ll]
he quho furst of all tuik it frome ye Bischoipes brother
callit Rannald Oige. "All ye men of eyllay ar ell[ls] cu$\tilde{m}$ to
S[r] Ja[es] and Calders haillie expellit q[r]of I am suir [your]
Lo. is not content.

To my werie guid Lord My Lord Secreter
        and Lord Beninge theis.

---

[1] Campbell of Ardchattan.

108. Privy Council to the King

30 *June* 1615

PLEAS ZO[R] SACRED MAIESTIE—We haif this moirning ressauit advertisement that S[r] James M[c]donald and his complices hes surprisit and tane the Castell of Dunnyvaig [1] and hes slane the Capitane and some of the keipairis thairof, sua that now thay ar enterit in an oppin rebellioun and will not faill to procure some grite disordour in the yllis gif a p̅n̅t and substantious course be not tane for preventing and suppressing thairof, And whereas the geving of thair landis over thair headis to the erll of Ergyle and his freindis is pretendit be thame to be the caus quhairby thay ar inducit to this disperat and treasounable rebellioun, and it being expectit that the said erll and his freindis sould not onlie haif retenit and haldin these landis vnder a perfyte and satled obedience sua that zo[r] maiestie nor zo[r] cuntrey sould neuir haif bene forder trublit in that mater, bot that thay otherwyse sould haif disabilled thir rebellis and lymmairis to haif attemptit ony disordour heirefter. We haif thairfore thocht meete that the chairge and burdyne of this seruice salbe layd vpoun the said erll, and that he and his freindis be send home with all diligence with a strait chairge and direction to him to accept vpoun him the lieutennandrie and chairge of this seruice, and to prosequute and follow oute the same in his awne persone with his haill pouer, freindschip and forces and with all kynd of celeritie and diligence, and for this effect, that he go in persone to Ila, and thair persew the house and the rebellis and neuir leave af the persute of thame quhill the house be recoverit, the rebellis dissipat and supprest or put af the cuntrey, and that the cuntrey be restorit to obedience and quietnes, And whereas zo[r] Maiestie had formarlie appointit a schipp with a pinnace to come to the yllis for the persute of Coill M[c]gillespik, We will humelie requeist zo[r] Maiestie, seeing

---

[1] Among the prisoners were the Prior of Ardchattan and his two sons. Sir James treated them well and set them at liberty.

zo^r Maiesteis cannoun can not be transportit frome hense
to Ila, That zo^r Maiestie wilbe pleased to gif new ordo^r
and directioun for sending of the ship and pinnace to
Ila provydit with cannonis and vther wearlelyke furnito^r
to attend zo^r Maiesteis seruice thair in the persute and
batterie of that house, And that zo^r Maiestie will resolue
with the erll of Ergyle agane what tyme he will vndirtak
to be thair with his forceis, to the effect zo^r Maiestie gif
vnto him a strait chairge and directioun to haif in cair of
the keeping of zo^r Maiesteis cannonis and that the same
come not vnder the pouer nor reverence of the rebellis
as he wilbe ansuerable vpoun his lyff, This being a mater
requiring haist and diligence we will humelie beseik zo^r
Maiestie to be so mutche the moir instant with the erll of
Ergyle to mak his address home to follow out this busynes,
So in all reverence recōmending zo^r sacred Maiestie to
godis divyne protectioun we rest, zo^r Maiesteis most
humble and obedient subiectis and seruito^{ris},

AL. CANCELL^s.   BINNING.   JO. PRESTOUN.
S. R. COKBURNE.   ALEX. HAY.   OLIPHANT.
DRUMMOND.

Edinburgh, the last of Junij 1615.

109

Vltimo Junij 1615

Vpon the first advertesment that come heere of the
taking of the Castle of Duneveg by Sir James Makdonald
the counsall immediathe directed a messinger in all haist
to the Lord deputye of Yreland with a close letter acquent-
ing him with the taking of the house, and willing him to
stay his Maiesties ship and pinnage to come fordward
whill he ressaue new derection outher from his Maiestie
or by his Ma^{ttes} appoyntment from the counsall heere,
Becaus the ship and pinnage can do no seruice now whill
a land force be prouyded to assist thame, and becaus diuers
of the rebells of Yreland doeth daylie repair from thense
heere, and doeth joyne with our rebelles, the Lord deputie
is desyred to tak some course wherby the resort of suspect

persones from Yreland towardes this countrey may be
stayed, and yf ony of our rebelles come there, to persew
thame, and he is lykwise desyred to have a care that no
supplie nor ayd in poulder, armour nor victuales come
heere to our rebelles from Yreland.

And wheras the erle of Ergyle is looked for to be send
home with all haist and diligence with a ample comissioun
of lieutenandrie for suppressing of this rebellioun, the
counsall beeng carefull to haue his owne boundes and
countrey vnder warning and in reddynes agane his home
comeing to joyne with him or such others as shall haue
comissioun from his Maiestie in this seruice, they haue sett
out a proclamation aganes all betweene sextie and sexteinth
yeeres within the Schirefdomes of Ergyll and Tarbett to
be in reddyness with all warrelyk provision and furnitour, and with gallayis and birlinges and fourtyes [1] [*sic*]
victuales and provision to joyne with his Maiesties lieuten-
nand and to pass fordward with him by sea and land, and
to conveane and meete at such dayes tymes and places as
they shalbe advertesed by new proclamatioun vpon sex dayes
warning vnder the paine of tinsell of lyf, land and goodes.

The Larde of Auchinbrek who hes the charge of the
countrey of Ergyll is wrotten to, to haue a care and re-
guarde of the dew executione of that comission and charge
whitche he vndertook vpon the xxij[th] of this instant, and
to rease and vse the whole powar and forceis within the
boundes vnder his charge for defence of the countrey,
persute of the rebelles and assisting of his nightbour
boundes who shall happen to be distressed by the rebelles.

Missiues ar derected to the tounes of Glasgo, Air and
Dunbartane chargeing thame as thay wilbe ansuerable at
there highest perrell that they suffar no pouldar, lead,
armour nor victuales to go oute of there townes to the
vse of the rebelles nor to be sold to ony suspect persones,
and they ar comanded to furnishe his Ma[tles] comissionars
who ar employed in this seruice with all kynd of necess-
ars vpone moderat and reasonable pryces.

---

[1] *Quære* forty days.

110. Copie of the names of these who betrayed the Castell of Dunywaige to Sr James McDonald in Junij 1615

Thair names who wes the tratouris to the hous of Dunyvaige

p. 275

      Johne M^cdoull vyre v^c donald
      Alex^r M^cdoull vyre his brother
      Sorill M^cdoull vyre his brother
      Coill M^cdoull vyre his brother
      Duncan M^cdouill vyre his brother who slew his
        maister Alex^r M^cdougall wth ane shoatt
      Johne M^calester v^c ean, ane vther servand of Alex^r
        who wes one of the ploteris and gaue his maister
        two straikes wth ane sword as is reportit.

Thair names who refussit to concur wth me and skaillet my [1] watter

      Coill M^cean v^c alester M^cdougall
      Alexander M^cdonochie vyre v^c allane
      Alex^r M^cdouill v^c alester
      Ewir M^cean v^c ewir, and
      Johne M^cean v^c ewir, tua of ye clanlaine.

111. Copie of my ansueir to Sir Rorie Makcloyde

Ult. Junij 1615

S^R—zo^r lfe of the 18 of this monethe wes this day delyuered to my lord Chanceller and me q^rby we persaue zo^r faithfull affectioun to do his Matie good seruice againes his rebellis q^rin I pray yow to perseuere constantlie following the exemple of zo^r foirbeares assureing yow that if zo^r weele doing desserue his Maties favo^r and liberalitie he is bothe als willing and more powarfull to recompence good seruice nor ony king that euer reigned in this Ile. We haue knawine this day that the rebellis hes teane the

---

[1] Cf *post*, p 265   There is nothing to show when or by whom this memorandum was written.

Castell of Duneveg, quhiche makis thair rebellioun moir manifest and odious, and will force his Maiestie and counsell to vse the greater powar and diligence to ouerthrow and puneis theme. I pray zou sick all good occasiounes to hairme the traito^ris and giue zo^r true concurrance with zo^r best forces to those quho sall persew theme be his Maiesties cōmissioune. Zo^r opinioun for thair persute mentioned in zo^r lr̃e is verie gude and weele allowed as yow will persaue be the cōmissiounes gevin to zo^r self and zo^r nightbo^ris principall commandares of the Iles and hielandes. His Maiestie is adverteised with the rebellis proceedingis with aduyce from the counsall to send schippis and cannons againes theme with all other neces- sare forces and prouisioune as forder salbe concluded zow salbe adverteised nather sall the wrangis done to zow be zour nightbouris be neglectit bot according to the tryell zow salbe repaired. In the mean tyme the counsall desyres zow to foirbeare all violence againes zour nightboures. Bot if they intend ony violence againes zow, defend zo^r selfis with all convenient moderatioun, least zo^r particulares bread hinderence to his Maiesties seruice. So hoiping zow will let me know with diligence all thingis falling furth quhiche zow sall think fit to be signified to the counsall I commit zow to the protectioun of god, Edinburghe the last of Junij,   Zo^r verie loveing freend.

My Lord Chancellare and the rest of the lordes of his Maiesties counsall hes desyred me to adverteiss yow that this letter must be accompted as an ansuer from the haill counsall.

I sall presenthe wryte to his Maiestie the contents of your letter and signifie to his hienes your faithfull purpose to give him pruif of your true hairt to do him seruice therfore I pray yow be cairefull to show it be good effects to eschew your owne repruif and myne which can not be done if efter so dewtifull promeisses yow aither kythe slewthfull or vndeutifull which I will nowayes suspect.

112. Earl of Argyll to the King

[*Undated*]

Sir—it hes Placsed god to uisit me so that I am not hable to undergo any long Jurnay, I haif thair for send by the secretaire ane nott of souch things as I think most fitt for your Matie seruice in the Iyls, wh^lk^ls I know will performe als mouch as I could haif done my self, whon I had helth I did bestow it in your Maties seruice, and now whon I am not hable, whone it placsis God to send me helth I schalbe as heirtofoir your Matie hes found me—your Matie obedient Subject, Argyll.

113. Copy, Sir James Macdonald to the Marquess . of Hamilton

July 1

My vere honorable good lord—Pleas your Lo. in respect my forebears hes beene dependars and servantes to zo^r Lo. house, I this far bould to entreat yor Lo. to do for me and accept of me : that according to my dewtie I and my whole race shalbe bund to serve zo^r Lo. hous, So long as any of ws leeves, And wherein I would haue zo^r Lo. to deall for me I haue wrotten the same at more length to yor Lo. kinsman and servant the captan of Arran to be showen to zo^r Lo. So abyding zo^r Lo. fauorable answere, Comitting zo^r Lo. in godes protection I rest—Zo^r lo. ever assuired frend and seruand, Sir James McDonald.

Ila, Julij the first.

Derected on the bak to my Lord Marques of Hamilton.

114. The same to Lord Binning

My verie honourabill gude lord—Pleis your lo. I wald haue writtin to your lo. long or now, had not I culd find no bearer, becaus nane of my awin dar go thair.

Aluyse, I will euer think myself bund for the fauour your lo. schew me at my being last in the Castell, whanne God knawis vtheris wes bent to wrong me be thair fals accusationis ; whose feir, and the report they gave out that my lyfe was onlye in thair willis, was the onlye motione of the braik of ward ; and no intentione nor desyre I had, or hes to live as ane Rebell or outlaw ; whiche traid, the Lord knawes, I abhore ; bot that I wald glaidlie live at libertye with my lyfe saif. And now, my lord, I beseik your lo., for the fauour of God and my perpetuelle seruice, pitie me and be my freind, that his Maiestie may be graciouslye moved not to zield to my vnfreindis, to ruit me and my whole race out, being fyve or sex hundreth zeiris possessouris, and now willing to obey and serwe his Maiestie, in all humilitie, I, seing how I and my pure freindis may live ; and if zour lo. culd find the meanis that his Ma^{te} and Counsall may be moved to let me posses this pure Iland, paying for it as anie vther may or hes zit offerrit to do, and getting my pardone, sall find sufficient suretie, both for my zeirlie dewtye and the peace and quyetnes of me and all that dwellis vnder me. Gif zour lo. may or will do me any guid in this, I will not onlie be ane to do zour lo. guid seruice, bot, with Goddis graice, let zour lo. sie my thankfulnes. I beseik zour lo., for Goddis cause, be playne with me, and if his Ma^{te} may not be moved to let me haue this Iland, diminissing nothing of his Ma^{tes} commoditie, that zour lo. will let me know, be zour advise, be what vther meanis his Ma^{te} may be moved to grant ane generall pardone to me and all myne ; and that we may haue to susteine ws in sum measour, leist we be forcit, being without oure living, to oppress vtheris. This abyiding zour lo. ansueir, committing zow to God, I rest, Zour lo. euir to command, SIR J. MAKDONALL.

Julij 1.

115. The same to the same

MY LORD—If his Maiestie be not willing that I sall be his heighnes tennent in Ila, for Goddis cause let his Matie

hauld it in his awin hand ; for that is certane, I will die befoir I sie a Campbell posses it.   And his Matie haulding it in his awin hand, his Ma^{te} may haue ane thousand merkis mair be that, nor Calder suld pay ; I making it quyt of me and my kin, whiche I will do vpoun suche reasonabill conditiones as I will schow zour lo., if ze may assure me that ze may get his Matie brocht to this poynt, and in the meintyme no imployment be gevin aganis me, till zour lo. sie how this may be brocht to pas.   As for this House of Duneveg, which I tuik in four and tuenty houris from Calderis menne, your lo. getting me fauour of his Ma^{te}, the house salbe to serve his Ma^{te}, and neuer to be keipit aganis his hienes.   And if his Ma^{te} awin Gaird or the Bischopes had bein in the House, befoir God I wald neuer persew it ; bot finding these in it, who crewellie opprest the pure cuntrie, wes the onlie suitteris of my lyfe and landis, I wald I culd do thame mair disgrace ! Referring all to zour lo. consideratione and ansueir, I rest, Zour lo. euer to be commandit,   Sr J. MAKDONALL.

Julij 1.

To my Lord Secretare.

116. The same to the Earl of Caithness

MY VERIE HONORABLE GOOD LORD—Pleas your lo. the ondeserued fauour and courtesee which I resaued by your lo., in showing your selue my frend, that tyme at Court, when my onfrendes did misreporte of me to his Maiestie, makes me now this bold to beseek your lo. to continew my frend, according to my reasonable sute.   And, in speciall, that your lo. will meane my caise to your frendes in Counsall ; for I protest my beeng ten yeeres in warde in the Castle of Edinburgh, and the disponeing of my kyndlie landes, made me not so much to tak that haistie resolution to esheap, as when I was assured, by his owine frendes reportes, that my lyf wes geven over in the Larde of Caddelles handis ; who beeing, as your lo. knowes, nowise my frend, or one to trust my lyf to ; alwise now I beseek

your lo., as yee shall till death have my poore service, try
by the Counsall, yf vpone any conditiones, not diminishing
his Maiesteis comoditie, I may have this peece of old
possessiounes, which is Illa, to susteane my selue and all
my kinne, that now followes me ; that his Maiestie may
have his owine, with honour and ease, and wee to leeve in
peece and offend no manne, and I, getting suretie of my
lyff and of this peece land, shall find sufficient suiretie,
both for my obedyance and good ordour, keeping by all
my kinne and frendes. As your lo. learnes in this, or can
be hable to do me fauour in getting me his Maiesteis peace,
your lo. will aduertese me. And I beseech your lo., so far
as you can, crosse the Campbelles to gett any employmintes
againes me—for they caire not how much they trouble the
countree and put his Maiestie to charges needles. As for
the House of Dwnoveg, I tooke it from Calderis menne, in
the speace of one day,—killed parte of thame, vpone the
Greene of the House,—chaised in the rest,—tooke there
watter [1] and the two Barmkines from them,—and forced
thame to yeeld in my will, the next morning. So I have
the House, neuer to be gevin to these that is not worthier
of it. But yett, his Maiestie may ever command it and
my selue, I seeng how I may leeve with the assureance of
my lyff and my poore frendes.—So, abyding your lo.
aduertesment, with the rememberance of my humble
seruice, I shall ever remaine, Your lo. assured frend to
serve yow,   S^R J. MAKDONALL.

Ila, 2 Julii.

I beseech your lo. let me know how my lord Secretar is
towards me ?—Or who is most for Calder ?—Or how he is
now thoght of be his Matie ?

To the Erle of Caithenes.

117. The same to the same

My Lord—Geve the Consall be curius to knaw whom it
was thatt Calder send to, he had the Warand for taiking

---

[1] Cf. *ante*, p. 260.

my lyfe. The Pryar of Ardchattan and M^ckwoll his sone, Allan M^cdowgall is my authours; and they will not, nor can not deny itt. Also Calder's avin agent, James Movatt, maid no secreitt thairof; for he tauld it both to the Erle of Crawfuird and to M^cintois. I wald not nov, becaus I had nott ane beirar of my avin, haisart to vryt to the Secrettar, bott itt is only in your lo. and his lo. thatt I trust. I know Calder and the Cambellis wilbe buissie to seik imployment of service aganes me; bott the same sall nott be neidfull, for your lo. and my Lord Secrettar may better bring me to that quhilk salbe most to his Ma^{te} commodite and the quyetnes of the contre, without bestoving oney chargis nor all the Cambellis liveand may or can do by his Ma^{ttes} fors, quhilk I will ever except, and honour, and respeck what zour lo. wryttis to me, onles the Consall dereck one to me. Zour lo. may send zour Letters to my lord Tuillibairne, to be sent be his lo. to the Officer of Lochaber, wha will send thame to me whair ever I be.—So abyding your lo. ansuer, I rest, Your lo^s ever to serve you, Sr J. MAKDONALL.

[*Without date.*]

To my verje honourable gud lord, my lord Erle of Caittnes.

118. The same to the Earl of Crawfurd

MY VERIE HONORABLE GOOD LORD—I wes not four nightes out of the Castle when I wrotte to your lo., but be not sure if your lo. hes ressaued my Letter. I have now wrotten thir few lynes, praying your lo. to remember me zour promese and conferrence with me. As for my selue, I am well, praised be God, and all my kyndlie men hes ressaued me most glaidlie. I will do all I can to have his Ma^{tes} peace, and find also good suiretie for my obedience and yeirlie dewtie as may suffice. And if my onefrendis crose me, I trest in God, how so ever the mater go, to be evin with thame. I pray your lo. see if it be possible yee may gett outher manne or boy to come speak with me, and aduertese me moir of all your awin estate and dyett, and of all such newes as occurs. Any of my bookes that your lo. can gett, send them to me, and vse your moyen to gett from the Erle of Atholl the bookes that wes tane from me at that onsett in Atholl. They gatt the thrie conversiones of England, Burnes book, and it that Phillip sett out on the controverted heades, it ze saw Makcartney wrotte, the Mekle old Cornikle, in wrett. Ther wes other bookes that I remember not, bot your lo. may seek thame all to your selue. I pray your lo. gett me word from Pittfindie, and try if I will gett my mounter and chister to lovse.

This wes the forme of the taking of Duneveg. We lay in ane buis about the hous, till the Captane and tuelf of his best men com out. We persewed ouer rashlie or they come far from the hous. The Captanes men fled, bot him selue and three or foure wer slane. We zeid in at the vtter Barmkin with the rest, but they closed the zett of the inner Barmkin. Or tuelf hours we took the vatter, the vtter tour, and the tuo Barmkyns from thame, and sett fyre to the zett of the inner Barmkin, brunt it, killed and hurt some of there menne in with our shott; for we shott from four in the morning till efter tuelfue. Tuo of myne wes killed, a shouldiour and ane boy; tuo lightlie hurt. The hous wes promesed to yeeld or ten hours the morn. And so wes the Pryour and all that come out gatt thair lyff and there cloathes.

I trest in God that all the Campbelles in Scotland, without his Maties powar, shall not recouer it, so long as they live. I heare Patie Kilchrist is troubled for me; bot I protest to God he is innocent of my break, and all that is in that Castle. No more, but remember me to all frendes, specialie to Margrate, to Cristian, and all your owne frendes in the breathing; and also my homble seruice remembered, I rest, Your lo. owin to command,

S^R J. MAKDONALL.

July 3, Fra Duneveg.
To The Erl of Craufurd.

119. The same to the Bishop of the Isles

MY VERIE GOOD LORD—Pleis your Lo. war not I hard your lo. was in Ireland, and could find no meanes to wreit to yow, I was not four nightes out of Ed^r, quhan I would have writtin to your lo. as to one quhom I haue euer found my friend. And now, my Lord, I protest, albeet I was xij zeires in waird, and all my kyndlie landis disponed to strangeres, my lyff left in his Maiesties handis, zett the same maid me not so mvche to braik ward as it did quhan I was offered be the Laird of Calderes awin freendis, quha can not deny it, that his Maiestie, be his secreit Warrand, had gevine ower my lyff in the Laird of Calderes handis. And now, my lord, I protest to God my desyre is not to rebell or truble the Esteat of the cuntrie, bot serue his Maiestie with all humilitie, and mak my kin and freindis paceable men, iff I may haue his Maties pace, with the assuirance of my lyff and the lyfe of my puir freendis, and some meanes to susteane ws rather nor to fors ws, for want, to opres otheres. Heirfoir I beseek your lo. seing my Race has bene tenne hundreth yeeris kyndlie Scottis men, vnder the Kinges of Scotland ; and war I willing to leive vpoun ane puir pairt of that quhilkis our foirbeiraris had, and I to find gud suirtie for all that becomes loyall subiectis to do, both for myself and my quholl kin that followes me, that zour lo. will, as ze euer did, interseed for me at his Maties handis to sie quhat grace or fauour zour lo. may obtein to me, and in speciall, to sie give, without diminisching his Maties commoditie, I may have the Iland to my self and my kin to susteine ws ; wtherwayis that zour lo. will get that fauour that no hesté curse salbe taine againes me, be geveing imployment to my onfreendis, till your lo. may have tyme first to speck with me ; att quhiche tyme, albeit I gett not the Iland, zett, provyding his Maiestie will hauld it in his awin hand, I will shaw your lo. how his Maties commoditie heir may be incressed, and I to be satisfied, and this cuntrie to be frie of ony truble of me or my freendis.

As for this House of Dunovege, I protest to God, give

aither his Maiesteis Gaird or your lo[s] men war keepares of it, I wald neuer enter within it, albeit it war without keeping—bot finding it suche as serued them quha foght my lyf and landis, and quho crewally opprest this puir Iland in such sort, that I protest to God thair desing was rather to waist it, nor mak it able to pay his Ma[tles] rentes. The same maid me preserwe the hous ; and albeit that Hous cost his Ma[tle] muche money in putting it in Calderis handis, it pleased God that, in one day (I took it), with the lose bot of one man.   And now if your lo. may get me fauourable conditiones be his Ma[tle], ze may assuir zour self I will give yow the Hous, provyding it be in your handis, and nane of the Cambellis to gett it.   As your lo. does in this, or is lyk to do, adverteis me.—And so, reposeing in your lo[s] constand freendschip, I committ your lo. to God, and restis, Your lo[s] ever assuired to command,

S[R] J. MAKDONALL.

In hope, with Goddis grace, 1 will geve zour lo. zitt ane better propyne, I pray your lo. send me ane Inventaré with this bearer, for I am far from the clock.

S[R] J. MAKDONALL.

To the Bischeop of the Illis.

120. The same to Mr. James Knox

RIGHT WORSHIPFULL—I have, for some bussinesse, pairtly concerning your father, sent this bearer to Edinburgh ; and geve my lord be gone to England, I pray yow faill not, as yee respect his lo. well, to send his Letter to him, with suretie that it may com to his handes ; for I hawe wrotten to his lo. the thing that I hope shall come to his lo. honour and credite ; and there is none leaueand vnder his Maiestie that I will do more to, till do be, and do him all the honour and credite I can.   Heir I will entreat yow, give ze be in Ed[r], and any of my Letters come to zour hand, yee will delyver thame to suche as I

have wretten thame to.   And so, reposeing in zour good
will, and assureing zow I am to serve and honour zour
father and zour selue, I rest, Zour assured frend to
command,   Sr J. MAKDONALL.

From Ila, 4 Julij.

(*Postscript.*)   SIR—Albeit it be too great paines, yet in
hope I will, God willing, do zow yett more seruice, send ony
of zour servandis with all the rest of my Letters to such
as thay are derected to, and what answer bees gotten,
geve it to the berar.   I rest, Zour assuired frend,
                                        Sr J. MAKDONALL.

To Mr James Knox, sone to my Lord Bishope of the
Illis and Raupho.

121. George Grahame his depositioun

the 6 of *Julij* 1615

At Edinburgh the saxt day of July 1615 in pñce of my
Lord Chancellair,[1] thesaurair depute and aduocat.

George Grahame haueing seene and red the lr̃e writtin
be him to Hector M^cneill he acknowledgeis the lr̃e to be
his awne lr̃e writtin be him self.
Demandit whome he maid Cap^{ne} of the Castell of
Dunnyvaig quhen the Castell wes delyuerit to him, deponis
that he delyuerit the Castell bak agane to Angus Oig
vpoun his promeis and oathe that he sould keepe the
same in his Maties name, and that he sould delyuer the
same to ony his Maiestie wold appoynt to ressaue the same.
Demandit yf when he come from Dunnyvaig he spak
with the Laird of Cadell his Maties lieutennent and desirit
him not to go to Ila, denyis the same.
Demandit yf he desyrit him to stay till his bak coming,

---

[1] It is rather startling to find Dunfermline presiding at the examination of
the scoundrel whom he had himself employed

deponis that he onlie aduisit him not to go to Ila vnles he wer weele accompanyit and had his Maties cannoun with him.

Demandit yf he desirit the lieutennent to go with him to Courte deponis that he desirit him to go to courte, and the deponner promeist to go with him, and if the pledgeis pleasit thay sould go w^t him.

Demandit yf he said to the Laird of Cadell that he wald tak the burdyne of his reteiring vpoun him, denyis the same.

Demandit yf Cadell promeist to the deponner that he sould do nothing in the yle quhill he send him bak worde frome the Counsell, deponis that Cadell said to the deponner, that he wald onlie go veu the Ile and that he wald do no thing thairin quhill the cannoun come.

Demandit for quhat caus he write suche thingis in his lr̃e as now he standis not to, deponis that he did the same rashlie and vpoun simplicitie. Sic subscribitur

G. GRAHAME.

122 [1]

Whereas G. G. hauing to the notable hinderance of o^r seruice in the Iles assured the rebels that he had warrant to stay the coming of o^r forces and canon frome Irland, and to stay o^r lieutenent frome coming to Ila willing them to keepe the house against all men whatsomever til they hard from him And being demanded both by o^r selfe and by some others of o^r counsell by what authority and vpon what warrant he did these thingis wee finde his answeres to varie so far both frome the report of otheris of good credite, from the depositiones of the rebels who haue stood to the treuth of them to the death And in some pointes frome his owne wordes and writtinges as wee can grounde no certeynty

---

[1] This item and the next are written on the same sheet of paper and endorsed 'concerning the service in Ila.' They seem to be drafts or copies of communications from the King, but it does not appear to whom they were addressed.

vpon them [1] And because yee are one of his owne name
and kinred whome in respecte of zo^r place and calling wee
psuade o^r selfe that he will reuerence wee haue thought
good be these presents to require zow earnestlie and effec-
tuallie to deale with him to declare vnto you the simple
treuth of all that busines and that he halte no longer by
concealing ony reason or circumstance of any pte thereof,
and so draw vpon him selfe the punishment eyther of his
owne waywardnes or of another man's offence assuring him
that if he deals vprightlie and sincerelie with you in his confession wee may be easelie moued to pardon his trespas But
if he shall persiste in his dissimulation, the nixte wilbe a
warrant to putte him in the boote, what he confesseth let
him eyther vnder his owne hand setle doun and giue to
you to be sent hither to vs or then ze zo^r selfe write it and
wee faythfullie promise to zou vpon the word of a king that
his said confession shall go no farther then o^r selfe so as
neyther shall he feare to be preeiudged nor any other
man endomaged thereby And in this pointe expecting the
best of yor endeuo^{ris} wee etc.

123

Whereas the B. of the Iles hauing complayned vnto vs
that Sr John Campbell of Calder wrongis him by challenging the Abbacie of Ikolmekille w^{ch} (as he affirmeth) hath
time oute of minde apperteyned to the B.B. of the Iles,
And wee hauing conferred with the said Sr John concerning that mater wee finde him so reasonable as he consentis
to submitte the decision of that controuersie to the said
Abbacie eyther to the ordinarie course of law, to the iudgement of such as wee shall appointe or to the arbitriment
of neutrall freindis Wee haue therefor thought good by
these pñts to require zow to examyne the title of the said

---

[1] Notwithstanding the great body of testimony in their favour and the
obvious mendacity of Grahame, Angus Oig and several of his followers were
tried and condemned for high treason on 3rd July and hanged at the Market
Cross of Edinburgh on 8th July. According to Calderwood (vol. vii. p. 200)
'the people thought hard of it.'

Sr John to the said Abbacie and if you sall finde it in-
sufficient that ye aduertise him to desiste from further
vsing the same, but if yee sall find it good and valide that
yee end the said controuersie vpon such equitable condicions as yee sall thinke sufficient and reasonable.

124. Archibald Campbell, younger of Ardchattan to Lord Binning

15 *July* 1615

RIGHT NOBLE LORD—I ressaued z^or Lo. letter of the
13 of June as whair your Lo. wrettes the trust and caire
of Duneveg wes cõmitted to me in furnisheing it with
victuell, poulder and lead, if your Lo. findes or heeres by
report that it laikit any of these prouisiones I am to be
blamed and byd z^or Lo. censure, and to pleace more men
I had no warrand of the Lard, for if those who were
appoynted to remaine within the house had beene trustie
to there maister it neidit no more men. The certantie of
that conspiracie and ploitt can nevir be cleerlie knowne
whill those who were within the saides house be present
afoir the Lordis. My Lord, at my comeing out of Ila I
mett with Sir James' Lady wha reported privatlie to me
for certantie that Donald Gorme, the captane of clanronnald and M^{c}cloyd had a speciall band between thame
and Sir James, as for Makcleane he wes not fullie resolued
at that present tyme, bot sade he would do no thing
againest tham, and yf he desyred to go against thame he
would not be verie earnest. Sence my comeing to Lorne I
mett with a man, who spak with her Ladiship, who reportes
that Makcleane hes latelie tunit with them, I can not
assuire your Lo. of this bot shee reported it to me for
verritie, and at my beeng in Ila Makcleane's brother
persewed me and my company hardest of any. My father
derected four boyes till Ila for a seek man and to enquyre
newes wha reportes Sir James with his companie ar bissie
repairing the yll of Loughgorme and Downnand, as for
Dunyveg they think it not hable to be manned. The

nomber of Sir James companie is about four hundreth;
I heir sindric Kintyre men ar going to him. I dout not
your Lo. hes hard how Ronnald McJames and the oyes
hes tunit with Sir James, I shall not faill to mak your Lo.
frequent with there proceedinges at euerie certane occasion
to which tyme I remain—zo^r Lo. ever to my power,

A. CAMPBELL.

Ardchattan, the 15 of Julij 1615.

125. Campbell of Ardchattan to Lord Binning

15 *July* 1615

RIGHT NOBLE LORD—I ressaued your lo. lettre of the
first of Julij as where your Lo. desyres that frendis may be
diligent in repressing these rebelles, your Lo. may see
there awne answer to the counsall where they discharge
them selues from medleing with that service whill they
see a lieutennant before tham, I can assure your Lo. till
the counsalles nixt aduertesment or the lairdes owine
presence there will be nothing done againes the rebelles,
as for newes of there proceedinges my sone Archibald hes
wrotten all that he could learne, for they put all there
trust in there strenthes, as for Dunyveag they lippin least
to it, and thinkes not to keepe it. Bot whill they heere
of armie comeing to the countrie So that there most
trust is in the yle and Downand be reason they think
them onvincibill, and they dar not mak to the seas for
fear of the shippes, my sone Archibald hes spyes in seuerall
partes and at euerie certan occasion your Lo. may be
assuired to heere all newes; My Lord, as to me or my
barnes all we haue is of his Maiestie and the larde of
Calder, and yf we haue offended his Maiestie and prowin
vntrustie frendes to the larde of Cadell we ar to byd zo^r
Lo. and the rest of the counsalles censo^r So that I beseek
zo^r Lo. not till geue credite till euerie reporte whill my
owine presence. The nomber of fourtie men ar verrie
vnhable to do anie thing to four hundrethe, the longer the

rebelles be vnpersued they mak the greater beild in there
streangthes and gettes the greatter nomber. So to zo^r
Lo. ansuer or new occasion I rest—zo^r Lo. to be cõmanded
with seruice,   AL. CAMPBELL of Ardchattan.

Ardchattan, ye 15 of July 1615.

126. Archibald Campbell, younger of Ardchattan to Lord Binning

16 *July* 1615

RIGHT NOBLE LORD—Efter the wreitting of this packat,
on of my spyes come to me, quha reportis that Sr James
company is pairt of Donald Gorme men, pairt of the
Capitã clanrannald mē and of McCloid mē. All the company
in Kintyre ar going with him. The traitouris of the Clan-
donnald owir quha betrayit thair M^r ar thair spayes in
thir boundis of Lorne. They expect no enemy to come on
them. Not having farder to new occasioune I rest—Zo^r L.
to my powar,   A. CAMPBELL.

v. p. 260

Ardchattan, the xvi of Julij.

127. Copie of the letter sent to me be Archibald Campbell, sone to the pryour of Ardchattan

29 *July* 1615

(Res. 4 *Aug.* 1615)

MY NOBLE LORD—I ressaved zo^r Lo. letter of the 22 of
Julij. I am certanelie informit be my spie that M^{c}fie of
Collinsay, Donald gigache in Jouray hes gone wth the rebels
and ar earnest transporting thair gudis to Ilay, they expect
no forces to go aganis them for the present. Sir James
wth the rest of the rebels ar for the present in Ilay and hes
endit thair strenthis, they ar daylie bounding for Kintyre ;
one of these men that was schot q^n the house wes rendered
is dead, Sir James sone is appoynted to keip Dunnyveg q^{ll}
they heir of schippis cūing about, Coll is appoyntit for the
Ile of Lochgorme : Thair is one of the rebels' servandis that

X dougald ??

Archbald Campbell of Kilmelphoure was cautioner for is gone wth thame as I am informit, I haue sum purpois in handis q^lk I dar not report to zo^r Lo. q^ll it tak sum effect one desyrit to know q^t he might luik for at my handis if he brought me a good blok, I dar wryt no more bot prayes zo^r Lo. let me know q^t I may promeis for good service. So to new occasion I remaine,

Zo^r Lo. ever to my power.

Ardchattan, 29 July 1615.

Please zo^r Lo. confer wth the bearar who can schew zo^r Lo. of o^r occident that was out of the houss be M^ccleane's brother and the cuntrie people.

128. Copie of the letter sent to me be Hector Makneill

29 July 1615

(Res. 4 *Aug.* 1615)

My Lord—My humble dewtie remembred. It will pleas zo^r L. that since I wrot to zo^r L. last, Donnald Gorme, Sir James bestardis sone came into Kintyre the number of tuentie four souldiours and finding the Kingis houss in Keanloch woid without any in it hes taine the same vpone Wednsday last, Sr James, Coill M^callisbit,[1] and the haill rebels of the number of foure hundreth come to Yla to Kintyre and ar gladlie ressaved of many of cuntrie me thair, The haill speciall inhabitants of Yla ar also wth the rebels, Two speciall me that held of Argyle befoir ar newlie rebellit wth thame, M^cduphe of Collinson [2] and his haill name, and Donnald Gigaich Makean who held Jura of Argyle, those two chiftanes ar gaine wth the rebels thriescore and foure and remaines in Kintyre in pairtis neirest Argyll as zit making thair boast and wowing to be at the Tarbert q^lk is nyne myls within Argyle's boundis this night or the morne

---

[1] Coll M'Gillespick.
[2] Colonsay

Auchinbrek hes convocat all that he could and is to resist
thame and to persew in cace they pas the boundis of
Kintyre he hes left cōpanies to keip all boundis and coistis
neir thair persute he is cairfull to dischairge ane honest
dewtie in that he hes taine in hand, many pairtis neirest
Kintyre castin weast in speciall my haill estate and my
frendis which if ye treuth war knowne to zoᵣ Lo. zoᵣ Lo.
wald lament it, the rebels in so ffar as I can learne presumes
to no les nor more then euer thair forebearis had, except it
please god and his Maᵗⁱᵉ to provyd sum suddane remedie,
for the rebels dispairis of any persute, and allures many
to follow thame be assuring thame of Argyle's death, so
Argyle's lang stay makis all thair pryde to increas all the
cuntries ar aloft qᵗ sall succeid zoᵣ L. sall heir as all
occasions offers, so lang as I bruik my liff zoᵣ L. sall be
assured of the poare service I may or can be able to do,
praying god for zoᵣ L. happines I rest and ever to death
sall remaine, Zoᵣ Lo. most humble and
always ready to serve zow.

Thyneis, 29 July 1615.

This day we ar all wairned be Auchinbrek and passes
fordward.

129. Sir Dougal Campbell of Auchinbrek [1] to the Chancellor

(Received Aug. 4, 1615.)

HONORABLE GOOD LORD—My humble dewtie remembrit,
please zour lo. to wit, that I am heer in the Tarbet, attending vpone our enemies coming farder in the cuntrie.
Zour lo. sall vnderstand, since my last wryting to zour lo.,
Sir James the traitour hes latlie directit out ane fyrie croce [2]
from the head of Lockerrane, quhair he makes his residence

---

[1] There is a valuable genealogical account of the Campbells of Auchinbreck and their cadets in the Advocates' Library (MS. 34. 6. 19); vide also *Highland Papers*, vol. ii. p. 96, note 2.

[2] Vide *Highland Papers*, vol. i. p. 305.

✳ Printed in Highland Papers, Vol. IV, pp. 63-89.

for the tyme, to the Tarbart, vpone the pretence that all maner of man betuix the Mull of Kintyre and the Tarbart sould come and tak land of him. And to preveine this, that the cuntree sould get no skaith, I have directit for to get more assistance of men throw Argyle and Lorne. Zour lo. sall know that I was not ansuerit, according to my Commissioun. The monyest that came to me was ane hundreth men; the number of the haill thrie hundreth men. Wishing zour lo. to tak ordour with the cuntries disobedience, for farder inconvenience; quhilk I fear will come to more skaith, if they be not punischit for thair fault. I sall give vp in sorow to your lo. the particular disobeyars. These Rebels ar in readines with fyve nichtis provisioun and lone. Quhair they ar to mak thair onset I know not; bot they ar mor in number than I wret to zour lo. in my last Letter. I dowt not bot zour lo. remembers the dait of my Commission, quhilk approchis neir to the sext day of August; quhairfor I thocht good to mak zour lo. forsein of this, that zour lo. may tak ane ordour farder with thir Rebels. So, not troubling zour lo. with farder writ, committis zour lo. to the protectioun of the Almighty God.—Zour lo. to be commandit to my powar, AUCHINBRECK.

Tarbart, 30 July, 1615.

130. Copy, Sir James Macdonald to Paull Hamilton, captan of Arran

31 *July* 1615

RIGHT LOVEING AND ASSURED FREND—I am many wise oblished to rander many thankes to zow for your loue and kyndnes to my poore kin and frendes in tyme of there gretest trouble, and in speciall to that poare boy my sone which fauour shall not be onrequett so far as my powar may be hable euer to do zow pleasour, and now for my owine parte althoght for the saifetie of my lyf I haue offended his Maiestie and counsall by braiking ward zett god is my wittnes my desyre is not nor neuer wes to rebell nor to trouble the peace of the countree But only to serue his Matie in all humbilitie for pairt of that which my forebeais hes had, Now S^r as zee haue beene a frend euer to me and myne So I will now entreat zow do me that fauo^r to go with this my letter to my Loid Maiques your Maister, which letter I would not close till yee first redd it that according therto zee may speak his Lo. and resolue me what I may look for at his Lo. handes, for it is kyndlie to his Lo. to do for me and my race, and it is our dewtie to serue his Lo. befor ony subiect in this land and for my owne pairte yf through yough^th and euill counsall I did ouersee my dewtie to his Lo. father or him selue in any degree I am most sorie for it, and shall redeeme my offence god willing with my seruice to his Lo. and his hous. Praying zow sir therefore to deall with my loid and see for my perpetuall seruice and all my kin that I may cõmand geue his Lo. wold tak a doing for me that his Matie and counsall wold not at the onlawfull desyre of my onfrendes seeke to roote me oute But rather suffer me to haue this poore iland doing to his Maiestie for it as ony onkyndly tennent shall do, And yf his Lo. will tak on him selue the setling of this erand his Lo. shall haue hono^r by it, for at his Lo. word I will come to him to Hamiltoun and do by his derection by all the subiectes hes Maiestie hes, And in the meantyme till his Lo. try how he may best do his Maiestie good seruice without charges and ws some good that his Lo. will stay otheres to gett employ-ment in that bussines to our prejudice Sir I beseech zow deall in this and as zee find, adverteis me and show Arch-bald Makallestar or Hector what newes yee haue for the present anent the counsalles mynd or the Campbelles towardis me. Lett this cõmend me harthe to zo^r kynd wyff and cõmend me to zo^r self I rest—Zo^r euer assuired to my powar,   SIR JAMES M^cDONALD.

July ye last.

Directed on the bak To Paull Hamilton, Captan of Arran.

131. Copy Letter, Lord Binning to Archibald Campbell, younger, of Ardchattan

4 Aug[t] 1615

TREST FREIND—zo[r] servand delyvered to me this night zo[r] lr̃e of the tuentie nyne of Julij. I thank zow for zo[r] adverteismẽt and will pray zow to continew dewtifull and diligent try and adverteis of the rebels' interpryses and proceidingis, for ze will w[th]in verie few dayes sic the erle of Argyle in the cuntrie with such forces be sea and land as will mak the owerthrow of the rebels suddane and easie w[th] godis grace, whair ze desyr to know of me what wairand ze may haue of ane recompans to ane man who sall do good service agams the rebels, I can not wryt to zou particularlie of any recompens, becaus ze wryt not to me of the qualitie of the service, bot ze knaw q[t] is promeised be proclamatioun both of remissioun and rewaird in money alwayes ze may be asured that whatever zou condition to any man for any worthie service to be done agams the rebels salbe faithfullie performed according to the mercit and qualitie of the fact, if ze had writtin more particularlie to me I sould haue sent ane more direct and speciall ansuer, bot I pray zou be diligent to procure the service to be done not dowting of ane condigne recompens and adverteis me oft of all the rebels' proceidingis. I haue inquyred of zo[r] man the maner of the rebels taking the houss, and Makclane's brothers persewing zou. I pray zow commend me to zo[r] father, whome wth zo[r] selff I cõmit to the protectioun of god. Ed[r], 4 Aug.,　　　　　　　　Zo[r] verie good fieind.

132. Copy of the Council's letter to Auchinbrek

4 Aug. 1615

RIGHT TRAIST FREIND—after oure verie hartlie commendatiouns by your lr̃e send to the Lord Chancellar we ar informit of the proceidingis and resolutiouns of the trayto[r] M[c]donald within the boundis of Kyntyre and of the preparationis maid be your selff for withstanding of his insolencyis and keeping of the countrie harmeles of him, whairin as you haif approvin your selff worthie of the credite and trust q^{lk} we did repoiss in you and for the q^{lk} we rander vnto you our hairtlie thankis, so we will gif notice yairof vnto his Maiestie who is nevir vnmyndfull of suche weill deserving serviceis, And whereas it appeiris by your lr̃e that you putt some questioun and doubt anent the terme of your commissioun q^{lk} you tak to be expyrit, ffor removing of this scioople we haif heirwith send vnto you ane ample commissioun within the haill boundis of Argyle and Lorne to indure to the hame comeing of the Erle of Ergyle and farder till the same be specialie dischargit   And we haif writtin to the Lairdis of Ardkinglas and Lochinzell to assist you with the forceis of Cowell and Lorne, And thairfoir these ar to requeist and desyre you to accept this new commissioun vpoun you, and as you haif weill begun that you will continew in the prosequutioun of the seruice and in speciall that you haif a speciall cair of the keeping of the countreis within your commissioun frie of the rebellis and to eschew the adventuring of the forceis of ye countrie raschlie quhairby the rebellis may draw yame in ony snair or ambushment, bot that your chief studie may be to defend the countrie and obedient subiectis from thair violence till the erll of Ergyllis comeing who is daylie expectit and wilbe so stronglie assistit with his Maiesteis forceis and shippis be sea and land as may enable him caselie to ouerthraw the rebellis without danger to his Maiesteis good subiectis, And so recommending thir premissis to your cairfull diligence as a point of seruice tuitcheing his Matie most heighlie in honno^r and quhairof the performance wilbe most acceptable to his Matie we bid you harthe fairweill from Ed^r the fourt of August 1615.

133. Copie of my ansuer sent to Hector Makneill

4 *Aug^t* 1615

S$_{IR}$—I have this day ressaved zo^r lr̃e of the 29 of Julij declairing the rebels cũing to Kintyre thair number, forces

and professioun to go aganis the rest of the cuntric to
the trouble and perrill of his Maties obedient subiects, I
schew to the counsall zo^r lře who wnderstud zo^r adverteisment to be trew becaus the Laird of Auchinbrek had
writtin to thame to that same effect. They have renewit
to Auchinbrek ane verie ample cōmissioun to convocat the
forces of the cuntrie to resist the rebels with strait command to all fensible peisons to assist him and becaus we
everie night expect the erle of Argyle's cūing to this towne
whome his Matie hes appoynted Lieutenant generall aganis
the rebels and is to furnische him waiged souldiours to
assist the cuntrey men for whome he is to send in two
of his schippis directit for that service wth artailzerie and
munitioun and all warlyk preparatioun and great number
of muskets, corslets, pikkis and vther veapons and armour
to arme the fied souldiouis who sould serve vpone land.
Such of the counsall as wer in this town have be o^r lře
desyred the Laird of Auchinbrek to draw togidder the
forces of the cuntrie and such as he sall find necessar to
resist the rebels and to hinder thame to do any harme or
violence to his Maties obedient subiects, and have re-
queested him to eschew soffar as may be that he adventure
not raschlie to giue any advantage to the rebels, or seiking
to owerthraw thame to indanger himselff and the forces
of the cuntrey vnles he be sure of advantage without
indangering himselff and his forces, for if they sould get
any victorie ower him, q^{lk} god forbid, it wald discourage
the cuntrey people and imboldin the rebels and give great
increas to thair reputation and forces, q^{ras} if the Laird
of Auchinbrek proceid wyshe and warlie being cheiflie
cairfull of the saftie of the cuntrie fiom skaith q^{ll} the erle
of Argyle's cūing to it q^{lk} will vndowtedlie be within verie
few dayes, he will come so stronglie provydit as thair is
no caus to dowt bot god will mak him caselie to owerthrow these traitours and mak the cuntrie quyte of thair
trouble for ever. Thairfor I pray zow go to Auchinbrek
and give him the best assistance ze can both wth zo^r
forces and counsall, and let him sie this lře to the effect
he may the more cleirlie know the counsal's mynd in his

proceidingis, q^rin wisliing to him and zou all happines I
rest, Zo^r verie assured freind.

    Ed^r, 4 Aug.

I pray zow faill not to adverteis me wth diligence of eveiie
thing that fallis furth in zo^r cuntrie fit to be knowne be his
Matie or his counsall.

134. Copie of my letter to the Erle of Argyle

5 *Aug.* 1615

MY MOST HONO^{BL} GOOD LORD—thinking my self assured
that zo^r Lo. wuld according to zo^r promeis contenit in zo^r
lf̃e of the 24 sent to me begin zo^r journey homeward vpone
the nixt day and endit at fardest within ten or tuell dayes
I certified to the counsall y^rof, and be letteris to Auchinbrek
and vtheris affirmed wndowtedlie that yor Lo. wald keip
that dyet, bot now wnderstanding zo^r lo. cairlesness of that
weightie chairge q^{lk} ze haue wndertaine aganis the tratours
who daylie growes in number, force and presumptioun
becaus they find no resistance, far les persute aganis thame,
q^rby they haue left some forces in Ila to keip Duneveg and
Lochgorme, and Makoneill self and sex hundreth wth him
having maid thame selffis maisteris of Kintyre ar so swelled
in pryde that they haue sent the fyre corss throw the
cuntrie and wairned all the inhabitants betuix Tarbert
and the Mull of Kintyre to tak thair land of the traito^r
Makoneill. We heir of so much boldnes in the rebels and
fear in the cuntrie people as we expect daylie to heir of
thair farder futting vpone zo^r Lo. cuntrie of Argyle which
zo^r owne people does fearfullie apprehend. We ar assured
of Auchinbrakis faithfulnes to his Matie and zo^r Lo. bot
do exceidinglie distrust his gouernement in respect of his
owne seiklines and disloyaltie of many of the Irische people
and boldnes and subtilitie of the rebels too able to kep
advantage of him, nather will I conceall that zo^r Lo. name
is envyed, zo^r owne autoritie and wounted estimatioun
infinitlie impared be your absence and neglect of zour
cuntrie and releiff of zo^r freindis engadged and wraiked for

zo^r debtis, and now if zo^r Lo. sall kythe cairles or slouth-
full and sluggishe in this great chairge ze will increas the
libertie of zo^r ewillwillars who haue boldlie spokin to zour
disadvantage and discredit, discourage his Maties good
subiects, embolden the rebels, and mak zo^r task more difficle
nor zo^r Lo. apprehend, my affectioun to my maister's
hono^r and respect and goodwill to zor Lo. selff makis me
to wryt more liberallie in this mater nor vtheris will, which
I hope and requeast zo^r Lo. may tak in good pairt, earnesthe beseiking zo^r Lo. all empeschments removed to
come heir with all possible expeditioun and resolutioun
to go fordward wth wisdom and diligence, zo^r Lo. will find
that zo^r following zo^r owne will aganis my opinion in pur-
chessing ane cōmissioun in this service to ane particular
number of the counsall will do hinder to the bussines, bot
the nixt best must be done, nothing being able to remove
all difficulties, bot zo^r Lo. presence and diligence, which I
recommend to zo^r Lo. as ze affect zo^r maister's favo^r and
zo^r owne hono^r, So luiking for zo^r Lo. extreame diligence
to amend bypast sleuth and ouersights I cōmit zo^r Lo. to
the protectioun of God.   Ed^r this fyft of August.

Zo^r Lo. verie affectionat to serve zou.

135. Lord Binning to the King

16 Augt 1615

Most sacred Souerane—Be the copies of the letters
writtin to me be the Laird of Auchinbrek and Hector
Maknell sent heirwith to your Maiestie the estate of the
hielands will be trewliest known and how necessar it is
that the erle of Argyle haist thither, his slow returne hes
emboldened the rebels. I persuaded the Archibischop of
Sanctandrois to stay in Ed^r till the erles cumming and I
came to this place to meit him and haist him, and this day
having rencontred him prayed him to dispatch letters
from the counsall to the cōmissionars of the Iles to be in
Ed^r vpon sonday at night the 20 of this moneth that he
being advysed and authorised be thame may with all

speid go to the hielandis aganis the rebels, he is this night
to wryte to his freindis in Argyle of his being in Ed[r] and
resolution to haist to that cuntrie, he is also to send to
Aire to learne Capten Wodis [1] estate if he can cum thither
and if he be not yet cum to direct the provest and bailzies
to mak him speidie wairning when the Capten sall cum,
I have not concealed from him what is talked of his slownes
and what opinion is consaued and vttered be sum that
since his infeftment and Cadels of the landis of Kintyre
and Ila hes driven thir rebels to attempt thir desperat
courses that thay having sufficient power to represse
thame sould do it bé thair owne forces and at thair owne
charges, he ansuers that he will do so for Kintyre, and
doutes not bot Cadell will do all that he can to debate
Ila bot they can not hinder the rebels to go to vther pairtis
of the Iles and mayne land whair thay can not be preassed
to persew thame, I did not insist in the purpose which I
onlie moved to wairne him of the danger of his reputation,
if he sall not proceid sincerelie and forwardlie in the bussines
whairin he professes verie dewtifull affection. None of
his freindis ar yet returned from court except Lundie,
Auchinbrek is vnfit for seruice which I think sall be best
supplied be Lawers.

Yisterday the Archbischop of Sanctandrois [2] caused your
Ma[tties] commandement concerning Sinclair, Wilkie and
Cruikschank ressettars of the Jesuites to be executed
with great secrecie well kept to the verie moment of the
expected execution and then caused convoy thame bak
to prison to be baneissed according to your Ma[tties] last
warrand.[3]

---

[1] He and Captain Monk commanded the two ships of-war which, with a hoy
carrying a battering train, were sent from England to assist Argyll

[2] Spottiswood, Archbishop of Glasgow, had been translated to St. Andrews
on 31st May 1615, in succession to Archbishop Gledstanes He had recently
taken a prominent part in the proceedings against Father John Ogilvy, who
after torture was sentenced on 28th February 1615 to be hanged and quartered,
and three hours later was hanged, being subjected even on the scaffold to the
ministrations of the Rev. William Struthers and the Rev Robert Scott. It is
said that the quartering did not take place.

[3] Cf. Calderwood, vol vii p. 202, where the indignation of the disappointed
multitude is noted.

It may please your Matie to cause tak ordour with the erle of Cassils for renunciation of his heritable bailzerie of Carrik. So beseiking god long to prescrue your Matie in helth, happines and contentment, I rest, Zour most sacred Maiesties most humble, faithfull and bund seruand,

BINNING.

Inveiuick, 16 Aug.

136. Earl of Dunfermline to John Murray of the Bed Chamber

31 Augt 1615

frome this I can write off na forder to yiou bot the E. Ergyle is gane fardwart hame, satisfied be the counsall in all he desired ; Wee will heir after of his success against the rebellis, quha in all apeirance can mak na resistance nor partie to his powar, if all be weill amangs thame, sua ending this with my dew remembrance to y^{r} half marrow restis wissing ziou all contentement—y^{r} louing Cousing, to sciue ziou, DUNFERMELINE.

frome Dunfermeling, last Augt 1615.

137. Copie of the Erle of Argyle's letter to me

13 Oct. 1615

(Res. 16 Oct. 1615)

MY VERIE GUDE LORD—As I wret to zo^{r} Lo. in my last lr̃es from the Lodumis in Ilay that efter I had landit my men, I maid ane onset on the rebels q^{r} they war incampit at Ilanomsa[1] in Ilay q^{r} the greatest pairt of the rebels boattis was apprehendit, and if it had not bene that sum of the tennents were neir to my camp and seing my forces row away in thair boattis—the moone shyning—who

---

[1] 'An iyle called by the Erisch Ellan-nese with ane kirke in it' (O.P.S., II. 1. 274)

presentlie maid on great beakins vpone the tope of ane
hie hill, The q^{lk} so sone as Sir James did sie befor my
men war at him be sex or seavin myllis of sea, he went
to his boat accumpanied with M^{c}rannald, Sorle McJames
and sum four and tuentie or threttie wth thame, vtherwayes he could not haue escaped ; as they war going into
thair boattís sum of the principall tennentis of Ilay
desyred him to haue stayed, and becaus they had hazard
all for him, and knew thair wald be no mercie schawin
to thame, they sould all die at his· feit, bot M^{c}rannald
perswadit him to the contrar ; efter his going from Ilay,
he maid his first cours towardis Inchedaholl ane ile vpone
the bak of Inchewin in Ireland : Sorle McJames [1] and his
cumpanie of Irishmen did leaue him thair and ar fled to
the woodis of Ireland, I haue writtin to the cōmanders
of these places to be cairfull in apprehending of thame ;
Ane vther of his boattis being manned with sum of the
tennenttis in Kintyre who neuer left Sir James wntill he
was brought to such extremitie ar fled from him and cum
to Kintyre, they affirme that Sir James his resolutioun is
to cast himselff in sum great man's lap, who will interceid
at his Maties handis for him, I haue sent spyes both to
Lochaber and to·the north Iles if he go thair, for in my
opinioun he dar not adventure to stay in thir pairtes.
I am certanlie informed thair is not ane man with him
bot thrie sum and himselff. At Sir James his way going
out of Ilay all the tennentis of the cuntrie stayed behind
him. Coll M^{c}gillespie having the keiping of the castle of
Duneveg and the ile of Lochgorme he stayed in his strenthis
and fallowed not Sir James, Befor the landing of his
Maties cannon to the castle, Coll submitted him selff and
cam in : he hes randerit both the castle and ile to me and
hes delyverit Coline Campbell of Kilberrie who was his
prisoner, Lykwayes he hes wndertakin to do such service
as may releif him selff. I haue apprehendit all the principall ringleadars and such as could be tryed to haue gone
willinglie with Sir James, Sum of them I am to send to

---

[1] A natural son of Sir James MacSorley Buy Macdonald of Dunluce.

the lardis commissioners and the rest I will execut heir.
I have presentlie employed Coll Mᶜgillespik in service
against these that ar outlawis whois succes zoʳ Lo. will
know at my nixt adverteisment. Mᶜrannald his sonnes
and Glengarrie his brother ar gone to thair owne cuntries
and I haue sent efter thame.   So sone as I haue endit heir
in Ilay I intend to returne bak to Kintyre and to spair
none that willinglie joynned with the rebell Sir James,
for the greatest part of thame ar in Kintyre and Arran,
So sone as I can try qᵗ pairt of his Maᵗᵗᵉˢ dominiouns Sir
James hes takin him to, yoʳ Lo. sall be assured I sall not be
long wnpersewing him, I sall lykewayes god willing tak
such ane ordoʳ with those that hes fallowit him as his
Maᵗᵗᵉ sall not neid to dowt of gude obedience in thir
pairtes in tyme cūing. My Lord, the extremitie of the
wether and distance of the place hes bene the caus that
I have bene so long in adverteising of yoʳ Lo. of my proceidings, So for the present I rest,

Zoʳ Lo. assured freind.

Duneveg, 13 Octob. 1615.

138. Copie of my letter to the Erle of Argyle
16 *Octr.* 1615

MY MOST HONOᴸᴸ GUD LORD—I ressaued this night zoʳ
Lo. lẽrs of the 13 of this moneth from Duneveg making
mention of Coles¹ incūing to zoʳ Lo. and Sir James his
escape with all these that euer I haid nammed principall
mẽ in his cumpanie, bot I hope zoʳ Lo. will haue cair so
ffar as can be to mak ane gud count of them to his Maᵗᵗᵉ;
zoʳ Lo. lẽrs haue cum heir with gud speid being writtin
vpõ the 13 at Duneveg bot ane paket sent from this to
court vpone the 12 of this instant conteinit adverteisment from my Lord Chancelloʳ to court of all that zoʳ lo.
lẽrs of the 13 has now broght to me qˡᵏ I sall signifie to
court wᵗʰ all convenient diligence exspecting better nowells
be zoʳ Lo. nixt adverteismẽt qˡᵏ I pray god to send at the

---

¹ Coll M'Gillespick

nixt meiting of the counsall. I think thair will be ane
great number of the cōmissioners to whome all yor Lo.
proceidings sall be cōmunicat. I think zo^r Lo. will do
wyslie to advyse q^t course is most fit to be tane wth his
Maties schippis, for if your Lo. haue no necessar vse of
thame thair staye in these seas idillie can awaill nothing
but may put his Matie to great charges and bring danger
to the schippis q^{lk} god forbid, alwayes so long as zo^r Lo.
hes necessar vse of thame, his Matie and the counsall will
wndowtedlie allow that zo^r Lo. reteine thame and imploy
thame in any neidfull service. This mess^r will bring to
yor Lo. ane lr̃e of the erle of Lowthian's q^{lk} missed the
last paket with sum vthers sent to me sensyne be M^r
Williame Brown ; thingis heir ar quyet praysed be god.
I think befor this tyme yor Lo. hes hard that vpone the
26 of Septēber, the Lady Arbella deceased in the towre.
In france the troubles increasses and nevertheles the King
goes fordwart to his mariage. So beseiking god to grant
zo^r Lo. the hono^r and happines to cut off the ruttes and
headis of the Iles rebellioun and exspecting that heirefter
zo^r Lo. fallowars or nighbo^{ris} sall not prevent zo^r Lo. in
the report of zo^r proceidings I rest,

Zo^r Lo. most ready freind
to do zow service.

✗ Barnbougall, Monenday at night 16 Octob.

139. Copie of Archibald Cambel's letter to me

20 *Octr.* 1615

(Res. 28 *Oct.* 1615)

MY VERIE HONO^{LL} GUDE LORD—zo^r Lo. lr̃es of the 4 and
5 of October from Ed^r and Barnbougall came heir to my
Lord vpone the 18 of this instant, the caus of thair stay
so long be the way, and that zo^r Lo. hes not more frequent
adverteismēt sent from this is the extremitie of the windis
and the currenttis that runis so stranglie in thir seas q^{lk}

makis it almost wnpassable betuix this ile and the mayn.
My lordis lr̃e heirin inclosed will sufficientlie informe zo^r
Lo. of the succes of his Ma^{tles} service, Those that ar
alreadie execut ar not of the number that Coll M^cgillespik
hes apprehendit, My Lord intendis to morrow, if wind
and weather serve, to go to Kintyre, and hes left a roll
of certane persones wth Caddle who ar to be takin ordo^r
with and to that effect hes geivin him commissioun So
that on my credit to zo^r Lo. thair is nothing left vndone
in Ilay that concernes the weill of his Ma^{tles} service or
can do gude to Caddle q^rof I dowt not he will acquaint
zo^r Lo. him selff. The greatest number of the rebels ar
in Kintyre : they ar watched so that they can not escape ;
I hope my Lord sall no sooner cum to Kintyre bot zo^r
Lo. sall heir of dew executioun. I can heir no certantie
if M^crannald be gone to his owne cuntrie, or if he be gone
to schift a bark or a schip to carie him away, bot it is
certane that he hes pairted cumpanie wth Sir James, as
I wret to zo^r Lo. befor my lord hes sent both to Lochaber
and Glengarie's boundis to sie q^t may be done against the
rebels ; zo^r [Lo.] may easelie considder how difficle a thing
it is to find out such a number of Runagates who drawis
them selfis to lurk in diverss coineris of the kingdome, zit
I hope in god although it be paines to the erle of Argyle
and to those that fallowis him his Matie sall haue a sufficient
compt maid or it be long of these vilanis, as concerning
the rest of the ilanderis. I will wryt nothing at this tyme
bot I hope the exact performance of this service sall mak
them a littill more tractable then they haue bein heirto-
fore. I beleif seing the service is cum to such perfection
that my lord exspectis not any more pay from the thesaurar
vnles it be for a verie few number and a schort tyme, qⁿ
zo^r Lo. heiris the particular I dowt not bot zo^r Lo. will
find it verie reasonable. I think it expedient that in zo^r
first lr̃e to my Loid, zo^r Lo. wryt that seing thair is no sex
of the rebels togidder it is thought expedient that thair
be no more pay sent wntill zo^r Lo. know from my Lord
q^t number is requisted, for the pñt I will not trouble zo^r
Lo. with remẽbrance of my particular any more nather

dowt I of zo^r Lo. favo^r if it be my gud hap to deserve it
as god knawis I am most desyrous and sall ever remane,

Zo^r Lo. to serve zow.

Duneveg, 20 Octob. 1615.

At my Lordis cuming to Kintyre he intendis to dismisse
the *Charles* and the bark q^rin the ordinances ar, seing
they ar chargeable to his Matie and is to keip Captane
Wood wth the oidinance wntill zo^r Lo. heir ane accompt
of the service, and that his Matie conclud q^t farder is to be
done in thir pairtes.

140. Copie of my letter to Archibald Cambell

[*October* 1615]

Loving freind—I ressaued yor lfē of the 13 of this moneth
from Duneveg bot no newes in thame becaus vpone the
12 day I hard the substance of all that zo^r lrēs beares, q^{lk}
that same 12 day was writtin to court be my Lord Chan-
cello^r. I am glad that my lord is maister of the se strenthis,
and sorie that all the principall men ar escaped except
Coll who hes gottin conditions, bot I hope that my lordis
diligence, wisdome and gud luk sall owertak thame and red
his Matie and the cuntrie of thair cummer, for if it sould fall
vtherwayes furth (as god forbid) zow know what construc-
tions men wald mak of the great preparatioun maid be sea
and land at so great charges to his Matie without any effect
bot the wrak of the poore beggerlie tennētis of Ilay and
Kintyre, for sinc Sir James and his sone and Glengaiie's
sone and M^csorle are all escaped and Coll pardoned I know
not q^t ringleadars these ar whome ye wryt ze ar to bring
in, alwayes it is gud that thair forces ar scattered without
harme or danger, zit so long as the heades ar all to the fore
the rebellioun will never be thought quenched, q^rfor I know
my lord will haue such cair as agrieth wth his hono^r and his
Maties expectatioun. I haue no certantie of the thesaurare
deputes dyet, bot I hope he will be heir about Hallowmes
and will assuredlie performe his promeis yours being ob-

served, q^{lk} I hartelie wishe, So remembring my loving cōmendatiouns to yor brother Collin[1] and praying you to prevent zo^r curious nighbo^{rıs} in the adverteisments of my lordis proceidings q^{lk} I wishe may be prosperous I rest,

Zor verie loving freind at power.

141. Copie of my letter to Archbald Cambell
25 *Oct.* 1615

LOVING FREIND—I haue according to my dewtie adverteised my Lord be my letter that the cōmissioners for the Iles and such of the counsall as conveened this day mervell my Lord wret nothing in his last lr̄ez concerning the dissoluing of his men at the end of this moneth before q^{lk} tyme they think the opportunitie, tyme and power to do all that force requyred, and if any thing sould y^{r}efter rest to be done he might easelie performe it be his privat meanes, y^{r}for sinc many ar so ready to turne his actions be thair report to the worst, I pray zow propone to his Lo. how small advantage it will be to keep men vnnecessarelie vpone his Ma^{tıes} charges, q^{r}off they will affirme the greatest pairt to cum to my lordis benefit. The mater being vnworthie of the scandall and able to hinder him in ane greatar purpose, So vnles his Lo. be able to qualifie iust and necessar causes of keiping men vnder pay I harthe wishe that his Ma^{tıe} may be fred of that neidles burdene; it is also expedient that so sone as the necessitie of the seruice may permit the returne of his Ma^{tıes} schippes that my Lord consent to it and vrge it, for besydes the great cost thair stay thair bringis to his Ma^{tıe}, thair danger vpon that stormie cost in this winter season is greathe to be considerit and ffar as may be eschewed, his Ma^{tıes} is exceiding desyrous to haue trew and speedie knawledge of my lordis proceidings q^{r}in I wishe my Lord may vse diligence at all occasions, and so till farder occur I cōmit zow to god. Ed^r, 25 Octob.,

Zo^r loving freind at power.

---

[1] Colin Campbell of Aberuchill

142. Copie of my letter to the Erle of Argyle

25 *Oct.* 1615

MY MOST HONO^{LL} GUDE LORD—zo^r Lo. last lr̃es conteining
the discours of zo^r Lo. proceidings against the rebels the
taking of thair boattis, dissipating thame selffis and puting
to flight so scattered and in so small number as zo^r Lo.
hardlie knew q^r to fallow ye leadars furnissing me wairand
to informe the counsall (as I wes requyred) of the account
of zo^r Lo. bypast actions I maid trew report y^rof and of
Cole's yeilding to yor Lo. and puting in zo^r handis the
houss of Duneveg and Lochgorme.   My lordis of Glasgow,
Clerk of register and advocat (the remanent cõmissioners
for the Iles being absent) considering the estat of the
affaires and that thair was no knawin vse of waiged men
now, qⁿ zo^r Lo. privat forces to be assisted be the power
of such pairtes of the cuntrie as any of the scattered rebels
war suspected to lurk into war more then sufficient to
fallow, schearch and owerthrow thame haue tho^t it
vnnecessar that his Matie sould be any longer burdened
wth intertening souldiouris vnder pay and that these who
haue ever bene ready vpon smaller occasions to speak
vnkyndlie of zo^r Lo. will tak advantage both to blame zo^r
Lo. if ze requyre any such pay and the cõmissioners if
they allow it vnles zo^r Lo. will qualifie any iust and
necessar cause in q^{lk} caice it will be most readelie furnissed ;
it is also tho^t most necessar that zo^r Lo. eschew all neidles
detentioun of his Maties schippes and so sone as zo^r Lo.
sall cease to haue vse of thame that ye haue speciall cair
of thair saif and speidie returne to England.

Be these who cum from court I am certified that his
Matie is most desyrous to be frequentlie adverteised of
zo^r Lo. proceidings and gud succes q^rin I pray zo^r Lo. to
giue his Matie all dew satisfactioun fra tyme to tyme, So
till farder occasion I cõmit zor Lo. to god,

Zo^r lo. veric affectionat
and ready to serue zow.

Ed^r, 25 October.

143. Copie of the Erle of Argyle's letter

25 *Octr.* 1615

(Res. 29 *Oct.* 1615 at night)

My verry guid Lord—as I wrait to your Lp. in my last lefês from Dumbar the xiij day of this instant that Coll Mᶜillespick befoir the landing of his Maᵗⁱᵉˢ cannon had geivin vp the Castell of Dunovaig and Ile of Lochgorme haid delyvered Colin Campbell of Kilberrie [1] and wes gone about to do forder service for himselfe So this day he hes returnit to me and hes brocht withe him nynetene of the rebellis that followit Sʳ James of thir thair tua or thrie of the cheif and prinĩls that were withe Sʳ James. One of thame had the commandement of fourtie men his name is Mᶜduffie. [2] I purpose to present sum of thame befoir zour Lõpˡˢ that zour Lõps may be moir certefeit of Sʳ James proceidings since his last rebellioun. The rest of thame [I] intend to caus execute heir. My Lorde the caus of my stay so long heir is waiting vntill I heir what Sʳ James intendis to do at the wryitting of my last lefês vnto zour Lõpˡˢ, I vnderstood not whiche way he wes gone out of Inchedaholl ane ile on the baksyde of Ireland to the which he went whenas he wes forcit out of this ile Bot I am now suirlie informed that he is pairted withe MᶜRannald and landit in a place callit Rowvalin [3] in Ireland neir whair the vmqˡᵉ Lord Terchonellis Ladye [4] duellis for sche is his father sister. His intentioun is as I vnderstand to go to the deputie and to delyver him-selfe in his handis So how soune as I haif donne what I intend god willing in Kintyre I will mak zour Lõpˡˢ certefeit of the whole estaite of the service whairwithe I hope his Maᵗⁱᵉ shalbe welle pleasit and my freindis sufficientlie satis-

---

[1] He had been taken prisoner some time before.

[2] Malcolm Macfie of Colonsay.

[3] Probably meant for Rathmullin on Loch Swilly.

[4] Ineen Dhu, daughter of James Macdonald of Dunniveg and the Glens, was married to Sir Hugh M'Manus O'Donnell. Her eldest son was the famous Hugh Roe O'Donnell who proved the scourge of the English till they succeeded in poisoning him in 1602. Her second son Rory was created Earl of Tyrconnel.

feit ffor I purpose god willing so to conclude it as thair salbe
no place left for any ever to attempt the like in thir pairtis.
Leaving to truble zour Lôp̃ls with any farder for this pñt I
rest—Zour Lôp̃ls assurit freind,   ARGYLE.

Downovaig, the 25 of October 1615.

Efter the wryitting heirof I am informit that Sr James
Mckoneill bocht four horssis on the cost of Ireland and ane
gentleman callit Mckarie hes followit him as I beleue he
can hardlie escape.   This day I haif causit execute nyne
of the prinlls and leaderis of the rebellis whois names I
haif heirwt sent to zor Lopls, I hoip now dayly to be busie
in executioun whill his hienes rebellis be brocht to ruine.

144. Copie of Capten Wod's letter to me

2 *Nov.* 1615

(Res. 22 *Novemb.* 1615)

RIGHT HONOLL AND MY VERIE GUD LORD—I ressaued zor
lfĩe of the 16 of october and thinkis my selff verie much
bund for zor honoll favor, my Lord of Argyll hes bene
verie cairfull and hes settelled thingis in Ilay and the
greatest he found thair adherent wth the rebels he hath
caused execut, vthers of them he hes brot heir to Kintyre and
hes possessed Sr John Campbell[1] [of Calder] peaceablie in
the two strenthis qlk the rebels did hold in Ilay ; the castle
of Armorchy is to be delyvered to his Lo. servand and
the keipars to pñt them selffis to his L. service.   Sir James
Mcconeill is discoverit and my lord knowis qr he is and
for the apprehending of him he hes sent ten sufficient mẽ
ather to attack him or kill him, he hes wrought all meanis
possible to affect the same as zor Lo. sall know in my nixt

---

[1] This treachery of Coll Ciotach only foreshadowed the treachery to which he
himself fell a victim at the hands of David Leslie and the Covenanters (cf.
Highland. Papers, vol. ii. p. 252).   *Ciotach* means cunning as well as left-
handed, so it is possible that it was in this sense that the epithet was applied to
him.

lr̃e; thair is heir ane great number in Kintyre q^lk hes bene associat wth the rebels and for that caus I haue desyrit his Lo. to keip aboord his Maties schippis to such tyme that his men repair from onsetts q^r he hes appointit them at q^lk tyme he will tak ordo^r with them, the rebels hes spoylled mightclie the land that the poore tennents is allmost vndone. I sie it will be neir the end of nov̄eber befor my lord mak ane end heir, y^rfor becaus it is the deid of winter I meine to remaine in sum gud harbo^r in Clyde q^r his Maties schippis may be in safetie except I receiue warrant from zo^r Lo. and the rest of ye counsell to the contrare I will be so spairing to burdene the cuntrey of Scotland as possiblie I can. My lord of Argyle tauld me he wald wryt to the c̄osell to know if I sall leive the munitioun heir q^lk is not spent, q^lk I could not do as I tauld his Lo. without speciall warrant from his Matie in respect I ressaued it by warrant from him and hes indentit for the same in the tour q^r I must be countable : all vther proceidings conceining me zo^r Lo. sall haue intelligence. This I humlie tak my leiue gewing thankis for all zo^r hono^ll favo^ris and sall euer remaine,

Zo^r Lo. servand.

From his Maties schip
the Bran in Lochkilkerran
in Kintyre, 2 of Novemb. 1615.

145. Copie of the Erle of Argyle's letter to me

7 *Nov.* 1615

(Res. 22 *Nouemb.* 1615)

My VERIE GUD LORD—having done q^t was requised for the weill of his Maties service in Ilay and in sum vther places nixt adiacent, I came wth his Maties schippis from thenc on ye 16 of October, airyued in Loch Kilcheren the nixt day a safe harbo^r for his Maties schippes. I had no sonner cum to that place q^n thair cam to me one that had bene of lat in Sr James M^cconillis cumpanie who schew me of all Sir James his proceidings, and that he and his sone war in

Ireland, lykwayes he hes vndertaken on certane conditions to himselff to bring sum of my servandis to the
place q^r Sir James is. My Lord, altho^t this be wthout the
boundis of commissioun to mak schearse for any of ye
rebels having fled to ane vther kingdome zit to ky^{t1} my
zeall in his Ma^{tles} service I haue sent sum of my speâll servandis accôpanied wth threttie of the ablest mê I had to
that place in Ireland q^r I am surlie informed Sir James is,
I hope in god they sall ather bring him to me, or vtherwayes atteitch him q^r he is in sick sortt that he sall not
escape. As to Sorle McJames his sone he and his few
cumpanie ar into the rowt, and thair about he hes obtenit
a two monthis respit from ye deputie of Ireland. As to
McRannald and his sonnes I haue derected ane onsett on
them as I wret to zo^r Lo. who I hope sall ather apprehend
them selffis or mak it knowin in whois boundis they haue
actuell residence, q^{r}by the landislord may be obleist to
present thame. As to Glengarrie his sone I haue the lyk
onsett on him. And if his Matie and zo^r Lo. will haue bot
a littill patience I hope in god to mak such a cleir reckneing
of the service as thair sall no man neid to dowt that in thir
ptis heirefter thair salbe the lyk attempt. Thair restis
sum thing zit to be done hen in Kintyre and in places
nixt adiacent q^{lk} I am pñthe about. My Lord I thank god
that the suppression of this rebellioun wes in tyme preventit
for on my credit if it had bene 20 dayes longer protracted
few of my cuntrie mê betuix Tarbert and Innerarey had
provin gud subiects mekill les could y^r haue bene any gud
expected of farder remot places q^r thair was no trew
obedience to his Matie at all.

At my cûing heir I haue dismissed Captane Merick and
the wittuellar q^{r}in the ordinance war, and hes stayed
Captane Wood wth the ordinance wntill I know zo^r Lo.
pleasour heiranent seing I am surlie informit that Captane
Wood his stay heir wilbe no more charges then if he war
dismissed from hence. Q^r zo^r Lo. blames me that I sent not
word before the begining of this month anent ye disolving

---

[1] Kyth, ' to show '

of his Maties fied soiours please zo^r Lo. that in regaird of my sending to Ireland and ye onsetis I haue sent to Lochaber and Glengarrie's boundis and these that I haue in pn̄t service against ane number of the outlawis that ar in thir pairtis, I fand not that I could dismisse any of my cumpanies, and I assure my selff q^n zo^r Lo. sall considder dewlie of thir my pioceidings zo^r Lo. will acknawledge I draw not his Matie to any vnnecessarie chaiges and heiin will abyd zo^r Lo. awin censure, and however zo^r Lo. pleas to deall wth me it sall be seine that I sall friehe adventur lyff, land and all, befor thair be any thing wanting that may accōpleiss his Ma^{tles} seivice, Sua laving the [rest] to the sufficiencie of the bearar I bid zo^r Lo. faii weill.

Zo^r Lo. assurit freind.

Campbeltoun, 7 Novemb. 1615.

146. The Earl of Argyle's Report[1] to the Privy Council of Scotland of his Commission of Lieutenantry [2]

[24 November 1615]

Immediathe efter that the Erle of Ergyle had re-ceavit his Maiesties Commissioun of Lieutennandrie over the Illis, he addressit him self, with all convenient diligence, in Duntroone, quhair the gieatest pairt of his forceis did meete him. And being suirlie informit, that the Traytour Sir James McConeill, and his complices, to the nowmer of sevin or aucht hundreth men of weere, for that present in Kintyre, and of full intentioun thair to remane, quhill thay wer by the gritter power forcit out of it, his lo. resoluit to mak ane onsett without ony delay, alsweill on thair veschellis as on the Rebellis thame selffis ; and thanfore commandit the Laird of Caddell, who had

---

[1] This report was submitted to the Council by Archibald Campbell on behalf of Argyll, who appeared and reported in person at a meeting of the Council on 21st December 1615 (*P. C. R*, vol x. p. 762)

[2] The commission is printed at length, *ibid.*, pp. 749 *et seq*

the conducting of the forceis of Lorne, to mak his onset
on their veschellis, quhair he could heir thame to be,
ather in Yle of Giga, the Ile of Cara, or on the Maine-Land
of Kintyre. Lykewyse so, his Lordschip gaif command
to the Laird of Auchinbrek, and to some speciall of Auchin-
brekis freindis, to merch over land to the Tarbart, with
his lordschipis forceis of Ergyle. My loid him selff, being
accumpaneid with the men of Coule, went by Sea to the
Tarbart, on the other syde of the Maineland. My lord
went from Duntroone on the [   ] day of September
and wes that nicht in the Tarbart, quhair Auchinbiek,
with the men of Ergyle, did meete him that same nicht.
Coll Mᶜillespik haiving [   ] Coline Campbell
of Kilbernie, set out to him, come with fyftie men the
foirsaid nicht to Loch Tarbeit, quhair he apprehendit the
said Coline, and some foure or fyve with him, quhome he
maid his prisonairis. Airlie the nixt morning, Coll Mᶜillespik,
being on his way back agane, towardis the Ile of Cara,
quhair he had left McRannald, and his sones, and Sorle
McJames, who wer appointit to remane in Cara, for keiping
of the Rebellis veschellis ; he being on his way, as said is,
persauit my Lord of Ergyle his forces of Lorne, sailling
towardis Gigza ; and some of thame, haueing gone in the
bak syd of Gigza, maid ane onsett on the Rebellis who
wer in Cara, bot wer preventit by some of the Laird of
Largy his servandis, who persauit my lord of Ergyle his
forces going towardis Ergyle, quhair the Rebellis wer, and
set on grite beikynis to mak thame warr. The foirsaid
Ila not being distant frome land above twa or thrie mylhs
of sea, zit before the Rebellis could get away in thair
boitis, thair wer some of McRannald his men apprehendit
and slane. Coll Mᶜillespik, as said is, being on his way to
the Ile of Cara, wes adverteist be a servand of the Laird
of Largyis, that my Lord of Ergyle had chassit McRanald
and those that wer with him out of the Ile of Cara, and
had plantit thame selffis thair ; so he immediathe was
forcit to land in Kintyre. Some of the Erll of Ergyle his
men, haueing forgadderit with him in his landing, killit
a fyftene or saxtene of his men, and took his foure vas-

chellis frome him. My lord of Ergyle, the foirsaid day,
send his forces of Couell and Ergyle, within twelf myles to
the place quhair Sir James McConeill and his complices
wer; bot he being adverteist that my Lord of Ergyle his
forceis wer comeing, by sea and land, vpoun him, fled
away to the Ile of Rachlie, quhair he remanit twa nichtis,
and thairefter went to Ila   My Lord of Ergyle being
adverteist thairof, and heiring that his Maties schippis wer
arryvit at the Ile of M^cacharunnik, his Lordschip went
with his forces of Lorne and some of the men of Ergyle,
who had thair veschellis on that syde of the Meane-land,
towardis his Maiesteis schippis ; quhair he was storme-
stayd for the space of thrie dayis. And thairefter went
to Loddummes in Ila, a harbour convenient for his Maiesteis
schippis to abyd in, and good for landing of his lordschipis
forces out of the danger of the enemey. Haueing stayed
thair twa dayis, for refiescheing of his men, and till he
sould heir quhair the Rebellis wer, immediatlie being
adverteist that Sir James, with his complices, wer in the
Rindes of Ila, and in a little Ile neir by, called Illannoursay,[1]
my Lord maid onset on thame, by sea ; quhairin his lordschipis men wer preventit by some, who set on beakynis
in the O of Ila, quhairby Sir James was advertest that my
lord his forces wer comand on him, so as Sir James, McRan-
nald and his sones, and Sorle McJames fled over that nicht
to Inchdachele, ane Ile on the coast of Ireland. Coll
M^cillispik haueing the keiping of the Castell of Dunyvaig
and the Ile of Lochgorme, randerit thame bothe to the
Erll of Ergyle and Colin of Kilbernie, quhome he had taikin
captiue ; and apprehendit M^ciphie, on of the principallis
who followit Sir James, and deliuerit him to the Erll of
Ergyle ; and I haue presentit him this day before your
Lordschipis, with vther fyve of Sir James his complices.
Efter that the Castell of Dunyvaig and force of Lochgorme

---

[1] ' At the West poynt of Ilay lyes ane iylle callit by the Erische Ellan Ouersay
ane myle in lenthe.   It hath ane paroch Kirke and is very guid for fishing
nhabit and manurit with ane right dangerous kyle and stream callit Corey
Garrache : na man dare enter in it bot at ane certain tyme of the tyde or ellis
he will perish ' (Dean Monro's *Western Isles*)

wer taikin in, my Lord apprehendit fyftene of the principall men of Ila, who wer leadairis of the poore ones, to follow Sir James; whome he causit be execute thair.   And haue-ing deliuerit the foirsaid Castell of Dunyvaig and the force of Lochgorme to the Laird of Caddell, his Lordschip come frome Ila in his Maiesteis schipis, and arryved in Lochil-carrane on the sextene day of October last.   His Lord-schip no shooner come thair, than thair come on of the said Sir James his followaris who went with him to Ireland, and vndirtook to bring some of my lordis servandis to the place quhair he left the said Sir James; and gif he were not to be found thair, he wes suire to find him in the toun of Galloway, in Ireland, in Vallentyne Blak his house, or Robert Blak his house, thair; two, who are alledgeit to be ressettairis of Jesuitis.   My Lord being thus suirlie informit of the said Sir James his proceidingis, hes directit threttie of his men, in two onsettis, to Ireland, efter him. As to Sorle McJames and the twa and twenty that he had with him, they ar in the Route and Glennes of Ireland: It is alledgeit that the sub-officer thair hes gevin thame promeis of protectioun for two monethis. As to McRan-nald and his sones, thay ar fled to Lochquhabir; and my Lord his forces ar in persute of thame thair.   As to Glen-garrie his sone, he is ressat in his fatheris boundis, and my Lord hes some of his servandis efter him.   At my Lord his comeing to Kintyre out of Ila, he apprehendit some of the principallis thair, who had followit Sir James, and those who maid wairning to the Rebellis of the Erll of Ergyle his forces comeing to Cara.   Lykwyse his Lord-schip dismissit Capitane Wood, Capitane Monke, with his Maiesteis Schipis, and the Bark quhairin his Maiesteis cannoun and munitioun wes, on the tent day of Nouember instant.

As alsua, the said Archibald Campbell gaif in the Articles following, quhaironto he craved the saidis Lordis aduise and Ansuer; off the quhilkis Articlis and Ansueris the tennour followis.[1]

---

[1] These are printed in *P.C.R.*, vol. x. p. 760.

147. Sir Alex. Hay to Mr John Murray of Loch-maben of his Ma^tIes bed chamber

Ed^r, 21 *Dec.* 1615

Thir pairtes affordes no^t nather muche nor grit mater, so long as it pleisis God of his Infinite mercye to prolonge o^r M^rs gratious governament over ws there is nothing to be expected heir bot all dewtifull obedience And albeit now and then there may fall out some incidentis so there is no bodye of nevir so goode constitutioun bot will haif a catharre or some other distemperature. Alwyes o^r Iyles service is finished and o^r lieutennant the erle of Argyle returned yisternight and wilbe w^t the counsell this day. By many it is thoght that If goode will did secunde the dewtye w^che they ar bounde to do, thir frequent Iyland imploymentes wald not occurre so often. I wrotte to yow in my former l^r̃es that accompt being taken what this Iyla hathe stoode his Ma^tIes cofferis into thir tuo voyages and specially in the accomptes of admiralitye there, I doubt if the rent of o^r whole Iyles will recompense it ten yeir. Sen it is now qyueted It is fitting the purchesseris of the new right ather secure it heirefter and disburdyne his Ma^tIes cofferis of furder chairge or then surrender it to his Ma^tIe, for when thir employmentis ar so proffitable in pn̄t pay and a preparation for making suite at co^rte for service done, how easie a mater it is to haif some of these vnhallowed people w^t that vnchristiane language readye to furneiss fresh wark for the tinker, and the mater so caryed as that it is impossible to deprehend the plotte.[1] Bot leiving this vntill the lieutennant mak a relatioune of his service.

148. Sir Gideon Murray to the same
5 *Janij.* 1616

Right Hono^ble—Pleas yow be remembered that a two yeares sence when I wes att court Archibald Campbell

---

[1] The writer seems to have well understood the cause of the frequent troubles in the West Highlands.

maid sume hard informationes to the Kingis Maiestie of
my lord Chanclour, whairvpon thair wes directioun gevin
to my lord Fentoun [1] to adverteis his Lop. that his Maiestie
tuik it exceidinglie evill that he beand the principall
officer of estait heir suld in place of doing good seruice
oppose him self to his highnes will when his Maiesteis
effaires cam to be treated of in counsell and geve you
remēber the Kingis Maiestie wes exceiding angrie and
did wter the same with great passioñ to my Lord Fentoun.
It wes my chance to be present when Archibald maid the
informatioñ and so when he returned home, he purged
him self and leyed the blame vpon me w^che my Lord
Chanclour tuik in very evill part. Now that my lord
Chanclour is to be thair, I will intreat yow to desyre the
Kingis Maiestie do me the fauo^r to cleir me of that mis-
taking. For it is verie far bothe frō my nature and custome
to wrong any man eft^r that maner.

149. The same to the same

6 *Janij.* 1616

RIGHT HONͦᴮᴸᴱ—The Erle of Ergyle now efter that he
hes endit the seruice of the west yles and left all thair at a
quyetnes as appeiris cumes vpp to render the kingis maiestie
ane accompt of his seruice, I am intreated earnesthe in
his behalf to recōmend him to your freindlie cair, wch I
will earnesthe intreat for him bot so as he burding not
the kingis maiesteis cofferis within this kingdome w^che he
hes faithfullie promesit, and intendis that any fauo^r w^che
is to be bestowed vpon him salbe socht thair. Archibald
Campbell hes bein actiue anughe in the yles bussines and
when all salbe weill setled and maid peaceable so as the Kings
Maiestie sall haue the rent owt of these yles thankfullie
payed, he may iusthe chalandge the recōpance of his
seruice, whairin I will mak him all the lawfull healpe I
can so sone as his travellis sall have a goode successe. The

---

[1] *Vide ante*, p 192

Lord Vchiltrie cumes not vp with my Lord Chancelair as he ones intendit. In a discours I held with him he appeired to cōplein that you wer his wnfreind, altho he had never deserued the same and withall desyred that by my meines he might haue the eielist [1] removed gene thair was any, w^{che} for my awne pairt I could willinglie bothe wishe and allow, as I haue my self put of all these quarrelles I had with him for any questione that wes betuixt us befoir. This muche I piomesit to wryt in all the particulars afoirsaid And so my affectionat dewtie remembered I tak my leiue and sall euer remane, Your assured freind to be cōmandit,   S. G. MURRAY.

Edinbru^t, the 6 of Januar 1616.

150. The same to the same

13 *Janij.* 1616

RIGHT HON^{BLE}—The Laird of Caddell hath earnisthe requested that he might have a letter of mync to yow in his favo^r whilk I culd not weell refuis, wherfoir I will entreat you to schawe him all the lawchfull favo^r you may and that it wald pleas you to countinance him so far in his adoes as he seames not to bring any burthene vpoun this estate heir. Lykwys thair is a matter questionable betuix the Bishope of the Iles and him [2] wherwith he sayes you have bene of befor acquanted, gif thair be any thair that will deall in it for the Bishope's part, he is verye desirous that you wold tak the hearing of it and setle the difference whilk also he intreates me to recomend to yow. So for the present having no vther thing to trouble yow I comit you to god and restis, Your affectionat freind to be cōmandit,   S. G. MURRAY.

Ed^r, this xiiith of Januar 1616.

---

[1] ' Eelist ' or ' eyelist,' an offence
[2] *Vide ante*, p 272

151
28 *Aug* 1616

Becaus the resset of the trayto^{ris} and rebellis of the Iles hes bene verie frequent and commoun throughout all the north Iles, and it being a mater of great difficultie, trouble and fascherie to bring all those who ar guiltie in that point to thair tryall heir, ather before the counsell or iustice, thairfore ane commission is past to the Lord Lovat, the shereff of Cromartie and the tutor of Kintaill,[1] or ony two of thame to call and conveine before them within the buigh of Invernes all and sindrie personis within the boundis of that sherefdome who ar guiltie of the said resset and to try thame thairvpone according to the forme of the law, and to report the proces to the counsell to the effect, they may determine vpone thair punishment, which point the Counsell hes reserved to themselffis, Lykas they have reserved to themselffis the tryell of Donald Gorme, M^ccleude of Hereiss, the captane of Clanrannald, McKyn- noun, and ane complainte of sum inhabitantis of King- horne already in dependance befoie the counsell against certane personis alledgit to be men and servandis of M^ccleude of Hereiss all quhilkis ar exceptit out of this commission.

152
Decimo octauo Septembris 1616

Conforme to his Maiesties missiue lr̃e producit and red this day in counsall, thair is ane act and warrand past in favouris of the Ilandouris to shote within a myle of thair owne housis for thair recreatioun allanerlie.

153. Lundie [2] and other Campbells to the King
22 *Oct.* 1618

MAY IT PLEIS ZOUR SACRED MAJESTIE---Quhen we had ressaued your Ma^{teis} most gracious lr̃e and thairin red

---

[1] Simon Lord Lovat, Sir Thomas Urquhart of Cromartie, and Sir Rory Mackenzie.

[2] Colin Campbell of Lundie, second son of the sixth Earl of Argyll

and considdered zour Majesteis extraordinaire loue and royall cair of the preseruatioun of the erle of Argyll our cheiff his hous,[1] we could not be conteanned from vttering to zour Majestie the vnvtterable joy that we have conceaved to sie our selffis so far overcum alsweill be your Majesties great kyndnes as fatherlie prouidence for our cheiff and ws both, bot in speciall for making choyce of such a fit and fauowrable donatour of our cheiff his escheit and lyvrent as Sir George Areskene and that for the better contentment of his creditouris and releif of ws that ar sautionaris Neuirtheles your Matie is to be aduertised that although this be the onlie and best meano to content both credito^{uis} and cautionaiis, zit it wantis not greit oppositioun Quhairfoir we ar in all humilitie to pray zour Majestie to gif comand to your chancellar and remanent senatouris of the colledge of justice to gif all furtherance to your Majesteis donatour according to justice that all pairteis may be the better satisfied and zour Majestie may be the les vexed with ye continuall misereis and complaintis of credito^{ris} and we salbe all the moir and moir encuraged and provokit to pray the euerlasting god for your Majesteis long and prosperous Regne.—Zour sacred Majesteis most humble and obedient subjectis,

> LUNDIE.
> S. D. C. ACHINBREK.
> S JAMES CAMPBELL off Laweris.
> COLIN CAMPBELL of Kilew.
> S. DONALD CAMPBELL.[2]
> S. J. CAMPBELL.[3]

Ed^r, 22 Octobris 1618.

---

[1] By this time Argyll had left the country (cf *ante*, p. 94).

[2] Of Ardnamurchan.

[3] Of Calder For a bond executed on 12th January 1619 by the leading 'baronnes and gentlemen of the name of Campbell . . convenit for the. taking ordour in the absence of the Erle ther cheife,' vide *Thanes of Cawdor*, p. 243

154

Decimo quinto Novembris 1618

Vpoun the ressett of the tua pacquettis of the fyft and
sevint of this instant quhilkis come heir the xiiij[th] at night
the haill Counsell wer conuenit this day in a frequent
nomber after the afternoone preatcheing, and his Ma[teis] tua
lr̃ez, the one anent the erll of Argyll, and the other anent
the commissioun for the Holland fisheing[1] wer red to the
Counsaill, and the directionis thairof wer ordanit to be
obeyit. The Commissioun wes exped and send to the
Chancellarie and is heirwith send vp and chargeis ar direct
aganis the erll of Argyll vpoun lx dayis wairning to compeir vpoun the fourte of februair. Thir chargeis ar execute
with all solemnitie with sound of trumpettis and displayit
coittis of armes at the mercat croce of Edinburgh and
shoir of Leythe, and ane herauld is directit to execute the
same lr̃es at Striuiling, Glasg[w], Dunbartane and Innerara.[2]

155. Privy Council to the King

2 *Feb.* 1619

PLEAS YOURE SACRED MAIESTIE—We haif bene eirnistlie
delt with on the behalff of the fewars and vasallis of Argyle
for granting vnto thame confirmationis of thair landis
quhilkis thay hald of the erll of Argyle, Bot we haif bene
spairing to meddle in that mater in respect of the proces
and dangeir w[che] the said erll vndirlyis vntill we vnderstand youre Maiestcis will and pleasoure thairanent. In
oure awne opinioun thair demand in this pointe is reasounable and aggreable to equitie and justice, and that youre
Majestie can ressaue no harme nor preiudice thairby,
becaus thay ar free of thir crymes quhairin the said erll
hes vnnecessarlie involuit him selff, and hes had no dealeing
nor handilling with him thairintill, and forder thay ar

---

[1] Printed in *P.C.R.*, vol. xi.

[2] *Vide ante*, p. 94.

fewaris and vassallis to the Lord of Lorne thair superiour quho is feare and heritable proprietair of the erldome of Argyle,[1] with the haill dependanceis and peitinentis thairof, and is youre Maiesteis immediat tennent of the same, and the erll his fader is onlie lyverentair, Bot remitting this to youre Maiesteis more judicious and princelie consideratioun, and attending youre Maiesteis directioun and answer thairanent at some conuenient tyme of youre Maiesteis leaser, we humelie tak oure leave, praying god to bliss your Maiestie with a lang and happie Reignn, frome Edinburgh the secund of februair 1619.—Youre Maiesteis most humble and obedyent subiectis and seruitouris,

                    AL. CANCELL[s], MAR, BINNING,
                    S. G. MURRAY, OLIPHANT.

156. Sir James Campbell of Lawers to the King

16 *Oct.* 1619

SACRED SIR—May it pleas your Majestie, the Lord of Loudoun hes maid choise of my sonne[2] to inherite his estate[3] failzieing of airs maill lauchfullie to be gottin of his own body and so to preserve the estate of his house to do your Majestie service. And now S[r] it restis only that your Majestie may be pleased to accept of his resignatioun in favo[rs] of my sonne and to grant your Majesties infeftment thairvpone according to your Highnes accustomed clemencie to all your Majesties loyall subjects, And seeing it pleased the almichtie that my foirbear obteined his estate for doing your Highnes predecesso[r] of woithie memorie acceptable service. and that all who hes succeeded since of that race hes ever bein most willing according to

---

[1] On Argyll's resignation a charter had been granted in favour of himself in liferent and his son Lord Lorne in fee, 16th March 1610 (*R. M S.*), quite a common practice

[2] Afterwards Earl of Loudon and Chancellor, notorious for his insolence to Montrose, his adultery, and the violence of his Covenanting views

[3] It will be noted that this and the next letter refer solely to the estate, and not to the dignity of Loudon.

their bound dewtie to adventure their lives and all to do
their prince good service   And for my pairt (God knowes)
it hes been my greatest ambitioun on earth that I was
thocht worthie of your Majesties imployment in regaird
whairof I am encouraged to tak the boldnes humbly to
beg for your Majesties favour in this particular and that
your Majestie may be pleased to tak my sonne and dispose
of him as may be best seeming to your Highnes, for the
which accordinglie to my bond deutie I sall euer pray for
your Majesties most happy and long reigne.—Your
Majesties most humble and obedient Subject,

S. JAMES CAMPBELL off Lawiris.

Fordew, the 16 of October 1619.

157. Lord Loudoun to the King
8 *Oct.* 1619

SACRED SIR,—Since it hathe pleased God to tak from
me my laufull soneis, I haue maid chose (with your Ma^{tels}
permission) of young Laweris ane kinsman of my owne
to inherite my estaite failzeing of heires maill of myne
owne body, whoe is lykwayis schortlie to marie my eldest
<u>oy</u>:[1] And so be that meane (if it may please god) I intend
to preserue my houss to do your Ma^{ttle} good seruice.

And thairfoir I humblie beseik zo^r Ma^{ttle} (in recompence
of my foirbearis and myne owne service done to your
Ma^{ttle} and yor hienes predecesso^{ris}) to resaue my resignation and to grant infeftment thairvpon according to yor
Ma^{tels} gracious clemencie to all yor hienes loyall subjectis.
ffor the whiche and many otheris yor Ma^{tels} gracious
fauo^{ris} done to me, I shall evir pray for yor Ma^{tels} longe
and moste happie regne. So kissing yor Ma^{tels} hand I
evir remane, Yo^r Ma^{tels} humbill and maist obedient
subject,   LOUDOUN.[2]

Lowdoun, 8 Octob. 1619.

---

[1] Margaret, elder daughter of George, Master of Loudon, who died in 1612.

[2] In the *Scots Peerage*, vol v. p. 498, it is stated that he was 'created Lord
Campbell of Loudon with destination apparently to heirs whomsoever on 30
June 1601,' but no authority is cited.

158. Earl of Morton [1] to the King

18 *Apr.* 1621

MOST SACRED SOUERANE—Wpon the sicht of a licence giuin be zour Matie to Mr Alexander Coluill for the freindis of the hous of Aigyll to deal with that erle to try if we micht recall him from that euill cours wharin he hes plungit him selue I as on who both by bluid and allyance am oblisit to wisch the standing of that hous did wret to him to kno if he grunded him selue upon anie resons in that cours wich he had takin as also I laborit to sie if zet he was cum to that sence of him selue as to wisch a retrait from his euill wayis his ansuer cam slolie to me and when I had it, I could gedder no uther thing by it bot that he ferit I had no uther pouer bot by my kynd wisches to procuir him a saif retrait ; heirupon I heue presumit humble to beg zour Ma^{tles} resolution if without offenc I may zet trauell with the erle of Argyll to bring him a just acknoledgment of his grait ouersicht and that he may mak such offers of amendiment as may be acceptable to your Matie, and in my trauels to this effect I will argue to scho my selue a kynd fiemd to him and to his hous, zet my gretest cair sall be that I do no thing wich may be unseimlie for Zour Matie most faithful subject and humble seruitor,   MORTON.

Neuhous, 18 Apryl 1621.

159. Privy Council to the King

7 *June* 1621

MOST SACRED SOUERANE—Thair hes beene tua remissionis signed be yor Matie laithe p͠uted to be exped be ws,

---

[1] William, sixth Earl of Morton   Argyll's first wife was Agnes Douglas, Morton's aunt, and Morton appears to have acted as one of the guardians of Lord Lorne after Argyll's departure from Scotland.

the one in fauouris of Sr James M^cdonald [1] and a nomber
of his compliceis for the slaughter of M^cclane, for breking
of warde oute of the Castell of Edinburgh, for surprising of
the Castell of Dunnyvaig, for fyre raising and all otheris
crymes committit be thame And the other in fauouris
of M^crannald and certane his complices, for convoying
of the said Sr James M^cdonald oute of the Castell of Edinburgh, for fyre raising at the Castell of Dunnyvaig, slaughter
of the constable thairof, and for all otheris crymes and
offensses committit be thame, And althoght we acknow-
lege zo^r Maties royall pouer and youre most gratious and
clement dispositioun to extend yor fauour and mercie to
such of youre Maties subiectis as hes offendit, yett the
truste w^{lk} zo^r Matie hes repoisit of youre affairis in ws,
oblisses ws in dewitie to present vnto yor Maties consideratioun oure humble opinionis concerning thir remissionis,
ffor in materis of this kynd importing the quyet of the
state, and concerning chiftanis of clannis in the Heigh-
landis and Ilis, who hes grite dependance and ar followit
be mony personis wickedlie and euill dispoisit zo^r Maiestie
hes beene pleasit to command that goode suirtie be fundin
for youre Maties peace and for thair futur obedience to
law and justice in w^{lk} pointe thair hes no suche offer beene
maid be thir personis, and howeuer we persuade oure
selffis that it is not youre Maties meaneing that thay sall
returne within this kingdome, zitt it is expedient for preuenting of all occasionis that may fall oute that they sall
find suirtie for the peace, ffor thay and thair freindis who
now lurkis and ar quyet, and who without doubt will
ryise and joyne with thame yf thay sal happin to returne
hes so far medlit with the lyves and bloode of nomberis
of yor Maiesteis subiectis that it may be certanelie expectit
mutuall revengeis wilbe huntit for on ather syde quhairupoun such disordour and confusioun will fall oute in the

---

[1] One of the ironies of history is to find that Argyll had not merely to flee the
country for his faith but was kindly treated in his exile by both Sir James and
Keppoch. In fact, one of the charges against him was that he had 'oppinlie
enterrit in verrie professed freindschip and suspitious dealing with our proclaimed
tratours Sir James M'Donald and olde M'Ronnald . . .' (*P.C.R.*, xi. p. 468).

Ilis, as will require grite paneis chargeis and expensses to pacifie the same, The consideratioun quhairof hes moued ws to continew the expeiding of thir remissionis till we vnderstand forder of youre Maiesteis pleasour thairanent And we will humelie beseeke yoᵣ Maiestie to vouchsaif youre gratious acceptance and fauourable constructioun of this oure humble opinioun, quhairin we haif no other respect, bot zoᵣ Maiesteis obedience and the peace of the cuntrey, and so praying the almightie god to protect youre Royall persone and to blisse youre Maiestie with mony lang and happie yeiris we rest, Zoᵣ Maiesteis most humble and obedient subiectis and seruitouris,

AL. CANCELLˢ.　　MAR.
MELROS.[1]
GEORGE HAY.　　OLIPHANT.
S. G. MURRAY.　　S. J. HAMILTON.　　KILSAYTH.

Edinburgh, 7 Junij 1621.

160. Licence to Alexander Macdonald of Keppoch

12 *October* 1621

JAMES R.—Wee by the tenoᵣ heieof giue and grante libertie and licence to oᵣ beloued Alexander Makdonald cōmonlie called Mak Ronald to iepaire into oᵣ kingdome of Scotlande there to remayne and do his lawfull affaires the space of six monethes nexte and iñediathe following the date hereof, inhibiting and discharging all and syndiie oᵣ officers and ministers of Justice whatsoeuer to calle oᵣ persew before anie iudge or iudges spirituall or temporall, or otherwise to trouble or moleste the said Alexander in his bodie or goodes for anie crime or offence cōmitted by him at anie time preceding this oᵣ presente licence and of their offices in that pointe. Giuen vndir oᵣ hand and seale At Royston the twelfth day of October 1621.

---

[1] Lord Binning was in 1619 created Earl of Melrose, a title which in 1627 he exchanged for that of Earl of Haddington.

161. Privy Council to the King

21 *March* 1622

Most Sacred Souerane—Haveing by oure former lr̄e
of the last of Junij presented vnto youre Maiestie oure
opinioun concerning the tua remissionis signed be zo͏ͬ
Maiestie, and desyrit to be exped be ws, the one in fauouris
of S͏ͬ James M͏ͨdonald, and the other in fauo͏ͬ͜ˡˢ of M͏ͨrannald,
with the ressonis moveing ws to superseid the passing of
the same till we sould vnderstand forder of zo͏ͬ Maiesteis
pleasour thairanent we knowe that the importance of
zo͏ͬ Ma͏ᵗᵉˡˢ more weyghtie affairis hes not offerrit the occasioun vnto zo͏ͬ Maiestie to returne vnto ws youre ansuer
thairanent, And now we vnderstand that M͏ͨrannald is come
to this cuntrey leaneing to a protectioun grantit be youre
Majestie to him vnder yo͏ͬ hand and signett, and without
ony directioun or warrand for taking ordour with him anent
his futur obedyence and quietnes, quhairin althoght we
will eschew to be curious towcheing the particularis of
youre maiesteis purpois in that mater, zitt the truste that
youre Maiestie hes repoised of youre affairis in ws oblisses
ws in dewtie and alledgeance to pn̄t vnto zo͏ͬ Maiestie o͏ͬ
simple opinionis concerning that man, whose bipast lyffe and
conuersatioun hes bene so lewde and violent in bloode,
thift, reafe and oppressioun, that to this hour he never
randerit obedyence, and he wes not onlie the contryvair
and plottair of the said S͏ͬ James his eschaip and brek of
warde bot a principall actor in the rebellioun that followit
thairupoun, the suppressing quhairof wes so chargeable
vnto zo͏ͬ Maiestie and troublesome to the cuntrie, and we
can expect no thing frome him in tyme comeing bot a
constant continewance in the villanyis quhairin he hes
bene broght vp, and hes spent the rest of his vnhappie
lyffe And whereas now the whole Ilis and continent
nixt adiacent ar in a maner reduceit to obedience, and no
publict dissobedyence profest bot be Allane M͏ͨeanduy¹   X
fader in law to this manis eldest sone, youre Maiestie may

¹ Cameron of Lochiel.

considder how far otheris lymmaris wickedlie disposit, and not yitt fullie satled in obedience may be encourageit v'poun the example of this man and hoip of impvnitie to offend And yf he with the other lymmair M^ceanduy sall joyne togidder according to thair wounted maner as appeirandlie thay will do, nomberis of insolent personis who now lurkis and ar quyet will brek lowse and follow thair fortounis quhairupoun griter disordour and vnquyetnes will aryise nor wilbe weele gottin satled, The consideratioun quhairof conjoyned with the example and consequence depending thairon hes enforced ws oute of that dewitie quhilk we owe vnto zo^r Maiestie most humelie and submissiuelie to showe vnto zo^r Maiestie quhat we apprehend concerning this particulair, quhairin we haif no other respect nor consideratioun bot the peace and quietnes of the cuntrey, And yf youre Maiestie salbe pleased to send vnto ws directioun concerning this man, we salbe cairfull to see the same execute accordinglie.

And so praying the almightie god to watche ouer youre Sacred persone, and to blisse yor maiestie with mony lang and happie yeires, we rest, Yo^r Maiesteis most humble and obedient subiectis and seruitouris,

AL. CANCELL^s.   MAR.
MELROS.   GEORGE HAY.

Haliruidhous, xxi of M̃che 1622.

162. Privy Council to the King

28 *March* 1622

MOST SACRED SOUERANE—Haueing by oure formair lr̃e of the xxi of this instant pñted vnto yor Maiestie oure opinionis concerning M^crannald, and quhat ressoun we haif to suspect his futur behauiour and cariage, he sensyne gaif in a petitioun vnto ws desiring that the protectioun grantit be youre Maiestie vnto him might be exped in Counsell, And becaus his petitioun maid no mentioun of his futur obedyence, it wes thoght meete afoir ansuer sould be gevin vnto it, that he him self sould be hard, and that this point anent his obedience and the peace of the cuntrie sould

be layed to his charge, w^lk being accordinglie done vpoun
the 26 of this instant being the dyet appointit for his compeirance befoir ws, he preast to eshew that point anent
his obedyence, alledgeing he could get nane who wald
vndertak suche a burdyne for him, bot we haueing vrged
the same vpoun him with the best ressonis we could, obiecting vnto him oure dewyteis vnto zo^r Maiestie, and how
that we could not be ansuerable to zo^r Maiestie yf in a
mater of this kynd importing the peace and quietnes of
the cuntrie we sould be silent and the rather seeing he
had a purpois to go home w^lk might gif occasioun of some
disordour and trouble, he then promeist to vse his moyen
and freindship to gif satisfactioun in this point. In the
meanetyme, we hait ordanit him to remayne in this burgh
till the same be done.[1] This being the effect of oure procedingis with him, we humelie beseeke youre Maiestie to
vouchaif vnto ws yor gratious allowance of the same And
so in sinceritie of humble and deutifull subiectioun, recommending yor Maiestie with oure vncessant prayeris to
godis divyne protectioun, we rest for euer, Youre Maiesteis
most humble and obedyent subiectis and scruitouris,

AL. CANCELL^S. MAR.

LOTHIANE. WINTOUN. MORTON.

ROXBURGH. NITHISDAILL.

Haliruidhous, 28 Marche 1622.

163. Sir James Campbell of Lawers ' To my most honorable and spesiall good lord My Lord Vicunt of Annan ' [2]

25 *Jany.* 1623

MY WERIE HONO^LL GUID LORD—I doubt not bot yowr
Lo. hes hard that the Lord off Lowdune was pleasid to

---

[1] Vide *P C R* , vol xii. p. 696

[2] This letter, it will be seen, deals with the dignity Lord Loudon had
executed a resignation for a regrant in favour of his son-in-law, and had died
before the resignation had been accepted and the new grant made An interesting question of peerage law thus arose If the resignation had not been effectual
the dignity passed to the next heir under the patent, whoever that might be, and

conferre his esteate on my eldest sonne. As lykvys, befor
he depairtid this lyffe, he maid resignatioune off his
dignitie in my sonnis fauowris. And y^{r}for I am to be ane
humble sutter to his Matie that his Matie may be graciously
pleasid in recompence off my seruice to accept of the
wmq^{ll} Lord off Lowdune his resignatiō off his dignitie in
fauowris off my sonne. The whiche as it will be ane meane
to inaible him to doe his Matie the bettir seruice, so I will
accompt it a very grecious recompence off my great lossis
susteind in his Maties seruice. My Lord I hawe had suche
proofe of your Lo. fauowre heartofoir that I assure my
selfe your Lo. will not deny me your fauowrable concurrence to mowe his Matie to grant this my reasonable and
humble suit ffor the whiche your Lo. sall be well assurid
to hawe me and my sonne euer to remaine Zow^r Lo. assurid
freindis to serwe yow,

                    S. JAMES CAMPBELL off Lawiris.

Ed^r, the 25 off January 1623.

164. The grevanceis givin in be the cōmissionaris of
        burrowis to the cōmissionaris appoyntit be
        his Maiestie for heiring and reforming of the
        iust grevanceis of his Maiesteis subiectis in
        the kingdome of Scotland, and the ansueris
        givin be his Maiesteis commissionaris to the
        saidis grevanceis

——— 6. The merchantis of this kingdome ar preiudged
in the payment of the exsyse and teynd fishe exactit be
the bischope of the Illis, quhilk^{is} tua burdeynis do presse

---

on principle it is difficult to see how by now accepting the resignation the King
could deprive the heir of the dignity which had vested in him or her. (But see
Riddell, *Peerage Law*, vol 1 p 53) A remarkable solution is offered in the
article ' Loudon ' in the *Scots Peerage*, vol. v., which states concerning Margaret
Campbell (p. 499), ' *She* appears to have inherited the Peerage under a
resignation made by her grandfather before his death *in favour of her husband* ' !
and concerning John Campbell, her husband (p. 506), ' *He* succeeded his
·ather-in-law in terms of the resignation in December 1622 ' '

ws so soire as thair is no gayne of oure fisheing and gif the
same be not reformed and the subiect fred thairof thair is
no hoip that the trade of fischmg sall cuir tak roote far
lese to mak any progres in this natioun, albeit the same
be ane of the maist profitable cōmodityes this natioun
dois affoord and vsefull both at home and abroad.

Ansuer

Becaus this matter concernis the Kingis Maiestie
and his officiaris and the bischope of the Illis it is
thoght meit that thay salbe hard heirvpone and gif it salbe
fund that oney extraordinar noveltie hes bene vsed in
the vplifting of this teynd dewitie, or that moir is exactit
nor is dew to be payed ordour salbe tane for redresse and
reformatioun of the abuse and the Lordis appoyntis ony
competent day in the begining of the nixt sessioun for
heiring of this matter.

July 1623.

165. Privy Council to the King

4 *Feb.* 1625

MOST SACRED SOUERANE—Thair wes a Signatour gevin
yn to ws vnder your Maiesties hand, and recommendit be
of our Maiesties lfē to be exped contening ane infeftment
in the Lordship of Kintyre in fauouris of the earle of Argyll
his eldest sone of the secund mariage,[1] After consideratioun
quhairof haveing callit to oure rememberance how that
the passing of this infeftment wes verie instantlie vrged
be the Earle himself the tyme of the Parliament in the
sex hundreth and sevinteene yeir of god, quhair your
Maiestie wes pñt, and how that grite oppositioun was
maid thairunto be the said earle his cautionaris as namelie
be the constable of Dundee, the lairdis of Lundie, Lawcris

---

[1] With Ann, daughter of Sir W. Cornwallis of Brome This son James was
created Lord Kintyre in 1626 and in 1642 Earl of Irvine.

and some otheris who constantlie affirmed that thay had no hoipes of releiff of thair grite ingadgementis for the said earle if that infeftment wer exped, Seing the Lord of Lorne the said earle his eldest sone stoode infeft in the fee of the whole rest of his leving and nothing wes restand wherupoun thay might gett reall executioun for thair releiff, And whereas your Maiestie oute of yo[r] gratious respect of thir gentlemenis releiff allowit of the staying of the infeftment at that tyme, we thairfoir thoght that we could not be ansuerable to your Ma[tie] if now without hearing of thame we should giue way thairunto And thairfoir we wret for thame and Lundie compeirand he renewit with verie grite instance the formair suite anent the staying of the infeftment and gaif in a note of threttie sex thousand aucht hundreth and three pund wheiin he yet standis ingadgeit for the said earle, besydis tua thousand pundis with some añuellis that he hes payit.

We having at lenth hard him as alsua the said earle his agent who attendit this bussynes, we haif maid choise rather to stay the infeftment [1] nor rashelie to giue way thairunto, till first we be consultit with your Maiestie thairanent, wherin craving yor Maties pardoun for the shorte delay, and being readdie according to o[r] bundin dewtie vpoun significatioun of yo[r] Ma[ties] royall will and pleasoure in this pairticulair to conforme o[r] selffis thairunto, We pray god to blisse your Maiestie with mony long and happie yeiris, and restis, Your Maiesties most humble and obedient subiectis and seruitouris,

GEORGE HAY.
MELROS.
OLIPHANT.

Edinburgh, the fourte of februair 1625.

---

[1] On 12th February 1626 a charter passed the Great Seal narrating that in respect of the Act of 28th June 1617 the King ratified Letters of Procuratory and Resignation made by Archibald Earl of Argyll, Lord Campbell and Lorne, at Madreill (*sic*) 20th July 1624, in favour of James Campbell, the eldest lawful son of him and his wife, Dame Anne Cornewallace, Countess of Argyll, and also the Instrument of Resignation following thereon, dated at Taybollis (*sic*) 17th

166. Privy Council to the King

29 *July* 1625

MOST SACRED SOUERANE—The charge and burding of youre Maiesteis seruice aganis the rebellis of the Claneane (be whome not onlie youre Maiesteis awne subiectis, bot the subiectis of otheris princes yor Maiesteis freindis and confederatis wer havelie distrest and robbed of thair shippis and goodis, and some of thame cruellie and barbarousli slayne) being committit to the Lord of Lorne,[1] He oute of his humble and dewtifull respect to yor Maiesteis obedience, not onlie willinglie vndertooke the seruice, bot he hes prosequute and followit the same oute with grite resolutioun and dexteritie and that with his awne proper freindship and forceis without ony trouble or burdyne to the cuntrey, in so far that whereas it is vsuall throughout the Ilis in expeditionis of this kynd that victuallis ar takin without payment, the said Lord wes so respective of his credite in that point, that haueing fyfteene hundreth men in his company, he tooke suche ane strait ordour with thame, that during the whole tyme of the seruice nane of thame durst meddle with ony victuallis, bot for pñt and reddy payment.[2] In the prosequutioun of the seruice he hes execute be course of justice ten of the rebellis, he hes slayne sax of thame, and he hes broght heir to the burgh of Edinburgh foureteene, who ar to vnderly thair tryall and punishement. He compeirit this day befoir youre Maiesteis Counsell, and gaif ane accompt of his diligence and procedingis in the seruice, wherin we find

---

September 1624, and of new granted to the said James the Lands and Barony of Kintyre therein specified, all which he erected into the free Lordship and Barony of Kintyre, and further creating the said James and his heirs male and successors therein 'liberos dominos et barones ejusdem cum honore et stilo domini et baronis ejusdem cum additione insignium, potestate sedendi in parliamentis,' etc.

[1] Having been born in 1607 he was at this date just eighteen years of age.

[2] This and other facts suggest that there is room for a study of the true character of the Marquess of Argyll So far, the nearest approach to an understanding of that somewhat complex personality seems to have been made by Neil Munro in *John Splendid.*

that he hes approvin him self ansucrable to the traist wes repoised in him, And whereas he is a young nobleman, and this is the first of his imploymentis wherin he hes worthelie and dewtifullie dischargeit him self, we could not forbeare to gif notice of the same to yor Maiestie, to the intent that yf the lyke occasioun of seruice fall oute in the Ilis or Heylandis of this kingdome, yor Maiestie may be assured of one who is bothe able and willing to serue yor Maiestie; And so in all humilitie recommending him to youre Ma^{ttes} fauour and his seruice to youre gratious allowance and acceptance, we pray the almightie god to watche ouer youre Sacred persone and to blisse youre Maiestie with mony lang and happie yeiris. And we rest for ever, Yo^r Maiesteis most humble and obedyent subiectis and seruitouris,

GEORGE HAY.   MAR.   MORTON.

PERTHE.   MELROS.   ROXBURGH.   WINTOUN.

Edinburgh, 29 July 1625.

INDEX

✗ 'his twa sones' 203.

to lord Lovat, etc., for the trial of resetters of the rebels, 305, letter to the king on behalf of the vassals of Argyll, 307, letters to the king on the remissions granted to the rebels, 310, 313, 314; letter to the king on a proposed infeftment of the lordship of Kintyre in favour of Argyll's son, 317 and *n*, 319
Pubill, in Kintyre, 82

Rabston, in Strathbogie, 56.
Radadell, 151
Rae, Adam, 229
Ramsay, major David, 6, 29, his cows bewitched, 16
Rannadaill, 75, 81
Rathmullin, 294
Rathven, increase of popery in, 56, the liturgy of the church of England introduced, 64 and *n*
Reache, in Kintyre, 18
Reginald, son of Somerled, 67
Reid, Adam, of Barskimming, 75
—— Peter, celebrates mass in Strathbogie, 56
Richart, George, 34.
Robertson of Straloch, 221
—— of Strowan, 217
Rosland, 85
Ross, John, earl of, 67
Rothesay castle, witches in, 14
Rowan, Patrick, 27
Roxburgh, Robert, earl of, 320
Russell, Clement, 229
—— John, advocate, 225 *n*

Sackville (Seckvile), lord George, 43 and *n*
Saddel abbey, 67.
St. John, sir William, admiral, 111
St Magnus cathedral, 188 and *n*
Schools in Fochabers having 'popish women' for teachers, 57
Scone, lord, record of the court held by him in Kintyre in 1605, 69, 79-85, 101, 109 *n*, 110
Scotodaill, 74, 81.
Scott, captain Caroline, 42 and *n*, 43, 44, 46, 51
—— George, an episcopal clergyman, intrudes into Aberlour church, 63 and *n*
—— rev Robert, 285 *n*
Scrymgeour, sir John, of Dudhope, 229.
Seaforth, earl of, 59.
Second sight in Barra, 59 *n*.

Sempill, Bryce, servant to bishop Knox, 163
Seton, *alias* Ross, Alexander, a priest, natural son of the earl of Dunfermline, 61
—— Robert, a jesuit priest in Ardoch, 60
Sharp, John, chaplain to her majestie's forces in America, intrudes into the parish church of Aberdeen, 63.
Shaw, Elizabeth, wife of John Murray of Lochmaben, 170
—— John, of Bargarran, 31 *n*.
—— Marie, wife of Robert Douglas of Auchintullich, petition on behalf of her husband, charged with the slaughter of William Lindsay, 34
—— Mary, wife of John Douglas, in Auchindinnane, 31 *n*
Shian of Barcalden, Loch Creran, 37-38 and *n*
Sinclair, a resetter of jesuits, to be executed, 285
Skene, sir John, of Curriehill, 101 and *n*
Smerbye, 73, 80, 85
Smith, Margaret, a witch, 25
Socach, in Kintyre, 77
Somerled in possession of Kintyre, 66
Somerset, Robert Carr, earl of, 156, letter to, from Campbell of Calder, containing a report of his expedition to Islay, 177-186
Sorak, in Kintyre, 83
Sorcery in Appin, 36-38
Spense, Elspeth, a witch, 13, 19, 26
Speresak, in Kintyre, 74, 81.
Spottiswood, John, archbishop of St Andrews, 120, 285 and *n*
Stephen, John, 'blasted with ane evill ey,' 24
—— William, shot by witches, 23, 24
Stewart, a priest, in Fochabers, 57.
—— Andrew, lord Ochiltree, *q v*
—— Archibald, provost of Rothesay, 23
—— Charles, celebrates the mass at Dumbennan, 56, 57
—— —— writer in Banavie, 48 *n*
—— Coline, burgess of Rothesay, 24, 27.
—— Cristeane, in Gartingewoche, 84
—— —— in Lochquhordill, 75, 78
—— James, burgess of Rothesay, 22, 23.

Printed by T and A CONSTABLE, Printers to His Majesty
at the Edinburgh University Press

RULES

1. THE object of the Society is the discovery and printing, under selected editorship, of unpublished documents illustrative of the civil, religious, and social history of Scotland. The Society will also undertake, in exceptional cases, to issue translations of printed works of a similar nature, which have not hitherto been accessible in English.

2. The number of Members of the Society shall be limited to 400

3. The affairs of the Society shall be managed by a Council, consisting of a Chairman, Treasurer, Secretary, and twelve elected Members, five to make a quorum Three of the twelve elected Members shall retire annually by ballot, but they shall be eligible for re-election

4. The Annual Subscription to the Society shall be One Guinea. The publications of the Society shall not be delivered to any Member whose Subscription is in arrear, and no Member shall be permitted to receive more than one copy of the Society's publications.

5. The Society will undertake the issue of its own publications, i e. without the intervention of a publisher or any other paid agent.

6. The Society will issue yearly two octavo volumes of about 320 pages each.

7. An Annual General Meeting of the Society shall be held at the end of October, or at an approximate date to be determined by the Council.

8 Two stated Meetings of the Council shall be held each year, one on the last Tuesday of May, the other on the Tuesday preceding the day upon which the Annual General Meeting shall be held The Secretary, on the request of three Members of the Council, shall call a special meeting of the Council

9. Editors shall receive 20 copies of each volume they edit for the Society.

10. The owners of Manuscripts published by the Society will also be presented with a certain number of copies

11. The Annual Balance-Sheet, Rules, and List of Members shall be printed.

12 No alteration shall be made in these Rules except at a General Meeting of the Society. A fortnight's notice of any alteration to be proposed shall be given to the Members of the Council

PUBLICATIONS

OF THE

SCOTTISH HISTORY SOCIETY

For the year 1896-1897.

26. WARISTON'S DIARY AND OTHER PAPERS—
JOHNSTON OF WARISTON'S DIARY, 1639.   Edited by G M Paul —
THE HONOURS OF SCOTLAND, 1651-52   C. R A Howden.—THE
EARL OF MAR'S LEGACIES, 1722, 1726.   Hon S. Erskine — LETTERS
BY MRS. GRANT OF LAGGAN.   J R. N Macphail
Presented to the Society by Messrs. T and A. Constable

27 MEMORIALS OF JOHN MURRAY OF BROUGHTON, 1740-1747.
Edited by R FITZROY BELL.

28 THE COMPT BUIK OF DAVID WEDDERBURNE, MERCHANT OF
DUNDEE, 1587-1630.   Edited by A H MILLAR

For the year 1897-1898.

29, 30. THE CORRESPONDENCE OF DE MONTEREUL AND THE BROTHERS
DE BELLIÈVRE, FRENCH AMBASSADORS IN ENGLAND AND SCOT-
LAND, 1645-1648.   Edited, with Translation, by J G.
FOTHERINGHAM   2 vols.

For the year 1898-1899.

31. SCOTLAND AND THE PROTECTORATE. LETTERS AND PAPERS
RELATING TO THE MILITARY GOVERNMENT OF SCOTLAND, FROM
JANUARY 1654 TO JUNE 1659   Edited by C. H. FIRTH, M A

32 PAPERS ILLUSTRATING THE HISTORY OF THE SCOTS BRIGADE IN
THE SERVICE OF THE UNITED NETHERLANDS, 1572-1782
Edited by JAMES FERGUSON   Vol. 1 1572-1697

33, 34   MACFARLANE'S GENEALOGICAL COLLECTIONS CONCERNING
FAMILIES IN SCOTLAND ; Manuscripts in the Advocates' Library
2 vols. Edited by J T. CLARK, Keeper of the Library.
Presented to the Society by the Trustees of the late Sir William Fraser, K C B

For the year 1899-1900.

35. PAPERS ON THE SCOTS BRIGADE IN HOLLAND, 1572-1782.
Edited by JAMES FERGUSON. Vol II 1698-1782

36 JOURNAL OF A FOREIGN TOUR IN 1665 AND 1666, ETC , BY SIR JOHN
LAUDER, LORD FOUNTAINHALL.   Edited by DONALD CRAWFORD

37. PAPAL NEGOTIATIONS WITH MARY QUEEN OF SCOTS DURING HER
REIGN IN SCOTLAND   Chiefly from the Vatican Archives
Edited by the Rev J. HUNGERFORD POLLEN, S J

For the year 1900-1901.

38 PAPERS ON THE SCOTS BRIGADE IN HOLLAND, 1572-1782
Edited by JAMES FERGUSON   Vol. III

39. THE DIARY OF ANDREW HAY OF CRAIGNETHAN, 1659-60.
Edited by A. G REID, F.S.A Scot

For the year 1901-1902.

40. NEGOTIATIONS FOR THE UNION OF ENGLAND AND SCOTLAND IN
1651-53   Edited by C. SANFORD TERRY

41. THE LOYALL DISSUASIVE   Written in 1703 by Sir ÆNEAS
MACPHERSON   Edited by the Rev. A D MURDOCH

For the year 1902-1903.

42. THE CHARTULARY OF LINDORES, 1195-1479 Edited by the Right Rev. JOHN DOWDEN, D.D., Bishop of Edinburgh.

43. A LETTER FROM MARY QUEEN OF SCOTS TO THE DUKE OF GUISE, Jan. 1562 Reproduced in Facsimile Edited by the Rev. J. HUNGERFORD POLLEN, S.J
Presented to the Society by the family of the late Mr Scott, of Halkshill

44. MISCELLANY OF THE SCOTTISH HISTORY SOCIETY, Second Volume— THE SCOTTISH KING'S HOUSEHOLD, 14th Century. Edited by Mary Bateson —THE SCOTTISH NATION IN THE UNIVERSITY OF ORLEANS, 1336-1538. John Kirkpatrick, LL.D —THE FRENCH GARRISON AT DUNBAR, 1563. Robert S. Rait —DE ANTIQUITATE RELIGIONIS APUD SCOTOS, 1594. Henry D. G. Law.—APOLOGY FOR WILLIAM MAITLAND OF LETHINGTON, 1610. Andrew Lang —LETTERS OF BISHOP GEORGE GRÆME, 1602-38 L. G. Græme.—A SCOTTISH JOURNIE, 1641. C H Firth —NARRATIVES ILLUSTRATING THE DUKE OF HAMILTON'S EXPEDITION TO ENGLAND, 1648. C. H. Firth.— BURNET-LEIGHTON PAPERS, 1648-168- H C Foxcroft —PAPERS OF ROBERT ERSKINE, Physician to Peter the Great, 1677-1720. Rev Robert Paul —WILL OF THE DUCHESS OF ALBANY, 1789 A. Francis Steuart

45. LETTERS OF JOHN COCKBURN OF ORMISTOUN TO HIS GARDENER, 1727-1743 Edited by JAMES COLVILLE, D Sc.

For the year 1903-1904.

46. MINUTE BOOK OF THE MANAGERS OF THE NEW MILLS CLOTH MANUFACTORY, 1681-1690 Edited by W. R. SCOTT

47 CHRONICLES OF THE FRASERS; being the Wardlaw Manuscript entitled 'Polichronicon seu Policratica Temporum, or, the true Genealogy of the Frasers.' By Master JAMES FRASER Edited by WILLIAM MACKAY.

48. PROCEEDINGS OF THE JUSTICIARY COURT FROM 1661 TO 1678. Vol. I 1661-1669. Edited by Sheriff SCOTT-MONCRIEFF

For the year 1904-1905.

49. PROCEEDINGS OF THE JUSTICIARY COURT FROM 1661 TO 1678. Vol. II 1669-1678. Edited by Sheriff SCOTT-MONCRIEFF

50 RECORDS OF THE BARON COURT OF STITCHILL, 1655-1807 Edited by CLEMENT B. GUNN, M.D , Peebles

51. MACFARLANE'S GEOGRAPHICAL COLLECTIONS Vol. I Edited by Sir ARTHUR MITCHELL, K.C.B

For the year 1905-1906

52, 53 MACFARLANE'S GEOGRAPHICAL COLLECTIONS. Vols. II. and III, Edited by Sir ARTHUR MITCHELL, K.C.B.

54 STATUTA ECCLESIÆ SCOTICANÆ, 1225-1559. Translated and edited by DAVID PATRICK, LL.D.

For the year 1906-1907.

55. THE HOUSE BOOKE OF ACCOMPS, OCHTERTYRE, 1737-39. Edited by JAMES COLVILLE, D Sc.

56. The Charters of the Abbey of Inchaffray. Edited by W. A. Lindsay, K.C., the Right Rev. Bishop Dowden, D D., and J Maitland Thomson, LL.D

57. A Selection of the Forfeited Estates Papers preserved in H.M. General Register House and elsewhere Edited by A. H. Millar, LL.D.

For the year 1907-1908.

58 Records of the Commissions of the General Assemblies (continued), for the years 1650-52. Edited by the Rev James Christie, D.D

59. Papers relating to the Scots in Poland. Edited by A Francis Steuart.

For the year 1908-1909.

60 Sir Thomas Craig's De Unione Regnorum Britanniæ Tractatus Edited, with an English Translation, by C Sanford Terry.

61 Johnston of Wariston's Memento Quamdiu Vivas, and Diary from 1632 to 1639 Edited by G. M Paul, LL D , D K S

Second Series.
For the year 1909-1910.

1 The Household Book of Lady Grisell Baillie, 1692-1733 Edited by R. Scott-Moncrieff, W.S.

2 Origins of the '45 and other Narratives Edited by W B Blaikie, LL.D.

3 Correspondence of James, fourth Earl of Findlater and first Earl of Seafield, Lord Chancellor of Scotland. Edited by James Grant, M A., LL B

For the year 1910-1911.

4 Rentale Sancti Andree; being Chamberlain and Granitar Accounts of the Archbishopric in the time of Cardinal Betoun, 1538-1546. Translated and edited by Robert Kerr Hannay.

5 Highland Papers Vol. I Edited by J. R. N Macphail, K C

For the year 1911-1912.

6 Selections from the Records of the Regality of Melrose. Vol. I. Edited by C. S Romanes, C.A

7 Records of the Earldom of Orkney. Edited by J S. Clouston

For the year 1912-1913.

8. Selections from the Records of the Regality of Melrose. Vol. II Edited by C. S. Romanes, C A

9 Selections from the Letter Books of John Steuart, Bailie of Inverness. Edited by William Mackay. LL.D.

For the year 1913-1914

10. Rentale Dunkeldense; being the Accounts of the Chamberlain of the Bishopric of Dunkeld, a d. 1506-1517. Edited by R. K. Hannay.

11 LETTERS OF THE EARL OF SEAFIELD AND OTHERS, ILLUSTRATIVE
OF THE HISTORY OF SCOTLAND DURING THE REIGN OF QUEEN
ANNE Edited by Professor HUME BROWN

For the year 1914-1915.

12 HIGHLAND PAPERS Vol II. Edited by J. R. N. MACPHAIL, K C.
(March 1916)
(*Note* —ORIGINS OF THE '45, issued for 1909-1910, is issued
also for 1914-1915.)

For the year 1915-1916.

13. SELECTIONS FROM THE RECORDS OF THE REGALITY OF MELROSE
Vol III. Edited by C. S ROMANES, C A. (February 1917)
14. A CONTRIBUTION TO THE BIBLIOGRAPHY OF SCOTTISH TOPOGRAPHY
Edited by the late Sir ARTHUR MITCHELL and C. G CASH.
Vol I. (March 1917)

For the year 1916-1917.

15 BIBLIOGRAPHY OF SCOTTISH TOPOGRAPHY. Vol. II (May 1917)
16 PAPERS RELATING TO THE ARMY OF THE SOLEMN LEAGUE AND
COVENANT, 1643-1647. Vol. I Edited by Professor C
SANFORD TERRY. (October 1917)

For the year 1917-1918.

17. PAPERS RELATING TO THE ARMY OF THE SOLEMN LEAGUE AND
COVENANT, 1643-1647. Vol II. (December 1917)
18 WARISTON'S DIARY. Vol. II Edited by D. HAY FLEMING, LL D.
(February 1919)

For the year 1918-1919.

19. MISCELLANY OF THE SCOTTISH HISTORY SOCIETY. Third Volume.
20 PAPERS RELATING TO THE HIGHLANDS. Edited by J. R N.
MACPHAIL, K.C

In preparation.

THE EARLY RECORDS OF THE UNIVERSITY OF ST ANDREWS Edited
by J MAITLAND ANDERSON, LL.D.
REGISTER OF THE CONSULTATIONS OF THE MINISTERS OF EDINBURGH,
AND SOME OTHER BRETHREN OF THE MINISTRY, SINCE THE
INTERRUPTION OF THE ASSEMBLY 1653, WITH OTHER PAPERS OF
PUBLIC CONCERNMENT. Edited by the Rev. W. STEPHEN, B.D
CHARTERS AND DOCUMENTS RELATING TO THE GREY FRIARS AND THE
CISTERCIAN NUNNERY OF HADDINGTON.—REGISTER OF INCH-
COLM MONASTERY Edited by J G WALLACE-JAMES, M B.
ANALYTICAL CATALOGUE OF THE WODROW COLLECTION OF MANU-
SCRIPTS IN THE ADVOCATES' LIBRARY.
A TRANSLATION OF THE HISTORIA ABBATUM DE KYNLOS OF
FERRERIUS.
PAPERS RELATING TO THE REBELLIONS OF 1715 AND 1745, with other
documents from the Municipal Archives of the City of Perth.
THE BALCARRES PAPERS.

Cabale (anno 1614) p. 171

cláirnench p.22

p.254 Sir J. Macdonald in Eigg

20
16
─────
120
20
─────
3²0

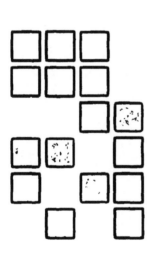

Lightning Source UK Ltd.
Milton Keynes UK
UKHW021315190221
379019UK00006B/1599